Righteous Cause or Tragic Folly

Michigan Monograph Series in Japanese Studies
Number 17

Center for Japanese Studies
The University of Michigan

Righteous Cause or Tragic Folly

Changing Views of War in Modern Japanese Poetry

Steve Rabson

Center for Japanese Studies
The University of Michigan
Ann Arbor, 1998

Published by the Center for Japanese Studies, The University of Michigan, 202 S. Thayer St., Ann Arbor, MI 48104–1608

Library of Congress Cataloging in Publication Data

Rabson, Steve.
Righteous cause or tragic folly : changing views of war in modern Japanese poetry / Steve Rabson.
ix, 287 p. 23.5 cm. — (Michigan monograph series in Japanese studies ; no. 17)
Includes bibliographical references and index.
ISBN 0–939512–77–7 (cloth : alk. paper)
1. Japanese poetry—1868– —History and criticism. 2. War poetry, Japanese—History and criticism. 3. Poets, Japanese—1868– —Philosophy. 4. Japanese poetry—1868– —Translations into English.
I. Title. II. Series.
PL733.57.W3R33 1998
895.6'1409358—dc21 96–48385
CIP

This book was set in ITC Cheltenham.

Jacket design by Seiko Semones.

Jacket illustration: *Women of the Air Defense Corps*, painting by Todoroki Mikichi. Courtesy of the Anne S. K. Brown Military Collection, Brown University Library. Caption accompanying photo reads: "A household fire brigade on stand-by alert, always ready to put out the flames from incendiaries or other bombs."

∞ The paper used in this publication meets the requirements of the ANSI/NISO Standard Z39.48–1992 (Permanence of Paper for Publications and Documents in Libraries and Archives).

Printed in the United States of America

Contents

Acknowledgments vii

Introduction:
Poets' Changing Views of War 1

1 Masaoka Shiki:
Troubled Journey to the Front 20

2 Yosano Tekkan:
The Pen As Sword 46

3 Takeshima Hagoromo and Miyazaki Koshoshi:
Harbingers of Protest 77

4 Kinoshita Naoe:
The Poetry of Pacifism 90

5 Yosano Akiko:
To Give One's Life or Not—A Question of Which War 107

6 Shimazaki Tōson:
Internal Conflicts 144

7 The "Democracy Poets" and
the Pacific War 175

8 Takamura Kōtarō and Saitō Mokichi:
War and Repentance 191

Conclusion:
Postwar Reflections and the Antiwar Revival 207

Notes 228

Bibliography 269

Index 278

Acknowledgments

The following publishers and individuals have generously given permission to use extended quotations from copyrighted works.

"To Any Dead Officer," "Silent Service," "Fight to a Finish," "Counter-Attack," "Kiss," and "Absolution," from *Collected Poems of Siegfried Sassoon* by Sigfreid Sassoon. Copyright © 1818, 1920, by E. P. Dutton. Copyright © 1936, 1946, 1947, 1948 by Siegfried Sassoon. Used by permission of Viking Penguin, a division of Penguin Books USA, Inc., and George T. Sassoon.

"Patience" by Tanikawa Shuntarō. Translation by John Solt. Published with the permission of Tanikawa Shuntarō and John Solt.

"Drafted" by Yamanokuchi Baku, translated by Steve Rabson, from his "Two Wartime Poems by Yamanokuchi Baku." *Salamander* 1.2 (Spring 1993). Used by permission.

"All the Hills and Valleys Along" from *Marlborough and Other Poems* (1916) by Charles Sorley. © 1922. Reprinted by permission of Cambridge University Press.

"Parting Sorrows of a Frontier Guard" translated in "The Man'yōshū" from *Records of Civilization*. Copyright © 1965 by Columbia University Press. Reprinted with permission of the publisher.

"The Death of a Soldier" from *Collected Poems by Wallace Stevens*. Copyright © 1923, 1951 by Wallace Stevens. Reprinted by permission of Alfred A. Knopf, Inc.

"The Death of a Soldier" from *The Collected Poems of Wallace Stevens* by Wallace Stevens. © 1955 by Faber and Faber Limited. Reprinted with permission of the publisher.

"Memorial Rain" from *Collected Poems 1917–1982* by Archibald MacLeish. Copyright © 1985 by The Estate of Archibald MacLeish. Reprinted by permission of Houghton Mifflin Co. All rights reserved. Originally published in *Streets of the Moon*, 1926.

"Give me Water" by Hara Tamiki, translated by John Treat, from his "Early Hiroshima Poetry." *Journal of the Association of Teachers of Japanese* 20.2. Used by permission.

"The Oath of Ōtomo" reprinted from *A Waka Anthology, Volume One: The Gem-Glistening Cup* translated by Edwin A. Cranston with the permission of the publishers, Stanford University Press. © 1993 by the Board of Trustees of the Leland Stanford Junior University.

"Evanescence" translated by Esperanza Ramirez-Christensen, reprinted from *Heart's Flower: The Life and Poetry of Shinkei* by Esperanza Ramirez-Christensen with the permission of the publishers, Stanford University Press. © 1994 by the Board of Trustees of the Leland Stanford Junior University.

"Those who Return to the Source" by Takamura Kōtarō, translated by Makoto Ueda, reprinted from *Modern Japanese Poets and the Nature of Literature* by Makoto Ueda with the permission of the publishers, Stanford University Press. © 1983 by the Board of Trustees of the Leland Stanford Junior University.

"In the Korean Mountains" by Yosano Tekkan, and "Announcing my Joy," "From a Reprobate—Offered to Bernard Leach," "Paris," "Polar Bear," "Men, Having Read my Poems, Went to their Deaths," "Mr. Chiang, Reflect on This!" and "The End of the War" by Takamura Kōtarō are from translations by Donald Keene in *Dawn to the West: Japanese Literature of the Modern Era (Volume 2)*. Copyright © 1984 by Donald Keene. Reprinted by permission of Henry Holt & Co., Inc.

"The Basic Principles of the New World" by Nishida Kitarō and "We are Standing for Justice and Life" by Takamura Kōtarō. Translations by Ben-Ami Shillony from *Politics and Culture in Wartime Japan*. Copyright © 1981. Reprinted by permission of Oxford University Press.

Translations and prose by Kenneth Strong from his book *Pillar of Fire*, © 1972 by Allan and Unwin, are reprinted with the permission of the beneficiaries of Kenneth Strong's estate.

Portions of chapter five are from "Yosano Akiko on War." *Journal of the Association of Teachers of Japanese* 25.1. Used by permission.

Portions of chapter six are from"Shimazaki Tōson on War," *Monumenta Nipponica* 46.4. Used by permission.

"The Palace of Slaughter," "The Day They Lost their Farm Fields," "Gloom at Sea," "Today, too, Parents of the Warrior Gods Plow their Fields," and "General Yamashita" by Shirotori Seigo. Translations appear by permision of Shirotori Kiyo.

"Handkerchiefs Waving from a Train," "The Pale Countryside," "The Song that Lives in Our Soil," "Gratitude," and "The Nine Warrior Gods of Pearl Harbor" by Fukuda Masao. Translations appear by permission of Fukuda Misuzu.

"For the Fallen" by Laurence Binyon is reprinted by permission of Mrs. Nocolete Gray and The Society of Authors, on behalf of the Laurence Binyon Estate.

Amy Vladeck Heinrich's translations of poetry by Saito Mokichi in chapter eight are from *Fragments of Rainbows: The Life and Poetry of Saitō Mokichi: 1882–1953* by Amy Vladeck Heinrich. Copyright © 1983 by Columbia University Press. Reprinted with permission of the publisher.

Translations of poetry by Saitō Mokichi in chapter eight are published by permission of Saitō Yuka.

"The Bayonet" from *The Collected Poems of Wilfrid Gibson* by Wilfrid Gibson. © 1929. Reprinted by permission of Macmillan General Books and Dorothy Gibson.

"Antwerp" and "On Heaven" from *Collected Poems* by Ford Madox Ford. © 1936. Reprinted with permission.

"Without Shedding Blood" by Geoffrey Johnson. Reprinted by permission of Carcanet Press Limited.

"The Send-Off" and "Exposure" by Wilfred Owen, from *The Collected Poems of Wilfred Owen*. Copyright © 1963 by Chatto & Windus, Ltd. Reprinted by permission of New Directions Publishing Corp.

"Bird's-eye" and "Notes on Hell" by Kaneko Mitsuharu. Translations appear by permission of Ken Mori.

"August 6, 1951" by Tōge Sankichi, translated by Richard Minear from *Hiroshima: Three Witnesses*. © 1990 Princeton University Press. Reprinted by permission of Princeton University Press.

"When I Was at My Prettiest" by Ibaragi Noriko. Translation appears by permission of the poet.

"Unsinkable Aircraft Carrier Okinawa" by Yamanokuchi Baku. Translation appears by permission of Yamaguchi Izumi.

"Okinawa" and "Then Came 'Postwar'" by Shiro Yū in translations by Steve Rabson from *Okinawa: Two Postwar Novellas* by Steve Rabson. © 1989 and 1996. Reprinted with the permission of the publishers, Institute of East Asian Studies, University of California, Berkeley.

"The Colored Race" by Arakawa Akira. Translation appears by permission of the poet.

Introduction: Poets' Changing Views of War

British poet Siegfried Sassoon (1886–1967) is best known today for his searingly graphic poems on the death and suffering of soldiers in World War I. Yet shortly before his two-year ordeal as a combat infantry officer, he wrote poetry he later disparaged as "the typical self-glorifying feelings of a young man about to go to the Front for the first time"[1]:

> The anguish of the earth absolves our eyes
> Till beauty shines in all that we can see.
> War is our scourge; yet war has made us wise,
> And, fighting for our freedom, we are free.
>
> Horror of wounds and anger at the foe,
> And loss of things desired; all these must pass.
> We are the happy legion, for we know
> Time's but a golden wind that shakes the grass.
>
> There was an hour when we were loath to part
> From life we longed to share no less than others.
> Now, having claimed this heritage of heart,
> What need we more, my comrades and my brothers?[2]

In "Kiss" (1916), one of his first poems written as a soldier, he compared the slashing of a bayonet to a "downward darting kiss":

> To these I turn in these I trust—
> Brother Lead and Sister Steel.
> To his blind power I make my appeal,
> I guard her beauty clean from rust.
>
> He spins and burns and loves the air
> And splits a skull to win my praise;

But up the nobly marching days
She glitters naked, cold and fair.

Sweet sister, grant your soldier this:
That in good fury he may feel
The body where he sets his heel
Quail from your downward darting kiss.[3]

Sassoon's friend and fellow poet Robert Graves (1895–1985) recalled that "Kiss" had been written initially as an expression of sincere bellicose enthusiasm, but that Sassoon presented it as satire after his battlefield experiences.[4] What he witnessed at the front moved him to write some of the most affecting poems on war ever published in English, many of which pointedly contrast the blissful ignorance of home-front flag waving with the reality of armed conflict.

You smug-faced crowds with kindling eye
Who cheer when soldier lads march by,
Sneak home and pray you'll never know
The hell where youth and laughter go.[5]

. . . .
The place was rotten with dead; clumsy legs
High-booted, sprawled and grovelled along the saps
And trunks, face downward, in sucking mud,
Wallowed like trodden sand-bags loosely filled;
And naked sodden buttocks, mats of hair,
Bulged, clotted heads slept in the plastering slime.[6]

Aside from exploding romanticized notions about armed conflict, Sassoon's poetry and prose express outrage at the press, popular attitudes, and the British government, which, he stated in 1917, had "deliberately prolong[ed] . . . these sufferings [of war] for ends which I believe to be evil and unjust."[7] His poem "Fight to a Finish" (1917) distills this anger into a gruesome fantasy of returning soldiers on parade, who take their revenge on reporters and politicians:

The boys came back. Bands played and flags flying,
    And the Yellow-Pressmen thronged the sunlit street
To cheer the soldiers who'd refrained from dying,
    And hear the music of returning feet.
"Of all the thrills and ardours War has brought,
This moment is the finest." (So they thought.)

Snapping their bayonets on to charge the mob,
    Grim Fusiliers broke ranks with glint of steel,

At last the boys had found a cushy job.

. . . .

I heard the Yellow-Pressmen grunt and squeal;
And with my trusty bombers turned and went
To clear those Junkers out of Parliament.[8]

For Siegfried Sassoon, however, the story does not end here. As Bernard Bergonzi notes, Sassoon's attitude toward war appears to have "swung full circle"[9] with poetry he published at the beginning of World War II. His "Silent Service" (1940) begins:

Now, multifold, let Britain's patient power
Be proven within us for the world to see.
None are exempt from service in this hour;
And vanquished in ourselves we dare not be.[10]

Valorization of power and sacrifice in this poem are typical of versified exhortations to battle everywhere, and Sassoon's assertion, with the Nazi defeat in 1945, that "a recurrence of Teutonic aggressiveness" was inevitable[11] reflects the national, ethnic, and racial stereotyping commonly found in writing that vilifies wartime enemies. Biographer Ian Hamilton wrote of British poet Stephen Spender (1909–): "He was the one who had believed the slogans—'Oh, young men oh young comrades'—and, after the war, the one who had recanted most shamefacedly."[12]

Changing attitudes toward war, such as those expressed above, can be observed in many countries at various times in this century. In the 1920s and 1930s a significant number of Americans and Europeans shared Sassoon's view that World War I had been prolonged unnecessarily and unconscionably, partly as a result of the influence of weapons merchants and others who profit from armed conflict.[13] Many also believed that Allied governments could have averted the war, and could prevent future wars as well, by the early application of diplomatic and economic sanctions. Yet after the United States entered World War II, which produced far less American or European poetry of note than did World War I,[14] Americans who publicly opposed U.S. involvement or refused conscription on philosophical grounds were limited mostly to Quakers, Jehovah's Witnesses, and others who objected to war within the context of established religious doctrines and institutions. World War II, now sometimes referred to as "the good war,"[15] had more widespread support than any in the nation's history. Harry Whitten, an American journalist, described his rapid conversion from pacifist to volunteer soldier with America's entry into the war:

> In the mid-30s many of us at the Southern Branch [of the University of Idaho] were pacifists. We read about the "merchants of death" and saw films about the horrors of World War I. A number signed the Oxford pledge that we would refuse to fight any future war. I was one of them. We organized a post of the "Veterans of Future Wars" which we thought was a good satire on the American Legion and Veterans of Foreign Wars.
>
> December 7, 1941, was a Sunday, and recruiting offices were closed. The next day, however, a long line of men stretched around the block from the recruiting office in Portland, Oregon, where I was living at the time. Guess who was one of those in line? My change from my pacifist days at the Southern Branch did not result simply from outrage at the attack on Pearl Harbor. For some time it had become evident that the United States would be forced into the war in Europe. It had also become evident that Hitler and Mussolini had to be stopped and that it was morally right for the United States to help stop them.[16]

More recently, many Americans called themselves "pacifists" or "conscientious objectors" during the 1960s and 1970s, when domestic opposition to United States military involvement in Vietnam produced numerous antiwar poems and songs.[17] Yet some of these same people were early supporters in 1991 of "Desert Storm," led by U.S. forces in the Persian Gulf. This brief but intensely destructive conflict produced little poetry by well-known poets in Europe or the United States, though it inspired American "rap" verses exhorting U.S. troops and vilifying Saddam Hussein, which were recited on television during the fighting.[18] However, in Japan, a widely circulated poetry magazine solicited poems from seventeen Japanese and twenty-eight foreign poets for a special edition on the Gulf War. Opinions among the Japanese ranged widely, with poets supporting the U.S. position, sympathizing with underdog Iraq, blaming both sides, condemning the human species generally, and despairing of any way to affect events. A contribution from Tanikawa Shuntarō (1931–), one of the country's leading free-verse poets, sums up an attitude shared by people in many countries who watched the Gulf War as television spectators:

> "Patience"
>
> with the t.v. as a side dish, I'm eating again today
> no matter what'll happen between now and death
> as usual eating and having it turn to shit
> anyway, that's all the desert soldiers are up to
>
> in the meantime they also shoot missiles
> enemies and allies base their launches in belief systems

because I don't carry such beliefs
and not knowing what to do, all I can be is patient
. . . .[19]

Among the "desert soldiers" of the Gulf War, none were Japanese. Yet in a nation frequently involved in armed hostilities abroad from the late nineteenth to the mid-twentieth century, including four major wars and numerous clashes and skirmishes, it is hardly surprising that poetry conveys wide-ranging attitudes toward armed conflict, or that Japanese poets have expressed sharply divergent views of war at various times in their careers.[20]

The Sino-Japanese War (1894–95) produced the first nationwide outpouring of poems in Japan supporting war, and they found a wide and enthusiastic readership in Japanese newspapers and magazines. It was a time when domestic demand for information about the progress of hostilities, hard to come by in the heavily censored dispatches from the front, significantly spurred the growth of Japan's print media.[21] The conflict, portrayed by Japanese poets in bellicose verses that often demeaned the Chinese, had its roots in rivalry between Chinese and Japanese forces vying for influence in Korea, and it escalated into all-out war with the Japanese naval attack on Chinese battleships off the Korean coast in July 1894. Using military technology only recently imported from Europe and the United States, Japan achieved a relatively quick and complete victory over a far larger Chinese force. The war's outcome surprised and impressed Western observers and established Japan as a military power. In Japan this victory was celebrated widely in poetry, stories, paintings,[22] and local festivals that sometimes featured dramatic re-creations of battles.[23] However, a few writers, such as novelist Izumi Kyōka (1873–1939) and poet Miyazaki Koshoshi (1864–1922), wrote highly critical depictions of death and suffering at the front and of militaristic influences on life in Japan.[24]

Meanwhile, not all Western nations were pleased with Japan's new prominence in East Asia. Alarmed by the territory and influence Japan had gained in this conflict, Russia spearheaded the Triple Intervention with Germany and France in 1895, pressuring Japan to withdraw from the Liaotung Peninsula, which had been occupied by the Japanese army after bloody battles against Chinese forces at Port Arthur and Weihaiwei. A public uproar ensued in Japan, and many writers, including poets, denounced the government's acquiescence to demands for the return of territory won on the battlefield (see chapter two).

Five years later Japanese forces drew praise from Western observers, especially the British, for helping in 1900 to suppress the Boxer Rebellion in China,[25] a military operation that was acclaimed in some Japanese poems and condemned in others (see chapter two). Japan subsequently signed a treaty of alliance with Britain in 1902, the first such arrangement between a Western and an Asian nation.[26] Two years later, lingering resentment in Japan over the Triple Intervention and growing rivalry with Russia for influence in Korea and Manchuria led to the Russo-Japanese War (1904–5), which opened with the Japanese attack on the Russian fleet at Port Arthur on February 8, 1904. Widely supported by the Japanese public, this conflict inspired another deluge of war poems and stories, most of which honored the sacrifices of Imperial forces, celebrated their victories, and vilified Russia. However, a few Japanese poets, novelists, and essayists risked government repression and public censure to write critically of this war and the sacrifices it imposed, even after the fighting was well underway (see chapters four and five).

There is less poetry to be found about the sporadic hostilities Japan was embroiled in over the next two decades. World War I, in which the nation was peripherally involved on the side of the Allies, produced a small number of Japanese poems lamenting the carnage in Europe.[27] The ill-fated Siberian Intervention (1918–22), undertaken to expand Japanese influence in the region, perhaps engendered the least public support in Japan for military operations abroad between the time of the Sino-Japanese War in 1894–95 and the end of the Pacific War in 1945. The deployment of forces inspired Fukuda Masao to write a poem that is often cited today as a landmark of modern Japanese antiwar literature. "Handkerchiefs Waving from a Train"[28] appeared at a time when many Japanese poets were writing odes to peace and democracy. Yet it was also a period that produced some famous and enduring "military songs" (*gunka*), praising the men and weapons of the Imperial Army and Navy.[29] These songs have become standards at bars and parties over the years, and some are still sung today with *karaoke* accompaniment.

The Imperial Army's dispatch of troops to Shantung in 1927 and 1928, which was undertaken ostensibly to protect local Japanese residents but was in fact intended to prevent the unification of China under Chiang Kai-shek,[30] inspired a poem of protest by Miyoshi Jūrō.[31] From this time on, however, poetry and prose in Japan became increasingly supportive of the nation's military policies as hostilities escalated in China. This support is especially noticeable among writers who visited Manchuria and Mongolia in the late 1920s (see chapter five).

There were isolated expressions of dissent. Graphic and sardonic poems on the fighting in China by Kaneko Mitsuharu (1895–1975), who had traveled extensively there, prompted official efforts to suppress his work in 1935 (see chapter five). In addition, stories published in 1938 by

Ishikawa Jun (1899–1987) and Ishikawa Tatsuzō (no relation, 1905–85), which depicted, respectively, growing militarization of life in Japan and atrocities committed by Japanese soldiers in China, led to government suppression of both works and to the prosecution of Ishikawa Tatsuzō (see chapter five).[32] More typical, however, were the copious verses produced by poets and would-be poets honoring the three Japanese soldiers who made what was portrayed, in official and popular accounts, as a suicide attack, carrying explosives into a heavily fortified Chinese garrison near Shanghai in 1932 (see chapters two and five).

Five years later, after full-scale war erupted between China and Japan with the Marco Polo Bridge Incident of 1937, more Japanese poets began turning out poems in support of the Imperial forces. In 1941 the opening of the Pacific War with the attack on Pearl Harbor touched off the greatest deluge of war poetry in the nation's history.[33] Over the next four years the vast majority of poets with national reputations, and countless amateurs besides, produced exhortative, ultra-nationalistic, and frequently vituperative verses that were recited over the radio and printed regularly in newspapers, magazines, and patriotic anthologies often published with government organizational and financial support.[34] Even poets known for writing against war a decade earlier, such as Fukuda Masao (1893–1952) and Shirotori Seigo (1890–1973), leaders in the "Democracy Poetry" movement of the early 1920s, now joined the battle with their pens.

Then, in what may be the most dramatic turnaround in the history of war literature, Japan's defeat in 1945 and the Japanese people's realization that the nation's military policies had been tragically misguided inspired an outpouring of poetry expressing revulsion toward war and militarism. Poets who had written enthusiastically in support of the recent conflict now found their wartime poems acutely embarrassing. Many refused to discuss this period in their careers and eliminated their wartime poems from postwar editions of their "complete works." However, Takamura Kōtarō (1883–1956) and Saitō Mokichi (1882–1953), perhaps the most prominent producers of gung ho war poems, reversed the direction taken a few years earlier by Fukuda and Shirotori to express regret openly and *in verse* for publishing poems that might have inspired young men to go to their deaths.

Poetry in Japan on World War II in retrospect tends to condemn the tragic folly of government policies and to lament the enormous losses and suffering they brought upon the Japanese people.[35] However, few poems mention the death and destruction the Japanese wrought in other countries such as China, where more than ten million died. This tendency, not limited to poets, to depict the Japanese only as the victims of the war has been criticized abroad, especially in China and Korea. Aspects of this one-sided portrayal that Chinese and Koreans find particularly objectionable are: the downplaying in public school textbooks of Imperial Japan's aggression; the occasional statements by older government officials who still insist publicly that Japan fought to protect other Asian countries and that such mass killings of civilians as the Nanking Massacre were "fabrications"; the continued enshrinement of wartime military leaders at Yasukuni, the Shinto sanctuary dedicated to the nation's war dead; and the reluctance of the Japanese government during the half-century since the war to offer apologies and compensation to victims of such wartime atrocities as prison-camp torture, forced labor, and sexual slavery.

Criticism focuses particularly on the Japanese Ministry of Education for a curriculum that fails adequately to cover Imperial Japan's wartime aggression and atrocities. Comparisons are often drawn with postwar Germany, where Nazi aggression and the Holocaust are taught extensively in the schools, as reported in a 1995 article by novelist Peter Schneider:

> The principal credit for the relatively widespread knowledge of the recent German past must evidently go to the schools. The curricula generally prescribe at least 14 hours (plus 7 optional hours) of instruction in "National Socialism and World War II." Many teachers introduce this material as early as the fifth or sixth grade. As a result, today no German child can graduate from school ignorant of this chapter in German history.[36]

Yet if such critical retrospectives are generally lacking in postwar Japan, notable exceptions can be found in the work of some writers, including Takamura Kōtarō, who dedicated "Apology in Shame to Mr. Chiang" to Chiang Kai-shek in 1948. Though short on specifics, this poem expresses remorse and self-criticism, emotions not often found in Japanese poetry on World War II. Having published a wartime poem ridiculing Chiang (see chapter eight, p. 196), Takamura now writes that he is "horrified at myself" for "poems of self-indulgent words" and "narrow pronouncements." He offers an "apology" to Chiang "with all my heart," and concludes that "there is nothing but to expose my own ignominy to the sunlight."[37]

Today large numbers of poems called "antiwar" are published singly and in collections or anthologies, an output stimulated periodically by the wars in Korea and Vietnam, by the anniversaries of the two nuclear attacks, and by protests against the U.S.-Japan Security Treaty, the prolonged American military occupation of Okinawa, and the continued stationing of approximately fifty thousand American forces over a vast network of bases in Japan. Some of these poems condemn armed conflict generally and lament World War II in retrospect, often describing Allied bombings of Japanese cities and the two nuclear attacks in particular. Others oppose U.S. military policies in Asia, along with the Japanese government's cooperation with them, and protest the continuing presence of American bases. Recent poetry on war varies widely in literary quality and philosophical perspective, and not a few verses convey anti-American overtones. Many poets, however, still occasionally recall the enormous relief they felt when the war finally ended and acknowledge that, in the words of Takamura Kōtarō, they "were saved from starvation by the Occupation Army."[38] Relief at the war's end and the comparative benevolence of the Allied Occupation also explains in part why many poets have embraced the democratic and pacifist ideologies that were promoted by Occupation authorities and why the Japanese sometimes look back on their occupiers as, in the words of Iijima Kōichi (1930–), "goodhearted Yankees,"[39] rather than as the child-eating devils portrayed in late wartime propaganda. Yet poets have not forgotten the Occupation's dark side, including G.I. crime, prostitution organized as a "safe outlet" for U.S. forces by Japanese authorities and unofficially sanctioned by Allied military commanders, and prepublication censorship. Poetry critical of the nuclear attacks and Occupation policies, unpublishable at the time, has subsequently appeared in recent collections and anthologies.[40]

Looking back, then, over the period from the late-nineteenth to the late-twentieth century, a proportionally larger number of poems on war have been published in Japan than in the nations of Europe and America, which also found themselves frequently caught up in armed conflict. To speculate on some possible reasons, it is important to note at the outset that the writing of poetry, traditionally considered a measure of status and accomplishment,[41] has continued to be highly valued and widely practiced in Japan. One need only consider the abundance of poetry magazines, featuring verses in both traditional and contemporary forms, that are published throughout the country, many by local poetry associations that hold regular meetings and specialize in one genre or another, such as *haiku*, *tanka*, free verse, or *senryū*. Although the readership for local poetry magazines is often limited to association members who are essentially reading their own poetry, poets in Japan generally have had more success than their counterparts in other countries publishing their work in magazines (local and national), newspapers (many of which have special poetry columns), and book-length collections and anthologies. Poets without established reputations are sometimes required to pay at least part of the printing costs and to do their own marketing, but many of them can publish.[42]

In addition to poetry's broader appeal, the long tradition of keeping diaries in Japan, which often include original poems on contemporary events, has meant that more poems have been written in recent times on the subject of war, not only by poets, but by prominent politicians, business leaders, and individuals in many other walks of life. It has also been more common in Japan for poets to include with their personal letters original poems on current events, some of which are subsequently published. Furthermore, with the growth of the modern mass media in the early twentieth century, the press and the public in Japan have often sought opinions from established poets and novelists on issues of the day, such as war, even if these writers have never claimed any special expertise in politics or international relations.[43] Finally, especially during the Pacific War there was considerable official, as well as popular, pressure for poets to write in support of the war effort. One must add that most established poets, far from being coerced, welcomed the emperor's declaration of this "sacred war" and joined willingly—even enthusiastically—in turning out heavy-handed verses that deified the emperor, exalted the *gunshin* (warrior gods), vilified enemy nations, and exhorted the Japanese people to ever-greater toil and sacrifice.[44]

Recent efforts by Japanese historians and literary critics to find poems from this period opposing, directly or indirectly, Japan's involvement in the Pacific War have yielded little. A few poets, such as Nishiwaki Junzaburō (1894–1982), who reportedly disagreed with the government's military policies, were able to maintain silence if they could afford to live without an income from their writing.[45] Some writers claimed that the antiwar poems they published after the war were written between 1937 and 1945, but these claims are hard to prove.

One notable exception was the poem by Yamanokuchi Baku (1903–63) entitled "Ōshō" (Drafted) published, perhaps by mistake, in 1943, more than two years after the government had imposed prepublication censorship, which explicitly forbade the printing of anything that suggested "criticism of the military" or that "might engender war weariness." Though low-keyed and sardonic in tone, this poem clearly conveyed the drabness and disruption of mobilized Japan, where even Buddhist priests, presumably opposed to the taking of human life, were conscripted to serve at the battlefront, unlike their Shinto counterparts, who, as practitioners of a "national" and state-supported religion, were exempted from the draft.

In the middle of the night,
who could it be,
knocking at my door?

Even he had turned the color of this world,
khaki from head to toe.
"I must leave at once," he said.
"At once."
It is the way of this khaki-colored world.
He had hurriedly thrown off his accustomed robes.
And now this priest, personifying that other world,
no longer looked like a man of the temple.[46]

Such grim depictions of the home front were extremely rare in poetry published between 1932 and 1945. However, after the war, in which many more Japanese experienced personal loss than, for example, did Americans, the shock of defeat and the revulsion against wartime ideology led to an outpouring of "antiwar poetry."

Thus, during the last century, each of these factors has influenced the production of more poems on the general subject of war, as well as on specific battles and military operations, in Japan than in other countries, even those that have frequently been embroiled in armed conflicts. Yet, if the production has been more copious in Japan, events, emotions, and philosophies are conveyed in ways that have much in common with what poets in other countries have written on war. Antiwar poetry in Japan, as elsewhere, tends to focus on individual experiences—of soldiers and their families, lovers, and friends—in wartime. It often expresses sorrow for the human losses imposed by armed conflict and anger at those who perpetrate and prolong it. Poetry advocating war also radiates anger, in this case at "the enemy," as well as pride—in the nation, the rightness of its cause, and the courage of its soldiers. Critic Clutton Brock outlined his criteria for poets writing in support of the British cause at the start of World War I:

> [I]t is the very essence of their business to be magnifying mirrors of that fraction of our life which is great and significant. And so, though they are more aware than they used to be of the ugly and stupid side of war, they will still, and quite rightly, for the most part pass all that by and insist that for them the thing that matters in war is not the waste and loss of the body and the goods of the body, but the escape of the spirit into that eternal world in which bodily death is as nothing compared with the triumph of an idea.[47]

Brock's admonition to poets reads like portions of the *Imperial Rescript to Soldiers and Sailors*, promulgated by the Meiji government in 1882, which exhorts military men to remember "the importance of 'Great Righteousness'" and "bear in mind that duty is weightier than a mountain, while death is lighter than a feather."[48] Though found less frequently in poetry, conceptions of war as righteous and inevitable have been identified by Frank J. Wetta as an essential part of American culture:

> Our nation was born, sustained, and expanded in warfare. In 200 years we've had at least 12 major wars, on the average a war every 16 years. I think that war is not an aberration in American history. I think it is something essential in American history . . . a kind of defining element.[49]

Poets in Japan have written more often than their counterparts in Europe and America on the willingness of soldiers to sacrifice their lives in battle, commemorating such suicide missions as those carried out by infantry units at Port Arthur during the Russo-Japanese War, by the "nine warrior gods" in the special naval attack force at Pearl Harbor, and by kamikaze pilots later in the Pacific War. These poems were intended to honor men who gave their lives, and to inspire greater dedication, both on the battlefront and the home front (see chapter eight).

Strong "group" identity among Japanese, as members of a family, employees of a company, soldiers in a platoon, or citizens of a nation, along with the country's long tradition of self-sacrificing warriors, has frequently been cited to explain such copious exaltations of war dead. During the conflicts in China and the Pacific, poets, particularly composers of *tanka*, specifically condemned "individualism" and "freedom" and praised the loyalty and self-sacrifice of Japanese who were said to be "rediscovering the true way of the warrior" (*makoto no bushi no michi*).[50] Thousands of *gunka* were inspired in 1932 by the attack near Shanghai in which three Japanese soldiers from Kyushu, carrying demolition canisters, plunged through barbed wire into a heavily fortified Chinese installation. All three died in the explosion that opened the perimeter for an invasion of Japanese forces. Japanese newspapers even ran contests for poems honoring "the three brave warriors," in which panels of poets chose the prize-winning entries. Yosano Tekkan (1873–1935) earned the prize at the *Tōkyō nichi-nichi shinbun* for "Human Bombs: The Three Brave Warriors," which concludes:

Aa Kōnan no ume nara de,
  sakete chiru mi o hana to nashi
Jingi no gun ni sasagetaru
  kuni no seika no san'yūshi.
	Ah, like the plum blossoms of Kiangnan,
	  bodies torn and scattered become flowers.
	The three brave warriors, flowers of our nation,
	  offered to the army of humanity and justice.

Chūkon kiyoki ka wo tsutae
  nagaku tenka o hagemashimu.
	The pure fragrance of their loyal spirits
	  will long inspire the nation.

Sōretsu muhi no san'yūshi,	With the unparalleled heroism of the three brave warriors,
hikari no meiyo no san'yūshi.	with the shining honor, of the three brave warriors.[51]

Although poetry explicitly honoring soldiers who die willingly in war is less plentiful in Europe and America, poems and the lyrics to patriotic songs sometimes mention them. Katherine Lee Bates's poem "America the Beautiful," first published in 1942 at the beginning of U.S. involvement in World War II, contains the lines:

O beautiful for heroes proved
In liberating strife,
Who more than self their
country loved,
And mercy more than life![52]

In earlier examples of American poetry specifically honoring the death of soldiers, the anonymous poem below was inspired by the clash between the battleships *United States* and *Macedonian* in the War of 1812, the same conflict that produced Francis Scott Key's *The Star-Spangled Banner*.[53]

Now chain-shot, grape, and langrage pierces through her oaken sides,
And many a gallant sailor's blood runs purpling in the tides;
While death flew nimbly o'er their decks,
Some lost their legs, and some their necks,
And glory's wreath our ship be-decks,
For brave Yankee boys.[54]

In "Boy Brittan" (1862), on the Battle of Fort Henry, Forceythe Willson praises the "immortality" of young men who died in the Civil War:

. . . .
And there at the captain's feet, among the dead and dying;
The shot-marred form of a beautiful boy is lying—
There in his uniform!

Laurels and tears for thee, boy,
Laurels and tears for thee!
Laurels of light, moist with the precious dew
Of the inmost heart of the nation's loving heart,
And blest by the balmy breath of the beautiful and true;
. . . .
And laurels of light, and tears of truth,
And the mantle of immortality;

And the flowers of love and immortal youth,
And the tender heart-tokens of all true ruth—
    And everlasting victory!
And the breath and bliss of Liberty;
And the loving kiss of Liberty;
And the welcoming light of heavenly eyes,
And the cover of God's canopy;

For all the brave who rest with thee;
And for one and all who died with thee;

. . . .
On the solid land or heaving sea,
    Dear warrior-boy—like thee.[55]

Like Tekkan, Willson compares fallen soldiers to flowers. Certainly none of the three American poems quoted above could be described as great literature written by a major poet. However, Henry Wadsworth Longfellow (1807–82), who has several works in the standard canon of American poetry, published poems that, like those of Siegfried Sassoon, opposed war at one time and supported it at another. Longfellow wrote "The Arsenal at Springfield," often included in collections and anthologies, reportedly after he and his new wife were appalled to see the array of weapons stored at this Massachusetts army depot that they visited on their honeymoon. "We grew quite warlike against war," Mrs. Longfellow wrote, "and I urged H. to write a peace poem." At this time the United States was mobilizing for war with Mexico. When hostilities commenced, Longfellow denounced "this shabby and . . . disgraceful war with Mexico." He urged that money be spent not on arsenals but on schools.[56] His poem, first published in 1845, reads in part:

Were half the power that fills the world with terror,
    Were half the wealth, bestowed on camps and courts,
Given to redeem the human mind from error,
    There were no need of arsenals and forts:

The warrior's name would be a name abhorred
    And every nation, that should lift again
Its hand against a brother, on its forehead
    Would wear forevermore the curse of Cain![57]

Yet a few years later Longfellow wrote "The 'Cumberland'" (February 6, 1862), a grandiloquent eulogy to a battleship sunk by the Confederate navy in the Civil War. Longfellow's poem concludes with this two-stanza tribute to sailors who died in an armed conflict he apparently deemed worthy of their sacrifice. For reasons discussed in the conclusion to this study, "The 'Cumberland'" has not been enshrined in the canon of American poetry.

> Next morn, as the sun rose over the bay,
>   Still floated our flag at mainmast head.
> Lord, how beautiful was Thy day!
>   Every waft of the air
>   Was a whisper of prayer,
> Or a dirge for the dead.
>
> Ho! brave hearts that went down in the seas,
>   Ye are at peace in the troubled stream.
> Ho! brave land! with hearts like these,
>   Thy flag, that is rent and twain,
>   Shall be one again,
> And without a seam![58]

Although the exhortation for soldiers and sailors to give their lives appears less frequently in American than in Japanese poems on war, verses written everywhere in support of armed conflict tend to emphasize collective goals and to treat individual suffering and death as necessary and honorable sacrifices for some larger cause. As noted above, however, sacrifices portrayed as necessary by a poet in one poem may be condemned as outrageous in another.

Like Sassoon and Longfellow, many poets in Japan have expressed contradictory attitudes toward war at different times, sometimes swinging "full circle" in their depictions of armed conflict. Government and public pressures in wartime have undoubtedly played a part in these changing views. In September 1914 Britain's Department of Information (that is, of propaganda) summoned several writers to urge the "organization of public statements of the strength of the British case and principles in the war by well-known men of letters." Such official exhortations accounted at least in part for the deluge that followed of some 3,000 English war poems by 2,225 poets during World War I.[59] Coercion was more direct and punitive in wartime Japan, where the government was armed with the broadened provisions of the Peace Preservation Law, originally promulgated in 1925, which authorities used to pursue even people said to have "dangerous thoughts" (*kiken shisō*). Harassment and arrests of socialist and anarchist writers escalated sharply after the Manchurian Incident in 1931. Several were released from prison and joined in support of the war after recanting their mainly Marxist beliefs by making ideological conversions called *tenkō* or *gise-tenkō* (fake conversions). Some refused to convert, however, and thus served long, hard terms in prison. Novelist Kobayashi

Takiji, for instance, died in prison from torture in 1933. Censorship, enforced erratically since the early Meiji period, became stricter and more systematic after the outbreak of full-scale war with China in 1937. Then, during the Pacific War, military censors could ban distribution, prevent publication, or expurgate portions of anything that, in their opinion, might imply criticism of the war effort or threaten public morale.[60] The situation was reversed after the defeat, when the Allied Occupation banned publication of noncritical references to war or the military, even to legendary ancient battles or mythical warriors in classical and children's literature.

Yet, in the light of biographical studies and historical accounts of contemporary conditions, it seems clear that poets wrote for and against war at different times in their careers mostly out of genuine conviction. As for Sassoon, his assertion in 1917 that the British government had "deliberately prolong[ed] . . . these sufferings [of war] for ends which I believe to be evil and unjust" sounds no less sincere than his exhortation to British soldiers twenty-three years later, in the face of Nazi aggression: "None are exempt from service in this hour. / And vanquished in ourselves we dare not be." Examples of Japanese poets who, like Sassoon and Longfellow, wrote on both sides of the issue can be found long before the China and Pacific Wars that produced the largest numbers of conversions. Yosano Tekkan turned out gladiatorial *tanka* in 1894 at the start of the Sino-Japanese War, asserting that he looked forward to the "killing of pigs" in this "thrilling" battle, and even offered "to take up the sword" himself. Yet three years later, Tekkan, who never served in the military abroad, denounced war as "murder" supported by "false sages" in a poem written after he had visited Japanese families bereaved by the conflict. Then by 1904 he had swung full circle with poetry praising the suicide missions of Japanese naval forces that year at Port Arthur and, later, extolling the "human bomb" attack by Japanese soldiers in 1932 near Shanghai (see chapter two).

Miyazaki Koshoshi also wrote in 1894 of how his "heart . . . was inspired by the sound of the guns that shot and sank the Chinese ships." In a poem published the following year, however, Koshoshi denounced "voices all around us shouting of victory and defeat" and pleaded for "a way to abolish war" (see chapter three). In "Song of the Assault," appearing in June 1904 at the height of the Russo-Japanese War, Ōtsuka Naoko (1875–1910) admonished Japanese soldiers "to die in battle" because "to retreat one step will disgrace you." Yet in a poem published seven months later she posed the wrenching dilemma of a soldier's wife asked to choose between her husband and "the nation." Her answer: "I shall not reply, but only weep." In 1904 Yosano Akiko (1878–1942), Tekkan's wife, who far surpassed him as a poet, published what has gained the reputation as Japan's most famous antiwar poem. Its title and refrain entreat her brother at the Russo-Japanese front, "Brother, Do Not Give Your Life" (*Kimi shinitamō koto nakare*), and it denounces armed conflict in which "men spill one another's blood and die like beasts." Yet Akiko later joined her husband in writing poetry lauding the 1932 "human bomb" attack in China, and in 1942 she published *tanka* praising "our brave soldiers" and urging her son, a navy lieutenant on a battleship in the Pacific, to "fight bravely" (see chapter five).

It is all too easy, looking back, to snicker at such inconsistency. Clearly, few writers anywhere maintain entirely static views on war or other large questions of the human condition, preferring to modify their ideas as careers develop and times change. Akiko's plea in 1904 for her brother not to give his life at Port Arthur is expressed in the context of her assertion that the goals of the war against Russia had no relevance for her family. Later, from the highly distorted information available in the Japanese press during the conflicts in China and the Pacific, she evidently became convinced of the rightness of Japan's cause, which she described in China as an effort to "restore peace" by "rescuing" that nation from the grip of battling and corrupt military cliques, and, in the Pacific, as "this sacred war" (see chapter five). With strict control of news from abroad, the government was generally able to persuade Japanese intellectuals, including writers, that the nation was fighting to preserve itself, and to liberate Asia from Western colonialism and racial prejudice. Many responded enthusiastically by publishing bellicose verses that later caused them embarrassment. The tendency of poets in Japan since 1945 to cover up their wartime writing, fearing ridicule, is regrettable because we all need to be reminded of war's profound effects on a nation's cultural life. Critical acknowledgment by Takamura Kōtarō and Saitō Mokichi of their wartime poems proves that inconsistency on this issue does not necessarily ruin writers' reputations or diminish their literary achievements.

It would also be much too easy, considering their respective sides in World War II, to commend Siegfried Sassoon for his "conversion" and condemn Yosano Akiko for hers. I hope to show in this study that, taking into account the circumstances in which poets have experienced wars and written about them, to pass such facile judgments would be an abuse of hindsight. It is in this spirit that I examine these changing views of war in historical and cultural context, focusing principally on the work of eleven poets.[61] I discuss their writing styles, philosophical perspectives, and professional associations, as well as their experiences of war on the battlefront and the home front. Many of their poems convey views of war congruent with contemporary public opinion and official propaganda, but there are also notable expressions of dissent. While the subject of war has inspired poetry of high quality that is now understandably included in the canon of modern Japanese poetry, a number of poems discussed in this study are humorous for reasons that their authors could hardly have intended. Recognizing this wide range in quality, I have included critical evaluations of poems throughout as well as some thoughts in the concluding chapter on what makes a "good" war poem.

I also examine how poets' writings on war were interpreted and evaluated when first published, as well as in subsequent years. Opinions of these works, which often vary widely among individual critics, have undergone considerable change over time with the shifting of popular, intellectual, and official ideologies in Japan and elsewhere. During the course of four or five decades the same poem might be praised, condemned, ignored, censored, and then praised or condemned again—judgments that often reflect prevailing philosophical and political trends, not only among literary critics and readers, but in the press and the government as well. With revulsion toward war frequently expressed in Japan since 1945, it is understandable that critics and historians tend to emphasize poets' antiwar poems and to ignore the poetry they wrote at other times in support of Japanese military actions abroad. However, this has sometimes led to confusion, as in the erroneous characterization of poet Yosano Akiko, who wrote both for and against war, as a lifelong pacifist. Furthermore, antiwar labels have recently been applied to poems by such prominent writers as Mori Ōgai (1862–1922) and Shimazaki Tōson (1872–1943). Although these poems describe the devastation of armed conflict, they do not express opposition to war generally, portraying it rather as an unfortunate necessity in some circumstances or as an inevitable manifestation of human nature.

Finally, a word on translations in this book, all of which are mine except where otherwise noted. Ideally, a successful translation of poetry should faithfully convey images and ideas in a diction and tone that correspond to the original. In practice, however, it is impossible to transfer all nuances, implications, and potential interpretations in a poem from one language to another. The task was, perhaps, a little easier in this study, which is limited to modern poetry on war, though, of course, the reader will have to judge the results. Modern verse, especially in Japan where it is usually dated from the 1870s, tends to be more explicit and colloquial than classical poetry. Furthermore, since virtually all poems in this volume deal with one subject, a focus is maintained that lightens the burden on the translator to provide contexts. To be sure, cultural divergences can sometimes make the impact of a word or image very different in two languages. Yet, with war being regrettably ubiquitous among humankind, the expressions and evocations of these poems in Japanese, especially concerning natural phenomena, often carry similar metaphoric implications in English that invite comparisons with British and American poetry on war.

Many people contributed invaluable assistance and advice to this project. I especially wish to thank Ann Berent-Johannsen, Amy Vladeck Heinrich, and Laurel Rasplica Rodd for their criticisms of the manuscript; Yuriko Saito for her criticisms of the translations; Seiko Furuhashi, Faye Mizusaki, George L. Newman, and Tazuko Wada for their assistance in obtaining reprint permissions; and Bruce E. Willoughby for his advice on many matters and astute final editing.

1 Masaoka Shiki: Troubled Journey to the Front

Poet Masaoka Shiki (1867–1902) was editing the *haiku* column for the newspaper *Nippon* when Japan and China declared war on each other in August 1894. From its founding five years earlier, *Nippon* had sought in its editorial policy to encourage the growing nationalistic sentiment in Japan that was finding expression in the country's political and cultural life. Japan had achieved much in the first two decades of the Meiji era (1868–1912). Determined to build a strong and prosperous nation that could resist pressures from Western powers, government leaders had embarked on a crash program to import European and American technology that spurred rapid industrialization. The vast transformation effected by railroads, electrification, factories, and compulsory education proved enormously productive, though the changes led to disruptions in traditional life-styles and marred areas of the landscape. The nation had benefited, too, from importations of art, literature, music, and philosophy from abroad. Yet overeager efforts to adopt Western styles of dress, dietary habits, and cultural artifacts began to provoke a backlash. By the end of the 1880s people in Japan were reacting against uncritical imitations of clothes, manners, and gadgets. Discontent was also growing over the continuance of the always-unpopular unequal treaties, which maintained extraterritoriality and other special privileges for the nationals of several Western countries. Resentment over these treaties helped to fuel widespread opinion that Japan should expand its influence on the Asian mainland in order to enhance its status in Western eyes as a powerful nation and thus to hasten revision of the treaties. Responding to the cultural and political climate of the times, influential people in and out of government called for a revival of indigenous traditions and for positive action that would assert Japanese interests abroad.[62]

As an ardent advocate of these views, *Nippon* sustained a temporary government ban in early 1894 for going too far beyond official policy in demanding immediate treaty revision. Shortly after resuming publication, it joined other Japanese newspapers enthusiastically supporting the war against China. *Nippon* competed vigorously with the press organs of the day to supply a public hungry for information about a conflict widely proclaimed by prominent Japanese intellectuals to be a "just war." The conflict was also viewed by many at home and abroad as the acid test of Japan's military, which had been developed as a primary component in the nation's costly industrialization program. *Nippon* dispatched several writers from its staff to the front as war correspondents, and Masaoka Shiki, though suffering from tuberculosis that had already caused a series of lung hemorrhages, volunteered eagerly to join them. In *Waga yamai* (My illness), a closely autobiographical novel published six years later, Shiki wrote that he felt "a terrible loneliness" sitting in the newspaper's office surrounded by the empty desks of writers who had already left for the front. Though he recalled worrying briefly about his own safety, he concluded, "Unless I could see service with the troops somehow, there would be no point in having been born a man."[63]

Shiki's earlier writings suggest that his wish to join the troops went well beyond a desire to validate his manhood. From his youth he had wanted to work in service to the nation, but chronically poor health prevented him from pursuing a career in politics. Later, he saw his mission as a writer partly in patriotic terms, as he sought to reform Japanese poetry by taking it back to its origins. His column fit well into the editorial perspective at *Nippon* and spoke to the revived interest among Japanese in the nation's indigenous artistic and literary forms overshadowed by the recent fascination with all things Western. In 1894 Shiki began advocating a return to what he viewed as traditional Japanese poetic ideals of sincerity and simplicity that he found expressed in *Man'yōshū,* Japan's first officially sponsored anthology of poetry, compiled in the eighth century. Shiki's rediscovery of *Man'yōshū* inspired him to write essays praising it as poetry coming directly from the heart and to imitate the language and tone of some of its poems in his own work.[64] He compared this anthology favorably with *Kokinshū* (905), in which he found too much imitation of Chinese poetry.

Shiki's essays honoring *Man'yōshū,* which were published shortly before the outbreak of war with China, reflect the trend in Japan toward renewed pride in the nation's cultural past. However, despite his reservations about *Kokinshū*, his sense of patriotic mission as a writer did not lead him to the xenophobic extremes that sometimes characterized mid-Meiji nationalism. Shiki accompanied his call for Japanese poetry to look to its roots with the assertion that Japanese literature also had much to gain from infusions of ideas from abroad. To defend the short, compact *haiku* from its recent detractors in Japan, Shiki cited the work of English philosopher Herbert Spencer (1820–1903), a strong advocate of stylistic economy, who wrote that "the shortest sentence is the best."[65] The same year that he embraced *Man'yōshū,* Shiki also began to advocate the principle of *shasei* ("realistic description" or "copying from life") as a basis for writing *haiku.* He had borrowed the term from Western-style painter Nakamura Fusetsu (1866–1943), who much admired the techniques and concepts of illusionist realism.[66] For Shiki, as for other poets and novelists, practicing the ideals of *shasei* meant writing from closely autobiographical sources about actual events, observed and experienced. Thus, his espousal of *shasei* in 1894 also helps explain why he found it "truly unbearable" that his illness would prevent him from witnessing firsthand a war that essayist Takayama Chogyū (1871–1902) called "this once-in-a-lifetime event," and why Shiki believed that going to the battlefront was his "duty as a writer."[67]

Shiki finally got his chance in February 1895, six months after the outbreak of hostilities. The staff at *Nippon* decided after a special meeting that he could travel to China despite his condition. Shiki later recalled:

> There was nothing to compare with my happiness at that moment. Of course, everyone at the newspaper was concerned about my poor health and urged me to abandon the idea. Even a doctor I knew told me not to go, as did everyone else with whom I discussed it. Still, I had no intention of giving up. . . . I did not care what happened to me. I was just happy to be going to the front.[68]

Masaoka Shiki remained a dedicated nationalist and continued to espouse the principles of *shasei* until his death seven years later from the illness that was severely exacerbated by his hardship-filled trip to China with the Imperial Japanese Army. But his writings on this journey to the war zone show that, like Siegfried Sassoon and other British poets who penned rousing platitudes about the battlefield before going off to World War I, he encountered horrors and deprivations that were beyond anything he had anticipated. No poet writing about war conveys a more rapid and profound change of attitude after witnessing the effects of armed conflict. Shiki's poems on the aftermath of battles at Chin-chou and Port Arthur express initial shock and revulsion followed by deep sorrow upon viewing the corpses of soldiers and civilians killed in the recent fighting and walking through villages abandoned and destroyed. His prose in *Jūgun kiji* (Record of my journey with the army, 1896) bristles with anger at the tyrannical and insulting treatment accorded Japanese writers who accompanied the Imperial Army to the battlefront. Of his ordeal he wrote, "What I learned and felt left a permanent mark on my heart."[69]

Shiki was still in a state of elation, however, when he set out on March 5, 1895 for Hiroshima, which was Japanese military headquarters during the conflict and the point of embarkation for troops and accompanying reporters. He later recalled experiencing a moment of concern about his own safety in a war zone as his train left Tokyo Station, but it "did not last as far as Kanagawa,"[70] Tokyo's neighboring prefecture to the west.

Perhaps Shiki was fortunate that the wheels of bureaucracy turned slowly after his arrival in Hiroshima. Tired of waiting more than a week for orders, he traveled to Matsuyama in Shikoku on March 15 to spend three days in his hometown and visit his father's grave. He was finally granted official permission for the trip to China on March 21, but he did not receive his departure orders for another two weeks. In the meantime, Chinese and Japanese forces had signed a cease-fire agreement on March 30, which cast doubt on Shiki's prospects for witnessing any actual fighting, a turn of events he noted regretfully in his diary: "Though I have received permission, I have not yet embarked. Now, already, a truce has been concluded. How much longer will I have to wait in discontent, my hopes unrestrained?"[71] Orders finally arrived on April 7 for Shiki to join the Imperial Army's Konoe Division in China, but on the eve of his departure he apparently had an inkling of what lay ahead. In a letter to Matsuyama dated the same day he received embarkation orders, Shiki wrote, "everyone complains that the Konoe Division is especially hard on reporters, and that baggage limitations are severe."[72]

As soon as Shiki boarded the troopship *Kaijō-maru*, bound for Manchuria, he realized that the rumors he had been hearing about the army's treatment of reporters were grossly understated. He describes with fierce indignation the constant harassment and calculated discomfort of his horrendous passage in *Record of My Journey with the Army*, published by *Nippon* in January and February 1896.[73] Though first appearing in sections, this work is not a series of dated dispatches of the kind Japanese journalists were sending back from China. Rather, Shiki presented a unified essay, with an introduction and conclusion, in which he tried to put his experience into perspective within the contexts of the war effort and the role of reporters who accompany soldiers to the front. His shock and outrage come through powerfully when he writes about the way he was treated by the army, yet his ordeal cannot be said to have diminished his nationalism or his belief in Japan's need for a strong military—views that, if anything, he expressed more emphatically after the Sino-Japanese War and the Triple Intervention. Still, his unsparing account of life for journalists traveling with the military is marked by acid portrayals of Imperial Army soldiers and by an accusatory tone.

In this essay he articulates both his harsh criticism and his subsequent proposals for reform in a manner that recalls "remonstrations of a loyal subject" from the works of Mencius (373–289 B.C.). Shiki was intimately familiar with Mencius, having been drilled assiduously as a child in the Chinese classics by his grandfather, a distinguished Confucian scholar.[74] Shiki's frequent use of parallelism and rhetorical questions in *Record of My Journey with the Army* also gives this piece the stylistic flavor of classical Chinese expository prose.

> In a nation there must be newspapers; in a war there must be reporters. They are assigned with the army, not for the benefit of one or two newspapers, but for the sake of the entire nation, including its officers and men. . . . So how can there be any disputing that common decency and courtesy should be observed?[75]

Besides stylistic similarities, Shiki follows a format typical of classical Chinese prose in moving from this statement of general principles to specific examples that illustrate the condescending attitude of Japanese soldiers toward journalists. He recalls hearing officers tell their troops to "think of reporters as thieves" and to treat them "the same as privates," the lowest-ranking enlisted men who were themselves notoriously abused physically and psychologically in the Imperial Army.[76]

> This goes beyond inhospitality and is demeaning. They insult us this way because, to them, we are like dogs or cats. Yet, as reporters traveling with the army, we are denied the right to object. Even if we had the right, complaining would only be to our detriment. As long as we are reporters with the army, we have to suppress our anger and endure these insults for the sake of our newspapers or the state.
>
> In ancient times there was a saying, "honor to officials, contempt for commoners," . . . but minor clerks reviling taxpayers are not just dreams from some distant past. Even in this Meiji period who could imagine that war correspondents, by whose efforts the exploits of battle are honored throughout the world, would be afraid to express their indignation when forced to kowtow to officers, commissioned and noncommissioned, or to beg for food and tea? . . . Such provisions are supplied by the state,

> but privates think of them as their property and make reporters feel like parasites at a stranger's house. We are, after all, as much citizens of Japan as they. Moreover, these soldiers talk proudly about maintaining strict discipline and using proper forms of address. Yet, they call reporters "paperboys," and we are expected to bow meekly to them. They see themselves as our masters and make us feel like moochers. . . . Reporters must be treated with respect![77]

In *Record of My Journey with the Army*, Shiki concedes that journalists should be prepared for hardships in the field, where the availability of food and lodging is dictated by local conditions. Yet he cannot forgive the Imperial Army's harsh treatment of him and his fellow reporters aboard ship, where they were "packed together like cattle" in spaces so cramped that sleep was impossible because their bodies were wedged between the ship's cargo and quarters for enlisted men, who were constantly yelling at them for taking up too much room. Shiki notes bitterly that Shinto and Buddhist priests, who traveled under official imperial appointments, enjoyed the privileges of sleeping and dining in first-class cabins. Of the food reporters ate in shipboard mess halls, he writes: "The rice was like pebbles [and] the few drops of tea [tasted as though] made from water heated in the bath. The one cup and pair of chopsticks issued us were caked with dirt, which made eating all the more unpleasant." Shiki characterized the way reporters were pushed and shoved when they lined up for meals in the mess hall as "a struggle for survival in which weaklings would starve." He writes that, when they tried coming for food after the troops had eaten theirs, the sergeant major in charge said feeding them late was too much trouble. Then, asked if someone might bring them their meals, the sergeant retorted, "Get them yourselves, fools, or you won't eat" (156–63).

If reporters' expectations seemed unrealistic at times, Shiki insisted that he was less concerned about the quality of the food and sleeping quarters than "the complete absence of courtesy toward us." He was particularly offended by disrespectful language, such as *dete ike* (get out) and *baka yarō* (idiot!): "I wouldn't have minded if such words were spoken once or twice in moments of anger, . . . but how can we not feel demeaned when they are used constantly . . . and with contempt that is obviously from the heart" (164).

After arriving at Chin-chou, Shiki went with other reporters to the Imperial Army's Fourth Division field headquarters to file a complaint over their treatment. What followed was the poet's first encounter with a classic military runaround in which officers at various levels of command first denied any responsibility for the problem and later insisted they had no authority to take action. "Two or three days later the staff officer told us, 'I passed your complaint on to the commander here, but he can do nothing because the sergeant major you speak of is in another unit'"(166). The reporters finally got results when some of them immediately requested permission to return to Japan. For a time things improved: they were given better quarters, canned goods, and even sake. Shiki writes that, although their cubicles at Dairen "resembled prison cells," at least they slept in rooms and were served food by "one Chinese boy" whom he refers to as *Chan hitori* (169).

Yet the reporters' troubles were far from over with their disembarkment in China. Shiki complains about the disdainful attitude and paternalistic restrictions they encountered constantly as they traveled with the Imperial Army to Chin-chou, Luang-tao, and Port Arthur: "[When arriving at new quarters] we always felt like young brides entering our father-in-law's house, and returning to Konoe Division headquarters was like going back to a mother-in-law" (161). Shiki observes that the men of the Konoe Division were proud of their reputation as an elite force and were deeply offended when no reporters showed up to welcome troops from the division returning to Hiroshima after completing their tours of duty. Konoe soldiers, according to Shiki, had expected that reporters, considering their status at the front, would be there to carry their baggage and generally wait on them at the pier (171).

However, by far the worst experiences Shiki describes in *Record of My Journey with the Army* occurred during his own return trip to Japan aboard the troopship *Sadogoku-maru*, nicknamed the *Umeboshi-maru* (*S.S. Pickled Plum*). He complains that the food and accommodations were, if possible, even more abominable than those aboard the *Kaijō-maru*. Not only did soldiers mistreat reporters, but they fought among themselves in what Shiki portrays as a complete breakdown of discipline and order. A riot nearly erupted, he writes, after several cholera patients died (169). In this piece he does not mention the relapse of his own illness, suffered aboard the *Sadogoku-maru*, but he later wrote of the severe lung hemorrhage that caused him to cough up large quantities of blood during the trip.[78] When at last the ship reached Kobe on May 23, 1895, he was carried to a hospital and was in critical condition. He remained there for two months and, at one point, was thought so close to death that doctors summoned his family from Matsuyama. Though he finally left the hospital and resumed writing, he remained bedridden for most of the remaining seven years of his life.

Though occasionally pompous and naive, Shiki's account of reporters' ordeals during the Sino-Japanese War has been confirmed by other writers. Sakurai Chūon (1879–1965), author of the best-selling book *Nikudan* (Human bullets, 1906) based on his later experiences as an Imperial Army lieutenant in the Russo-Japanese War, recalled that Japanese journalists assigned to cover the conflict with China were treated worse than cavalry horses aboard troopships and were sometimes suspected of being spies. They were denied food and blankets in some locations, where they were forced to sleep outside the barracks and scrounge wild plants for nourishment. Furthermore, the army refused to let reporters mail their dispatches from camp, ordering them to walk long distances to field post offices where they had to submit all written materials for censorship before mailing.[79] Kuroda Koshirō, a reporter for the *Tōkyō nichi-nichi shinbun*, met Shiki in China and urged him to return to Japan as soon as possible. "You are sure to get sick here," he warned, "and if you die, you'll be thrown away in a field like a dog or a cat." Of Shiki's death at thirty-six, Kuroda later wrote that "the army killed him."[80]

Considering Kuroda's indictment and Shiki's own outrage, the poet's "Conclusion" to *Record of My Journey with the Army* seems remarkably mild. He advises Konoe Division soldiers to show reporters some respect if they want better press. He recommends that the army formulate reasonable standards in the future for the treatment of journalists accompanying the troops. He calls on officers, in particular, to take the lead in preventing the kind of abuses reporters endured during the Sino-Japanese War. While his criticisms of the army are severe, Shiki frames them in this conclusion as the pleas for reform of a loyal subject determined to be of service to his nation by improving relations between its armed forces and the press, not as the denunciations of a protester against the inherent ruthlessness of military organizations or the ultimate folly of war. In fact, he had even expressed regret earlier for "returning ignominiously" from China "without hearing the sound of a cannon, seeing the rain of shells, or feeling even one new bruise on my arm" in dated journal entries of poetry and prose that *Nippon* published as *Jinchū nikki* (Diary at the front) in July 1895.[81] One wonders, of course, how long his eagerness to witness combat would have lasted had he actually come under hostile fire. Still, in Shiki's case, it is perhaps understandable if he thought he might have fared better in an enemy attack than at the hands of "friendly" forces.

It is precisely because Shiki's horrendous experiences do not lead him to more far-reaching philosophical and political conclusions that *Record of My Journey with the Army* has been faulted by recent literary critics in Japan. That he did not extend his criticism of the Imperial Army to arrive at a more broadly critical view of Japan's military establishment, of its influence on the nation as a whole, of the Meiji government's foreign policy, or of war itself, has been called a "weak point" of this work.[82] Such judgments would seem to require that Shiki reach conclusions about the Sino-Japanese conflict similar to those that Uchimura Kanzō (1861–1930) did in 1895 after initially supporting it as a "just war." Surely, this would have been difficult considering Shiki's fundamental ethic of loyalty to the Meiji state, grounded in his early Confucian training, which contrasted sharply with Uchimura's Christian, internationalist, and (after early 1895) pacifist views. Beyond this, Uchimura was primarily a philosopher who often expressed moral and religious opinions about contemporary events, whereas Shiki was a poet who saw his primary mission as "realistic description" (*shasei*) of them. If there is a philosophical strain in *Record of My Journey with the Army*, it can perhaps best be summed up in Confucian terms as a remonstration against soldiers who fail to act in a soldierly way that should be characterized by discipline and courtesy, and who consequently hurt the reputation of the army and the cause of the nation they are serving. In this essay Shiki echoes the mixture of Confucian principles and *bushidō* codes of conduct expressed in the Meiji government's 1882 *Imperial Rescript to Soldiers and Sailors*, which admonishes that military men

> who . . . appreciate true valor should in their daily intercourse set gentleness first and aim to win the love and esteem of others. If you affect valor and act with violence, the world will in the end detest you and look upon you as wild beasts. Of this you should take heed.[83]

Shiki's criticisms and his limited calls for reform are stated within an expository framework, but *Record of My Journey with the Army* achieves its impact more from depictions of his own experience than from the rigor of his argument, which contains some notable inconsistencies. Demeaning, epithetic reference to Chinese, even at the time of this war, seems out of place in a work that appears to borrow structurally and rhetorically from Chinese prose models, though Shiki was hardly alone among Japanese in this incongruence. Images abounded in Japan of China as a once-great nation that had fallen into corruption and disarray. A more central problem in this piece arises with Shiki's strong objection to the "unequal treatment" of reporters in comparison with Shinto and Buddhist clergy, which rings hollow when he complains that he and his colleagues were being treated "the same as common soldiers" (*ippei-sotsu dōyō*). At a climactic moment when Shiki reached the point where he could no longer bear to suffer indignities in silence, his outrage was triggered, he writes, by a staff officer at Chin-chou who informed him that journalists were considered to be of the same status as privates:

> Until then I had suppressed my feelings and tried to talk politely. . . . Now anger welled up inside me. "Privates? Privates? We are like privates?" I could barely speak.
>
> "Yes, just like privates."
>
> This cut off any chance for further discussion. I turned resolutely and went back to my room.[84]

What he writes about privates, with whom he had to contend for sleeping space aboard ship, tends to demean them and, inadvertently, to inspire sympathy among readers today for the plight of lower-ranking enlisted men in an army famous for imposing cruel hardships on young recruits. In Japanese society, where considerations of status are pervasive, it is perhaps understandable that a distinguished poet would resent being quartered with these men. Yet, while he depicts the beleaguered state of reporters effectively, he fails to consider that the privates who are his special nemeses might have been venting their own frustrations over harsh treatment at the hands of their superiors. The reader can readily share Shiki's indignation, but one suspects that his problems were exacerbated because, as he says himself, "We were all shocked, being entirely unaccustomed to military discipline" (157). He later maintains, of course, that it was the "lack of discipline" that most troubled him.

Shiki's references to Chinese are demeaning in *Record of My Journey with the Army*, but his portrayals of them are decidedly mixed in his other writings on this trip to the war zone. He wrote highly sympathetic poetry on Chinese soldiers and civilians victimized by the fighting, and even a tribute to one soldier's devotion to duty. Besides *Record of My Journey with the Army* and *Diary at the Front*, he published *shintaishi* in *Kinshū zasshi* (Miscellaneous poems on Chin-chou, 1896) and *Omoideru mama* (As I remember it, 1895), which is an essay on his impressions of contemporary Chinese culture, and another series of *haiku* and *shintaishi*, entitled *Meiji 29* (1896), on the war in retrospect. Because the two sides signed a truce while he was still delayed at Hiroshima, Shiki arrived in China too late to witness any fighting. However, he visited the fortresses at Chin-chou and Port Arthur that the Japanese army had recently seized after battles with Chinese defenders, which, in the case of Port Arthur, led to charges of atrocities on both sides. Heavy shelling had wreaked widespread damage at Chin-chou, where Shiki came upon the corpses of Chinese soldiers and civilians in fields surrounding the fortress and observed the post-battle desolation of nearby villages. From what was perhaps his first encounter with violent death came his most affecting poems on Chinese victims of the war. However, he portrays the Chinese at other times in highly stereotypical ways and makes pointedly unfavorable comparisons between China and Japan. Describing what he saw en route to Chinchou in *Diary at the Front*, Shiki finds in the refusal of a Chinese onion peddler to lower his prices an example of "the stubbornness of these people" and "their quick eye for profit." Later, examining the impressive array of weapons and ammunition captured by the Imperial Army at Port Arthur, Shiki echoes widespread opinion in Japan that Chinese soldiers were inept and cowardly:

> Among the many large cannon emplaced here, some sixty feet above the ocean, are two with calibers of twenty-four centimeters. The one on the right, called a rotating cannon, is a weapon not yet seen in Japan that can be fired by one person in any direction. But inanimate objects need people to operate them, and in the hands of the Chinese they were as useless as junk. And speaking of things they failed to make use of before fleeing their coastal battery under fire, everything from the gunpowder storehouse to the iron rail that carried shells underground was left intact. (88–89)

Shiki's appraisals are more varied when he sketches his impressions of Chinese calligraphy, architecture, music, and theater in *As I Remember It*. He makes no claim to expertise in this short essay but speaks as a traveler observing what he encounters with a critical eye. He describes Chinese houses, which are usually one story, as cramped compared to those in Japan, but he adds that they have a certain "archaic elegance" (*koga*). He finds calligraphy in China to be quite good on the whole, noting that even characters over the doorways of ordinary people's homes were drawn more skillfully than those found on houses in Japan. Comparing Chinese to Japanese theater, he writes that works for the stage in China, as in Japan, seemed to be divided into historical plays, usually long and serious, and plays on contemporary life, mostly humorous and frequently depicting love affairs. However, he complains about multiple characters and what he calls a lack of discernible focus for the action in Chinese plays, which have large numbers of actors entering and exiting the stage "as in a military drill":

> It goes without saying that, in this respect, Chinese drama is undeveloped and cannot be discussed in the same breath with theater in Japan. In sum, their plays lack the classical elegance of Noh drama. They are also inferior to the realism [of our

modern plays] and consist mainly of meaningless dances crudely performed. (101)

In *Diary at the Front* Shiki writes of the poverty, "unspeakable" sanitary conditions, and a generally "depressing" atmosphere in the Chinese cities he saw, understandable impressions for any first-time visitor from a country where circumstances were better than in war-torn areas of China. In a series of *haiku* entitled *Shinsenryōchi* (Newly occupied territory), however, he goes beyond a portrayal of wartime conditions to ridicule *Tōjin*, another derogatory term for Chinese people used in Meiji Japan:

Tōjin no Nihongo tsukau gyokei kana	Here the Chinamen greet us in Japanese.[85]

Shiki even denigrates China's natural scenery in comparison with Japan's. In his entry for April 15, 1895 he concludes his description of a Chinese landscape seen on his way to Chin-chou with another *haiku* exuding sarcasm:

taikoku no yama mina hikuki kasumi kana	The mountains of this big country— how short they all look in the mist![86]

Shiki's disparagement of foreign scenery foreshadows comparisons made in later Japanese literature on war and its aftermath. Imperial Army soldiers are often pictured in novels on the China War (1937–45) as marching across endless, barren plains and through teeming, dusty cities, while nostalgically recalling gentle green valleys and quiet villages back in Japan.[87] Ariyoshi Sawako (1931–84) draws a particularly scathing comparison between foreign and domestic cherry blossoms in her novel *Hishoku* (Beyond color, 1967), set during the period immediately following World War II. Her protagonist, a Japanese war bride who comes with her American husband to live in the United States, concludes that the cherry trees along the Potomac River in Washington "must have undergone a dreadful transformation" since arriving as a gift from the Japanese government in 1912. The blossoms appear to hang stiffly from their branches "like cattail ears," and their color seems thick and glossy "as in an oil painting." By contrast, the blossoms she remembers from Yasukuni Shrine in Tokyo are said to possess a pale delicacy that is retained even as they scatter in the wind.[88]

In *Diary at the Front* Masaoka Shiki, too, associates cherry blossoms with nostalgia for Japan, but they also remind him of the possibility that he might not return alive from the war zone. As emblems of perishability, cherry blossoms are traditionally associated in Japan with soldiers who fall in their prime on the battlefield at the moment of their fullest flowering of devotion to duty. Although a cease-fire had been in effect since March 30, treaty negotiations were dragging on at Shimonoseki when Shiki arrived at Chin-chou in mid-April. He first witnessed the aftermath of battle there and expressed again the uneasiness that had briefly clouded his exuberance two months earlier as he boarded the train from Tokyo to Hiroshima. He tells how reporters at Chin-chou reacted when shown the heavy damage that artillery fire had inflicted on the fortress:

> We were traveling with the army but had seen no fighting. Now we listened to a description of the recent battle with feelings of emptiness. The briefing stirred our ambitions, but what we heard caused some of us to worry about what might lie ahead.[89]

In the entry for April 16, Shiki mentions feeling homesick, remembering the cherry blossoms in Tokyo, and concludes with the following *tanka*:

Karayama no	In the mountains of China
kaze susabu nari	the wind stiffens.
furusato no	The cherry blossoms at home
Sumida no sakura	along the Sumida River—
ima ka chiruran	are they scattering now?[90]

The next day, April 17, the Treaty of Shimonoseki was signed, virtually ending Shiki's prospects for witnessing combat, about which he had expressed mixed feelings.

Though his writing in *Diary at the Front* conveys a preference for Japanese landscapes, Shiki has much praise for the flowers that were blooming abundantly at the height of spring in China. Furthermore, like his memories of Japanese cherry blossoms, the beauty of the flowers in China seems to heighten his awareness of being in a war zone. In *tanka*, *haiku*, *kanshi*, and *shintaishi* from *Miscellaneous Poems on Chin-chou*, Shiki expresses the shock and revulsion he felt at his first sight of war dead. He shares the sentiments of other poets in other times when he notes the incongruity of nature's luxuriance in the aftermath of war's devastation:

mononofu no	No one to tend
shikabane osamuru	soldiers' corpses—
hito mo nashi	violets blooming

sumire hana saku haru no yama kage	in a mountain grove in spring.
nakihito no mukuro o kakuse haru no kusa	Hide from sight the corpses of the dead, grasses of spring.[91]
kojō ya sumire hana saku ishi no ma	At this old fortress violets bloom among the stones.[92]
Sanki no yama o uchikoete ikusa no ato o tomekureba, koko mo kashiko mo murasaki ni sumire saku no no sarekōbe	Crossing the San-ch'i Mountains to see the aftermath of battle, here and there in the field where purple violets bloom—human skulls.[93]

In juxtaposing human remains with less disturbing natural phenomena, these poems resonate with certain echoes from *Nozarashi kikō* (Records of a weather-exposed skeleton), a travel journal of poetry and prose by Matsuo Bashō (1644–94) describing a long and hazardous journey he made through a dozen provinces west of Edo in 1684–85:

nozarashi o kokoro ni kaze no shimu mi kana	A weather-exposed skeleton Haunts my mind: how the wind Penetrates my body![94]

Bashō, too, writes of contemplating human remains while traveling, yet his rendering differs from Shiki's in an important way. Bashō's piercing wind conveys a feeling that is consonant with the poem's mood, while Shiki's violets blooming in a field set the stage for a shocking reversal of tone with the poem's last word. The jolting incongruity of finding the remains of war dead amid thriving plants has also been noted in British literature from World War I. Describing his impressions of the French front in 1917, Edmund Blunden carries this juxtaposition a step further in a startling simile:

> In the afternoon, looking eastward . . . , I had seen nothing but green fields and plumy grey-green trees . . . ; it was as though in this part the line could only be a trifling interruption of a happy landscape. . . . [Yet] at some points in the trench . . . skulls appeared like mushrooms.[95]

British poet Charles Sorley quips bitterly at nature's apparent indifference to war's suffering in a disturbingly prophetic poem written shortly before his death in October 1915 at the Battle of Loos:

Earth that never doubts nor fears,
Earth that knows of death, not tears,
Earth that bore with joyful ease
Hemlock for Socrates,
Earth that blossomed and was glad
'Neath the cross that Christ had,
Shall rejoice and blossom too
When the bullet reaches you.[96]

Writing on the lines below from Allen Tate's (1899–) "Ode to the Confederate Dead," Cleanth Brooks, R. W. B. Lewis, and Robert Penn Warren could be referring to Shiki's *Miscellaneous Poems on Chin-chou* when they observe that "nature is oblivious of man, quite unmindful of his aspirations and heroism."[97]

Row after row with strict impunity
The headstones yield their names to the element,
The wind whirrs without recollection;
. . . .
Autumn is desolation in the plot
Of a thousand acres where these memories grow
From the inexhaustible bodies that are not
Dead, but feed the grass row after rich row.

Although Masaoka Shiki arrived in China after the killing had ended, he noted repeatedly the irony of flowers blooming luxuriantly in the aftermath of battle. In *Diary at the Front* he describes what he saw at Chin-chou by alluding to "A Spring View" by Tu Fu (712–70), a Chinese poem so commonly cited in Japanese literature on war that it has become almost a cliché:

> I climbed to the top of a hill and looked around at the scenery inside and outside the fortress. All the apricot blossoms had scattered, and now peach, pear, and rape blossoms seemed to vie with one another as they bloomed in profusion—for whose benefit I did not know. Even the rich verdure of the parade ground was deepening, unaware that this was the soil of a ruined nation. In spite of myself, I recited "Though the nation is destroyed, the mountains and rivers remain," and was saddened.[98]

Although Shiki does not refer to it, there is, of course, another irony in the fact that he quotes classical Chinese poetry and borrows Chinese poetic and prose forms for his writing about this war.

For his poems on the men who fought in the conflict, Shiki seemed to prefer classical Japanese language, using such words found repeatedly in *Man'yōshū* as *masurao* for brave soldier and *ōkimi* for emperor. None of these poems can be said to represent his best work, and he lapses into uncharacteristic clichés in his *Miscellaneous Poems on Chin-chou* on the Japanese who died in the battle there. Below he pays homage in highly conventional ways to the soldiers killed in the assault on the fortress:

Samo are, warera masurao wa shisubeki toki ni shisuru o ba homare to sunari. Naka naka ni urayamashisa yo, sono saigo. Kimira mitama o yasunzeyo. Kinshū-jō wa tachimachi ni waga te ni ochinu. Kore mo mata kimira ga tateshi isao nari.	You brave men, determined, proud to die when you had to. Oh, how I envy your final moments! May your souls rest in peace. All at once, Chin-chou fortress fell into our hands. This is yet another of your great deeds![99]

With its formulaic expressions and anticlimactic ending, this *shintaishi* is indistinguishable from the reams of war poems composed in Japan during 1894–95. The lack of any particulars about the battle or the fallen soldiers makes it difficult for the reader to appreciate their sacrifices and causes the poet's assertion of "envy" to ring hollow and platitudinous. This poem could easily have been written by someone who had never visited the war zone.

In other *Miscellaneous Poems on Chin-chou* Shiki portrays the feelings and circumstances of the Japanese who survived the battle there with greater depth and sensitivity. "Kokyū" (Chinese violin)[100] includes a dialogue between two Japanese soldiers visiting a shrine just outside the gate of the fortress. Shiki's rendering of the passage of time in this poem through floral imagery is, to be sure, a well-worn convention of Japanese poetry. Still, the focus here on individual emotional experience makes this poem a far more compelling evocation of men sent to war in a foreign country than the one above, even though it makes no direct reference to the battlefield:

"Kuni o ideshi wa kyonen no hodo kiku tsubomitaru hodo nariki. Haha wa wakare o oshimitsutsu kaeri koran hi o itsu to toi kaesarete, ima sara ni nagusamekanetsu 'sore yo sore yo, Sumida no sakura saku koro ni miyage ninau te kaeru beshi.'"	"When I left Japan last year, chrysanthemums were in bud. My mother, lamenting my departure, asked again and again what day I would return. Now I cannot console her with 'There, there. I'll come back carrying souvenirs when the Sumida cherry trees bloom.'"
"Chikaishi koto wa wasurenedo tsukihi wa ware ni todomarazu.	"I have not forgotten what I promised, but time does not stop for me.

Haya haru kurete kono kuni no
hana mo sakari to miru kara ni,
tada natsukashiki furusato no
sakura wa yuki to fukaru ran.
Ima ya kaeru to hahabito wa
munashiku tateru mon o soto."

Already spring is ending,
and when I see the flowers
of this country in full bloom,
I think the cherry blossoms
in my hometown,
for which I long with all my heart,
might be blowing like the snow.
Perhaps even now my mother stands
  in vain outside our gate,
  awaiting my return."

Hitori ga ieba mata hitori
"ware mo zaisho ni nokoshi oku
tsuma koso ko koso ikani shite
kono hitofuyu o shinogikeme.
Kane wa okuredo henji nashi.
Fumi kakan ni wa muhitsu nari.
Mohaya ikusa no owari zo to
kiku mo ureshiya, kinō kyō."

When he had spoken, another asked,
"I left behind at home
my wife and child, too.
How did they get through the winter?
I send money, but there is no reply.
Though I write letters, they cannot.
How glad I was to hear the other day
that now the war is over."[101]

To have soldiers at Chin-chou in 1895 speak in classical language reminiscent of *Man'yōshū* heightens the sense that they share a timeless predicament with troops everywhere stationed far from home. The soldier's ever-present concern for loved ones with whom communication has become impossible is, in fact, the subject of a poem by Ōtomo no Yakamochi entitled "Parting Sorrows of a Frontier Guard" from book 20 of *Man'yōshū*:

haha no mikoto wa
mimo no suso
tsumiage kakinade
chichi no mi no
chichi no mikoto wa
takuzuno no
shirahige no ue yu
namida tari
nageki no tabaku
kagojimono
tada hitori shite
asatode no
kanashiki wagako
aratama no
toshi no o nagaku
aimizu wa
koishiku aru beshi
kyō dani mo

My mother
picking up the hem of her skirt,
Stroked me with it
and caressed me.
My father
said regretfully
with tears streaming
Down his beard
white as the *taku* rope:
"My fawn,
my only son—how sad
Your parting in the morning,
dear child!
I shall miss you
when I see you not
For such long years.
Let me talk to you
If only for to-day."

kotodoi semu to
oshimitsutsu
kanashibi maseba
wakakusa no
tsuma mo kodomo mo
ochikochi ni
sawa ni kakumi i
harutori no
koe no samayoi
shirotae no
sode nakinurashi
. . . .

He sighed and moaned.
My wife and children
gathering about
here and there,
Wailed
like the birds of spring,
Their sleeves
all wet with weeping.
. . . .

haroharo ni
wakare shi kureba
omou sora
yasuku mo arazu
kouru sora
kurushiki mono o
. . . .

Having left my dear ones
far behind,
My mind knew no rest
While the pain of longing
wrung my heart.
. . . .

iebito no
iwae ni ka aramu
tairakeku
funade wa shinu to
oya ni mōsanu

Oh, tell my parents
That I have set sail;
and all is well
Because, I think, my folks
are praying for me.

misora yuku
kumo mo tsukai to
hito wa iedo
iezuto yaramu
tazuki shirazu mo
. . . .

Though men say
Traveling the sky
Is a messenger,
I know no means
To send home my presents.
. . . .

shimakage ni
waga fune hatete
tsuge yaramu
tsukai o nami ya
koitsutsu yukamu

Though the ship stops
at an island haven,
There is none
by whom I may send word home—
So I must sail on in vain![102]

When portraying anguish and devastation wrought by the Sino-Japanese War, Masaoka Shiki did not confine his sympathy to the Japanese. Though at times he disparages China and its people in his writing, his poetry also expresses compassion for Chinese caught up in the conflict. Two of his *Miscellaneous Poems on Chin-chou* describe the loneliness of abandoned homes and villages near the battlefront:

"Kūson"

Kasasagi sawagu karekodachi,
yūhi no hikari hiyayaka ni
yama ni katayoru hitomura no
sekibaku to shite hito mo nashi.

"Deserted Village"

Magpies squawk from dead trees,
and shafts of evening sunlight,
slanting coldly toward the mountain,
fall on this village, now lonely and deserted.

"Akiya"

Nakaba kuzureshi michi no be no
ie no entan ni uruwashiku
sakeru anzu o mejirushi ni
kaerikiniken, tsubakurame,
kyonen no furusu o tazunetsutsu
kanai nozokeba ko wa ika ni,
kamado tsumetaku kaze samuku
aruji mo ko mo kage o mizu.

"Abandoned House"

Perhaps the swallows have returned
to visit last year's nest
marked by apricots that bloom
gracefully from the eaves
of this half-crumbling house by the roadside.
Peeking inside, they may wonder why
the hearth and wind are cold
and no parents or children are to be seen.

In "Wakana" (Young greens) he wonders sadly about a little girl he sees gathering plants:

"Wakana"

Kinshū no kuruwa no soto ni
wakana tsumu unai otome.
"Nare ga ie wa izuku no hodo zo,
nare ga toshi wa ikutsu ni nareru.
Tsumi tsumite kago ni amaru
sono wakana dō ni ka tsumeru.
Nare ga haha ni susumuru ryō ka,
machi ni idete yo ni kauru ka.
Yo hoshikuba kaete torasen.
Hi kururu ni haha koso matame.
Toku kaere," ieji o sashite.
Aware kono ko, kuni horobishi to
nare wa shirazu yo.

"Young Greens"

Outside the gate of Chin-chou fortress
a little girl picks young greens.
"Where is your house?
How old are you?
Why do you pick on and on
until you fill the basket?
Will you give them to your mother,
or go to town and sell them?
If you need money, let me buy them.
The sun is setting and your mother
must surely wait for you.
Hurry home," I say as I point the way for her.
The poor child knows nothing
of her country's devastation.[103]

In another firsthand account of civilian victims in the Sino-Japanese War, an Imperial Army officer describes how Japanese soldiers provided special care for Chinese children abandoned or orphaned in the aftermath of battles, even if it meant delaying or neglecting their military chores:

> There were many small children abandoned on the battlefield. These children, it turned out, were looked after and loved with

> remarkable tenderness by the Japanese soldiers, who were called Oriental devils and were indeed destructive and cruel otherwise. As far as my company was concerned, the importance of following military rules came only after the need to protect the abandoned children of the enemy. Toward evening, after a day's march of fifty kilometers, we would enter a village and find children abandoned there. The soldiers would not begin their routine duties of the military life, such as taking care of horses and guns, until they cooked the little food they carried and had fed the children. Even though I, as platoon leader, yelled at them, they paid no attention to me, saying, "The kids are crying, sir."[104]

In his poetry, Shiki moves beyond sympathy for civilian victims of the war and makes an ambitious attempt to portray the conflict from the viewpoint of a Chinese soldier in "Shin-jin ni kawarite kokorozashi o nobu" (Stating a man of China's resolve):

ten to aogu waga Ōkimi no tame naraba hi ni iru inochi o shikeku mo nashi	For the sake of the Emperor whom we revere as heaven, I plunge into flames begrudging not my life.
kono yūbe tachi motōrite naku karasu naku koe kanashi yokeku ya Kimi wa	Evening comes and crows call mournfully as they fly overhead. Would the Emperor look upon me with favor?
sora kakeru chōgon towaba yakko ware nao ni ari to Kimi ni tsuge koso	If you crows who circle in the sky can speak, please tell His Majesty that I, unworthy soul, still live in this world.
sashinami no Yamato no kuni wa semakeredo tami yutaka nari nori ni torubeku	Though the Yamato nation lies in a narrow island chain, its people are abundant, and we should take them as our model.
koto no naru to ina to ni arazu yoshi ya ware shini suru inochi Kimi no kuni no tame	Whether we prevail matters not to me. To die for the Emperor's nation is my command.

nakatsu kuni no tami to umarete Ki no Kawa no sumeran miyo ni awade yamame ya	Born into this world, will I give up, never to see an age when the Yellow River runs clear?
kuni no tame inochi o suteshi waga tomo ni okurete aran ware nara naku ni	No, I will not be unequal to my countrymen who gave their lives for the nation.
kuni no tame shini suru ware o hi no moto Yamato no hito yo aware to wa miyo	Oh, people of Yamato, nation of the rising sun, grieve for me who dies for his country.[105]

Even speaking as "a man of China," Shiki does not neglect to praise Japan, "nation of the rising sun," where the people are abundant and exemplary. This *tanka* series, like his earlier *shintaishi* ode to Japanese soldiers killed at Chin-chou, consists mostly of platitudes, making it difficult for the reader to "grieve" for a persona whose personal reflections emerge only in his momentary doubts about whether he is up to making the ultimate sacrifice. Still, this plea for Japanese to sympathize with a Chinese soldier's determination to die for his nation, even in a losing war against Japan, speaks to an enduring tradition in Japan where warriors from Minamoto Yorimasa (1106–80) to Saigō Takamori (1827–77) have become heroes in defeat.[106] This man's "resolve" is conspicuously at odds with Shiki's earlier characterization of Chinese defenders hurriedly abandoning their positions at Port Arthur, leaving behind large stores of weapons and ammunition, a portrayal that reflected widely disseminated stereotypes in Japan of Chinese troops fleeing from battle and eagerly surrendering to become prisoners of war.

If Shiki's writing expresses growing sympathy for the Chinese in defeat, the poetry he later wrote on Japanese veterans of the conflict warns that victory is not something to be celebrated. Having witnessed the results of the fighting, Shiki urges in "Jūgun kishō" (War medal, 1896) that soldiers should not be decorated amid tales of glory. His poem does not mention the wild and sometimes violent victory rallies that followed China's defeat, portrayed critically by other Japanese poets and novelists. However, he finds the awarding of combat medals to be an occasion for sadness and solemn reflection, not for exulting over battlefield triumphs:

Aware masurao. Nare mo mata	Alas, my valiant, again
mune ni kakeshiyo kinenshō.	a medal is pinned on your chest.
Kōkun ari to mo yoshi sareba	Though you served with distinction,
isao kataru na. Kunshō wa	let us not talk of glorious deeds.
warera ga nozomu koto narazu.	Medals are not to be wished for.
Yamato danshi ga Kimi no tame	Yamato men earn them with their blood,
inochi suteten to takakaite	giving their lives for the Emperor.
chi o mote etaru kinenshō.	Medals are cast from melted cannon,
Bundoshitaru taihō o	captured from the enemy.
tokashite itaru kinenshō.	Their commemoration is sad and solemn,
Shison ni kataritsutaemashi.	speaking to future generations.[107]

To this *shintaishi*, Shiki appended the following *haiku*:

Kinshū ni	Those who fought
tatakaishi hito yo	at Chin-chou
hatake utsu	now plow their fields.[108]

Here Shiki indicates that he is honoring the citizen soldiers who filled the lower ranks of the Japanese army after the government instituted universal male conscription in 1873. During the Sino-Japanese War, it was more often enlisted men, and not their professional-soldier commanders, who became popular heroes in the press, perhaps partly because more readers could identify with them. In yet another manifestation of Shiki's changing view of the conflict, the two poems above suggest that his observations in China had the effect of softening his earlier resentment, expressed in *Record of My Journey with the Army*, toward privates who had bullied him and other reporters aboard the troopship *Kaijō-maru*.

"War Medal" is one of the few poems about the conflict that Shiki wrote after 1895. He characterized his experiences in China as deeply affecting personally, but as having little enduring impact on his poetry.[109] He did, however, publish two highly sardonic poems on the war's outcome. In "Nisshin jōyaku" (Sino-Japanese Treaty, 1896) he recalled the toll of the fighting on both nations and wryly depicted the official reestablishment of diplomatic relations:

Kuchibiru horobite ha samushi.	Our lips gone, our teeth cold,
Nare areba koso ware areba koso.	we have come to coexist.
Ima yori ato wa nare to ware to	From now on let us meet,
kakusu koto naku majiwaran.	hiding nothing from each other.[110]

The appended *haiku* suggests that Shiki had doubts about how long peace would last. Considering conditions in 1896, however, especially heightened tensions between Japan and Russia over the previous year's Triple Intervention, it seems unlikely that his warning in this verse refers to China:

inazuma no ushiro no hō ni yudan su na	Behind the lightning flashes, keep watch! (386)

Shiki's humor turns vitriolic in "Shōkin shūyō" (Accepting the indemnity, 1896). He notes the acute humiliation felt by many in Japan over the return of the Liaotung Peninsula dictated by the Triple Intervention:

Shōkin gosen yo man ryō Shinkoku harai ware ukenu. Gaikoku-jin wa kore o mite meiyo to ya sen. Ryōtō no kanpu o hazuru kokoro ni wa shikaku shōkin nani ka aran.	The indemnity exceeds 50 million *ryō*. China pays and we receive. Maybe this brings us honor in the eyes of foreigners, but what good is an indemnity to hearts ashamed by the return of Liaotung? (379)

The appended *haiku* is an especially bitter parody of a poem that has become the text for the song "Kimi ga yo" (The reign of our emperor). Adapted from an anonymous *tanka* in the tenth-century collection *Kokinshū,* the poem was set to music in 1893 by Hayashi Hiromori (1821–86), a composer in the Imperial Household Ministry, and has been required singing at public school ceremonies to this day. Such highly disrespectful reference to the Meiji emperor's reign as Shiki's mocking *haiku* cannot be found even in his angriest denunciations of the Imperial Army's treatment of reporters during the Sino-Japanese War. The text of "Kimi ga yo" reads:

Kimi ga yo wa chiyo ni yachiyo ni sazareishi no iwao to narite koke no musu made	The reign of our Emperor— a thousand ages, eight thousand ages, until a pebble grows into a rock covered with moss.

Shiki lampoons it:

Kimi ga yo ya kogane kusarite koke no hana	The reign of our Emperor— rotting gold and a mossy flower. (379)

Ridiculing the emperor's reign might seem uncharacteristic, but Shiki's postwar poems expressed the indignation many Japanese felt over the return of Liaotung, and indicated his own views on the nation's future *vis-à-vis* potential adversaries. As noted above, neither his outrage at the treatment he received from the Imperial Army nor his shock and sorrow at seeing the results of the fighting in China diminished his nationalism or his belief that Japan needed a powerful military force. Although recent literary critics and historians might have preferred that such experiences had led him to a critical view of the government's military expansion policies and of war generally, they concede that, if anything, his support for a strong army and navy increased after the Sino-Japanese War and the Triple Intervention.[111] There is even a certain romanticization of military hardware in his 1896 poem "Gunkan haken" (Battleship deployed), in which Shiki eulogizes one of the Japanese warships that launched the opening engagement of the Sino-Japanese conflict off the Korean coast:

Minami no sora o mite areba	Seen in the southern sky,
ayashiki kumo koso hashirikere.	a mysterious cloud glides along.
Kemuri o tatete isamashiku	Its smoke rising valiantly,
Manira ni mukau Yoshino-kan.	the battleship *Yoshino* heads for Manila.[112]

Shiki's veneration of the *Yoshino* contrasts sharply with his bitter complaints about the Japanese naval vessels he traveled aboard in his *Record of My Journey with the Army*. Yet he articulated his postwar nationalism with comparative restraint amid the xenophobic furor that erupted after the Triple Intervention. In fact, Shiki explicitly opposed the views of those revivalists of *Nippon-shugi* (Japanism) and *kokusui-shugi* (national essence-ism) in the late 1890s who advocated the purging of foreign influences from Japanese life and culture. He stated his continuing determination to "study and learn from all literature, old and new, high and low, East and West,"[113] and he seemed little concerned that such views had become unpopular in the current climate of public sentiment. Asserting, as he had in 1889, that foreign literature could have a positive effect on Japanese poetry, Shiki collided with ultraconservative opinion both among the staff members at *Nippon*[114] and among its readers. In "Uta-yomi ni atauru sho" (Open letter to *waka* poets), published by *Nippon* in 1898, Shiki responded to a reader who had accused him of threatening "the ramparts of Japanese literature" and the nation's very well-being for suggesting that foreign elements could be successfully assimilated into Japanese poetry:

> I have no intention of destroying the national poetry—I only want to strengthen the walls of Japanese literature a little. . . . To consider the tanka as the foundation and ramparts of

> Japanese literature is like fighting with bows and arrows or swords and lance—it is out of place in the Meiji Period. After all, paying out vast sums of money to foreign countries for warships and cannons is only to strengthen the Japanese nation. I want to keep importing the literary thought of foreign countries, which we can purchase for a song, to strengthen the ramparts of Japanese literature.[115]

Shiki was especially critical of contemporary *tanka*, which he believed had grown moribund because custom severely restricted its vocabulary and subject matter. He denied that the use of foreign words and ideas would destroy the integrity of Japanese poetry, pointing to Japan's long history of successfully assimilating forms and materials from other countries:

> Even if one writes a poem in Chinese, or a Western language, or, for that matter, Sanskrit, it is part of Japanese literature as long as its author is Japanese. A government organized by Japanese is a Japanese government even if the ranks and their associated colors are modelled on the Chinese system and the uniforms are in the Chinese style [as was the case in Japan under the Taihō Code of 701]. Even if we win a war with warships bought from England and cannons from Germany [as in the Sino-Japanese War of 1894–95], it is Japan's victory as long as the people using them are Japanese. . . . We cannot rely exclusively on Japanese things.[116]

Shiki's copious use of military metaphor in these writings also suggests the importance he attached to military power for Japan. On this point he was in full agreement with his conservative critics, even if he rejected their xenophobic inclinations. Though he once dreamed of becoming a statesman, Shiki was not given to analyzing his nation's foreign policies in his poetry and prose, or to protesting the hardships imposed on people in Japan by increased military expenditures. He remonstrated with the country's leaders on occasion, criticizing the Imperial Army's treatment of reporters and voicing indignation over the return of Liaotung. Still, he maintained the role of a loyal subject who did not question his government's motives, as Uchimura Kanzō had, or let his own disturbing experiences traveling to the front lessen his belief that Japan should be a nation fully armed. Shiki died in September 1902, a year before some writers in Japan expressed opposition to the continuing military buildup and to the nation's drift toward war with Russia (see chapters four and five). It seems unlikely that he would have joined them, or followed the dramatically shifting course of his friend and fellow poet Yosano Tekkan, whose far more strident support for the Sino-Japanese War was followed a few years later by poems that went well beyond sympathy for the victims of armed conflict to denounce war as "a senseless crime" and "evil disguised" by the teachings of "false sages."

2 Yosano Tekkan: The Pen As Sword

The disparity between the poems on war that Yosano Tekkan (1873–1935) wrote during the conflict of 1894–95 and those he wrote after it is all the more striking because he began not only by supporting Japan's war against China but gloating over it in a way Masaoka Shiki never did. Tekkan's early poems on the Sino-Japanese War proclaimed his own readiness to fight, exuberantly celebrated Japanese victories, and demeaned the Chinese. Reviled by literary critics then and now, his *tanka* and *shintaishi* welcoming the start of hostilities and offering to take up his sword to kill "the pigs" might charitably be described as gladiatorial:

fude toraba sono fude o motte tachi toraba sono tachi o motte iza tsukaeten	If taking up the pen, then by the pen, if taking up the sword, then by the sword, I will serve.
waga ikusa kachinu to ieri buta kirite ide hitotsuki no sake wa nomitemu	In our battle we will win, once we've killed the pigs. Let us drink a cup of sake.[117]
mi no tame ni mi wa itawarazu ware mo mata mesaba tattoki Kimi no mitate zo	I do not care for my own safety. If I, too, am summoned, I will be His Majesty's shield.
itazura ni nani o ka iwan	Why should I waste words?

koto wa tada kono tachi ni ari tada kono tachi ni	My words are only in this sword, only in this sword.[118]
Omoshiroshi, senzai-ichigū kono ikusa, ōdanshi, shinubeki toki koso kitari kere kyō kikeba Heijō no ikusa mo, kateri to ka.	Thrilling, once-in-a-lifetime, this war. The time for great men to die has come. I hear today that in the battle of P'yŏngyang, too, we are victorious.[119] . . . .

For the psychoanalytically inclined, the braggadocio of Tekkan's early war poetry might be read as an effort to compensate for his own unfulfilled dreams of joining the battle. Like Masaoka Shiki, Tekkan harbored political ambitions in his youth. However, while Shiki had aspirations of becoming a government official in Japan, Tekkan envisioned himself furthering the cause of the pro-Japanese faction in the tumultuous world of politics in Korea. He traveled to Korea four times between 1895 and 1898, spending close to eighteen months there in a variety of pursuits that ranged from teaching the Japanese language to an ill-fated venture in exporting ginseng. His published reminiscences indicate that he also found time for a considerable amount of sight-seeing, partying, womanizing, and, of course, poetry writing. The exact nature of Tekkan's involvement in Korean politics remains a matter of much speculation among his biographers, but he claimed to have played a role in plotting two violent intrigues, one of which led to the brutal assassination of Queen Min and many of her followers in October 1895.

Tekkan also shared Shiki's desire to return Japanese poetry to the ideals of *Man'yōshū,* but he interpreted them quite differently. Instead of seeking a simplification of rhetoric or a more direct expression of emotion, Tekkan initially wanted to purge Japanese poetry of what he called its effeminate preoccupations, particularly its concentration on love. He blamed the prevailing schools of *tanka* not only for what he saw as the decadent state of contemporary Japanese poetry, but also for a moral decline that he perceived in the nation as a whole. He advocated the revival of a poetry of "manliness" (*masuraoburi*), which he found exemplified in poems from *Man'yōshū* with a martial theme and tone.[120] Like Shiki's 1894 appeal for a return to "*Man'yō*-style" simplicity and sincerity, Tekkan's call for "manly" poetry struck a highly responsive chord on the eve of the Sino-Japanese War. His manifesto on the subject, *Bōkoku no on* (Tones ruinous to the nation, 1894–95), attracted a wide readership, as did the deluge of war poems that followed.

The later turnabout evident in Tekkan's writing on love, war, and poetry has sparked lively discussion among literary critics and historians. Some attribute his reversal in part to the initial intensity of his love for Yosano Akiko, his wife after 1901, who is generally acknowledged to have been a better poet than he and is the writer of perhaps Japan's most famous poem denouncing war, "Kimi shinitamō koto nakare."[121] Others have cited his own explanation that the belated effects on him of the violence and turmoil occurring while he was in Korea, together with the realization that he was not really cut out to be a mover of coups d'état, later caused him to write critically of war and to ridicule his earlier macho posturing.[122] Although radically shifting portrayals of war can be found in the work of other writers in Japan and elsewhere, the poetry and prose chronicling Tekkan's spectacular reversal make his literary persona seem at times like a character in a turbulent saga that wavers between melodrama and farce.

Itsumi Kumi, whose critical biography examines Tekkan's poetry and prose on his trips to Korea, suggests that Tekkan's early fascination with violent political intrigue can be traced to his childhood in Kyoto.[123] Tekkan's father Yosano Reigon, a Buddhist priest and a poet of some distinction, had close ties to *shishi* (fervent patriot activist) court loyalists before the Meiji Restoration, and he enthusiastically embraced the ideology of the new state, which was based on self-sacrificing devotion to the emperor. Reigon taught his son, known by his given name Hiroshi before he adopted Tekkan as a pen name between 1890 and 1905, to compose poetry in traditional Japanese forms and encouraged him to read the classical literature of Japan and China. Though Tekkan is said to have studied hard, he failed to gain admission to middle school. His father subsequently arranged for him to take orders at the age of sixteen as a Buddhist priest, and he was assigned to a temple in Yamaguchi Prefecture. However, Tekkan found little satisfaction in his father's vocation, and three years later he left the temple and his family to move to Tokyo. There he became a pupil of the influential *tanka* and *shintaishi* poet Ochiai Naobumi (1861–1903) in 1893, and the following year Naobumi arranged for him to edit the arts and letters column of the newspaper *Niroku shinpō*, in which Tekkan published his manifesto on "manly" poetry.[124] When Tekkan left Tokyo in April 1895 on his first journey to Korea, fellow poet Kawai Suimei (1874–1965) was impressed with "how deeply he was swayed by political passions, . . .

determined to devote himself to the cause of the nation, even to the point of becoming a martyr."[125]

In another biography, Yano Hōjin writes that Tekkan's expressed desire to be where the action was received added stimulus from his older brother, who served during the Sino-Japanese War as a Buddhist chaplain.[126] Both Tekkan and his mentor Naobumi passed military physicals in 1893 but were assigned to reserve units not activated during the conflict. Tekkan's wartime poems vowing to "take up the sword" without "care for my own safety" and to become the emperor's shield "if I, too, am summoned" suggest that he would have welcomed his call-up. Still, for some reason, he did not leave his job in Tokyo until the fighting had ended, when he chose to travel to Korea where Japanese forces had prevailed early in the war. To be sure, for Tekkan to have left Tokyo before his mentor gave permission could have been detrimental to his literary career in its fragile early phase.

Naobumi arranged for Tekkan to publish not only his manifesto advocating "manly" poetry but also the poems he wrote to exemplify his creed in *Tōzai nanboku* (East, west, north, south, 1896), his first solo collection. Literary critics often characterize these poems on the war in China and the poet's first trip to Korea as examples of Tekkan's "sword-and-tiger style." This label originated with an incident that Tekkan wrote of, but others disputed, in which the poet supposedly had a close run-in with a tiger (or tigers) while traveling in the Korean mountains. Perhaps telling of this encounter gave Tekkan an opportunity to capture in his writing some of the "action" he had missed out on, traveling to a nation where fighting in the Sino-Japanese War had ended more than six months earlier.

As it turned out, Tekkan went to Korea initially at the invitation of Naobumi's younger brother Ayukai Kaien (1864–1946), a minor poet who was known more for his business acumen than his writing. Kaien founded and managed five private elementary schools in Korea with the support of the Korean Ministry of Education. He hired Tekkan in 1895 to teach Japanese language and literature at the new Itsubi Academy, scheduled to open shortly in Seoul. The poem Tekkan wrote, later published in *Tōzai nanboku*, to commemorate the school's opening suggests the perspective of Japanese nationalism from which he saw his mission in Korea:

Kara yama ni, sakura o uete, Karabito ni, Yamato onoko no uta utawasen.	In Korean mountains I plant a cherry tree, And I shall teach Koreans To sing the songs Of the men of Yamato.[127]

More than seven hundred students attended Itsubi Academy, and among Tekkan's pupils were children of the Korean nobility. Having been afforded this opportunity to promote his views, Tekkan expressed the fear in the summer of 1895, when he lay in a Seoul hospital stricken with typhoid fever, that if he died, "the poetry of true men would again be cast aside."[128] Itsumi Kumi notes that, from Tekkan's writing at this time, it is clear that what he meant by planting a cherry tree in Korea went well beyond teaching *tanka* to Korean children: "Behind his effort to implant the Japanese spirit by teaching Japanese literature and song were political ambitions."[129]

There is precious little evidence that Tekkan's oft-stated ambitions were translated into action. His poetry and prose on this trip apparently reflect an inflated sense of self-importance that led him to exaggerate his role in events unfolding in Korean politics. However, he seems at least to have been acquainted with some of the perpetrators of the assassination of Queen Min and the coup d'état that followed. When he first arrived in April, he stayed for a time at the Japanese legation in Seoul and became friendly with Deputy Minister Horiguchi Kumaichi (1865–1945),[130] whom an official inquiry later identified as a conspirator in the plot against the queen, in which Tekkan also claimed to be involved.[131]

The animosity Tekkan expressed toward Queen Min, at least in his poetry, was widely shared in Japan. She was deeply resented for effectively organizing opposition to Japanese influence in the Korean court and government after the Sino-Japanese War. According to Japanese government pronouncements, often echoed in the press, this "just war," ignited in reality by a conflict between Chinese and Japanese interests in Korea, had been fought in order to guarantee that nation's independence. However, soon after China's defeat, the Japanese government launched a series of repressive "reforms" in Korea, which ranged from ending the power of the court in affairs of state to cutting off the topknot traditionally worn by male Koreans as a symbol of manhood.[132]

When Tekkan arrived there, Korean resistance to the Japanese-sponsored "reforms" was already growing, as were protests over the activities of Japanese businessmen who came to Korea in large numbers after the war. Koreans charged that they were insulting and unscrupulous in their dealings with local residents.[133] Meanwhile, the Japanese press was portraying Queen Min as an enemy of Japan who operated behind the scenes to subvert Japan's foreign policy. In her efforts to oppose Japanese interests and influence, she was said to have sought the assistance of foreign diplomats in Korea, particularly those from Russia, a nation viewed with much antipathy in Japan for its leading role in the Triple Intervention.

The extent of Tekkan's involvement, if any, in the plot against Queen Min that was organized and directed by Japanese diplomats in Seoul may never be known. The official accounts of the incident do not mention him, nor do the records of the pro forma trial held in Hiroshima after Japanese complicity in the assassination came to light. Only Tekkan's reminiscences, published in "Sajō no kotoba" (Words on the sand, 1925),[134] claim specifically that he joined Ayukai Kaien and Horiguchi Kumaichi in formulating a plan (*kensaku*) for the assassination.[135] This planning supposedly occurred when the two men visited him in the Seoul hospital where he was recovering from typhoid fever in the summer of 1895. During his two months in the hospital, Tekkan wrote a series of *tanka*, each beginning with the line "Kara ni shite, ikade ka shinamu" (How can I die in Korea?). The series was later published in *Tōzai nanboku*. In these poems he contemplated, without undue modesty, how his premature death would inflict a terrible loss on his family, his mentor, and the cause of "manly" poetry, and would prevent him from carrying out his self-proclaimed mission to participate in some violent act:

Kara ni shite, ikade ka shinan. Yamato ni wa, chichi mo imaseri, haha mo imaseri.	How can I die in Korea? In Japan I have a father and a mother, too.
. . . .	. . . .
Kara ni shite, ikade shinan. Shi no kimi no, fukaki nasake mo imada mukuizu.	How can I die in Korea without even repaying the deep kindness of you, my teacher?
. . . .	. . . .
Kara ni shite, ikade ka shinan. Ware shinaba onoko no uta zo, mata sutarenan.	How can I die In Korea? If I die, the poetry of true men would again be cast aside.
. . . .	. . . .
Kara ni shite, ikade ka shinan. Ada ni shinaba, ie no takara no, tachi zo naku beki.	How can I die in Korea? If I die in vain, the sword that is my household treasure would surely weep.
. . . .	. . . .

Kara ni shite ikade ka shinan. Shinubekuba, tōtose no ato no, ikusa mite koso.	How can I die in Korea? If I must die, let it be seeing the battle of ten years hence.[136]

If Tekkan does not specify the nature and timing of the violent act he was contemplating (Could he be predicting the Russo-Japanese War of 1904–5 in the last poem quoted above?), he hints at its desired targets in the poetry and prose he composed after leaving the hospital. In a prose passage from *Tōzai nanboku* he tells how a Korean female entertainer (*kiseng*) he became friendly with could barely restrain him, when in his cups one night, from attacking a Korean official:

> She is eighteen years old and possesses great wit and beauty. She even has some education and is a cut above most of this country's so-called "official dancing girls." Her exceedingly favorable attitude toward Japanese was a rarity. . . . After the first night we met, I saw her often, though, alas, she was shy and not amorously inclined. . . . When I tried to read some Korean novels, she was the one who tore them up, saying they were pornography unfit for a gentleman. It was she who stopped me . . . from killing a Korean official after I had unsheathed my sword in a drunken rage.[137]

Tekkan's introductory headnote to a poem in the same collection observes: "Kaien and I compose poetry together on the first day of autumn in Seoul. Now the tyranny of Queen Min grows day by day, and the power of the pro-Japanese faction has fallen rapidly."[138]

Kara yama ni, aki kaze tatsu ya, tachi nadete, ware omou koto, naki ni shi mo arazu.	In the Korean mountains The autumn wind has risen; As I stroke my sword I am by no means wanting in righteous indignation.[139]

Tekkan wrote in "Words on the Sand" that he and Ayukai Kaien were supposed to participate in the "dramatic spectacle" (*engeki-teki kōkei*) that had been scheduled for early November 1895. He explains, however, that unexpected developments in Seoul forced an earlier launching of the coup on October 8 while he and Kaien were traveling in the mountains far from the capital: "When we got back as far as Inchon on October 15, a pro-Japanese cabinet had already been formed."[140] Thus, by his own account, he missed out on this opportunity to "take up the sword" as he had missed out on the Sino-Japanese War.

As we shall see, this would not be the last time he would be somewhere else at the moment of crisis in a violent action he claimed to have helped plan. Still, Itsumi Kumi gives enough credibility to Tekkan's version of events to conclude that the poet was "involved indirectly" in the plot of October 8, though he did not join in carrying it out. Itsumi adds, however, that "the deep emotion Tekkan was feeling in Korea might have caused him to confuse fantasy and reality" as to the extent of his involvement. Itsumi compares the situation to the tigers Tekkan thought he heard roaring on his travels with Ayukai Kaien in the mountains, tigers Kaien later said never existed.[141] Even Tekkan himself conceded thirty years later that he might have had an exaggerated sense of his own importance to events: "When all my government and civilian associates were rounded up and placed in Hiroshima prison, I was conceited enough to think that Kaien and I alone were left to carry out their aims."[142]

Tigers or no tigers, the assassination and coup of October 8, 1895, organized by the minister of the Japanese legation in Seoul, General Miura Gorō, and his first secretary, Sugimura Fukashi, involved Tekkan at least to the extent that it resulted in the closing of Itsubi Academy where he taught, and in his involuntary repatriation to Japan. The Japanese government apparently suspected at first that he was somehow connected with the incident and included him among the Japanese nationals ordered to return by chartered boat to Hiroshima. A trial was scheduled there after official denials of Japanese involvement could no longer be supported by the evidence and after severe criticism of Japan began to spread abroad.[143] Tekkan gives a first-person account of the boat trip taken by the Japanese suspects from Inchon to Ujina and describes the circumstances surrounding the trial at Hiroshima:

> On October 17 the situation changed abruptly. The Japanese government stopped believing Consul General Miura's reports, and Komura Jutarō was appointed to replace him. Public prosecutor Andō Kensuke was sent to make an investigation, and all Japanese connected with the incident were transferred under escort to Hiroshima.[144]

Tekkan characterizes these actions as the response of "a government fearful of the Great Powers." In prose and poetry published earlier in *Tōzai nanboku*, he wrote of the trip back to Japan and indicated his attitude toward events:

> To fight the boredom aboard ship, my friends amused themselves with poetry and sake. I also composed several poems at the time, and here is one I remember:

Kara kara to,	I was ashamed
warau mo yo ni wa,	to laugh in public
habakarinu.	about Korea "ha ha,"
Nakinaba ika ni,	but how can people
hito no togamen.	blame me if I cry?[145]

With its rather crude wordplay on *kara kara* (*Kara* is an old Japanese name for Korea; *kara kara* is onomatopoetic for laughter), this poem only hints at Tekkan's feelings about what had transpired in Korea. However, it might well have indicated his uncertainty, while aboard ship, as to whether or not he was to be treated as a suspect once he and his friends arrived in Japan. Showing too much regret for the turn of events in Seoul, when the Japanese government decided to recall Miura and the others after the initially successful coup, could have brought him under suspicion. In "Words on the Sand" he wrote that, upon their return, more than forty Japanese were held in the Hiroshima jail, but "I was exonerated as the result of a preliminary hearing when it became clear that I had not entered the royal palace on the night in question."[146]

After his release, Tekkan visited those among his friends who were imprisoned to await trial. He then left Hiroshima, stopping briefly in Kyoto to see his family, and made his way to Tokyo where he related his adventures to Ochiai Naobumi and the staff at *Niroku shinpō*. Tekkan's writing in *Tōzai nanboku* indicates that, like the crowds of well-wishers who welcomed the suspects back to Japan as conquering heroes, he held strong sympathies for them. His *tanka* on the imprisoned defendants sounds almost as if he had longed to join them in their cells:

Tsumi nakute,	To be summoned
mesaruru mo mata,	though guiltless—
fūryū ya.	how elegant!
Hitoya no tsuki wa	The moon over the prison,
ika ni teruran.	how it shines![147]

Having expressed his sympathy for the defendants, Tekkan did not remain in Japan for their trial, which has been characterized as "farcical"[148] and "a deliberate miscarriage of justice designed to protect the culprits."[149] He also missed the celebration that followed their acquittal, leaving before the year was out for his second visit to Korea, which lasted from December 1895 to May 1896. His avowed purpose on this trip was to pursue a business venture, but the exact nature of the enterprise he planned remains, like his earlier political involvement there, largely a mystery. Tekkan later wrote that he had expected Japanese influence in Korea, restored temporarily by the coup of two months earlier, to benefit him commercially. He visited the Japanese legation shortly after arriving in Seoul and tried to renew his contacts with the pro-Japanese faction that, for the moment, controlled the Korean government. He was evidently unprepared for the change in attitude at the legation, after General Miura's compulsory departure, toward those who had been friendly with Miura's aides. He writes in "Words on the Sand" that he met with newly appointed Minister Komura Jutarō and other officials to discuss his plans but was sorely disappointed by the reception he got and decided in the end to abandon his venture: "In a short time the situation had changed completely in Korea. . . . The embassy and consular officials were unpleasant toward me. So, after explaining my plans to new Minister Komura, I left on a trip to Kwangwon-to, braving the December snows, for the purpose of writing poetry."[150]

Tekkan does not indicate how he financed this trip, but he describes his travels through the snowy province of Hamkyung-Nam-to as filled with hardship and danger. He tells how a mob of religious fanatics threatened him, causing a rumor to reach Seoul that he had been murdered. He barely managed to escape, he explains, by dressing as a Korean, adding that it had been an unfortunate Japanese peddler who was killed by the mob.[151] He also writes that he heard the roar of a tiger (or tigers) three times on this journey, and he cites this experience as the source for his best-known poem on encounters with these animals:

Onoe ni wa,	From the mountain ridge
itakumo tora no,	how furious
hoyuru kana.	is the tiger's roar!
Yūbe wa kaze ni	Tonight a storm
naran to suran.	is sure to rise.[152]

While Tekkan was traveling in the mountains, another violent upheaval occurred in Seoul that he says inspired him to make a second and final try at political intrigue on behalf of the pro-Japanese faction in Korea. This was the coup organized by Russian diplomats, called the February 11th Incident in Japan, that temporarily installed the pro-Russian faction as the dominant force in Korean politics.[153] Tekkan writes that he had been on his way to the city of Inchon when the coup occurred:

> I heard that the Korean king and crown prince had been brought into the Russian legation, and that members of the cabinet, from the prime minister on down, had been murdered, their corpses mutilated. This was the result of a plot by the pro-Russian faction to depose the pro-Japanese faction. Soldiers of the pro-Russian faction went searching for officials of the pro-Japanese faction who had disguised themselves as Japanese. Many of them fled Seoul to Inchon, where they hid in Japanese shops.[154]

To this point, Tekkan's description of events squares with historical accounts. However, he also claimed to have initiated a mysterious plot in support of the beleaguered pro-Japanese faction. This scheme, as he later described it, sounds strangely like a combination of an earlier coup supported by Japanese in 1882 and an aborted attempt by disgruntled Korean officers to kidnap the Korean king when he was scheduled to leave the Russian legation in November 1896, six months after Tekkan had returned to Japan.[155] From his account of this plot in "Words on the Sand," Tekkan seemed unconcerned in February 1895 that the highly volatile nature of politics at the turn of the century in Korea, where several nations vied ruthlessly for influence, offered little prospect that power could be retained very long, even following an initially "successful" coup:

> After the February 11th Incident, I resolved, for the sake of the Koreans in the pro-Japanese faction, to do what I could to restore their fortunes once more from the present decline. I gathered a few like-minded persons, and, having heard a rumor that the Korean king was to be moved shortly to the Myŏngye Palace in the vicinity of the Russian legation, we made a plan to start a fire near the palace that would deprive the king of a safe escape route back to the legation. We then intended to escort him to the Japanese legation. Japanese government officials, owing to their lack of moral courage, declined to join our approximately twenty comrades, who included Suzuki Jōzō, later a diet member in the Seiyūkai during the Taishō era. We rented a Korean mansion near the Myŏngye Palace, where we stored a large number of oil canisters. The Japanese who worked in the store Suzuki managed were recruited to start the fire and to serve as reinforcements under his command. However, Russia's scrupulous vigilance prevented us from carrying out our plan. When April passed into May and the king was still not moved to the Myŏngye Palace, I suspected that word of our intentions had leaked to the pro-Russian faction. I also became aware that the long delay had diminished the state of readiness among our comrades. Therefore, I abandoned the plan and returned to Japan at the end of May.[156]

History records that negotiations were taking place in March and April 1896 over Minister Komura's request that the Korean king leave the Russian legation and return to the royal palace. The Russians were troubled by Japan's insistence on maintaining a reduced number of troops in Seoul and were unsatisfied with government pledges to control the *sōshi* (swashbucklers).[157] Despite Russian suspicions, however, these assurances seem consistent with Japanese officials' refusal to aid Korean military officers in the planned November coup, and with Tekkan's claim that he was denied their assistance in the swashbuckling scheme he had hoped to carry out seven months earlier. Still, like his other adventures and misadventures in Korea, his claims about this scheme and his role in it remain uncorroborated. Another question arises as to whether he went home out of disappointment over his aborted plan or because his mentor Ochiai Naobumi summoned him by telegram in March to return to Tokyo, where he was to be appointed chief of the editorial section at Meiji Shoin.[158]

What is clear from Tekkan's writings after he returned in the spring of 1896 from his second odyssey in Korea is that he was now resolved to abandon his attempts at violent political intrigue. Most of the poetry in *Tōzai nanboku,* published in July of that year, represents his earlier "sword-and-tiger style." This collection, however, also contains later, more reflective poems on the Sino-Japanese War and his experiences in Korea that are occasionally self-mocking. A jolting incongruity results when the two kinds of poetry appear side by side. Perhaps the most startling contrast occurs when a series of poems from 1894 celebrating Japan's victories over China is followed immediately by a later poem portraying a Japanese war widow's refusal to let her child go out and watch a noisy victory parade.

Unfortunately for Tekkan, literary critics have chosen for the most part to evaluate *Tōzai nanboku* on the basis of the earlier poems, which comprise the bulk of its 279 *tanka*, 45 *shintaishi*, and scattered *renga* (linked verse) sequences. Thus, despite enthusiastic prefaces by literary luminaries Masaoka Shiki and Mori Ōgai, the collection has fared badly with reviewers then and now. The year it appeared, Ōmachi Keigetsu (1869–1925), a poet who certainly shared Tekkan's ultranationalistic views (see chapter five), wrote in the magazine *Teikoku bungaku* that "Tekkan swears his determination, talks of the sword, and pulls tigers out of the poems he writes in Korea. It is all too strange, like a boor's courage."[159] Miyazaki Koshoshi, known for writing some of the first successful lyric poetry in *shintaishi* (see chapter three), was still more condemnatory in his review the same year for the magazine *Kokumin no tomo*: "In sum, his failings are insincerity and wild exaggeration. His chaotic and impetuous poetry reads as though it is dashed off as soon as he picks up his writing brush, with little reflection or preliminary drafting. Two-thirds of this collection is scribblings."[160] More recently, Donald Keene has written that "despite Tekkan's insistence on 'manliness' (*masuraoburi*) in poetry, most poems in the collection that do not specifically describe Tekkan polishing his sword or listening to tigers roar are conventionally pretty rather than intense."[161]

As suggested by such criticism, *Tōzai nanboku* remains of interest today mostly for humor that Tekkan never intended. Yet, looking beyond the swords and tigers, one finds a few poems in which he expressed sympathy for the victims of armed conflict and mocked his own recent bluster, acknowledging that he was unsuited to a life of violent intrigue. Reflecting on his dreams of glory in combat, Tekkan wrote the following *tanka* after his second trip to Korea. It stands in remarkable contrast to his earlier sword-brandishing poems in *Tōzai nanboku*:

Fude torite, araba arubeki, ono ga mi o, tachi ni kaete to, nani omoiken.	For me, best suited to take up the pen, to change to the sword— what could I have been thinking?[162]

In explaining the transformation in Tekkan's poetry on war, Itsumi Kumi locates the turning point as a "rude awakening" Tekkan received when he visited Japanese families bereaved by the Sino-Japanese War. This experience is said to have inspired the *shintaishi* "Gaisenmon" (Arch of triumph, 1896) included toward the end of *Tōzai nanboku*[163]:

Itsu totosama wa kaerimasu, kaerimasu zo to tou mono o, kaerimasazu to tsuge mo seba, osanaki mune no sakeya sen. Miyako no ichi no asakaze ni, hata no kazukazu uchinabiki, shōri o iwau gungaku ni, hanabi no oto mo majiru nari. Kiku ni kokoro no isamarete, hito wa mi ni iku gaisenmon, taii no ie no sono tsuma wa, waza to waga ko o mi ni yarazu.	"When will Dad come back?" If Mother answers that he won't, the child's heart would break. In the morning wind of the capital countless flags are flapping. Mingled with the martial music celebrating victory, are the sounds of firecrackers. People rush out, spirits high, to listen and to view the arch of triumph that the wife at this captain's house will not let her child go to see.[164]

On the one hand, this *shintaishi* might be subject to Donald Keene's criticism that most of the poems in *Tōzai nanboku* not in Tekkan's "sword-and-tiger style" lack intensity. Yet, in this case, whatever success "Arch of Triumph" achieves can perhaps be attributed to its very understatement. The reader appreciates the mother's feelings more because Tekkan communicates them indirectly, through her interaction with the child, rather than describing them explicitly. The contrast he draws between crowds of victory celebrants and an individual family bereaved is also the subject of short stories set in Japan during the Sino-Japanese War by Miyazaki Koshoshi and Izumi Kyōka.[165] Furthermore, the sounds of a victory parade, hateful to those grieving a war's victims, is also the subject of poetry elsewhere, as in "The Drum" by John Scott of Anwell (1730–83):

> I hate that drum's discordant sound,
> Parading round, and round, and round;
> To thoughtless youth it pleasure yields,
> And lures from cities and from fields,
> To sell their liberty for charms
> Of tawdry lace, and glittering arms;
> And when Ambition's voice commands,
> To march, and fight, and fall, in foreign lands.
>
> I hate that drum's discordant sound,
> Parading round, and round, and round;
> To me it talks of ravaged plains,
> And burning towns, and ruined swains,
> And mangled limbs, and dying groans,
> And widows' tears, and orphans' moans;
> And all that Misery's hand bestows,
> To fill the catalogue of human woes.[166]

From the arrangement of poems in *Tōzai nanboku*, the poignant contrast of glory and grief in "Arch of Triumph" reads like a contradiction to four of Tekkan's earlier *gunka*-like *shintaishi* that immediately precede it, in which the poet urges Japanese soldiers to give their lives "without regret" and tells their wives to hope only for success in battle.[167] To be sure, Tekkan is not the only writer to have published poems with reverse views of the same war, but perhaps never have they appeared so close together in one collection.

The changed perspectives on war and personal mission that Tekkan expressed in his poetry did not prevent him from making a third visit to Korea, lasting from July 1897 to March 1898. His stated purpose was, again, to go into business, but this time his mentor Ochiai Naobumi firmly opposed the trip. Tekkan later recalled that his ultimate goal had been to make enough money in Korea so that he could travel to Europe and study foreign languages and literature as distinguished novelist Mori Ōgai had done a decade earlier. This would turn out to be yet another of his large but unfulfilled dreams, and Naobumi, who had more immediate plans for Tekkan, tried hard to keep him in Tokyo. Besides arranging the editorship at Meiji Shoin, he hired Tekkan to help him compile a Japanese language dictionary and recommended him for a job teaching Japanese literature (at Yamaguchi Higher and Middle School). Tekkan wrote that he was "deeply moved by the warm devotion of my teacher," but felt compelled to "betray" him by purposely staying overnight at friends' homes to avoid Naobumi, who came to visit almost every night after work in an effort to dissuade Tekkan from leaving Japan.[168]

Tekkan's account of what happened to him after he arrived in Korea suggests that he should have heeded Naobumi's advice. His aim on this trip had been to get rich quick in the ginseng trade. He knew that ginseng brought high prices as a much sought after stimulant, aphrodisiac, and cure-all medicine. He had also learned that Japanese were involved in an elaborate black-marketing system that circumvented the considerable vigilance of police and customs officials in Korea, where exporting ginseng without a license was a capital crime.[169] He wrote three years after this trip that he had led seventy men with seventeen horses and oxen into the ginseng fields of Kŭmch'ŏn. He blamed his failure in this venture on "unscrupulous landowners" who told the authorities he and his band of entrepreneurs were stealing. He describes how they fled, pursued by Korean soldiers, over treacherous terrain in freezing weather until they were barely able to reach safety on the coast of the Yellow Sea:

> We traveled continuously for nine days without sleep. . . . All of us were starving, and our feet were frozen cold as stone. At last we asked ourselves angrily why we were suffering these hardships in a land far from home. Our daily pay . . . was high, but it seemed foolish to risk our lives in such an ordeal with all the profits going to others.[170]

Whether or not Tekkan's troubles in Korea this time were quite so dramatic, Itsumi Kumi believes that they were caused not so much by double-crossing landowners as by Tekkan's own lack of business acumen, which made him easily exploitable by other merchants. Noting the many poems Tekkan composed about female entertainers on this trip, Itsumi concludes that Tekkan spent much of his remaining time in Korea consoling himself with drink and *kiseng*.[171] If his second visit there had led him to abandon his dreams of violent political intrigue, his third trip convinced him that he was not cut out for wheeling and dealing in the black market. Looking back two decades later, he wrote, "I have many regrets about the crude and shallow nature of my earlier ideas, words, and actions."[172] "When I think back on it now, I can barely force a smile. In those days, though unfit for the role, I had played at being a *shishi*, like a little Don Quixote."[173]

The shifting perspective evident since 1896 in Tekkan's poetry on the Sino-Japanese War and the turmoil in Korea suggests that his views had begun to change long before these statements were published in the 1920s. Several poems in Tekkan's third collection, *Tekkan-shi* (1901), take up the thread from "Arch of Triumph," published five years earlier, to depict the suffering caused by armed conflict as well as the futility of recent Japanese military interventions abroad. He wrote not only of the ultimate failure of the October 1895 coup and assassination to restore Japanese influence in Korea, but also of the loss of expected rewards from the Sino-Japanese War and the deployment of ten thousand Japanese troops to Peking during the Boxer Rebellion of 1900. One poem in this collection denounces war so totally and vehemently that it reads like a pacifist declaration. If these works are not always successful as poetry, their criticism of the horror and futility wrought by armed conflict is often pointed and explicit. In one *tanka* from a series entitled "Myōjō" (Morning star, not to be confused with the famous magazine of the same name that Tekkan edited with Akiko), he comments wryly on the results of Japanese attempts, in which he claimed a part, to gain influence in Korea:

nonoshirade	I cannot help berating myself,
ware mo e arazu	for I, too, made a failed effort.
Karayama ni	In the Korean mountains
asahi no mihata	the flag of the rising sun
chikara naki mireba	looks flaccid.[174]

In another *tanka* he writes of the coup organized by the pro-Russian faction in February 1896, after which the Korean king ordered the beheading of those who had served as ministers under the deposed pro-Japanese cabinet:

hidarite ni	Hoisting
chi ni somu kōbe	seven bloodstained heads
nanatsu sagete	in his left hand,
sake nomi oreba	he drinks a toast.
kimi mesu to iu	"The king ordered it," he says. (96)

The aversion to violent acts expressed here runs counter to Tekkan's earlier poems in which he celebrated the killing of Chinese and vowed to take up his own sword against the enemies of Japanese influence in Korea. It is, of course, the *allies* of Japan whose beheading he deplores in this poem. Yet, even on the subject of enemy number one, Queen Min, his poetry undergoes a remarkable change. According to Tekkan's headnote, the following *tanka* is from a series of six "written in the autumn of the third year after the death of Korea's queen." This 1898 poem on her brutal assassination conveys a poignancy that diverges sharply from his denunciation of her "tyranny" three autumns earlier:

watadono no chishio no nagori ima mo kiezu chisaki miashi no ato zo nioeru	In the corridor traces of bloodstains yet remain, and your small footprints are still fragrant. (109)

In another poem in this series on the assassinations in Korea, Tekkan echoes the observations of Tu Fu, Masaoka Shiki, and many other poets who have noted the incongruity of nature's luxuriance that remains after the destruction of human life in armed conflict:

ōniwa ni sutetaru kabane tsuchi to narite ima sakari nari akikusa no hana	Discarded on the palace grounds, the corpses have turned into earth where now autumn flowers thrive. (109)

This poem also recalls a popular suspicion that certain flowers are nourished by the blood of those cut down by weapons. British poets Isaac Rosenberg (1890–1918) and Keith Douglas (1920–44) drew on this gruesome notion for poems about World Wars I and II, respectively. Douglas writes: "the body can fill / the hungry flowers." According to Rosenberg, "Poppies whose roots are in man's veins / Drop, and are ever dropping."[175]

Bloodshed is the central motif of Tekkan's most fervent and thoroughgoing denunciation of war, oddly titled "Kessha-ka" (Poem limned in blood), which also appears in *Tekkan-shi*. Although its stark polemics are less affecting than the understatement of "Arch of Triumph," this *shintaishi* is notable for its tone of outrage and for evocations of bereaved families and spilled blood that Tekkan's wife Akiko is thought to have drawn on a few years later for her more successful poem denouncing war, "Brother,

Do Not Give Your Life."[176] Tekkan dates this poem's composition to November 1897, during his second visit to Korea. It was first published in the November 1898 issue of the magazine *Kokoro no hana* before appearing in *Tekkan-shi.* Itsumi Kumi describes the first stanza as "criticism of the brutal, amoral civil war in Korea that Tekkan had experienced during three visits there."[177] Although Tekkan could well have gleaned material for this poem from his travels, no country is mentioned specifically. Rather, the poem's first stanza and the six that follow seem to express a more general condemnation of war, and of those who advocate and glorify it:

seigi to wa
akuma ga kaburu kamen nite
kōmyō wa
shi o yorokobasu majutsu kana

So-called "justice"
is a mask for evil.
"Glorious deeds"
are sorcery that brings death delight.

onaji sekai ni umareidete
oya mo ari
tsuma mo aru ko o
na o tsukete
isamashiki na no chanpion
kawai ya na
ikusa ni yareri harubaru to
mi mo shirazu
nare mo senu
banri no sora no hito no kun

Born into our world,
a son with parents
now has a wife, too.
Dubbed with the name "bravery,"
how handsome!
Then, he is sent
far away to war
under distant skies in a foreign country
he does not know
and cannot get used to.

kashikoshi to
hokoreru hito no
nishi ni ari
higashi ni mo ari
nani hodo no
kashikoki hito zo
mukashi yori
ma ni miirarete
ima mo nao
mayoi wa samezu

In the East
and in the West
are people bragging of their wisdom.
But how wise are they
who remain bewitched
from ancient times
by demons?
Even now
they awaken not
from their delusions.

aware ya na
hito o koroshite namida naku
osoroshi ya
ikichi ni akite zange sezu
eiyū to
ware kara hokori
gōketsu to
issei o gu ni su

Such sorrow there is
in killing without tears!
Such horror there is
in spilling life's blood without remorse!
"Heroes"
they call themselves proudly,
and make fools of everyone.

hone o tsunde hana wa kaoru kinden gyokurō chi o nutte hoshi wa kagayaku kunshō hōju aa hyakusen no zaiaku o soko ni ichibu no bunmei-shi	The palace of fragrant flowers is built on piles of bones. Medals and jeweled ribbons that sparkle with stars are lacquered in blood. Ah, the crimes by the thousands that fill this one chapter in the history of "civilization."
itawashiki kana chichi haha wa oite tayori no ko ni hanare aware naru kana taoyame wa nisei no otto ni wakaretsutsu ijirashiki kana chichinomigo wa mada teteoya no kao shirazu	Those grievous spectacles— of father and mother left as they grow old without the son they depended on. Of the young wife whose husband is taken from her. Of the dear child still nursing who will never know his father's face.
"chūgi ni wa nao kaegatashi appare tegara shita zo" to wa aa aa hito o koroseyo to ese-seijin no oshie kana	Though they speak of "unwavering loyalty" and "glorious deeds," murder alone is what the false sages teach.[178]

The distance Tekkan has traveled from 1894, when he wrote of "thrilling . . . war" as "a time for great men to die," to 1897, when he wrote of war as "murder" preached by "false sages" and the "horror [of] spilling life's blood without remorse," would seem to be measurable in light years. If there is a common strain, it is the passion with which he first exalts war and then later denounces it in tone and terms strongly reminiscent of "Evil" from Arthur Rimbaud's (1854–91) *Eighteen-Seventy*, inspired by the Franco-Prussian War:

. . . .
The criminal justice that deceives
and rules us, lays our corpses end on end,
then burns us like the summer grass or leaves;
La Patrie is avaricious to this end!

She is a god that laughs at Papal bulls,
the great gold chalice and the thuribles.
She dozes while our grand hosannas drown

the guns and drums, and wakes to hear the grief
of widows or a mother who lays down
her great sou knotted in a handkerchief.[179]

Perhaps even more startling than the reversal of philosophical perspective evident in "Poem Limned in Blood" is the reversed application of language in this and other poems on war from *Tekkan-shi*. Tekkan uses the same words found in *Man'yōshū*, such as *ikusa* (war), *ōkimi* (emperor), and *mitami* (emperor's subjects), for his earlier poems glorifying war as he does in these later poems deploring it:

hingashi ni oroka naru kuni hitotsu ari ikusa ni kachite anadori ukenu	In the east is one foolish country. Victorious in war, yet scorned.
Ōkimi no mitami o shini ni yaru yo nari hito no hikiiru ikusa no naka e	It is an age when His Majesty's subjects have been sent off to die, led into a foreign war.
te o oite tanka no ue ni ko wa eminu aa wazawai ya hito o korosu michi	Lying on a stretcher, a wounded boy is smiling. Ah, how cursed is this murderous path![180]

The disturbing specter of "a wounded boy . . . smiling" also has parallels in European verse, with perhaps the best-known example in Robert Browning's (1812–89) "Incident of the French Camp":

. . . .
Then off there flung in smiling joy,
And held himself erect
By just his horse's mane, a boy:
You hardly could suspect—
(So tight he kept his lips compressed,
Scarce any blood came through)
You looked twice ere you saw his breast
Was all but shot in two.[181]

If Tekkan refers only indirectly to the Sino-Japanese War in these three *tanka* from the series "Morning Star" in *Tekkan-shi*, he mentions this conflict explicitly, as well as Japan's growing rivalry with Russia and the Boxer Rebellion, in later poems expressing skepticism toward the nation's military involvements abroad. "Nihon o saru uta" (Song of farewell to Japan, 1901), composed in honor of a friend's trip to China, is a lengthy *shintaishi* condemning the "immorality, villainy, and corruption" Tekkan finds manifested in everything from Japan's foreign policy to drunken womanizing among the country's Buddhist priests. Such denunciations recall the pompous moralism of *Tones Ruinous to the Nation*, the manifesto Tekkan published six years earlier blaming what he perceived then as the nation's ills on the state of Japanese poetry. Yet "Song of Farewell to Japan" conveys a cynicism and disillusionment not found in *Tones Ruinous to the Nation*, which was intended as a clarion call for reform. In this poem Tekkan laments the country's recent military adventures, which, he writes, have resulted only in useless killing and thwarted expectations. Of Korea he asks:

Nijū shichi-hachi nen no eki
nan ga yue ni fuso no shison
  o koroshite
kōrai hantō no sanga
munashiku hokui no jūrin ni
  ishitaru

For what purpose
did the war of 1894–95
kill the descendants
of our forefathers,
  only for us to yield in futility
  to Russian infringement
  in the hills and rivers
  of the Korean Peninsula?[182]

Similarly, he questions why Japan bothered to send ten thousand men to help an approximately equal number of European and American troops quell the Boxer Rebellion in the spring of 1900. Tekkan notes that Japanese soldiers did most of the fighting. The defeat of the Boxers was followed by the arrival in Peking of several companies of foreign troops under the command of German Field Marshal Count von Waldersee. This officially designated "relief force" then proceeded to pillage the city for several weeks.

Tenshin o otoseshi wa dare zo
Pekin o otoseshi wa dare zo
hei o mochiiru fuso Hideyoshi
  o hazukashimezu
shikamo Wa-gensui wa
  nan no kuni no hito zo
aa tanin no tame ni
  kai o nuu mono

Who was it that subdued
Tientsin and Peking,
not to disgrace our forefather,
  Hideyoshi, leader of soldiers?
But Field Marshal Waldersee—
  what nationality is he?
Alas, we only sewed a wedding gown
  for the sake of another.[183]

Tekkan's use of sexual metaphor seems appropriate here inasmuch as rape, along with robbery and murder, was repeatedly committed by the "allies" in what became known as the sacking of Peking.[184] Looking back on Japan's recent military interventions abroad, Tekkan concludes in "Song of Farewell to Japan" that the nation's traditional warrior ethic has little relevance in the modern world:

omoe gen arishi fuso no ken	Our ancestral swords, once so decisive,
ima rekkoku no warai o kau no gu ni sugizu	buy us nothing now but scorn from the Great Powers.
mizukara ken o totte mizukara kizutsukuru wa	To take up the sword and bring wounds upon ourselves—
aa waga fuso Jinmu Tennō no michi ka	Alas! Was this the way of our forefather Emperor Jinmu?
. . . .	. . . .
ware nijusseiki no Nihon ni mitari	What I see in Japan of the twentieth century
. . . .	. . . .
	makes me ask, if things have come to this,
Yamato-damashii ya bushidō ya kaku no gotokun ba nan no atai zo	"the Japanese spirit" and "the way of the samurai"— what use are they now?[185]

Although "Song of Farewell to Japan" does not express the unequivocal condemnation of war found in "Poem Limned in Blood" and "Morning Star," it deplores the futility of Japan's recent military ventures. Literary critics today have praised these poems for their critical view of armed conflict,[186] but Tekkan is not identified with Miyazaki Koshoshi, Takeshima Hagoromo, and Shimazaki Tōson as a progenitor of modern antiwar poetry in Japan. Perhaps he is too well known for the virulently bellicose verses of his "sword-and-tiger" days. Or, perhaps it is remembered that his poetry on war took another 180-degree turn with *gunka*-like *shintaishi* he published during the Russo-Japanese War and the escalating conflict with China in the early 1930s.

Tekkan's poems on the Russo-Japanese War not only contradict the sentiments expressed in his poetry on war three years earlier but also seem inconsistent with his own published criticism of the new effusion of war literature that accompanied the outbreak of hostilities with Russia. He wrote in the February 1904 issue of the magazine *Myōjō*: "Now in this eventful time of a nation at war, we read such dilettantish writings, but they certainly do not represent the sensibilities of the people of a great nation."[187] Yet three months later two of his own poems that were very much in the current mainstream of exhortatory war literature appeared in *Dokugusa* (Poison herbs), a poetry collection he published with Akiko on May 29, 1904.

In both these poems he applauds the Japanese navy's efforts, at the cost of many lives lost, to blockade Port Arthur, heavily fortified under Russian control. "Ryojun-guchi fūsa-tai" (The blockading squadron at Port Arthur) singles out for special mention Commander Arima Ryōkitsu, subsequently lionized in Japan as a "warrior god" (*gunshin*). Arima led seventy-seven sailors, selected from two thousand volunteers, on a suicide mission in February 1904 designed to block the Port Arthur harbor entrances by blowing up their own boat in the channel. Tekkan's *shintaishi* of twelve four-line stanzas reaches a feverish pitch vilifying Russia in the portion below:

aa ima Ryojun no fūsa-tai meiyo no sen o kōmuru wa Arima chūsa o hajime to shi kesshi nanajū nana yūshi	Ah, those honored with selection to the blockading squadron now at Port Arthur! Led by Commander Arima are seventy-seven brave warriors ready to die.
kuni ni wa oya mo tsuma mo ari ko mo ari to ie tatakai ni shinuru inochi o oshimanu wa Yamato no bushi ga narai nari	Though back home they have parents, wives, and children, too, they do not regret giving their lives in battle, for this is the code of Japan's samurai.
mashite yaban no Ro o korashi sekai no teki o nozoku beki seigi no gun ni shinan koto ika ni warera ga homare zo ya	What an honor it is to die serving in the army of justice that must chastise savage Russia and annihilate this enemy of the world.[188]

Starting with his "sword-and-tiger" poems of 1894–95, Tekkan comes a full 360 degrees in 1904 as he applauds the sacrifices of war by precisely reversing the effect of language and imagery from the pacifistic "Poem Limned in Blood" that he composed in 1897. The parents, wives, and children he mourned then as bereaved in a "war under distant skies" are now left behind without regret. The "justice" (*seigi*) that was but "a mask for evil" in 1897 is now "the army of justice [*seigi no gun*] that must chastise savage Russia." Resentment of Russia, growing in Japan since the Triple Intervention, had been expressed earlier by Tekkan in his poetry on Korea (see p. 66). This poem, however, goes much further to promote hostility in a way that both recalls his poetry of 1894 vilifying China and previews the countless verses published forty years later by prominent Japanese poets calling for the "chastisement" of "savage" England and America during the Pacific War.

Tekkan's other war poem to appear in *Dokugusa* is "Aa, Hirose chūsa" (Ah, Commander Hirose). It tells the story, which later became a legend in Japan, of Navy Commander Hirose Takeo, who died in the second suicide mission at Port Arthur carried out on March 27, 1904. Again, Japanese sailors sank their own ships in an effort to blockade the harbor. According to official accounts of this action, Hirose carefully laid explosives to destroy his own ship, the *Fukui-maru*, and after it blew up, searched desperately, but in vain, for his missing chief warrant officer. Finally, with great reluctance, he left his sinking ship to board a lifeboat that an enemy shell immediately destroyed. A scrap of Hirose's flesh was recovered and later carried through the streets of Tokyo under falling cherry blossoms in an enormous funeral procession. He was posthumously promoted and awarded the nation's highest military citation. In addition, a bronze statue of him was erected in Kanda, and the newspapers proclaimed him another "warrior god," a designation revived during the Pacific War to honor those who gave their lives in the attack on Pearl Harbor.

Like his tribute to Arima, Tekkan's poem honoring Hirose is a *shintaishi* of twelve stanzas, but this time the four lines in each stanza are followed by a two-line tag. This structure makes this poem particularly adaptable for a composer to set to music, as Tsuji Junji did with Tekkan's more famous 1932 *gunka* "Bakudan san'yūshi" (Human bombs: the three brave warriors), which eulogized the three Japanese soldiers who died that year detonating explosives they carried into a heavily fortified Chinese installation on the outskirts of Shanghai. The first four stanzas of "Ah, Commander Hirose" refer to the failure of the earlier mission at Port Arthur and warn that this time the harbor must be blocked at all costs:

teki no minato no yōgai ni
goshō no fune o shizumete wa
kyūshi no naka ni ikitarishi
Ryojun fūsa no kesshi-tai
  isamashiki umi ikusa
  chishio ni somanu hito mo nashi

When they sank five ships
off the fort in the enemy's harbor,
some of the suicide squadron
  blockading Port Arthur
narrowly missed death.
In this courageous battle at sea,
  all were stained with blood.

. . . .
. . . .

. . . .
. . . .

nao mo minato o sukima naku
fusagiezaru wa haji nari to
   waga isao o hokorazaru
   Yamato no bushi no yukashisa yo
	But now, unless they can block the harbor,
	leaving no gaps, shame will befall them.
	   Not to be proud of their own deeds
	   is the modest way of Japan's samurai.

Tekkan shifts to a narrative mode to describe the naval officers sinking their own ships in the channel amid the "sky-rending" fire of enemy shells. Then he focuses on Commander Hirose aboard the *Fukui-maru* and tells of his unsuccessful attempts to rescue Chief Warrant Officer Sugino:

naka ni aware ya Fukui-maru
mizukara shizumu bakuyaku ni
funazoko fukaku hi o sasu to
heisōchō wa kudarishi ga
   teki ga sashi suirai yo
   anaya kono toki meichū shi
	Among the ships,
	how sad is the *Fukui-maru*!
	Her chief warrant officer receives
	   the order to sink her
	by firing explosives deep in her bilge,
	   but just then an enemy torpedo
	   suddenly hits its mark.

subete hashike ni utsuredomo
heisōchō wa kaeri kozu
katabuku fune o aogedomo
heisōchō wa orite kozu
   kanpan ni mizu tsukite
   fune wa shidai ni shizumiyuku
	The crew transfers to a sampan,
	but the chief is not among them.
	They gaze upward at the listing ship,
	but still he does not come down.
	   The water rises to the deck
	   and the ship begins to sink.

fune no shirei wa chin'yū no
Hirose chūsa to kikoetari
nasake shiritaru hito nareba
heisōchō o sukuwan to
   mitabi made hikikaeshi
   aa mitabi made fune no ue
	The ship's commander is famed Hirose,
	quietly courageous,
	and a man of compassion.
	To rescue the chief,
	   three times he goes back.
	   Ah, three times he boards the ship.

abunaki naka o mono to sezu
konata kanata to hase motome
Sugino Sugino to na o yobedo
heisōchō wa iraenu ni
   shinashitari kuchioshi to
   ima wa hashike no tsuna tokinu
	Ignoring the danger all around him,
	he runs this way and that in his search,
	calling "Sugino, Sugino!" over and over.
	When the chief does not answer,
	   he grieves his death
	   and unties the sampan's line.

ima wa hashike no tsuna tokinu
kono aware naru ketsubetsu ni
chūsa o hajime sen'yū wa
hashike o kozori mina mugon
   ori kara o susamajiku
   hito-kiwa masaru tama no ame
	He unties the sampan's line,
	and in their sorrowful farewell,
	the commander and his men
	gather silently in the sampan.
	   Just then, with dreadful swiftness,
	   comes a sudden rain of shells.

aa sono setsuna hitobito no	Ah, in that instant the men's brows
hitai ni sosogu chi no keburi	are splashed with blood
awaya to mireba funabata no	and when they look again,
chūsa no kage wa nakari keri	the commander has vanished overboard.
batsugun no isao arite	Having carried out a supreme feat,
chūsa no kage wa nakari keri	the commander has vanished.[189]

Again, Tekkan has traveled a great distance, in a reverse direction, from denouncing "glorious deeds" and "heroes . . . vaunted foolishly by everyone" in 1897 to extolling "a supreme feat" and "famed Commander Hirose" in 1904. The imagery of bloodshed is retained from "Poem Limned in Blood," condemned in this 1897 work as "the horror of spilling blood without remorse" but honored in 1904 as marking "this courageous battle at sea" and Hirose's sudden splattering demise. To be sure, Tekkan goes beyond glorifying gore in this poem when he describes Hirose's compassion in attempting to rescue Chief Sugino and notes the sorrow of leaving behind a fallen comrade. However, both feelings are posed firmly in the context of the very samurai ethos Tekkan had ridiculed as a useless anachronism three years earlier in "Song of Farewell to Japan." Now he valorizes men who confront danger with selfless determination and endure their grief in silence.

Expressing the view that these two poems represent a temporary aberration and not a full-fledged reversion in Tekkan's attitude toward war, Itsumi Kumi emphasizes that both "The Blockading Squadron at Port Arthur" and "Ah, Commander Hirose" were omitted from the second printing of *Dokugusa*, which appeared in September 1904.[190] Itsumi also quotes *haiku* poet Naitō Meisetsu (1847–1926), who wrote in the July 1904 issue of the magazine *Myōjō* that he had received a letter from Tekkan insisting again that "true artists do not involve themselves in war."[191] It is not known if Tekkan's wife Akiko, co-contributor to *Dokugusa*, influenced the decision to eliminate Tekkan's two war poems from its second printing. However, September 1904 is the same month she published her famous antiwar *shintaishi* "Brother, Do Not Give Your Life." Subtitled "An Appeal to My Younger Brother with the Besieging Forces at Port Arthur," her poem deplores the Imperial Japanese Army's long siege, resulting in massive casualties, of the same fortress that the Japanese navy attempted to blockade, an effort Tekkan had hailed in his poetry four months earlier. Itsumi speculates that Akiko's "Brother, Do Not Give Your Life" borrowed from Tekkan's earlier poetry condemning war but does not consider the possibility that her work might have had some influence on him.

Tekkan's silence in his autobiographical writings on his motivation for including, and later deleting, these two poems makes it difficult to confirm assertions that, despite their publication, he had "sobered up from his intoxication with war" and essentially maintained an abhorrence of armed conflict derived from his observations during the aftermath of the Sino-Japanese War in Japan and Korea. However, Tekkan's highly popular 1932 *gunka*, rarely mentioned by recent critics and biographers, that extols the "human bomb" mission near Shanghai[192] would seem to cast doubt on the "temporary lapse theory" of his poetry on war. As in the case of his poems praising Japan's military successes against Russia, his publication of a *shintaishi* lauding the Imperial Army's actions in China was preceded by denunciations of an age when military influences held strong sway over life and literature in Japan. Akiko's biographer Yamamoto Fujie quotes from Tekkan's letter dated November 30, 1931, written to Kobayashi Masaharu, a businessman and novelist who had been a longtime supporter of the Yosanos:

> An age has come of a despotism, wielded by military men, that has extended its pressures to the business world, of course, and even to people who have no involvement [in business or politics]. . . . With the severe hardship of making a living, people endure unspeakable suffering.[193]

Yet, despite this 1931 denunciation of "military men," whose "despotism" he blamed for the poverty of many, including himself, the following year Tekkan published his popular *gunka* on the "human bomb" attack in China. This charge by three Japanese soldiers from Kyushu, who carried explosives through barbed wire into a heavily fortified Chinese installation near Shanghai, was widely celebrated as a suicide mission in Japan's press. However, Ueno Hidenobu wrote in his 1989 book *Tennō Heika banzai: Bakudan san'yūshi josetsu* that the three soldiers, members of Japan's long-oppressed Burakumin minority, had been told that, after detonating the explosives, they could escape back through the hole in the fortress opened by the blast. They discovered only after igniting the detonator cord that it was too short for them to get clear of the explosion, and their bodies were blown to bits. Ueno further related that, amid the frenzied public celebration that followed, the mother of one of the men declined an interview and her share of the "consolation money" raised in a nationwide collection because she was afraid that the location of her home would reveal her family's Buraku origins.[194]

The truth about this mission notwithstanding, three major newspapers, *Asahi*, *Hōchi*, and *Tōkyō nichi-nichi*, joined the frenzy and ran nationwide contests soliciting *gunka* lauding the "suicide" attack. Tekkan's entrance into the *Asahi* competition was criticized by some who considered it unfair that the work of a prominent professional poet should be judged alongside poems submitted by amateur contestants that included schoolchildren. Tekkan fared better at the *Tōkyō nichi-nichi*. His entry won the contest there, and a revised version was recorded to the accompaniment of music composed by Tsuji Junji and performed by the Toyama Army Academy Band. "Human Bombs: The Three Brave Warriors" became the most popular by far of the several *gunka* released by record companies that competed to sell songs eulogizing the soldiers.[195] The first published version of this ten-verse *shintaishi* reads:

1.

Byōkōchin no teki no jin,
ware no yūtai sude ni semu.
Ori kara kōru kisaragi no
nijū-ni nichi gozen goji.

Our comrades-in-arms
have already attacked
the enemy's camp, Miao Hsing Chen.
It was 5:00 a.m.
on a freezing February twenty-second.

2.

Meirei kudaru, shōmen ni
hirake, hohei no totsugekiro.
Sōchi no ma nashi, tenka shite
hakaitō o ba dakite ike.

The order was given: "Open the way
for a frontal infantry assault.
There's no time for emplacements.
Ignite the fuses of the
demolition canisters and carry them out."

3.

Kotaete "hai" to, kōhei no
Sakue, Kitagawa, Enoshita-ra
rin taru kokoro, sannin ga
omou koto koso hitotsu nare.

Replying "Yes, Sir"
were engineer corpsmen
Sakue, Kitagawa, and Enoshita.
Their hearts inspired,
the three were thinking
a single thought.

4.

Warera ga ue ni itadaku wa
Tennō Heika no ōmiitsu
ushiro ni ou wa kokumin no
ishi ni kawarareru omoki nin.

We receive with humility from above
the august virtue
of His Majesty, the Emperor,
and bear on our backs
the heavy responsibility
for the will of the nation's people.

5.

Iza kono toki zo, dōdō to,
fuso no rekishi ni kitaetaru
tetsu yori kataki "chūyū" no
Nihon danshi o arawasu wa.

Now is the time! They demonstrate
gallantly the loyalty and bravery,
firmer than steel, of the men of Japan,
that has been forged
through the history of our ancestors.

6.

Machikanetari to hase-izuru
kao ni kesshi no bishō ari.
Ta no sen'yū ni nokoseru mo
karoku "saraba" to tada ichigo.

On their faces, as they rush out
impatiently, are the smiles
of men ready to die.
For their other comrades-in-arms
they leave behind but one word,
a casual "farewell."

7.

Tenka no mama no hakaitō,
dakiaitaru hakaitō,
tetsujō-mō ni tadoritsuki,
waga mi morotomo mae ni nagu.

With the demolition canisters ignited,
the demolition canisters they carry,
they reach the barbed wire and,
holding them, hurl their bodies forward.

8.

Gōzen okoru bakuon ni
hiraku misuji no totsugekiro,
ima waga-tai wa ara-umi no
ushio no gotoku to odoriiru

In the thundering explosions,
three assault paths are opened,
and now our forces rush inside
like a storming sea.

9.

Aa Kōnan no ume nara de,
sakete chiru mi o hana to nashi.
Jingi no gun ni sasagetaru
kuni no seika no san'yūshi.

Ah, like the plum blossoms of Kiangnan,
bodies torn and scattered
become flowers.
The three brave warriors
are the flowers of our nation,
offered to the army
of humanity and justice.

10.

Chūkon kiyoki ka o tsutae
nagaku tenka o hagemashimu.
Sōretsu muhi no san'yūshi,
hikari no meiyo no san'yūshi.

The pure fragrance of their loyal spirits
is bequeathed,
and will long inspire the nation.
The unparalleled heroism
of the three brave warriors,
the shining honor
of the three brave warriors.[196]

It seems unlikely that newspapers in England or the United States would run contests for poems on the subject of a soldiers' suicide attack. As noted above, however, poetry eulogizing young men who went to their deaths in battle is not uncommon in Europe and America. Whereas Tekkan writes of "the flowers of our nation" and "shining honor" to describe the "three brave warriors" who gave their lives at Shanghai, Forceythe Willson writes in "Boy Brittan" (1862) of "the flowers of . . . immortal youth" and "laurels of light" to describe the "warrior -boy[s]" who died at the Battle of

Fort Henry, Tennessee, in the American Civil War. The resulting poetry is, arguably, even worse than Tekkan's:

> And laurels of light, and tears of truth,
>   And the mantle of immortality;
> And the flowers of love and immortal youth,
> And the tender heart-tokens of all true ruth—
>   And everlasting victory!
> And the breath and bliss of Liberty;
> And the loving kiss of Liberty;
> And the welcoming light of heavenly eyes,
> And the cover of God's canopy;
>
> For all the brave who rest with thee;
> And for one and all who died with thee;
> . . . .
> On the solid land or heaving sea,
>   Dear warrior-boy—like thee.[197]

Yamamoto Fujie compares "Human Bombs: The Three Brave Warriors" to Tekkan's early "sword-and-tiger" poetry, and she tries to explain why he produced a poem in 1932 exalting soldiers that contradicts the disdain he expressed the previous year for "the despotism" of "military men" in his letter to Kobayashi Masaharu. She notes the severe financial hardship that plagued the Yosanos and many others at the bottom of the depression and speculates reluctantly that the five hundred-yen prize (a very large sum of money in 1932) offered by the newspaper might have inspired Tekkan to write this poem.[198] His published reminiscences mention only that he regrets being rushed to submit it in time for the contest deadline, before he could make it "sufficiently polished to portray the exploits of the three brave warriors":

> In fact, when I saw the reports of the heroism exhibited by those three brave warriors, I was most deeply moved and spontaneously composed the first two verses of this poem. Just at that time it was announced in your newspaper that a contest was being held soliciting poems on the three brave warriors; furthermore, the judge was my old friend Mr. Usuda, so I felt inclined to submit an entry. I was surprised to learn that my poem was honored with the prize, but simply the fact that it was a "Poem to the Three Brave Warriors" made it a special honor and a joy for me, and I felt deeply moved anew. However, I regret that there had been so little time. With a little more, I could have composed a poem sufficiently polished to recount the mission

> of the three brave warriors as if readers were seeing it with their own eyes. Although the poem is inadequate, I put all my efforts into writing it because these soldiers represented the aspirations of their countrymen to celebrate the glory of His Majesty, the Emperor, by offering their flesh and blood. There was another reason. Since *gunka* had formerly not been considered works of literature, I wanted to write one myself. Yet, on this point, as noted above, I am extremely sorry that I had to submit this poem while it was still very unsatisfactory.[199]

The poet's reservations about it aside, "Human Bombs: The Three Brave Warriors," published three years before Tekkan's death, seriously undermines Itsumi Kumi's theory that his *gunka* written during the Russo-Japanese War were only a "temporary aberration" for a writer who essentially opposed armed conflict. Biographer Sunaga Asahiko has another explanation for the 360-degree rotation evident in Tekkan's poetry on war:

> "Human Bombs: The Three Brave Warriors" was written in response to a public appeal for poems [by the newspapers]. . . . It is similar to "Ah, Commander Hirose" and other poetry in the collection *Dokugusa* (1904). Tekkan maintained a strict purism closely connected to his early nationalism, which remained somewhere inside him throughout his life, rising up on occasion.[200]

Tekkan's death from pneumonia in 1935 meant that, unlike Akiko, he did not live to see the start of the Pacific War. Yet, despite poetry against war that he produced during his career, it is difficult to imagine that he would have hesitated to join her and all the other poets who wrote poetry supportive of the cause espoused by Japan's military leaders in this conflict.

3 Takeshima Hagoromo and Miyazaki Koshoshi: Harbingers of Protest

Identified today as progenitors of modern antiwar poetry in Japan, Takeshima Hagoromo (1872–1967) and Miyazaki Koshoshi (1864–1922) did not always publish poems on war that consistently or explicitly opposed it. Like Yosano Tekkan, Koshoshi came to write against armed conflict after publishing verses in support of Japan's war against China. Although Hagoromo's best-known poetry is reprinted in recent anthologies of antiwar literature, he launched his career with help from influential writers remembered, like Yosano Tekkan, for their bellicose pronouncements.

As a student of Japanese literature at Tokyo University in the mid-1890s, Hagoromo received crucial early support from his senior schoolmates (*senpai*) Takayama Chogyū, who berated Japanese writers for not advocating "patriotism and courage" during the Sino-Japanese War, and Ōmachi Keigetsu, who publicly accused Yosano Akiko of treason for the poem urging her brother not to give his life during the Russo-Japanese War (see chapter five). By the time Hagoromo graduated in 1896, he had already gained a reputation as a promising poet of the neoclassical school who wrote in the "new style" (*shintaishi*) form with lines in the seven-five syllable pattern.[201] Keigetsu brought him into the prestigious Akamon (Red Gate) poetry group, named for the landmark that still designates the main entrance to Tokyo University, and Chogyū's generous praise of his work provided him with recognition and publishing opportunities in wider literary circles.

Recent identification of Hagoromo with dissident literature is also ironic because these early contacts and his scholarship in classical Japanese poetry brought him an official appointment to the O-Utadokoro (Poetry Bureau) in the ultraconservative Imperial Household Agency. Moreover, the poem "Senshi-sotsu" (A fallen soldier), which earned him the reputation as a progenitor of modern Japanese antiwar poetry, was published in an 1896 anthology *Hana-momiji* (Flowers and red leaves), which also included the work of Keigetsu and Shioi Ukō (1869–1913), a neoclassicist associated with Yosano Tekkan's mentor Ochiai Naobumi and an editor at *Teikoku bungaku* (Imperial literature) magazine.

Besides following the *shintaishi* structure that was the preferred medium for Meiji neoclassical poetry, Hagoromo composed the eight stanzas of "A Fallen Soldier" entirely in classical Japanese. While Yosano Tekkan and Masaoka Shiki borrowed expressions from *Man'yōshū* for poems about war, Hagoromo's use of such words as *tsuwamono* for soldier and *koma* for horse gives this poem the flavor of Japan's medieval warrior tales.[202] It moves in a circular pattern, beginning with a plaintive evocation of the soldier's death in battle, shifting to focus on his despondent and embittered family back home, and then returning to the lonely spectacle of his corpse lying in a deserted field. The first three stanzas tell how he died:

Ochikata shiroki kogarashi ni,
chishio no tsuyu no tama chirite,
kaze mo iro aru suenohara,
tsuwamono hitori taoretari.

Far away in a white winter wind,
blood scatters like drops of dew,
coloring even the gusts that blow
over the desolate field
where a fallen soldier lies.

Isameru koma no hitosuji ni
kao mo somukezu susumi ken.
Sobira ni kizu wa owanedomo,
hitai ni tama no ato shigeshi.

Urging his brave horse straight ahead,
he had advanced,
never turning his face aside.
Hence, on his back there are no wounds,
but his forehead is covered
with the marks of piercing bullets.

Kimi ni tsukushishi magokoro o,
tomurau hito no kage mo naku,
kuyashi namida ni museburan,
kabane ni sosogu kusa no tsuyu.

With no one present to mourn
this offering of true devotion
to the Emperor,
the grass sprinkles dew,
as though sobbing with tears of regret,
over the soldier's corpse.[203]

To express sorrow by likening dew to tears is one of the familiar metaphorical devices from classical Japanese poetry that Hagoromo draws on for this poem. The soldier's death provokes "tears of regret" but is described as a supreme act of loyalty with no hint of irony or sarcasm that could suggest protest at this point in the poem. However, the four-stanza sequence that follows, which portrays the grief and resentment felt by the soldier's family when they finally come to acknowledge reluctantly that he is dead, has been cited recently by literary critics as one of the earliest examples of implied protest against war in modern Japanese poetry:

Yūkage shigeki furusato ni,
ooshiki chichi mo uchishiore,
sonata no sora o nagametsutsu
"Aware waga ko ya ikani seshi."

As the evening shadows deepen
in his hometown,
even his stout-hearted father
gazes on and on despondently
toward the distant sky.
"Alas, my poor son,
what has become of him?"

"Kaeranu mireba sari tomo to
omoishi waga ko mo usenu meri."
Iitsutsu haha wa fushishizumi,
kagiri no sama ni uchinakinu

His mother in the depths of grief
says it over and over—
"He does not return, so it must be true
that I have lost my beloved son"—
and weeps bitterly
that his life should end this way.

Tsuma wa tsuyukeki samushiro ni,
"Waga se no kimi wa nakimono to,
omoitsutsu nao waga mi ni wa,
ima mada imasu kokochi shite."

His wife speaks
from straw mats stained with tears:
"Though I know my husband is dead,
I cannot help feeling in my heart
that he is still alive."

Yami ni shi mayou tarachine no,
namida ya ame to narinu rashi,
uramuru tsuma no magokoro ni
sora mo aware ya shiriniken.

The tears of his parents,
lost in grief, fall like the rain,
and from his embittered wife comes
such true devotion that even the sky
might know her sorrow.

Hagoromo again draws on conventional metaphors, not limited to Japanese poetry, when he compares tears to rain. What is particularly affecting about these four stanzas is the response of the soldier's family, whose first reactions to his death are manifested in various shades of disbelief. Writers who observed families in Japan bereaved by the Sino-Japanese War remarked on this tendency, which is shared by people everywhere when confronted with the news of a loved one's violent death. After disbelief, anger often follows as the next stage in the bereavement process, and Hagoromo focuses on the soldier's "embittered" widow. Had the poet chosen to condemn war explicitly in "A Fallen Soldier," this might have been a good place for it. However, he does not elaborate on her bitterness or suggest that its target goes beyond the cruelty of her husband's fate. Nevertheless, the intense concentration on her feelings and those of other family members contrasts sharply with verses popular during the

Sino-Japanese War and subsequent conflicts exhorting soldiers' families in Japan to ignore their personal concerns and urge their men to fight bravely and to die if necessary. In its final stanza "A Fallen Soldier" returns to the site of the recent battle:

Miwatasu hate mo aranohara,
  sora to hitotsu ni shiguretsutsu,
kusamusu kabane otozurete,
  urasabishiku mo sosogu nari.
	Stretching even to the horizon,
	  the deserted plain merges with the sky
	that sends rain pouring down forlornly
	  to fall on the corpse overgrown with grass.

Here Hagoromo evokes not only rain in the manner of *waka* to express sorrow but also the stark desolation of a recent battlefield where only a single corpse remains. The bleakness of the landscape in this "desolate field" emphasizes the terrible separation of the soldier from those who mourn and honor him. American poet Wallace Stevens (1879–1955) evokes such separation as "a season of autumn," also associated with parting and loneliness in Japanese literature, in his similarly titled and articulated "The Death of a Soldier":

Life contracts and death is expected,
As in a season of autumn,
The soldier falls.

He does not become a three-day personage,
Imposing his separation,
Calling for pomp,

Death is absolute and without memorial,
As in a season of autumn,
When the wind stops,

When the wind stops and, over the heavens,
The clouds go, nevertheless,
In their direction.[204]

The effect of natural imagery in both poems is powerful, but Hagoromo's apparent allusion in the phrase *kusamusu kabane* to a famous ancient battle song praising those who gave their lives in service to the emperor presents another obstacle to reading "A Fallen Soldier" as an antiwar poem.[205] In fact, the text of this same song was set to music twice during the second Sino-Japanese War for two of Japan's most popular and enduring *gunka*, both entitled "Umi yukaba" (When we go to sea), by composers Shinji Kiyoshi in 1937 and Tōgi Rihō in 1938.

Nevertheless, Murata Masao finds protest implied in "A Fallen Soldier" with the contrast between the soldier's willingness to die for the emperor and the anguish his death is causing his family, though Murata concedes that this might be stretching the point.[206] The poem effectively depicts the suffering caused by armed conflict, but Hagoromo's use of the word *magokoro*, an expression of high approbation, to describe both the soldier's devotion to the emperor, manifested by his willingness to die, and his wife's bereavement after his death makes an antiwar reading problematic. Murata is on firmer ground when he points out that "A Fallen Soldier" must be considered distinctive in the context of its time, when Hagoromo's mentor Takayama Chogyū and others were successfully promoting a hostile ultranationalism in the wake of the Triple Intervention.[207] For bucking the current of its day, this work is perhaps best viewed, then, not as an antiwar poem in itself but as a forerunner to Tekkan's "Poem Limned in Blood" (1897), Akiko's "Brother, Do Not Give Your Life" (1904), and later Japanese poetry explicitly condemning war.

The other poem that has been cited, perhaps more justifiably, as an early example of modern antiwar poetry in Japan is "Ensentō" (Weary of war, 1897) by the innovative poet Miyazaki Koshoshi.[208] Also active as a novelist, essayist, and Christian minister, Koshoshi is credited with writing some of the first successful lyric poetry in the *shintaishi* form. Literary historians also cite his work as a strong influence on authors whose reputations far exceeded his own, particularly Shimazaki Tōson (1872–1943), who became a major novelist after initially establishing himself as a writer of lyric poetry in *shintaishi*.[209]

As a poem condemning armed conflict, "Weary of War" sparked controversy in Japan, both at the time of its first publication and after World War II, when it was reprinted in anthologies of antiwar poetry. Recent critics who praise it as an early modern poem against war have also noted that it expresses a view that sharply contradicts the celebratory tone of *gunka*-like verses Koshoshi published three years earlier, marking the opening of hostilities with China. Back when it first appeared, Miyazaki Koshoshi's antiwar views provoked a very different response, inspiring novelist Hirotsu Ryūrō (1861–1928) to make him the model for the villain Hakozaki Kanekichi in his story "Hikokumin" (The traitor, 1897), which portrays an eccentric, Christian pacifist poet and church elder who denounces Japan's role in the recent conflict with China.[210] Ryūrō's targeting of Koshoshi can be explained in part because, while Hagoromo's "A Fallen Soldier" is limited to a depiction of the suffering war causes, Koshoshi explicitly criticized bellicose fervor and called for war's abolishment.

However, the fact that Koshoshi attracted more hostile attention than Hagoromo also had much to do with the widely divergent backgrounds, associations, and temperaments of the two poets.

Unlike Hagoromo, who maintained close connections with writers of the neoclassical school known for their ultranationalistic views on literature and politics, Koshoshi was associated with Min'yūsha, a press that printed the work of younger writers, such as Kunikida Doppo (1871–1908) and Tayama Katai (1872–1930), who had reputations as innovators widely read in European literature. Doppo and Katai produced their own unsparing autobiographical accounts of the Sino-Japanese and Russo-Japanese Wars, respectively,[211] with Katai's novel *Ippeisotsu* (One soldier, 1908) later subjected to expurgation of passages that government censors considered antimilitary.[212] Both of these writers also published poems in *Jojō shishū* (Lyric poetry, 1897), the same Min'yūsha anthology in which Koshoshi's "Weary of War" first appeared.

Koshoshi also produced other works containing overtones of dissent, including stories and essays critical of the popular values in late Meiji urban Japan that placed primary importance on acquiring wealth and social status.[213] In these writings he often advocated a return to what he considered the more idealistic values of rural life, though he conceded he could not bring himself to abandon Tokyo to live in the countryside. Koshoshi framed his ideas in an eclectic combination of Eastern and Western thought, drawing especially on Taoism and Christian philosophy. Known for his translations of Thomas More and William Wordsworth, he also infused his poetry and fiction with biblical imagery and allusions that he sometimes posed in highly unconventional ways.

Koshoshi's eclectic approach to religion and philosophy was shared by Kinoshita Naoe and other writers who embraced Christianity in post-Restoration Japan. Banned by the Bakufu government during most of the Tokugawa period (1600–1868), Christianity was legalized in 1873 under pressure from European and American governments. There were some Catholics among the missionaries who came subsequently to establish churches, schools, and charitable organizations, but most were Protestants from the United States and Canada. Though the numbers of missionaries and converts were comparatively small, Christianity as a system of beliefs had a powerful impact on Japanese writers and intellectuals, including the leaders of prominent labor and socialist movements founded in Meiji. Its importation also brought Western ideas to literature and the arts in Japan, which utilized religious texts, symbols, and subjects.[214]

Koshoshi's activities as a Christian, which later fueled the controversy that surrounded him, began quietly in 1886 with his baptism at the

Ushigome church in Tokyo. He became an elder there in 1891 and maintained his affiliation until 1898. It was during his years at Ushigome that he published his best-known writing on war, starting with a series of decidedly bellicose *tanka* that appeared in the *Kokumin shinbun* of August and September 1894, shortly after hostilities had erupted with China. These verses are indistinguishable from the hundreds of war poems appearing at the time and seem especially uncharacteristic of a poet known as a pioneering lyricist. They bear such titles as "Bushi-damashii" (Warrior spirit), "Shukushō-ka" (Victory song), and "Kaisen-shi" (News that the war has begun), quoted below, on the cruiser *Naniwa*'s July 25th destruction of two Chinese ships off the Korean coast:

Shina fune o uchishizumetaru tsutsu oto ni kokoro ugokanu hito nakaru ramu	There is no one whose heart was not inspired by the sound of the guns that shot and sank the Chinese ships.[215]

If Koshoshi's heart was inspired by the guns of July 1894, by the end of the following year he was publishing poetry that drew on biblical allusions to denounce war as ignorant folly. Literary historians have explained the change in Masaoka Shiki's writing on the Sino-Japanese War as the result of his experiences traveling with the army (see chapter one). Yosano Tekkan's more spectacular turnabout has been attributed to his meetings with bereaved families and his observations in Korea (see chapter two). Koshoshi did not leave Japan during the Sino-Japanese War or its aftermath, but his poetry condemning bellicose fervor and his prose depicting the painfully ambivalent situation of Japanese families with loved ones serving in the conflict indicate that he had become a sensitive observer of home-front Japan.

For Koshoshi the turning point seems to have come with the short story "Tsuru ga buji" (Tsuru is safe) , published by *Kokumin no tomo* magazine in January 1895,[216] only four months after his prowar *tanka*. Wartime excitement was now at its peak in Japan with crowds waiting eagerly for reports from the front, gazing through store windows at fanciful *nishiki-e* paintings of one-sided battles, and celebrating each victory as it was announced in briskly selling newspapers.[217] Koshoshi's story does not explicitly condemn this fervor or war itself, as his later poems did, yet it is a highly sympathetic depiction of families with loved ones at the front who were unable to conceal their true fears amid the reveling of everyone around them. Hunger for information from the war zone plays a crucial part in the story, narrated by a friend of Tsuru's who gives an elaborate oration on the tide of battle in China before a crowd of villagers hanging on his every word.

The village is Tsuru's hometown in Kyushu, where his father Tōkichi and his mother O-kane had watched, with sharply differing responses, as their son was drafted into the army, sent for training to Fukuoka, and then deployed to the China front. Portrayed mostly through his letters and the recollections of his family and friends, Tsuru is described by the narrator as undergoing a profound change after his conscription, from a frail and gentle boy to "a brawny and splendid soldier," though he is still said to have his mother's smile. He had suffered at first from the harsh discipline and relentless drill of military training, but he gradually became accustomed to army life thanks, in large part, to a unit commander who was so kind to him that Tsuru came to think of him as a father.[218] Tsuru also reports that, despite the hardships, he and the other soldiers are always inspired by the thought that they are doing their duty to the emperor and the nation. Koshoshi's Tsuru is, in this sense, much like Hagoromo's fallen soldier in his unquestioning devotion to the emperor.

Tsuru's father Tōkichi, who speaks often of duty to the emperor, listens proudly to the narrator's description of Tsuru as a young recruit and does not yet betray any misgivings about his son's mobilization. Tōkichi owns a metal-forging shop specializing in gun repair and is himself an expert marksman. Koshoshi portrays him as a heavy drinker, a carouser, and something of a braggart who likes to sing ballads from *jōruri* dramas and play the *biwa* when in his cups. He is said to prefer his son Tsuru to his two daughters, but he has never liked Tsuru's slightly effeminate manner, which is another reason he is happy to hear that the boy has become a "splendid soldier."[219]

Tsuru's mother, O-kane, expresses her worries about Tsuru's conscription much earlier and more directly than her husband, however. Koshoshi effectively contrasts Tōkichi's initial feelings of pride with the disappointment O-kane feels when Tsuru is drafted, which turns to deeper concern as the crisis in Korea leads to hostilities between China and Japan. Shortly after the outbreak of fighting is reported in the newspapers, the family attends a meeting of the villagers at a local school during which everyone is urged to support the war for the sake of the emperor and the nation, even if this means sacrificing their beloved sons. Koshoshi comments that, as they listened to this, the villagers "looked like people struck by disaster." Even Tōkichi is shocked when the family returns home to discover that Tsuru, who telegrammed earlier that his unit would soon be deployed, has made out a will. O-kane weeps bitterly as she reads it, asking over and over, "What will become of him?" Tōkichi insists that she quiet herself out of respect for the emperor, but at this moment O-kane "did not feel gratitude toward the emperor" (*tennō heika no arigataki to shirazariki*). "It's as though I'm seeing Tsuru dragged off like a calf to the slaughterhouse," she wails.[220] This is more than Tōkichi feels he can tolerate, and he orders her out of the house. Although posed here initially as a dispute between husband and wife, the conflict felt in Japan by families caught between pressures to support the war and concern over the safety of loved ones at the front soon touches Tōkichi himself when heavy casualties in Tsuru's unit are reported in the newspapers.

In this story Koshoshi does not explicitly criticize Japan's expansion of the conflict. However, in describing the course of the war, he notes that Tsuru's unit, the Sixth Division, is not deployed until the fall of P'yŏngyang in September 1894. He refers to British and American offers in October and November to mediate, rejected by the Japanese government, as "rumors of peacemaking." He then tells how Tsuru's Sixth Division is combined with the First Division under the Second Army for the bloody assault on Port Arthur, commenting that "peace had now become a vain hope."

Tsuru sends his parents another telegram when his unit is ordered to the front and asks them to come to Fukuoka for a farewell visit. Tōkichi has fallen ill so O-kane goes there alone. When she returns, she tells Tōkichi at his bedside that Tsuru "smiled, saying it was for the emperor's sake, and got on the train. . . . He did not seem like my little boy." She repeats her impression of "a calf going to the slaughterhouse." At this point Tōkichi is still proud to hear of his son's brave departure and to see a Japanese flag, brought back by O-kane, that was given to Tsuru by his commanding officer, who inscribed it with the words "loyalty, courage, and service."[221]

Tōkichi's attitude undergoes a profound change shortly after the fall of Port Arthur. The narrator describes the scene in the village when news of the Japanese victory arrives with the delivery of the *Fukuoka nichi-nichi shinbun*. Japanese flags are hung from the eaves of houses on both sides of the street, and the whole village is hastily decorated, as if for the annual sports day (*undōkai*), for a large victory celebration. Later, people gather in front of the shrine to drink, dance, and sing such favorite *gunka* as "Nihon no guntai" (The Japanese army) and "Chan-chan bōzu" (The Chinks). The mood of celebration remains at a high pitch while the narrator travels to Fukuoka for more detailed information on events at the front. When he returns, he stands before the villagers and gives a long and elaborate oration on the battle at Port Arthur. He describes the actions of various units, emphasizing the bravery of soldiers from Kyushu who had advanced through hails of gunfire and suffered heavy casualties in the final decisive assault. He even quotes a foreign military observer who had witnessed the attack and called it "unparalleled in the world" (*sekai muni*). The narrator notes the high pitch of his own excitement as he feels "my listeners responding in their hearts to my every word. I was overcome with emotion, sensing the greatness of this deed of our nation." He also becomes aware that all are not celebrating. When he assures his listeners that those who died at Port Arthur will receive high honors, he discovers that some in the audience are far more concerned to learn the fate of individual soldiers than to hear about the successful progress of battle:

> The pitiable ones were the families of soldiers at the front. All of them had been invited as guests of honor and were seated at the head of the gathering. The soldiers from each family were honored one by one. While most in this group joined the ceremonies, there was one person who did not. (59–60)

Tsuru's father Tōkichi, always the life of the party, now sits apart from the others. Sunk in despair, he refuses even the food and drink his family urges on him. In portraying Tōkichi's growing fears for his son and his resentment toward the celebrants around him, Koshoshi employs biblical imagery in an unusual and arresting way to suggest the scene of the Last Supper:

> The sake reminded him of the blood of his son, and in the sliced meat he saw his son's flesh. . . . He did not feel enmity toward his fellow villagers, but he could not help seeing his friends as cruel. They seemed oblivious to the families' anguish in their great hurry to eat and drink, unable to postpone their feasting until the war had ended and the troops had returned home. (60)

For Tōkichi the war has finally come home, and he is neither inspired by news of victory nor consoled by the thought that, if killed in battle, his son would receive posthumous decorations. At this point O-kane comes rushing in breathlessly to deliver the message that serves as the title of the story. She says that a letter has just come from another soldier who fought at Port Arthur to his family in the village with word that "Tsuru is safe." Immediately, the mothers of two other soldiers at the front press O-kane for news of their sons, but she tells them that only Tsuru was mentioned in the letter. Now Koshoshi notes the contrast between Tsuru's family, joining the crowd in celebration, and the two other families whose renewed fears are tinged with disappointment and envy at the good fortune of Tōkichi and O-kane.

Tōkichi is suddenly his old self again. Apparently cured of his illness as well as his depression of a few moments before, he returns home dancing and singing. Hugging the narrator, he offers an invitation: "Let everyone come to our house and celebrate our victorious army. Come one, come all! Don't leave anyone behind." The party that follows lasts until dawn with Tōkichi leading the festivities. The narrator notes that "Tōkichi celebrated the army's victory . . . and could not wait for the war to end and his beloved son to return" (64). The story concludes with this ironic comment on Tōkichi's inconsistency.

Appearing while the conflict was still going on, "Tsuru is Safe" is an early fictional portrayal of the disturbing impact of the Sino-Japanese War on soldiers' families in Japan. The negative side of victory celebrations, also depicted in Yosano Tekkan's poem "Arch of Triumph," is the subject of later fiction by Izumi Kyōka.[222] Critic and literary historian Nishida Masaru, writing in 1983, cautions that "it would be difficult to call 'Tsuru is Safe' antiwar."[223] Yet Nishida identifies it as one of a small number of works published during and immediately after the conflict with China "focusing on the anguish war causes."[224] Far more direct condemnation of war and the popular agitation that accompanies it can be found in a poem Koshoshi published in the November 1895 issue of the same magazine, *Kokumin no tomo*, in which "Tsuru is Safe" had appeared ten months earlier. "Tashiro-zaka yori kokyō mioroshite yomeru chōka" (Overlooking my hometown from Tashiro Hill, 1895) predates his more famous "Weary of War" by nearly two years. It also opens by evoking pastoral imagery to suggest bellicose fervor:

Yo wa ima ya ikusa no saichū, hito wa sawagu susuki no gotoshi.	In this world now at war people are like seething *susuki* grass.

In a subsequent verse, Koshoshi again employs a biblical allusion, this time to denounce armed conflict specifically:

Ana utate kami no tsukurishi, hito wa mina onajiki mono o, kotonareru mono ni omoite, hima naku zo hito wa arasou.	How it saddens me! Created by God, all people are one. Yet, thinking they are different, they fight on without respite.[225]

Two years later in "Weary of War" Koshoshi again likens bellicose fervor to plants disturbed by the wind, and he calls for an end to all wars:

Kachinu makenu to yo no naka no, nonoshiri-sawagu koe kiku wa, kozue o harau akikaze no, otozure yori mo nao tsurashi.	The voices I hear all around us shouting of victory and defeat disturb me far more than the sound of the autumn wind blowing through the treetops.
Waga yo tanoshimu tami no tame, ikusa o yamuru sube araba.	If only there were a way to abolish war for the sake of people who merely seek some happiness in their lives.
Mono-sawagashiki kono koro wa, sabishiki nobe mo kai arazu. Ashima o wataru kaze ni sae, odorokasaruru waga kokoro.	In this time of boisterousness, a lonely field gives no relief. Even the wind sweeping through the reeds stirs fear in my heart.[226]

The plaintive reflections of Koshoshi's observer in this poem lack the emotional intensity Hagoromo conveys in "A Fallen Soldier," which voices the grief and bitterness of the soldier's family. However, "Weary of War" is more explicit in advocating war's abolishment. Asserting the ultimate meaninglessness of victory and defeat, Koshoshi leaves no room for honoring battlefield sacrifice in devotion to the emperor that Hagoromo praises in "A Fallen Soldier." If one can question the inclusion of Hagoromo's poem in anthologies of antiwar literature, poet and critic Tsuboi Shigeji seems justified in concluding that "Weary of War" is "clearly an antiwar poem. Though one senses a certain weakness in its protest feeling, . . . it is of monumental significance as the first work of modern Japanese poetry to condemn war."[227]

Given the atmosphere of hostile ultranationalism that prevailed at the time, it is not surprising that Hirotsu Ryūrō penned his caricature of Miyazaki Koshoshi as "The Traitor" following the publication of "Weary of War." During this period Koshoshi also came under attack for his activities as a Christian. Many prominent Christians in Japan had supported the nation's involvement in what they believed to have been a "just war." Koshoshi was particularly vocal in his opposition to the policies of the church hierarchy and switched sects twice after 1898, finally leaving his third church in Tokyo's Hongō Morikawa-chō district to become an independent pastor in 1905. By then he had gained a reputation as a radical among Japanese Christians, though his departure from Morikawa-chō was thought to have resulted less from a doctrinal or policy dispute than from gossip surrounding an affair he was rumored to be having with the niece of his deceased wife.[228]

Koshoshi is often compared personally and professionally to Shimazaki Tōson, his better-known successor among early writers of lyric poetry in the *shintaishi* form. Tōson, too, composed poetry about the Sino-Japanese War that has been called antiwar, and he is said to have had an affair with a niece. However, while Tōson's work is often praised for its compelling expression of individual emotion, Koshoshi's often seems lacking in affective power, being more detached and introspective. In his poetry on the Sino-Japanese War, Tōson writes, as does Hagoromo, from the first-person perspective of men and their families caught up in the conflict. Thus Tōson's "Nōfu" (The farmer, 1898) achieves greater emotional impact than Koshoshi's poems on war, which are stated as the impressions and opinions of an observer. Yet, as we shall see, despite the greater affective power of "The Farmer," attempts by recent critics to categorize it with "Weary of War" as an early modern antiwar poem do not seem convincing when this work is read as a whole. Though less distinguished as a poet, Miyazaki Koshoshi seems more deserving than either Tōson or Hagoromo of recognition as the first Japanese writer after the Meiji Restoration to publish antiwar poetry.

4 Kinoshita Naoe: The Poetry of Pacifism

Kinoshita Naoe (1869–1937) is remembered far more for his prose and social activism than for his poetry, but he produced a number of poems opposing war during the years he was writing his better-known fiction and essays. A Christian convert and talented orator, he advocated universal suffrage, equal distribution of wealth, and laws against prostitution. He also condemned war and Japan's military policies. His pacifist convictions initially put him at odds with leading Japanese Christians, such as Uchimura Kanzō, who had spoken out in support of Japan's war against China in 1894–95. Uchimura later renounced his earlier views and embraced pacifism himself, but Naoe grew increasingly estranged from influential clergymen and the established Christian churches in Japan, eventually severing his ties with them almost completely. Looking back on his initial divergence with Christian leaders over the Sino-Japanese War, he wrote in 1906:

> I had always believed that war and Christianity are diametrically opposed, and I was shocked when prominent Christians from Tokyo began traveling all over the country making speeches in support of this so-called "just war." Perhaps they misunderstood the gospel. Or, if not, they were certainly acting hypocritically to avoid accusations of being anti-*kokutai*.[229]

Despite the pacifism that put Naoe at odds with Christian leaders during the Sino-Japanese War, he joined other writers after the war in denouncing the Japanese government for agreeing to return Liaotung Peninsula, occupied by the Imperial Army after bloody battles at Port Arthur and Weihaiwei,[230] to China, as demanded by Russia, Germany, and France in the Triple Intervention of 1895. No country can claim a writer who more fervently and consistently opposed war in his poetry and prose. Unlike the other authors discussed in this study, Naoe never wavered in his writing from opposition to war. Still, his speeches at this time, which criticized the government for "ignoring the popular will," seem somewhat out of character for one whose philosophy would presumably lead him to condemn the armed conquest of another nation's territory. Recently, some literary historians have suggested that he was simply using antigovernment sentiment over the Liaotung issue to inspire public opposition to other official policies, such as the denial of universal suffrage.[231]

Whatever his motives for denouncing the return of Liaotung, Naoe is firmly established today as the Meiji writer who produced some of the earliest literature condemning war, having completed a novella in 1897 on the desperate plight of farm families bereaved by the conflict with China. "Ichiya no karine" (One night's rest)[232] is a story told by an elderly widow living in a mountain cottage whose son-in-law died of illness on his way to the Sino-Japanese front. She describes her grief and hardship to a younger widow spending a one-night stopover at the cottage. Because her son-in-law was not killed in battle, she was denied survivor benefits, despite the fact that during the conflict with China more than twice as many Japanese soldiers died of cholera as of war wounds.[233] After his death left her shorthanded in the fields, she was unable to raise enough crops to pay the rent on the family farm, which was seized by the landlord. She then went to work in a textile mill but was denied her salary when the business fell on hard times. She denounces the hypocrisy of such slogans as *kimi no tame* (for the sake of the emperor) and *kuni no tame* (for the sake of the nation), which exhorted people to make sacrifices, pointing out that the wealthy in Japan were able to escape conscription while it was the poor who were sent off to risk their lives, often leaving their families destitute. Writing in 1983, Okano Yukie praises this work for its impassioned protest against social and economic inequities in Japan and its moving affirmation that soldiers are not the only victims of war. However, Okano faults Naoe for relying too heavily on the central character to articulate the author's philosophy and finds this work to be lacking in the "realistic" description and crisp dialogue found in fiction by Izumi Kyōka and Hirotsu Ryūrō on the Sino-Japanese War and its aftermath.[234] Read today, this work seems at times less like a story than a testimony from one of Naoe's parishioners whose suffering wrought by war is placed by the minister in moral context.

Naoe published *Hi no hashira* (Pillar of fire, 1904) seven years after his completion of "One Night's Rest." Often called modern Japan's preeminent antiwar novel, this work has come in for criticism on similar grounds. During the intervening years Naoe produced a series of newspaper articles, widely admired today, that vigorously opposed war in general and the increasingly likely war with Russia in particular. In "Sekai heiwa ni tai suru Nihon kokumin no sekinin" (The Japanese people's responsibility toward world peace, *Mainichi shinbun*, March 17–19, 1899), he urged people in Japan to agitate for acceptance of the Peace Declaration of Tsar Nicholas II and condemned the arms build-up of powerful nations as a result of "competition for profits," a theme he was to repeat often in his later essays and fiction. In subsequent articles he condemned the notion that the Japanese are a "superior race" as "an excuse for aggression," and he criticized emperor-centered nationalism that, in his view, resulted in "totalitarian oppression" of the individual and "fostered militarism." In its place he urged people to redirect their energies from nationalism to internationalism and advocated pacifism and socialism based on Christian ethics, asserting that "capitalism is the ultimate cause of war." He wrote that governments have consistently exploited popular fears of external threats to justify large armaments, higher taxes, and internal repression.[235] Katō Shūichi has praised these essays as "deadly accurate attacks" on government policies and pronouncements of the time.[236] Okano Yukie finds in them "continued relevance for today."[237]

As war with Russia seemed increasingly inevitable, Naoe's protests became more impassioned, sometimes bordering on the shrill. On May 11, 1903 he wrote in *Mainichi*:

> Alas, the Japanese are fonder of war than the people of any other nation in the world. Their delight is in the sword and in bloodshed, their skill lies in the razing of castles and the slaughter of men. What has this skill done for them? Enabled them to crow over China; given them more recently a "distinguished" share in the exhibition of foreign military force in North China—and nothing else at all. . . . Why must Japan pursue so diligently such immoral, brutish courses?[238]

As editors at *Mainichi* came under increasing pressure to support hostilities against Russia, Naoe joined socialist activist-writers Sakai Toshihiko and Kōtoku Shūsui to start the weekly newspaper *Heimin shinbun*. Unlike *Mainichi*, *Heimin shinbun* continued to oppose war with Russia in its articles and editorials long after the fighting was under way. Naoe was dissuaded, however, from quitting *Mainichi*, in which the editors later permitted him to publish *Pillar of Fire* in three months of serialized episodes between January 1 and March 20, 1904.[239] He also managed to slip into *Mainichi* an article condemning wartime censorship, war reporting, and, by implication, the war itself. In the edition of March 25, 1904, published six weeks after war was declared, he wrote:

> Some go to the front leaving behind wives. Some kill children. Newspaper reporters take up their pens to laud what they call *gishi* (martyrs) and *yūshi* (brave warriors). . . . The "loyalty and patriotism" they extol are nothing but cheap demagoguery and cannot be called true love of country. Yet if we dare to expose such "patriotism" for the shallow provocation that it is, we are slandered as "corruptors of public morals."[240]

Five days before this article appeared, *Mainichi* had already published the last installment of *Pillar of Fire*. Kenneth Strong speculates that the government did not move quickly to ban this work because it was fiction, not an essay, appearing in a newspaper with a still small circulation that, in any case, was printing highly supportive coverage of the war extensively and prominently in its "news" sections. The initial book version of *Pillar of Fire*, which appeared in May, was also spared censorship until some six years later when the government confiscated all the copies it could locate. Subsequent editions published in 1929 and 1930 were heavily expurgated, with a full text printed again only in the 1950s.[241] Still, the fact that *Pillar of Fire* was not banned immediately seems remarkable, considering its protagonist's outspoken condemnation of the war against Russia and of social and economic inequities in Japan. For their writing against war and social injustice, Naoe's colleagues at *Heimin shinbun* spent time in prison during 1904 and 1905, while their newspaper died in January 1905, the victim of government prosecution in the courts and police harassment at the newsstands where it was sold. Naoe himself had been detained the year before by the police for giving an antiwar speech. He was later fined for the March 25, 1904 *Mainichi* article, quoted above, which denounced government censorship as well as contemporary war reporting. Still, considering the content of *Pillar of Fire*, on the whole he seems to have gotten off rather lightly.

As to its literary quality, Naoe himself conceded later that at the time *Mainichi* editors agreed to serialize the work: "I hadn't had the remotest idea of writing a novel. Now at least I got what I wanted—space to myself and plenty of it where I could write against the war."[242] Katō Shūichi shares the view of many critics today:

> [This work] is somewhat polemical and rather scrappy in style and characterization but perceptive in its exposure [of] and attack on a society directed by financial and political power.

> The actions and thoughts of the hero give a clear picture of the author's Christian socialist beliefs.[243]

While also acknowledging its shortcomings, Kenneth Strong observes that Naoe was breaking new ground, with few past examples to draw on:

> [T]o publish a novel preaching an undiluted Christian-inspired pacifism abroad and something resembling Christian Socialism at home demanded a degree of independence and courage that was rarely equalled by the "proletarian" writers of the 1920s and 1930s who, though they faced harsher repression, were less isolated in their beliefs than Kinoshita. Neither for his pacifism nor for his brand of socialism did Kinoshita have any body of opinion behind him in Japan, nor was there any literary tradition to serve as a model, except for the fanciful and allegorical "political" novels of the early Meiji era, such as *Kajin no kigu* (Strange encounters with beautiful women, 1885) by Tōkai Sanshi (1852–1922). *Pillar of Fire* is a great advance on these. If it is still a thesis-novel, with no great attempt at characterization, what makes it readable today is the sheer force of feeling behind it: where the allegorical novels dealt in abstractions, *Pillar of Fire* conveys with sincerity and power a dissident view of the realities of Japan in 1904—war and growth-at-any-price capitalism.[244]

Although as a novel written from a particular philosophical perspective it might have lacked precursors in Meiji literature, *Pillar of Fire* shares with other Japanese fiction of its time a closely autobiographical strain and a cast of characters and sequence of events based on obvious models from contemporary life. Its protagonist, Shinoda Chōji, resembles the author not only in his uncompromising philosophy but also in the circumstances of his life. He is a writer, a social activist, and a Christian, whose outspoken opposition to government policies at home and abroad leads to his expulsion from his church and his harassment by the police.

Aside from its highly recognizable protagonist, the novel includes several characters whose names and official positions clearly identify them with prominent persons of the day. Portrayed as villains are the super-rich and corrupt merchant Ōhora Rihachi (for Ōkura Kihachirō, 1837–1928, founder of the Ōkura zaibatsu); the ruthless and lecherous Itō Kōshaku Kakka, "Prince Itō" (for Itō Hirobumi, 1841–1909, prime minister, elder statesman, and notorious womanizer); and Shōgun, "the General" (for Yamagata Aritomo, 1838–1922, powerful Meiji leader who held office as prime minister, home minister, and war minister and was the chief architect of the Imperial Japanese military). Such unconcealed reference to Itō and Yamagata makes one wonder again why this novel was not banned earlier. Naoe depicts in a more positive light Shinoda's fellow activists Gyōtoku Akika (for socialist and later anarchist Kōtoku Shūsui, 1871–1911) and Watabe Isoo (for Christian socialist Abe Isoo, 1865–1949), who are his colleagues at *Dōhō shinbun*, translated by Strong as the *Fellowship Daily* (for *Heimin shinbun*, translated as the *People's Daily*).

Actual events of the day, such as the organizing of miners in Kyushu, police repression of socialists, and, of course, the coming of war with Russia, figure prominently in the narrative. It seems clear that Naoe wanted no uncertainty among readers of *Mainichi* in 1904 as to the time and place he is writing about or the persons and policies he is criticizing. This is consistent with the novel's polemic conception, especially considering that Naoe himself has acknowledged that it was written for the purpose of communicating his opposition to war to the newspaper's readers.

To summarize the story reduces the novel to incidents that seem contrived and melodramatic in synopsis. It is important to show, however, how components of the narrative work to express Naoe's socialist and pacifist views. The story is propelled by the long-simmering love from afar between Shinoda and Yamaki Umeko, the idealistic daughter of Ōhora's corrupt business associate Yamaki Gōzō. Umeko is betrothed, against her will, to the boorish naval captain Matsushima so that her father can retain lucrative contracts with the navy despite his company's shoddy workmanship, which has already cost the lives of many young sailors. Shinoda's expulsion from the church is arranged by its obsequious minister Hasegawa so he can continue to receive generous contributions from Umeko's father, who is convinced that Shinoda's pacifist views are corrupting his children. On the eve of a socialist rally, Shinoda is betrayed to the police by one of his fellow journalists in urgent need of money. The stakes are raised for everyone when Prince Itō himself, an acquaintance of Captain Matsushima and the Yamakis, offers to serve as go-between at the wedding and agrees to arrange for the arrest of the troublesome Shinoda.

Among its stereotyped characters, the story contains an evil stepmother (Umeko's) who connives to leave the girl alone with Matsushima at Ōhora's country villa. It is here that the novel's climactic scene occurs when Umeko tells Matsushima she will not marry him. In his rage Matsushima attacks her in a rape attempt, which she foils by poking out his eye with her thumb. Thereafter, she flees her family to be with Shinoda, and they finally consummate their love shortly before he is arrested by the police on trumped-up charges of treason. The story concludes with Shinoda resolutely facing his arrest and Umeko vowing to be strong for the ordeals that lie ahead.

The novel is infused with Naoe's views on prostitution and capitalism, but opposition to war remains its central motif. In one of its first scenes Umeko's father, thoroughly corrupted by his ill-gotten wealth, explains to Reverend Hasegawa why he intends to stop sending his family (and his contributions) to the church unless Hasegawa arranges to have the "traitor" Shinoda expelled:

> "This Shinoda of yours—Chōji Shinoda. He's making a song and dance about war being wrong—'pacifism,' he calls it, or some such word. Not that I'd call that rag of his a newspaper, mind you: so there's no call to take much notice of the crazy utopian notions he fills it with. But now he's up to something new, my daughter tells me—spouting in the church, if you please, about the 'duty of every Christian to oppose war,' or some such dangerous nonsense. . . . Umeko seems to have caught the infection; . . . he's against war with Russia, which makes him a traitor, if there ever was one." (56)

The connection Naoe makes in his essays between war and lawless government repression is plainly personified in a character called simply "the General" (for Yamagata Aritomo), who orders the banning of a socialist rally in Tokyo where Shinoda is scheduled to be the featured speaker:

> "What speech—where?"
>
> "At the Youth Hall in Kanda. He's billed to speak against war with Russia."
>
> "The devil he is!" The General frowned. "Whether we go to war or not is the Emperor's business, and nobody else's. As for a ruffian like that—he'll be committing treason the moment he opens his mouth. Why hasn't the Home Minister banned the meeting? That's what's wrong with you bureaucrats, I keep telling you—what can you ever get done by sticking to the letter of the law? If we hadn't broken half the country's laws thirty-five years ago, how could we have put through the Restoration? Phone that Minister as soon as we get in, and tell him he's to stop that meeting—my orders! The shameless villains—in the middle of the capital!"
>
> The young man bowed. (164)

Despite the heavy thematic overtones in such dialogues and speeches, it is not impossible to imagine powerful men expressing themselves this way in private conversations. The narrative suffers, however, when Naoe attempts to portray the plight of the miners whom Shinoda's group of socialist activists is trying to organize in Kyushu. Unlike the wealthy and powerful individuals who speak for themselves in the novel, these workers remain in the background, a nameless mass whose "hearts" nevertheless echo Naoe's ideas about war and capitalism:

> By the middle of January there was widespread and mounting enthusiasm for an early war with Russia. The workers, however, ignored for so long by the rest of society as an inferior breed of beings, had at last begun to seriously awaken to their ever-increasing hardships, the pain of which war-fever could no longer disguise. Deep in their hearts they could hear a voice, faint but insistent: suppose Japan *does* win—we shall be worse off than ever. (146)[245]

Similar problems arise when Naoe touches late in the novel on the desperate circumstances of impoverished farmers after the Sino-Japanese War, the central concern of the novella "One Night's Rest" he wrote seven years earlier. Their situation is portrayed indirectly in the words of an elderly acquaintance of Shinoda's family, whom the protagonist meets by chance on a rare visit to his hometown. The older man's account of the hard times in the village since Shinoda's departure reads like a poignant antiwar testimonial but gives the reader little sense of the people whose troubles are described:

> You're famous now, they say. Like your father was before you. Things have gone just as he said they would—higher taxes every year, though the harvest stays the same, and they won't let us take timber from the woods, or even make a bit of hay out in the wild like we used to. . . . We have to borrow money, and sell our fields, a bit at a time. How many of us up here are working our own land, d'you reckon? On top of everything else, there's another burden. Conscription, they call it. It's a terrible thing. And there's talk of another war, too. There's three or four been taken from my village already. It's always the poor they take for soldiers. You can see why: they're working so hard always, they're bound to be the strongest, so it's them the army wants. A few days ago a man from the county office came up to our place—one of those queer Western hats he had on—and preached about what a beautiful thing it was to die for Japan. Did you ever hear such nonsense? One of our young folk was killed in the China War a few years back. A great honour for the village, we were told. They put up a stone monument to him in the shrine grounds: a whole lot of government people came when it was ready—I don't know how much we spent on the dedication, everybody was so excited, it was like a regular festival. But the boy's old father and mother—they'd no one else to support them, so the landlord took back their land, the government took

> their furniture because they couldn't pay the tax, and the money-lender took the bit of cash they got by mortgaging their cottage, which wasn't much more than a stable anyway. In the end they hanged themselves from a tree a few feet from the monument the village had put up for their son. (171)

At one point in the novel Naoe even inserts expository prose summing up his opposition to war in the form of a handwritten draft for one of Shinoda's planned newspaper articles, which the police have seized as evidence of "treason." Freed from the necessity to state his philosophy through his novel's characters or narrative, the author takes full advantage of this opportunity for communicating his antiwar views to readers of *Mainichi shinbun*:

> Those who clamour for war with Russia say it will be a fight between freedom and tyranny, between civilization and barbarism. In my opinion they are utterly mistaken. It will merely be a war between two governments each as tyrannical, as barbarous as the other . . . the privileges of property, the antics of the aristocracy . . . the Emperor's name invoked to justify every crime. (185–86)

Finally, as Shinoda Chōji and Yamaki Umeko spend their last moments together before his arrest, Shinoda gives full throat to Naoe's view of war and government repression as the inevitable results of capitalism. It was such passages as these that led to *Pillar of Fire* being banned, along with ninety other books, in a government crackdown on socialist literature in 1910[246]:

> "Give up church religion, Umeko-san. Leave to the hypocrites the kind of charity that does nothing to cure the causes of misery. How dare they say the massing of wealth in so few hands, the gap between rich and poor, is nothing but a material problem, to be smoothed over by their miserable handouts! There is no greater immorality than the rich getting richer and the poor poorer year after year. Robbery is the only rule of life nowadays, for men and for nations. What the law calls thieving is a childish game. In God's eyes it is our laws themselves that are guilty—our laws and our 'patriotism,' that society values so highly. The sacred rights of property, the duty to fight and kill, what are they but code words for theft and plunder? And of all the victims, Umeko-san, it is women who suffer most. Socialism, in a word, is God's will, as Christ revealed it." (196)

The initial reviews of *Pillar of Fire* were, like more recent critiques, decidedly mixed. The work was faulted for roughness of style and lack of background description but praised for its "richness of philosophy" and "extraordinary power."[247] As for its readership, the novel is said to have been a popular item in *Mainichi*, and to have sold well in its first full-length publication by Heiminsha, which used the proceeds to fund its activities supporting socialism.[248] *Pillar of Fire* is also thought to have exerted influence at the time on such younger writers as Mushanokōji Saneatsu (1885–1976), who later wrote poetry condemning war.[249]

In defense of its oft-cited flaws, Okano Yukie speculates that Naoe sacrificed background description and fuller characterizations to meet the space requirements of newspaper serialization and to attract a wider audience early on. Okano detects evidence of Naoe's *hansei* (self-reflection over past failures) in a later novel, *Ryōjin no jihaku* (Confessions of a husband, 1904–5), which presents characters that are more fully developed and settings that are more convincingly rendered.[250]

Still, with all its shortcomings, *Pillar of Fire* makes for compelling reading today, powerfully articulating—in passages that are sometimes more oration than dialogue—issues of worker exploitation, unequal distribution of wealth, government repression, and war that continue to plague societies everywhere. Shinoda's speeches are inspiring advocacies for abused mine workers, indentured geishas, and impoverished farmers, much as Naoe's speeches and sermons must have been. If its characterizations seem formulaic, the events of the novel engage the reader's sympathies for victims of economic and political repression and arouse indignation at those who manipulate others to satisfy their appetites for money, power, and sex. Naoe does not shrink from revealing the seamier sides of political and financial power in mid-Meiji Japan, and *Pillar of Fire* effectively ignites outrage.

The recent terms of praise for this novel's "passion" (Kenneth Strong) and "perception" (Katō Shūichi) can also be applied to the poetry Naoe wrote against war, though it too has its shortcomings. Like his novels, Naoe's poems represent an early effort in Meiji Japan to articulate pacifist philosophy in a literary context. As with *Pillar of Fire*, Naoe had few precedents to draw on. The two short poems cited in chapter three by Miyazaki Koshoshi from the Sino-Japanese War, while condemning armed conflict, do not address the causes or results of war specifically and had little impact among writers in Japan at the time. Naoe's poetry against war, by contrast, explicitly describes war's human toll and denounces the cavalier attitude of those who are not directly affected by its death and suffering. In addition, his poetry reflects the view of socialist pacifism by drawing a connection between the waging of war and the perpetuation of political and economic inequities. The first of these works, written in a combination of seven-syllable and free-verse units, appeared in *Mainichi shinbun* on October 19, 1903, four months before Japan declared war on Russia. By this time the editors at *Mainichi* were beginning to bow to pressures to support hostilities, but they continued to permit Naoe to publish his writings in opposition to war.

. . . .

saredo kuni yori mo chi yori mo ten yori mo
sara ni tōtoki mono ware ni ari
oitaru haha nari wakaki tsuma nari osanaki ko nari

. . . .

ware wa chikoute teki o korasaji
amanjite teki no katana ni taoren iza saraba
kenshinsha yo chūshisha yo to utaisawagu
murabito no mujō no ten'yu ni
tsukinu hiai o shibashi nagusametamae
natsukashiki waga haha yo, tsuma yo, ko yo

. . . .

My possessions are more
precious than country, or earth, or heaven:
An aged mother, a young wife, an infant child.

. . . .

I will kill no "enemy," I swear it;
I will fall by his sword, gladly.
Farewell, "Brave, loyal hero—
he died for his country!"
The villagers will clamour, without feeling.
Deaden your grief with their hollow praises,
My mother, wife, and child![251]

Considering the bellicose sentiment prevailing at the time and Naoe's detainment two weeks earlier by the police for making a speech against war, we can admire his courage in publishing this poem, especially since it explicitly puts a soldier's family before his duty. The following year Yosano Akiko was denounced as "a traitor" for advocating similar priorities in her famous poem, "Brother, Do Not Give Your Life" (see chapter five). One is inclined to agree, however, with Kenneth Strong's judgment that this early effort at verse by Naoe is "not great poetry." There is little in it to help the reader identify with either the soldier's despair as he faces the possibility of death in combat, or with the sorrow of those he left back home. Aside from his determination to die rather than kill (he apparently shares the author's pacifism), his personality and his family's circumstances are barely sketched in language that is stiff and prosaic. Like much of his fiction on war, this poem expresses Naoe's philosophy but lacks individualized personae and concrete description. Still, if this work has redeeming literary value, it is in communicating (1) the bitter realization of soldiers in every conflict that those back home have not the slightest inkling of what it is like to go to war, and (2) the hollow ring of wartime slogans intended to console bereaved families. Like the elderly widow in "One Night's Rest," the soldier in this poem repeats, with potent sarcasm, the platitudinous words and phrases heard during wars everywhere—"enemy," "brave, loyal hero," "died for his country." A similarly powerful irony can be found in Siegfried Sassoon's "To Any Dead Officer," composed during World War I, which parodies the words of those back home in England, who are rooting safely and obliviously from the sidelines:

> Good-bye, old lad! Remember me to God,
>   And tell Him that our Politicians swear
> They won't give in till Prussian Rule's been trod
>   Under the Heel of England . . . Are You there? . . .
> Yes . . . and the War won't end for at least two years;
> But we've got stacks of men . . . I'm blind with tears,
>   Staring into the dark, Cheerio!
> I wish they'd killed you in a decent show.[252]

Naoe also mocks popular wartime slogans and symbols in his series of three short poems in *shintaishi* form entitled "Sensō no uta" (Songs of war, 1904–5). The first of these describes a lonely visit during the rainy season to the graves of war dead:

"Aoyama bochi nite" (At Aoyama cemetery)

yamazakura
chiru o homare to utawareshi
"gunshin" no ato kite mireba
samidare kuraki gentō ni
shirushi no kui wa shirokeredo
kaze ni hanawa no mukuro midare
itomo arawa no funbo
kokoro arite ya masakaki no
aoba no sode ni uchiōi
namida to bakari tsuyu o taru
tojinshi no uta wa hana yori saki ni karete
ame no Aoyama tou kage mo nashi

"To fall like the wild cherry blossoms
is an honor," it is sung.
I come to visit the remains of "warrior-gods"
on the parade ground darkened
    in the early summer rain.
The grave markers are neatly white,
but the wreaths of flowers marking the corpses
    are tousled in the wind.
How exposed these graves are to public view!
Standing compassionately nearby
    are the sacred Shinto trees,
their leaves like sleeves showered
    with the dew of falling tears.
The songs of the townspeople
have faded even before the flowers do,
and no one visits Aoyama in the rain.[253]

A specific location, concrete description, and selected natural phenomena instill this poem with an immediacy that is often lacking in Naoe's earlier fiction and poetry on war. He effectively contrasts cherry blossoms, a well-worn symbol of soldiers who fall in battle, and the parade ground for "warrior-gods" (*gunshin*) with the actual scene—a graveyard that is dark, rainy, and deserted. Flower wreaths disheveled in the wind recall the tangled corpses below, and trees are personified in sorrow, their leaves covered with dew like tear-stained sleeves in another traditional metaphor of Japanese poetry. The last two lines, which read like a refrain, contrast the fleeting quality of honors for war dead (songs that fade faster than flowers) with the permanent reality of lives lost (graves visited only in good weather).

Archibald MacLeish (1892–1982) writes in a similar vein on the hollowness of eulogies for war dead buried under a deserted landscape, describing a visit to Flanders where his brother died in World War I:

Memorial Rain
for Kenneth MacLeish

Ambassador Puser the ambassador
Reminds himself in French, felicitous tongue,
What these (young men no longer) lie here for
In rows that once, and somewhere else, were young
. . . .
He, too, dead was a stranger in that land
And felt beneath the earth in the wind's flowing
A tightening of roots and would not understand,
Remembering lake winds in Illinois,
That strange wind. I had felt his bones in the sand
Listening.

. . . Reflects that these enjoy
Their country's gratitude, that deep repose,
That peace no pain can break, no hurt destroy,
That rest, that sleep . . . the flag . . . a grateful country
. . . .
Under the dry grass stem
The words are blurred, are thickened, the words sift
Confused by the rasp of wind, by the thin grating
Of ants under the grass, the minute shift
And tumble of dusty sand separating
From dusty sand. The roots of the grass strain,
Tighten, the earth is rigid, waits—he is waiting—
And suddenly, and all at once, the rain![254]

From an emblematic posing of natural imagery, Kinoshita Naoe returns to his more characteristic polemic mode for the epigrammatic second poem in the "Songs of War" series:

"Shin-taishō" (The new generals)

sensō gokagetsu narazu shite	The war not five months old,
taishō shichinin haya arawarenu	and already seven new generals appear,

yamome to koji to wa kazu shiranedo
gahyō wa chijō ni michimiteri
	while the number of widows and orphans
	    grows incalculable,
	and the earth teems with people dying of
	    starvation.[255]

The political and economic inequities exacerbated by war are tersely and pointedly summarized in this poem, a sharp departure from the overflowing emotion and traditional metaphor in the verse that preceded it.

The last work in this series recalls Naoe's earlier poem on conscription, published in 1903 before hostilities had begun. As in its predecessor, the conscripted persona regrets leaving his loved ones behind and rejects the wartime slogans intended to motivate soldiers and console their families:

"Shōshūhei" (Draftee)

nokoru saishi ya shiraga no oya no
asu o shinobeba
kokoro ga sakeru
meiyo meiyo to sawaide kurena,
kuni no tame to no seken no giri de,
nani mo iwazuni tada me o tojite
namida kakushite
shi ni yuku
	Trying to endure
	    the thought of tomorrow,
	when I must leave behind my wife,
	    children, and white-haired parents,
	my heart breaks.
	Do not holler of "honor and glory."
	Since it's "a citizen's duty" for "the sake
	    of the nation,"
	I will say nothing, but only close my eyes,
	hide my tears, and go off to die.[256]

"Draftee," composed mostly in seven-syllable units, lacks the explicit expression of pacifist protest found in Naoe's similarly structured poem on conscription, quoted above. Yet the plaintive lament of a soldier resigned to his fate reveals, as in the earlier work, the hollowness of wartime slogans for many who face the possibility of death in war that leaves their families without a father and husband.

Protest rings out loud and clear, however, in what is perhaps Naoe's best-known poem, "Ponpoko uta" (Song of the banging drum). This stinging indictment of political and economic inequities in Meiji Japan appeared first in his novel *Confessions of a Husband* and subsequently in the 1906 anthology *Socialist Poetry*, later banned. Poet and critic Tsuboi Shigeji has called this work an early forerunner of the proletarian literature that flourished in Japan two decades later, noting particularly its sarcastic tone and the lampooning of those with economic and political power. He also finds it "more like a song in need of a melody than a poem"[257]:

Kazoku no mekake no atama ni	What is that shining on the heads
hikaru wa nan desue.	of peers' mistresses?
Daiyamondo?	Diamonds?
Ie ie chigaimasu.	No, no. It's not.
Kawai hyakushō no abura-ase!	It's the sweat of our beloved farmers!
Poko pon-poko-pon-poko pon.	Poko pon-poko-pon-poko pon.
Daijin taishō no mune ni	What is that gleaming on the chests
hikaru wa nan desue?	of ministers and generals?
Kinshikunshō?	The Order of the Golden Kite?
Ie ie chigaimasu.	No, no. It's not.
Kawai heishi no sharekōbe!	It's the skulls of our dear soldiers!
Poko pon-poko-pon-poko pon.	Poko pon-poko-pon-poko pon.
O-kanemochi-shū no koppu ni	What is that sparkling
hikaru wa nan desue?	in the glasses of the rich?
Shanpēn?	Champagne?
Ie ie chigaimasu.	No, no. It's not.
Kawai kōjo no chi no namida?	Isn't it the tears of blood
	shed by our beloved factory girls?
Poko pon-poko-pon-poko pon.	Poko pon-poko-pon-poko pon.[258]

The deliberately strident, sing-song quality recalls comic ditties sung at the time by geishas to the accompaniment of a banging drum, except that the message of this poem is far from humorous. In its three pithy stanzas, Naoe manages to articulate the three major concerns of the socialist pacifism that infused his writing and lecturing: the exploitation of farmers and industrial workers, the oppression of women, and the human costs of war. "Song of the Banging Drum" might also be compared to such American protest ballads as "Sixteen Tons," a 1947 union song on the exploitation of coal miners, and "The Beat Goes On," a 1967 rock tune on the Vietnam War. "Sixteen Tons" is sung in a heavy, sing-song rhythm that suggests the tedium of hard labor in the mine, and includes the lines "You load Sixteen Tons, / what do you get? / Another day older / and deeper in debt. / Saint Peter, don't you call me / 'cause I can't go. / I owe my soul to the company store."[259] "The Beat Goes On" is punctuated with repeated nonsense syllables for rhythmic emphasis, called *hayashi-kotoba* in Japanese, which convey the monotony of lives that always seem to be controlled by outside forces. It includes the lines "Drums keep pounding rhythm to the brain, / La da da da di, / La da da da da. / . . . And men still keep on marching off to war, / 'Lectric'ly they keep their baseball score, / And the Beat Goes On."[260]

Naoe left the socialist movement in 1908, partly because of the heavy toll police harassment was taking on his personal life and partly because he despaired of radical reform in the Japan of his time.[261] Although his writings and conversations indicate that he maintained his socialist and pacifist views until his death in 1937 at the age of 69, he never resumed his active role as a protestor and polemicist. He spent much of his time after 1910 in religious study and teaching, having joined a group of Zen meditation (*seiza*) practitioners led by Okada Tarajirō. Naoe came to believe deeply in the redemptive powers—spiritual and physical—of *seiza* and assumed a leadership role in Okada's group for a time after the founder's death in 1920.[262]

Naoe's lectures and writings during the remaining years of his life dealt mostly with religion in general terms but occasionally touched on disturbing contemporary events, at least indirectly. In *Kami, ningen, jiyū* (God, man, and freedom), a collection of his essays published in 1934, he makes implied criticism of growing militarism and suppression in Japan by alluding to a time described in the New Testament when "God was murdered by the Law and the Palace. . . . I muse on these events that happened so long ago in a foreign land—and this frail old body of mine can only bow its head in . . . shame. O for a liberator—a liberator to set God free again."[263] Meanwhile, he had given permission for the publication of a heavily expurgated version of *Pillar of Fire* in 1929 and 1930, the original, complete book version of 1904 having been banned in 1910 with all the publisher's copies confiscated.

In more explicit criticism, Naoe expressed his anger at Japan's involvement in Manchuria in letters to friends a few months before his death. And, according to at least one source, in his final years he had even considered resuming his former activism. Historian Ienaga Saburō recalled:

> Even after Kinoshita retired, he occasionally considered speaking out publicly on politics. . . . He consulted with me any number of times during his last years about starting the socialist movement again. No one knows of this, but I told him to wait a while because it was a time of rising militarism after the Manchurian Incident, and there was no prospect for success. While waiting, he died.[264]

Yamagiwa Keiji cites a postcard Naoe sent to a friend that explains how he voted for the Proletarian Party candidate Suzuki Shigesaburō in the election of April 30, 1937, though "of course he lost" (312). Yamagiwa reports that, in private conversations with those close to him, Naoe expressed anger at the victorious Social Masses Party's adulation of the military, declaring that "the time has come for me die" (313). Three months later the Marco Polo Bridge Incident of July 7, 1937 led to all-out war in

China, and by mid-September Naoe was ill on his deathbed. He recorded his thoughts and feelings from his final two months in "Byōchū-gin" (Writings while ill). An entry dated October 24 reads: "The whole world is truly in a whirlpool of upheaval, while the hearts of all the people yearn for peace" (313).

Naoe died on November 5, 1937, the same day forces of the Imperial Japanese Army landed at Hangchow on China's northern coast. His death received only brief mention in the newspapers. The renewed interest in his life and writings after World War II can be explained in part by the eagerness of Japanese historians and literary critics to locate examples of antiwar dissent among Japanese writers before 1945. Such recent critics as Okano Yukie have found in Kinoshita Naoe not only a courageous opponent of military expansion writing at a time when popular sentiment strongly supported it, but also one offering an example for writers today who, in the view of these critics, should more actively oppose the current Japanese government's military and economic policies. Yet, unlike the literary critics associated with the proletarian literature movement, who evaluated poetry and fiction almost exclusively according to ideological criteria, Okano, Strong, and Katō also address such literary concerns as style, characterization, and description. All three find shortcomings, but each acknowledges the power of Naoe's writing against war and social injustice.

5 Yosano Akiko: To Give One's Life or Not— A Question of Which War

No Japanese poem denouncing war has gained wider renown or been subjected to more varied uses and explications than "Kimi shinitamō koto nakare" (Brother, do not give your life).[265] Yosano Akiko (1878–1942) first published this forty-line *shintaishi* in the September 1904 issue of *Myōjō* magazine, after having sent it with a letter as an impassioned plea to her younger brother Chūzaburō, then serving with the Imperial Army in the Russo-Japanese War at Port Arthur. Japanese soldiers were rumored to be volunteering for suicide missions in the protracted assault on the fortress there, and Akiko was afraid that Chūzaburō's highly impulsive nature would cause him to forget the family that depended on him back home. She learned only after the poem's publication that his unit had not been deployed in this long and bloody siege during which so many did give their lives[266]:

> Oh, my brother, I weep for you.
> Do not give your life.
> Last-born among us,
> You are the most beloved of our parents.
> Did they make you grasp the sword
> And teach you to kill?
> Did they raise you to the age of twenty-four,
> Telling you to kill and die?
>
> Heir to our family name,
> You are master of this store, old and honored, in Sakai.
> Brother, do not give your life.
> For you, what does it matter
> Whether Port Arthur fortress falls or not?

The code of merchant houses
Says nothing about this.
Brother, do not give your life.
His Majesty the Emperor
Goes not himself into the battle.
Could he, with such deeply noble heart,
Think it an honor for men
To spill one another's blood
And die like beasts?

Oh, my brother, in that battle
Do not give your life.
Think of Mother, who lost Father just last autumn.
How much lonelier is her grief at home
Since you were drafted.
Even as we hear about peace in this Great Imperial Reign,
Her hair turns whiter by the day.

And do you ever think of your new bride,
Who crouches weeping behind the shop curtains
In her gentle loveliness?
Or have you forgotten her?
The two of you were together not ten months before parting.
What must she feel in her young girl's heart?
Who else has she to rely on in this world?
Brother, do not give your life.[267]

The story of wide-ranging and conflicting responses to this poem over time is, in many ways, a story of changing intellectual and popular currents of opinion in twentieth-century Japan. Vilified as traitorous when first published at the height of the conflict with Russia, "Kimi" drew Akiko into a rancorous debate with prominent poet and critic Ōmachi Keigetsu and led to stonings of her house.[268] Twenty-five years later it was attacked again during the peak of Japan's proletarian literature movement, this time for allegedly failing to confront the true causes of war in its focus on the poet's family and their confectionery business, revealing, it was said, a "bourgeois worldview."[269] Yet, since World War II "Kimi" has drawn high praise variously as the finest modern Japanese antiwar poem, as an eloquent expression of democratic values, and, more recently, as a powerful literary assertion of women's concerns. High school teachers assigned it for memorization in Japanese literature classes during the 1950s, and Takeda Takako was one of a number of composers who set it to music in songs that became protest anthems for postwar student activists. In 1972 an Osaka woman sewed its text into the fabric of *noren* curtains that were distributed in several countries abroad to spread the message of the antiwar movement.[270] Still, as we shall see, even evaluations of it since 1945 have not been entirely favorable.

Although she is known today in many countries for what is Japan's most famous antiwar poem, Yosano Akiko did not always write against war during her long and productive career. Her poetry and prose on this subject underwent a remarkable transformation after a trip with her husband, poet Yosano Tekkan (see chapter two), to Manchuria and Mongolia in the spring of 1928. Between the time of her return from China and her death in 1942 she published poems and essays supporting Japanese military involvement in both China and the Pacific. These works are rarely touched upon by the critics and biographers who have written on her life and work since 1945, some of whom have characterized her as a life-long pacifist. Nevertheless, the fact that Akiko did not express views of war that were consistent throughout her career in no way diminishes either the value of the poetry and prose she wrote on the anguish war caused women in Japan or her courage in publishing such poetry at the height of the conflict with Russia.

First appearing amid another deluge of *gunka* in 1904, "Kimi" was one of a small number of poems published between 1903 and 1905 questioning the sacrifices of young lives in the Russo-Japanese War. Nevertheless, such works were far more numerous and prominent than poems published a decade earlier lamenting death and suffering in the Sino-Japanese War.[271] Aside from "Kimi" and Kinoshita Naoe's poetry discussed above, the best-known among them in Japan today is the *shintaishi* "O-hyaku-do mōde" (A hundred visits to the shrine) by Ōtsuka Naoko, published in the January 1905 issue of *Taiyō,* four months after "Kimi" had appeared in *Myōjō.* Naoko's poem tells of one woman's "hundred visits," repeated trips made to a shrine or temple in order to pray for something, usually of a personal nature, such as a relative's recovery from illness or a child's success in college entrance examinations:

> With my first step, I think of my husband.
> With my second step, I think of my country.
> But with my third step, I think again of my husband.
> Is a woman's heart to be condemned?
>
> This nation of Japan that glows with the rising sun—
> There is only one in all the world.
> This man who pledged his love and calls me wife—
> There is but one in all the world.
>
> If asked which I value more,
> My country or my husband,

I shall not reply, but only weep.
Oh, am I to be condemned for my hundred visits to the shrine?[272]

Although her poem might seem tentative and fragmentary when compared with "Kimi," Naoko joined Akiko in bucking the torrent of exhortatory and bellicose verses of the day to depict the wrenching dilemma of Japanese women with loved ones at the front. Evaluations of "Mōde" have also ranged widely, from those that criticized its comparatively subdued tone, characterizing the poem as but one more literary rendering of a *giri-ninjō* conflict of duty versus love,[273] to those that praised it for expressing, however reservedly, a woman's doubts about war.[274] Takenaga Yoshimasa has attributed the differences between "Mōde" and "Kimi" to Naoko's membership in Sasaki Nobutsuna's (1872–1963) Chikuhaku-en poetry group, which emphasized refinement and restraint in *tanka* composition, in contrast to the Myōjō-ha group, led by Akiko's husband Tekkan, which encouraged more passionate self-expression.[275]

Best-known today for "Mōde," Naoko reportedly read warrior tales extensively when she was growing up and produced other writings during her brief career depicting the disruptions and sacrifices of war. Her story "Ōbohei" (Enlisted soldier) appeared in the November 1894 issue of *Fujo zasshi* (Women's magazine) just after the outbreak of hostilities with China; in April 1906 she published "Waka-goke" (Young widow), a story about a woman who lost her husband in the Russo-Japanese War. Yet Naoko did not always portray armed conflict sorrowfully, and in light of her renown today for "Mōde," it is surprising to read the poem she published in the June 1904 issue of *Taiyō* (the same magazine that would print "Mōde" seven months later), which reads precisely like one of the numerous *gunka* appearing at the time. Her "Shingeki no uta" (Song of the assault), in the voice of an Imperial Army officer, contains no trace of sympathy for those caught up in war. On the contrary, its strident refrains admonish Japanese soldiers to cast aside "disgrace[ful]" reservations about the dangers of armed conflict and to attack "though bullets fly like rain," so they might make their wives "proud" back home. "Song of the Assault" urges the "men of Yamato" to charge relentlessly forward in the emperor's cause and to welcome the prospect of death in battle. Naoko even appeals to interservice rivalry, frequently intense in the Japanese military, exhorting army soldiers not to be outdone by their navy compatriots who had already suffered heavy casualties defeating a large force of Russian battleships off the coast of Port Arthur, a costly victory celebrated by Yosano Tekkan in his *gunka* from the Russo-Japanese War (see chapter two).

Forward, forward, all of you!
Into bitter battles of fierce fighting unparalleled.
Why prove unequal
To those gallant naval officers?
What is there to fear?
For we are the men of Japan.

Forward, forward, all of you!
Aim to crush the enemy at one blow,
In reverence of His Majesty's Imperial Command.
Hoist the sacred flag of the rising sun.
What is there to fear?
For we are the men of Japan!

Forward, forward, all of you!
Young, old, rich and poor alike.
Compatriots, don't drink yourselves half to sleep,
But wipe away your tears.
What is there to fear?
For we are the men of Japan.

Forward, forward, all of you!
Before us lies glorious death in battle.
Think of our loyalty and bravery
That will make our wives proud.
What is there to fear?
For we are the men of Japan.

Forward, forward, all of you!
Fill heaven and earth with gunpowder smoke.
Forged with the Spirit of Yamato,
We are honored as the flowers of the world.
What is there to fear?
For we are the men of Japan.

To retreat even one step will disgrace you!
Earn your fame in the Sea of Port Arthur,
And think of life's end as heroic.
Oh, soldiers of this nation under our Emperor's Reign,
What is there to fear?
For we are the men of Japan.

To retreat even one step will disgrace you!
Rip to bits the eagle badge of Russia!
Japan's army, justly enraged,
Must rout the Russians as though splattering the dew on rugged plains.
What is there to fear?
For we are the men of Japan.

To retreat even one step will disgrace you!
Our hearts throb with patriotism
As we look forward to our sacred nation's victory,
Seeking to die in battle!
What is there to fear?
For we are the men of Japan.

To retreat even one step will disgrace you!
Backed by the righteous indignation of our homeland,
We reflect our parents' achievements,
And bring honor to our children.
What is there to fear?
For we are the men of Japan.

To retreat even one step will disgrace you!
Though bullets fly like rain,
The men of Yamato hoist their honor high.
Ah, this is where to show your samurai spirit!
What is there to fear?
For we are the men of Japan.[276]

Almost never mentioned in post-World War II studies of Ōtsuka Naoko's work, this poem shows again how poets' views of war changed over time. The fact that its existence has been widely ignored since 1945 shows how critics tended later to tell only one side of the story.[277] Naoko's writing on war, like Akiko's, also underwent a remarkable transformation, although in a reverse direction. Yet, despite her June 1904 exhortation to battle, Naoko, like Akiko, took certain risks in publishing poetry seven months later that questioned wartime sacrifices just as the conflict with Russia was reaching its height.

When they printed "Kimi" and "Mōde," Akiko and Naoko were bucking not only the bellicose trend of the day but lingering social, cultural, and legal constraints in Meiji Japan that strongly discouraged women from expressing dissent. Despite egalitarian rhetoric in the 1889 Meiji Constitution, which initiated limited *manhood* suffrage, political activity by women, individually or in groups, continued to be barred explicitly by a so-called Peace Preservation Law.[278] Furthermore, nearly universal acceptance of traditional female roles discouraged women from availing themselves of the few opportunities offered to them under Meiji law. "Compulsory education for all children" was proclaimed as official policy in the early years of the new era, but families who registered their daughters' names on class rosters, as legally required, rarely sent them to school, still believing that a woman's place was in the home. Even in later Meiji, when the government began enforcing female school attendance, girls studied a separate curriculum that emphasized home economics and the "traditional arts," subjects thought to be appropriate preparation for a good wife and mother.[279]

Yosano Akiko found little of interest in the home economics courses her parents insisted she take as part of the "Supplementary Program" at Sakai Girls' School.[280] However, it was during her years there that she developed a lifelong commitment to one of those "traditional arts," literature. At Sakai she was taught by Oda Sugao (d. 1894), a renowned Kokugaku scholar, although she seems to have read on her own the literature that most appealed to her. Her family apparently did little to encourage this interest, despite the fact that her father was himself an avid reader of Japanese literature who dabbled in writing *haiku*.[281] When asked later about his daughter's literary talents, he is said to have lamented that she had not been born a boy.[282]

Besides dictating what Akiko studied at school, her parents insisted that she spend her hours at home in Sakai minding the family confectionery store and keeping its accounts, responsibilities she was expected to assume full-time after graduation. Yet even in the face of onerous family expectations Akiko showed that she was not one to be easily discouraged. Known in those days as "Shō," an alternate pronunciation to "Aki" for the character meaning "crystal" in her given name, she seems to have maintained a determination of crystalline solidity. She snatched every possible moment from her daytime chores and spent the hours from ten to twelve midnight reading in her room, where she was locked in at night, perhaps partly to prevent her from engaging in the kind of nocturnal adventures described in *Genji monogatari* and the other Heian classics that were her favorite works. She is even said to have read as she walked down the street on her way through town, oblivious to the sidelong glances and giggles of passersby.[283] By her late teens she had gained an extensive knowledge of Japanese literature, starting from the Heian classics that she borrowed from her father's collection and extending to recent works by Ozaki Kōyō (1867–1903), Kōda Rohan (1867–1947), and Higuchi Ichiyō (1872–96).[284]

Post-World War II scholarship on Akiko portrays her as a strong personality with more than enough assertiveness and determination to pursue what mattered to her in her personal and professional life, despite family pressures and social constraints. Her choices of both a literary career and a controversial marriage partner were at odds with what her family had expected of her. After first experimenting briefly with fiction and drama, Akiko settled on *tanka* as her preferred medium and almost immediately created a sensation in the usually staid and proper world of traditional Japanese poetry. She published several poems depicting, in verses of startling explicitness, her turn-of-the-century romance with her future husband, Yosano Tekkan, also a *tanka* poet, who was married to another woman at the time.[285] Her mention of breasts (*chibusa*) in one poem brought a scathing rebuke in the magazine *Kokoro no hana* from poet Sasaki Nobutsuna, Ōtsuka Naoko's mentor, who pronounced her guilty of "mouthing obscenities fit for a whore" and "corrupting public morals."[286] However, these fiery love poems, which she published in a collection suggestively titled *Midaregami* (Tangled hair, 1901), struck a highly responsive chord among younger Japanese, readers and poets alike, inspiring numerous imitations at the time and encouraging a freer expression of individual emotion in *tanka* that has affected the course of Japanese poetry to this day.

Aside from her literary innovations, Akiko is credited with being a central figure in the earliest awakenings of a movement for women's liberation in twentieth-century Japan. The first issue of the progressive journal *Seitō* (Blue stockings), published in September 1911 by critic Hiratsuka Raichō (1886–1971) and dedicated to the cause of women's rights, included Akiko's famous poem on women's activism entitled "Yama no ugoku hi" (The day the mountains move). The following year Akiko's observations on a trip to Europe deepened her concern for the status of women in Japan. Her writings and activities soon established her as a social critic on a broad range of issues. In a 1918 article she denounced Japan's "ruling and military classes" for "deliberately blocking the adoption of a truly moral system in an effort to protect the wealth and influence of their families. They hurry to invoke the power and precepts of the old totalitarian moral codes to direct the lives of Japanese citizens." She condemned "militarism" as "barbarian thinking [that] is the responsibility of us women to eradicate . . . from our midst."[287]

Still, of all the controversies Akiko kindled in Japan by expressing her unconventional and reformist views, she was drawn into the most hostile firestorm for publishing "Kimi," a poem that implored a Japanese soldier to put his family before his duty in the midst of what can only be described as a highly popular war. Her poem provoked outrage because perhaps no military organization in history demanded and received greater obedience than the Imperial Japanese Forces to the doctrine that its soldiers' highest mission was to die for the cause of the nation.[288] The 1882 *Imperial Rescript to Soldiers and Sailors* required that Japanese troops "with single heart fulfill their essential duty of loyalty, and bear in mind that duty is weightier than a mountain, while death is lighter than a feather."[289]

Patriotic stoicism was also expected of parents, who were urged to tell sons departing for the front to fight bravely and not to return alive, although, as Yosano Akiko wrote, during the Russo-Japanese War many parents pleaded for their sons boarding troop trains to come back safely.[290] Furthermore, numerous writers and the vast majority of the public in Japan enthusiastically supported the war with Russia, having shown a general willingness during the previous decade to shoulder heavy burdens of taxation, even on daily necessities, for the purpose of building up the nation's military forces. This broad consensus prevailed largely because, as the "hypothetical enemy," Russia was the hated prime mover behind the Triple Intervention (with Germany and France), which had forced Japan to relinquish the Liaotung Peninsula won on the battlefield during the Sino-Japanese War.

In Japan at the turn of the century, war against Russia was thought to be inevitable, "a bitter struggle for vengeance" (*gashin shōtan*), further necessitated by Russian refusal to withdraw forces stationed in Northeast Asia that were seen as threatening to Japanese interests in Manchuria and to Japan's considerable influence in Korea.[291] In 1903 the press campaigned with *gashin shōtan* and other ringing slogans for the government to open hostilities against Russia even while possibilities were still being explored for a negotiated settlement. In 1905, after Japan's string of military victories, popular opinion urged that the war be pursued ever deeper into enemy territory, beyond the Imperial Army's conquests in Korea and Manchuria, which had already cost some 100,000 Japanese lives and nearly exhausted the national treasury.[292] In fact, it was depleted financial resources and the dwindling supply of munitions, rather than the enormous casualties, that compelled the Japanese government to agree to lesser terms in the Treaty of Portsmouth than its negotiators and the public had demanded. When news of the treaty reached Japan in September 1905, protest riots broke out that led the government to declare martial law.[293]

Despite the level of bellicose fervor, a few determined Japanese writers consistently and courageously opposed the war with Russia, even after it was well under way. The most prominent dissenters were associated with the newspaper *Heimin shinbun*, founded in 1903 by socialist-activist authors Kōtoku Shūsui (1871–1911) and Sakai Toshihiko (1871–1933), which advocated pacifism and social reform. As noted above, Kinoshita Naoe joined the staff of *Heimin shinbun* during the Russo-Japanese War, portraying the newspaper and its staff through thinly veiled pseudonyms in his 1904 novel *Pillar of Fire*. This small weekly, with a circulation of less than five thousand, continued to publish until January 29, 1905, eleven months after hostilities had begun, despite censorship litigation and tactics of intimidation employed against it by the government, as well as condemnation heaped on it by other newspapers and the public.[294] Kōtoku wrote in the January 17, 1904 issue: "We remain absolutely opposed to war." Antiwar opinion was published again in the newspaper's next issue on February 14, appearing three days after hostilities had been officially declared, and in subsequent issues until the paper's demise a year later. *Heimin shinbun* maintained the most consistent opposition to the Russo-Japanese War, but it was not the only forum for dissent.[295] As late as the spring of 1904, Kōtoku printed two articles in the newspaper *Yorozu chōhō* entitled "In Opposition to Opening Hostilities" (May 1) and "The War Craze" (June 19). Two weeks later, on June 30, the same newspaper printed Uchimura Kanzō's "For the Abolishment of War," in which the author states, "War kills people and is nothing but an enormous crime." On March 25, six weeks after war was declared, *Mainichi shinbun* published "The Press in This Age of Militarism," in which Kinoshita Naoe condemned the "loyalty and patriotism . . . lauded by newspaper reporters as nothing but cheap demagoguery and . . . shallow provocation."[296]

A few writers also criticized those in their profession thought to be capitalizing on "the war craze" to sell their work. A March 1904 editorial in the magazine *Jidai shichō* condemned "claptrap dealers" who sought to profit off people infected with wartime hysteria by hastily turning out "shallow, phoney junk."[297] In April of the same year, *Myōjō*, the magazine that had published Akiko's celebrated early poems, printed a scathing article by poet and critic Takizawa Shūgyō (1875–1957) condemning writers of war literature for "kowtowing to the war gods in search of profits." In the June 1904 issue of the same magazine, appearing three months before the September issue containing "Kimi," poet and critic Hiraide Shū (1878–1914) published a similar article entitled "Rejecting So-Called War Literature." Perhaps best known today for his eloquent opposition to censorship, Hiraide shared Takizawa's disdain for the pen-wielding profiteers of war: "Lacking the slightest trace of an idea, such claptrap feeds the bottomless appetites of booksellers and panders to popular fads. If writers are so easily stampeded in the war craze, how can we ever expect them to produce works of true literary value?"[298] Furthermore, in the two monthly issues of *Myōjō* preceding the appearance of "Kimi," other poets published *tanka* lamenting the war, now six months under way, though their poems did not approach the impassioned outrage Akiko unleashed in September:

mi-ikusa ni koyoi ta ga shinu sabishimi to kami fuku kaze no yukue mimamoru	In this war, who will die tonight? With loneliness I gaze toward the destination of the wind blowing through my hair. Ishigami Tsuyuko (July)
mi-ikusa ni kuroginu ōi hoshi suete wagayo narinu to yoru no kami tatsu	In this war, wearing black, he stands shrouded in stars. "This is my world," says the god of night. Tamano Hanako (August)[299]

Writing a century earlier on the Napoleonic Wars, Lord Byron (1788–1824) makes similar associations with the nocturnal world in his long poem *Don Juan*, comparing man at war to "this spoiled child of the night [who] could decree / More evil in an hour, than thirty bright / summers could renovate."[300]

Antiwar *tanka* in Japan made a very small ripple against the torrent of exhortative and jingoistic verses that poured out during the Russo-Japanese War, but they show that Akiko did not write "Kimi" in a vacuum. There is evidence, however, that it was not this *tanka* by other Japanese poets but an antiwar essay of a foreign novelist—a Russian no less—that provided Akiko with literary inspiration for her celebrated poem. Her published reminiscences state that from the age of eighteen or nineteen she had read Japanese translations of Leo Tolstoy's (1828–1910) work.[301] Furthermore, the time and circumstances of the appearance in Japan of *Bethink Yourselves!*, his pacifist manifesto specifically opposing the Russo-Japanese War, suggest that its similarities with "Kimi"—in content and language—are more than coincidental.

Dated by Tolstoy to May 21, 1904, three months after the opening of hostilities, *Bethink Yourselves!* was first printed in English a month later in the June 27th edition of *The London Times*. This essay in twelve parts, running to fifty pages of English text in small book form, offers a wide range of philosophical objections to war and makes an outraged protest against the waging of the current conflict. Written in an alternately imploring and condemnatory tone, it is a stirring document that begins: "Again war. Again sufferings, necessary to nobody, utterly uncalled for; again fraud; again the universal stupefaction and brutalization of men."[302] Among other objections, Tolstoy complains that nations go to war, at least in part, to benefit rich people and professional diplomats, as well as certain academics and journalists who "thrive" selling it. Meanwhile, the young and the poor are sent off to suffer and die for a cause irrelevant to their interests, leaving their families in ruin. He states that those who call themselves Christians and Buddhists are only cynically exploiting religion to incite feelings of hatred and racial antipathy, and he calls for a true practicing of these religions that have produced, respectively, the golden rule and strictures that forbid even the killing of animals. On the current conflict, Tolstoy acknowledges Japanese military superiority, demonstrated by the defeat of the Russian Navy at Port Arthur, and quotes from the letters of a Russian soldier who, denouncing the catastrophic folly of war, vows, "Through me not one Japanese family shall be orphaned" (45).[303] The essay concludes with Tolstoy honoring such war resistors and stating that Russia has no need for more land in Manchuria.

Aside from its alternately imploring and condemning tone, *Bethink Yourselves!* closely parallels portions of "Kimi" that (1) suggest that soldiers sent to war have no stake in battlefield objectives, (2) observe pointedly that a nation's monarch does not himself face the dangers and sufferings at the front, (3) deplore war's effects on soldiers' families back home, and (4) compare men in armed combat to animals.

In addition, the two works share a number of other conceptual and lexical features. For example, mourning those "who have needlessly and so dreadfully perished" at Port Arthur, Tolstoy writes of "unfortunate men drawn from all parts of Russia [who] have been torn from honest, reasonable, useful, laborious family life [to be] placed on a cruel, senseless machine for slaughter . . . *without any need or any possibility of advantage* from all their privations, efforts, and sufferings, or from the death which overtook them" (31–32).[304] "Leave us in peace," he demands, "to plough, and sow, and build,—and also to feed you" (42). Speaking from the other side of the war's longest and costliest battle, Akiko begs Chūzaburō not to give his life at Port Arthur, asking "*For you, what does it matter* / Whether Port Arthur fortress falls or not? / The code of merchant houses / Says nothing about this." As for those in whose exalted names the battle is being waged, Tolstoy condemns "all these insolent, mendacious speeches about devotion to, and worship of, the Monarch, about readiness to sacrifice life (or one should say other people's lives, and not one's own)" (9). Elsewhere, he demands to know why "heartless Tsars, Mikados" do not "*go . . . under these shells and bullets*" (42). Akiko similarly notes that "*His Majesty the Emperor / goes not himself into the battle.*"

Of the deprivations inflicted on soldiers' families, Tolstoy writes that Russia's military leaders, at the behest of

> their adored Monarch . . . *tear away the fathers and the bread-winners from their orphaned families, preparing them for slaughter.* . . . And the same thing is going on in Japan. The benighted Japanese go in for murder with yet greater fervor, owing to their victories; the Mikado also reviews and rewards his troops; various generals boast of their bravery, imagining that, having *learned to kill*, they have acquired enlightenment. So, too, groan the unfortunate working people torn from useful labor and from their families. . . . And scores of thousands of [Japanese and Russian] *wives, fathers, mothers, children, are bemoaning their bread-winners*; uselessly destroyed. (39–41)

Protesting that Chūzaburō was not raised by his parents to study war, an outraged Akiko asks her brother, "Did they make you grasp the sword / *And teach you to kill?*" Of the family he left behind, she demands to know, "And do you ever think of your new bride, / Who crouches weeping behind the shop curtains / In her gentle loveliness? / *Who else has she to rely on in this world?*" Akiko begs him to "*Think of Mother, who lost Father just last autumn, / How much lonelier is her grief at home / Since you were drafted.*"

In characterizing armed conflict, Tolstoy draws several comparisons between men at war and animals. He finds that "this evil" makes "people stand on the plane of animals and even lower," transforming men into "*beasts*, ready any minute to tear each other to pieces" (20–21). "[B]oth Japanese and Russians . . . like wild animals, nay worse than wild animals, throw themselves upon each other with the sole desire to destroy as many lives as possible" (41). For Akiko war forces men "To spill one another's blood / *And die like beasts.*"

Besides textual similarities, the connection between "Kimi" and *Bethink Yourselves!* is suggested by the essay's wide exposure in Japan and the date of its appearance there, which would have given Akiko just enough time to read and digest it before composing her poem. A full translation was first published in the August 7, 1904 edition of *Heimin shinbun* as "Nanjira, kuiaratameyo" (Yourselves, repent!). This Japanese rendering of a Christian admonition made a suitable title for an essay that deals at some length with religion and bears an English title that is a quote attributed to Jesus Christ in the New Testament.

Despite overwhelming support in Japan for the war against Russia, this essay created a minor sensation when it came out in translation. Reprints were hastily published to keep up with a demand that far exceeded *Heimin shinbun*'s normally limited circulation. Thus, it was already sparking widespread debate when it was reissued in book form a month later as *Nichi-Ro sensō ron* (On the Russo-Japanese War).[305] Inasmuch as the deadline on manuscripts for the September 1904 issue of *Myōjō* was August 18 or 19, Akiko would have had nearly two weeks to contemplate Tolstoy's essay between its first appearance and the final day for submitting "Kimi."[306] Furthermore, as we shall see, Akiko herself stated, while she was under attack for her poem, that she had been reading the antiwar opinions published in *Heimin shinbun*, though she spoke of them disapprovingly.

Bethink Yourselves! carried messages similar to those conveyed by the few Japanese writers openly critical of the war. However, while writings opposing the war continued to appear in print long after hostilities were under way, a government crackdown on dissenters was taking a heavy toll by the time Akiko published her poem in September 1904. Sakai Toshihiko at *Heimin shinbun* had already spent two months in prison earlier that year. Then, in November, Kōtoku Shūsui was sentenced to five months in prison for violating the Press Laws.[307] Meanwhile, their newspaper was under siege in the courts and by police who were harassing newsstands and subscribers, "advising" people to change papers.[308] *Myōjō* itself was no stranger to government pressure, having been banned temporarily in 1900 for printing two French drawings of nudes, and "Kimi" provoked a hostile reaction from readers and a prominent critic. Yet there was no official response either against its author or the magazine. No statement or action emanated from the Home Ministry's notorious Censorship Division during the acrimonious controversy over the publication of "Kimi."

If Akiko angered readers for urging a soldier to put his family before his duty, she outraged them by her mention in the third stanza of the emperor and his absence from the battlefield:

> His Majesty the Emperor
> Goes not himself into the battle.
> Could he, with such deeply noble heart,
> Think it an honor for men
> To spill one another's blood
> And die like beasts?

Critics have widely disagreed on the degree of inflammatory connotation in this passage. Without a doubt, however, these lines were astonishingly bold for their time. Biographers of Akiko have noted recently that less critical references to the emperor led to the jailing of writers during this period.[309] One theory on the official silence and inaction regarding

"Kimi" postulates that the government never expected one female voice to have any significant national impact.[310]

Nevertheless, if officials of the Home Ministry chose not to act, a high minister of the literary world took it upon himself to launch a crusade against "Kimi" and its author.[311] From November 1904 to January 1905, Ōmachi Keigetsu, then chief literary editor at *Taiyō* magazine, published condemnations of this poem as "an expression of dangerous thoughts which disparage the idea of the national family," "a vilification that the Japanese people must not allow," and "a case of *lèse majesté*." He called Akiko "a traitorous subject, a rebel, a criminal who deserves the nation's punishment."[312] In pointed contrast, Keigetsu praised Ōtsuka Naoko's "A Hundred Visits to the Shrine," when it appeared four months later in the magazine he edited, as an appropriate expression in wartime of a woman's reserved and maidenly emotion,[313] and he chose a decidedly mild interpretation of the line "I shall not reply, but only weep" from "Mōde." Yet he made perhaps the most inflammatory reading ever propounded in print of the third stanza in "Kimi," which he paraphrased: "The Emperor himself does not risk the dangers of the battlefield, but from the safety of the palace he heartlessly urges on the sons of others to shed blood like beasts, assuring them that it is glorious to die."[314] In the course of his ensuing debate with Akiko and her defenders, Keigetsu insisted these lines meant that the emperor was cruelly sending men off to die at Port Arthur, a military objective that meant nothing to them.[315] Thus, with Keigetsu's vitriolic opening salvo attacking the third stanza, the long history of the explication and appropriation of "Kimi" had begun.

Initiating her own defense, Akiko countered with an "Open Letter" (*hiraki-bumi*) in the November 1904 issue of *Myōjō*. Her very different reading of "Kimi" so downplayed any suggestion of criticism, either of the emperor or of the war, that, had her interpretation obtained thereafter, this poem might never have gained its worldwide reputation as a distinguished work of antiwar literature. She conceded that, as a woman, she disliked war, but said she had wished only to express a desire for her brother's safety and for the earliest possible victory to restore peace. She urged Keigetsu to go to Shinbashi Station, where families were sending their sons off to the front, so he could hear for himself that they were voicing the same feelings she had expressed in her poem. She insisted: "No one has more love than I for this country of my birth, or feels more profound respect for the Emperor." She turned Keigetsu's charge of "dangerous thoughts" back on him, asking if it wasn't really more dangerous to proclaim that dying is the only way to serve one's country. Finally, she wrote that, while like any woman she disliked war, she "trembled at the arguments of such people as those at *Heimin shinbun*."[316] With this concluding statement, Akiko disassociates herself from the antiwar dissent of Kōtoku Shūsui and Sakai Toshihiko but indicates, as noted above, that at least she had read such dissent in this newspaper, which had also printed a translation of Tolstoy's *Bethink Yourselves!*.

Unmollified by Akiko's disavowals, Keigetsu responded in his January 1905 column by calling Akiko "a poison-tongued menace" whose "treasonous crimes against the nation cannot be tolerated by the Japanese people." With Keigetsu suggesting that Akiko should be punished as a criminal, Yosano Tekkan arranged to pay a personal visit to Keigetsu with Hiraide Shū, an eloquent law-school graduate, to head off a wider public brouhaha. Their "dialogue" was subsequently published in *Myōjō* where, not surprisingly, Keigetsu, who evidently stuttered, came out looking like the loser.[317] In the meantime, another writer had come to Akiko's defense. In the November 13th Sunday supplement of *Yomiuri shinbun*, the critic Kakuda Kin'ichirō, writing under the pen name Kennan, agreed that Akiko was only expressing a personal wish for her brother's safety, which hardly constituted "dangerous thoughts." Keigetsu retorted in the December 1904 issue of *Taiyō* that, with the nation at war, it was no time for such "personal feelings." In the December 11th issue of *Yomiuri*, Kennan addressed an article "To Ōmachi Keigetsu" in which he contended that Keigetsu's attack on Akiko showed that "in pandering to nationalism, he has himself fallen into irrationality."[318]

The defense of Akiko, carefully orchestrated by Tekkan and Hiraide, centered on the contention that Keigetsu had grossly misread the controversial stanza on the emperor. According to Hiraide, who put forward what Jay Rubin has called "the weakest of readings"—perhaps the *least* inflammatory reading ever proposed in print—all Akiko was really saying was how difficult it must be for the emperor to send his subjects to war, "even though [he] has no opportunity to see the battle first hand."[319] Hiraide fails to mention the ironic reference in the poem's fourth stanza to "peace in this Great Imperial Reign," which raises serious doubts about such an innocuous paraphrasing. Nevertheless, Keigetsu reportedly agreed in the discussion that this was a conceivable interpretation, though he said it made for rather tedious poetry. Furthermore, he conceded that he had perhaps overreacted in calling Akiko a traitor. Hiraide broached the larger question of whether poets shouldn't write their true thoughts even if Keigetsu might call them "dangerous." Keigetsu replied that, in his opinion, they should at least refrain from publishing them, a position Hiraide called cowardly and stifling of creativity. Their dialogue concluded with Hiraide and Tekkan telling Keigetsu to burn his writing brushes and admit his failure as a literary critic.[320]

While Keigetsu seems to have suffered a defeat in this affair, recent literary critics and historians agree that his initial outrage at "Kimi" represented the majority response in the press and in the country at large.[321] An article in the February 1905 issue of *Shinsei* that purported to be an overview of the controversy concluded that Akiko's poem might have been acceptable in "normal" times when expression of individual views could be permitted, but that in wartime it was reprehensible because its influence could lead to social disruption. The article deplored "Kimi," in the final analysis, as "the mindless complaining of an uneducated woman."[322] What this more widespread reaction strongly suggests is that, at the time, many more people had made the kind of inflammatory reading put forward by Keigetsu than the innocuous reading proffered by the poet and her defenders. Readers and critics have continued to differ sharply as to the intensity and target of protest in "Kimi" down to the present day.

The poem seems to have provoked little public debate during the years following the Russo-Japanese War when Akiko was broadening her concerns to write in protest of both government policy affecting women and popular attitudes toward them.[323] In the period just after the celebration in Japan of the armistice ending World War I, a time when much Japanese poetry was written advocating peace and democracy, "Kimi" became established as a "representative work" of antiwar literature. A decade later, however, this designation made it once again the subject of controversy at the height of Japan's proletarian literature movement.

Much maligned by American scholars during the Cold War period, this movement, factionalized and intolerant as its leaders often were, encompassed a number of talented authors who had varying degrees of allegiance to it and who produced some literary works of high distinction. As critics justifiably note, writers associated with it also turned out poetry and fiction that were long on ringing calls of protest and propagations of ideology but short on stylistic subtlety, compelling drama, and credible characterizations.[324] In contrast to their limited reputation in North America, writers identified with the proletarian literature movement have been the subject of extensive study since 1945 in Japan and in Europe, where numerous translations of their best-known works have appeared in such languages as Italian, Russian, Polish, and Serbo-Croatian. Even in the United States during the more frigid years of the Cold War, proletarian writers were grudgingly acknowledged for portraying laborers, fishermen, and farmers, often living in poverty, who comprised the majority of the Japanese population in the early twentieth century. Donald Keene should be commended for publishing a portion of Kobayashi Takiji's (1903–33) *Kani kōsen* (The cannery boat, 1929), considered a "representative work" of proletarian literature, in his 1956 anthology of modern Japanese literature in translation. Keene noted in his "Introduction" that, while they were often unsuccessful when judged by current literary criteria, "the great virtue of proletarian writings was that they dealt with aspects of Japan largely ignored by more famous writers."[325] Perhaps the proletarian literature movement's greatest failings were (1) constant infighting and factional division; (2) the insistence of its leading theoreticians that all literature must be judged on the basis of whether or not it serves the cause of socialist revolution, there being no other legitimate criterion for evaluation; and (3) efforts by a number of its devotees to dominate, sometimes through tactics of defamation and intimidation, literary societies, journals, and publishing houses.[326] With such a highly theoretical orientation, it is not surprising that many of the movement's most influential writings have appeared in the medium of expository prose, including literary criticism that evaluates the work of writers inside and outside the movement from a Marxist perspective.[327]

In his widely read essay "Hansen bungaku-ron" (On antiwar literature, 1929), Kuroshima Denji (1898–1943) sharply criticized recent Japanese novels on war and singled out one poem, "Kimi," for mostly negative comment. Kuroshima drew on his extensive reading of war literature and his personal experiences in the Imperial Japanese Army to write his own literature on war, as well as to evaluate what others, such as Akiko, had written. Sent as an infantryman with the 73,000 Japanese troops invading Siberia in 1918, he is best known for the stories based on his ordeal in Russia. His work is featured in the anthology *Sensō ni taisuru sensō* (War against war), printed by Nihon Sayoku Bungeika Sōrengō in 1928 and called "the first collection of antiwar literature ever published in Japan."[328] Yet, while his target in these stories is a war and a military that he portrays as cruelly aggressive and imperialistic, other authors associated with the proletarian literature movement criticized him a few years later for a lack of revolutionary ideology in his fiction. For his part, Kuroshima led a small number of writers in a November 1930 defection from one group within the movement because of what he termed "differences of political opinions." Within a few weeks his former comrades were accusing him in print of being, among other things, "nothing more than an ultra-left romantic" with a petit-bourgeois interest in money.[329] In the highly volatile atmosphere of the proletarian literature movement, such invective was tossed around indiscriminately in any number of disputes by all sides. Still, it is ironic that Kuroshima was attacked for being a romantic and petit-bourgeois writer, the same charges he had leveled at Yosano Akiko a few years earlier in "On Antiwar Literature."

In that essay, which appeared in the 1929 collection *Puroretariya geijutsu kyōtei* (Principles of proletarian art),[330] Kuroshima effectively summarizes Marxist-Leninist views of war and explains why he finds that works of Japanese literature most often identified as antiwar fail ideologically from the perspective of socialist realism. The author states that, unlike "bourgeois pacifists" and anarchists, the proletariat should not be opposed to all wars: "A historical distinction must be drawn between wars that oppress us and those that lead to liberation. . . . There are various kinds of war—wars of aggression and conquest, defensive wars, and wars of revolution and popular liberation."[331] He condemns wars fought for the purpose of perpetuating or expanding economic and political exploitation. While conceding that war is often brutal and tragic, Kuroshima calls for it to be retained as one option in the "struggle" (*tōsō*) of peasants against landowners, and of workers against capitalists for liberation from an evil class system. One must recognize, he writes, that such wars further the advancement of humanity, and that war itself can never totally disappear until the abolishment of class societies and the victory of socialism.[332]

It is noteworthy that the language and metaphor in Kuroshima's writing, as in much of Marxist literature in Japan and elsewhere, drew amply on military terms and war imagery. Repeated calls for "struggle" and "combat" (*tatakai*) came in magazines with names like *Bungei sensen* (Arts battlefront) and *Senki* (Battle flag); as noted above, Kuroshima's best-known fiction appeared in the collection *Sensō ni taisuru sensō*. The copious use of military language by leftist writers and their insistence on maintaining the option of armed struggle made it easier for them to support official military policies in the 1930s even though they had consistently opposed the government on a wide range of issues in the 1920s. Ben-Ami Shillony describes this process:

> In the 1930s, as the war clouds thickened and the demands for a national-defence state increased, intellectuals began to involve themselves more in the justification and propagation of the official goals. The non-conformist writers of the 1920s gave way to the conformist writers of the 1930s and early 1940s, who generally supported the international claims of their country. Marxism was no obstacle to this trend. Many left-wing intellectuals, having been disillusioned with Moscow, espoused the cause of Japan as the world's underdog. Their self-image as society's vanguard helped to propel them to the position of the new nationalist standard-bearers.[333]

In "Hansen bungaku-ron," Kuroshima condemned what he viewed as the essentially class-bound nature of literature opposing war. Beginning with passages in the Old Testament that condemn war and advocate peace, he quickly dismisses such "old stories" as outdated and irrelevant, moving on to show how modern antiwar literature in Japan is basically bourgeois. The problem, as he sees it, is that while such works might be emotionally moving, they concentrate too narrowly on individual suffering and ignore the wider issues revealed by armed conflict. The so-called "awakening of individualism" often ascribed to these writings is, in Kuroshima's opinion, nothing more than the rise of a bourgeois worldview that only serves to perpetuate oppression of the vast numbers of individuals in a capitalist society, belying the label "humanitarian" that is also frequently applied to such works.[334]

Among three specific examples, he is most critical of Tayama Katai's *Ippeisotsu*, based closely on the author's excruciating experiences at the Russo-Japanese front. Kuroshima cites this novel as a prime example of the narrowly passive viewpoint assumed by writers associated with Japanese naturalism. He briefly summarizes the story, in which the protagonist barely survives the overcrowding and squalor of an army field hospital at the Manchurian front until his suffering compels him to leave for his unit, even though his beriberi has not been sufficiently cured. In constant pain, the soldier drags his heavy rifle and sick body across the endless prairies, refused assistance by other soldiers and haunted by memories of civilian life, only to die of heart failure shortly after he finally reaches the PX. Kuroshima sees merit in Tayama's portrayal of the horrifying and disgusting aspects of war but finds his depiction of the battlefront as a huge, inescapable prison to be itself overly confining. Yes, military life is shackling of the individual. Yes, a peaceful life is more desirable. Yes, war is full of terror, squalor, and death. But Kuroshima maintains that the author's failure to move beyond "passive" description of individual suffering finally traps this novel inside Tayama's own bourgeois worldview.[335]

Kuroshima finds Akiko's poem, if anything, even more revealing of this bourgeois worldview than Tayama's novel, although he detects some desire in "Kimi" to "seek the causes of war." Furthermore, he takes a most dim view of Akiko's work in general: "Her other poems trifle with art, dabbling in love, and we find them most disagreeable. We shall certainly not touch on any of them here." Nevertheless, he concedes that "in this one poem, though shackled in the old-fashioned 7-5 *shintaishi* form, there overflows a genuine expression of feeling." He quickly adds, however, that the emotion is evoked "only as concern for a blood relative." In quoting from the text of "Kimi," he explains that he has himself written "X" marks (*fuseji*) in place of words "certain to be censored today [1929]." These words refer to the emperor and are, in the original, *sumera mikoto* (the emperor) and *omizukara* (himself).[336]

Unfortunately, Kuroshima fails to specify what it is in "Kimi" that suggests for him "a slightly broader conception [than in other works of bourgeois antiwar literature] and a desire to seek the causes of war." Whether this conception has anything to do with Akiko's mention of the emperor or not, her ideas are judged finally by Kuroshima to be "half-baked and half-hearted opposition to war deriving solely from individualistic emotion."[337] It was perhaps what Kuroshima grudgingly called its "slightly broader conception" that inspired critics after World War II to find expressions of democracy and women's liberation, as well as pacifism, in "Kimi," conveyed through its impassioned plea. For Kuroshima and other proletarian movement writers, however, philosophical implications in a poem are not enough. He is dissatisfied in the end because Akiko's feelings against war, however movingly expressed, are insufficient to make for a successful work of protest literature.[338]

Kuroshima's objections to a bourgeois worldview and a family-centered focus are repeated in evaluations of "Kimi" after World War II. However, almost all post-1945 literary criticism of her poetry on war, while including a few negative appraisals, begins and ends with this poem. With very few exceptions, recent critics and biographers have chosen to ignore poetry she published in the 1930s on Japan's escalating conflict with China, and in January 1942 on the Pacific War. One finds little mention after 1945 of (1) *tanka* she printed after a 1928 visit to China, where she was in Mukden during the first of the notorious assassination "incidents," the one that bears that city's name; (2) a lengthy *shintaishi* entitled "Nihon kokumin asa no uta" (Citizens of Japan, a morning song, 1932), in which she lauded the celebrated "human bomb" suicide attack by three Japanese soldiers near Shanghai as an example for Japanese women of patriotic devotion; (3) "Kōgan no shi" (Rosy-cheeked death, 1932), another *shintaishi* on the fighting in China; or (4) *tanka* she contributed one month after the attack on Pearl Harbor to *Tanka kenkyū*'s "Special Edition Marking the Imperial Declaration of War."

Akiko wrote poetry on the fighting in China during a visit there with Tekkan in the spring of 1928. These two poets were among the many artists and academics from Japan invited annually, all expenses paid, by the Japanese-owned South Manchuria Railway Company to make sightseeing tours of Manchuria and Mongolia. The couple traveled some forty days during May and June, visiting, among other places, Liaotung, Port Arthur, Harbin, and Antung, as well as Mukden. Two years later Akiko published poems she composed about this trip in a collection entitled *Man-Mō yūki* (Travels in Manchuria and Mongolia, 1930), coauthored with Tekkan. Her visit to Port Arthur, the scene of murderous battles in two recent conflicts, inspired the following *tanka*, an effective adaptation of traditional *waka* metaphor to convey the sorrow of war:

nakazu shite	How hard it is
Ryojun no yama o	to climb the hill at Port Arthur
yukigatashi	without crying.
koboruru suna mo	Even the sand falls through the rocks
musebu ne zo suru	with a sobbing sound.[339]

On the return leg of their journey the couple happened to be staying at the Hotel Yamato overlooking the railway station at Mukden when, very early in the morning of June 9, 1928, they heard what Akiko later described as "a strange noise." The sound turned out to be the detonation of an emplacement charge set by the Japanese army to explode along the railroad tracks. The blast destroyed four cars of a passing train. Among the passengers killed in this bombing were Chang Tso-lin, the military leader of Manchuria who was the intended victim, and his son Wu. In the aftermath of what became known as the "Mukden Incident," the Japanese army in Manchuria falsely accused Chinese vagrants of the attack, which the army tried to use as a pretext for occupying all of Manchuria. This crude plot was quickly exposed and thwarted by the government in Tokyo, but pressure from the Army Ministry prevented disciplining of the scheme's perpetrators.[340]

The Mukden Incident apparently had special significance for the Yosanos because, earlier during their travels in China, they had reportedly come to know Wu's wife, widowed by the attack. According to one account, she had invited the couple on a boat trip during which everyone had enjoyed the scenery of willow trees and exchanged poems. Akiko is described in a biography by Yūri Kaoru as having been deeply saddened to hear of Wu's death. She was also said to have been relieved when a report that his wife had subsequently committed suicide proved to be untrue. Yūri explains that these events and an upsurge of fighting elsewhere in China caused Akiko and Tekkan to cancel their planned trip to Peking, a city she had especially wanted to visit.[341] Yet, if these depictions of Akiko's feelings and circumstances are accurate, the *tanka* she published in *Man-Mō yūki* on the death and destruction resulting from the bombing at Mukden seems surprisingly lighthearted, especially its reference to Chang Tso-lin:

sono nakaba	Inside the half-burned train
kogetaru kisha ni	are the white cards
shōgun no	from the poker game
moteasobitaru	the general was playing.[342]
shihai no hakushi	

Another *tanka* in this travel journal offers cheery reassurance to the people of Manchuria, which had been administrated by Chang, that his death would not have unfavorable consequences for them. The place-name Tungsan denotes the three eastern provinces that comprise Manchuria:

hata aoshi	Tungsan,
Tōsan-shō wa	with fields of green.
horobu nashi	Do not worry, good neighbor.
wazarau nakare	You will not go to ruin.[343]
yoki tonaribito yo	

On events elsewhere in China, Akiko wrote the following poem on the end of factional fighting in Peking between the forces Chang Tso-lin had commanded before his death and Chiang Kai-shek's Kuomintang army. The Japanese government viewed with growing concern the increasingly unified resistance in China, after Chang's assassination, to Japanese expansion, which had proceeded with relative smoothness at first. Another of Chang's sons, Chang Hsueh-liang, who had once been pro-Japanese, now placed his father's forces under Chiang Kai-shek's unified command and raised the Kuomintang flag in Manchuria, much to the consternation of officials in Tokyo.[344]

Enkyō no	In Tungsan, too,
ikusa hajimaru	disturbing news
owarinu to	that the battle in Peking
mimi sawagashi ya	has started and ended.[345]
Tōsan-shō mo	

In one of the very few post-1945 studies of Yosano Akiko to mention her poetry on war after "Kimi," biographer Yamamoto Fujie emphasizes that Akiko and Tekkan were only tourists in China, and that they had no connection with governmental, military, or diplomatic affairs.[346] It is also important to remember that, after returning to Japan, they had no access to information on the situation in China beyond what was available to them in the Japanese press.

Four years after their visit, Akiko wrote that reading a newspaper article had moved her to compose "Rosy-Cheeked Death" in the aftermath of the first Shanghai Incident of January 1932. According to her accompanying headnote, this poem was inspired by a dispatch from Shanghai by *Yomiuri shinbun* reporter Andō Satoru. "Rosy-Cheeked Death" contains a sympathetic portrayal of young Chinese soldiers killed in a conflict escalated by events she had witnessed at Mukden. However, from reading Japanese newspapers, she could hardly have known any more of the truth about the Shanghai Incident of 1932 than she had about the Mukden Incident of 1928. As in the earlier case, the Japanese military instigated another murderous assault and blamed it on the Chinese in order to justify further aggression in China. This time, a number of Japanese Buddhist priests strolling peacefully in Shanghai were attacked by what the Japanese military claimed were "villainous" Chinese, with many deaths and injuries resulting. Units of the Japanese navy and army were sent into Shanghai to "avenge" the priests by making what they thought would be short work of the Chinese troops stationed in the city. Highly motivated Chinese resistance, however, led by the 19th Route Army commanded by General Ts'ai T'ing-k'ai and supported by citizen volunteers, fought the invading forces to a standstill and compelled Japanese commanders to summon reinforcements. Faced now with overwhelming firepower, the 19th Route Army was eventually forced to withdraw, and a truce was arranged, based on a proposal by England and the United States.[347] Referring again in her poetry to a Chinese military leader, Akiko explicitly denounces General Ts'ai in "Rosy-Cheeked Death," comparing him unfavorably to Sun Yat-sen, founder of the Chinese Republic in 1911, who had been considered friendly to certain companies and political groups in Japan[348]:

> To the west of the river
> We see something in the trenches.
> Approaching, we find enemy corpses—
> Enemy corpses, lying one upon another.
>
> The saddest among them
> Are the two hundred student soldiers.
> Youthful at seventeen or eighteen,
> None have faces over twenty.
>
> How could their gentle mothers
> Bear to see this?

Sons so young
Who probably had pretty fiancées
Chosen for them in the old Chinese custom.

Perhaps they had read a little,
With sufficient knowledge of the world
To have known the name of Sun Yat-sen,
Who prayed for the peace of their nation.

Who is it that deceives them,
With their youthful naive hearts,
Teaching them to hate
Their good neighbor, Japan?

Who is it that entices them
To turn in their pens for swords,
And scatters their young lives to the winds
Before the plum flowers bloom in spring?

It is the foolish Ts'ai T'ing-k'ai,
Commander of the 19th Route Army.
He did not know that, before the day is out,
His regiments must fall.

To the west of the river
We see something in the trenches.
Two hundred rosy-cheeked youths
Lie mired in blood and dirt.[349]

Although the poem depicts a different people in a different war, it is not without parallels to "Kimi." Once again, Akiko deplores the sending of young men, in this case Chinese, into a conflict that takes them away from their lives and families back home. Her mention of their bloodstained corpses, covered with mud and piled in trenches, recalls the death of beasts she referred to in "Kimi." However, "Rosy-Cheeked Death" conveys an attitude toward Japan's conflict with China that sharply contrasts with the attitude expressed in her earlier poem toward the conflict with Russia. In "Kimi," Akiko initially vents her outrage at the irrelevance of this war to the interests of her brother and his family by pointedly asking, "For you, what does it matter / Whether Port Arthur fortress falls or not?" She then laments the brutality of armed conflict and mentions the emperor in stanzas containing varying degrees of critical specificity and intensity depending on which reading one accepts. In "Rosy-Cheeked Death," however, she condemns General Ts'ai as a fool for tricking youthful Chinese students into joining the battle, not because war is wrong in itself or irrelevant to civilian concerns, but because this war is unwinnable and because Japan is really China's "good neighbor" and not the enemy that such men as Ts'ai "deceive" uninformed youngsters into believing it to be. Assertions that the Japanese military was invincible and that misguided Chinese leaders were wrongly turning their people against a Japan that was only trying to "develop" and "reform" their country were repeated ad nauseam in Japanese newspapers and magazines during the early 1930s. Akiko echoes another recurrent motif in the Japanese press of the time when she contrasts China's traditional customs and former leaders, representing the wisdom and beauty of the nation's glorious past, with the foolishness and deception of China's current leaders, who were blamed for dragging the country to the depths of despair and corruption.[350]

Once again, it must be emphasized that, with the benefit of hindsight, it is all too easy to forget the difficulty for even the most informed readers in Japan of finding accurate reports of the situation in China during this period. Literary critic Aono Suekichi (1890–1961) complained at the time that "journalism's *Shina-ron* and its so-called on-the-spot reports from China are almost always superficial or even nonsensical."[351] In fact, the press played an important role generating popular support in Japan for the government's military policies in China, with articles and books that sensationalized the battles, glorified soldiers and sailors, and sounded alarms about the "Manchurian lifeline" and the "national crisis." The wide popularity of these articles and books, some of which were produced for children, has been credited with pulling the Japanese publishing industry out of its own depression-era sales crisis.[352]

A few years later, with the continuing preponderance of such writings, the graphic and shocking depictions of the conflict in China published by novelist Ishikawa Tatsuzō and poet Kaneko Mitsuharu came as an unpleasant surprise to officials at the Home Ministry, who acted to suppress their work.[353] Yet neither Kaneko's poems nor Ishikawa's story on the war had appeared when Akiko wrote "Rosy-Cheeked Death" or her *tanka* on the fighting in China, so she lacked the benefit of even these tiny beams of reality in a dark sea of tabloid journalism and relentless propaganda. On top of this, the press in Japan constantly pursued prominent poets and novelists for their opinions on events in the conflict, despite the fact that these writers could not reasonably be expected to possess any special expertise in international affairs. As one who had traveled recently to China, Akiko would have been particularly sought after for comment. Nevertheless, even considering these circumstances, her lines in this poem lauding the military might of China's "good-neighbor" stand in jolting contrast to her 1918 declaration against militarism in Japan.[354]

A work that diverges even more strikingly from her earlier writing on war and the military is the poem "Citizens of Japan, A Morning Song," published in *Nihon josei* (Women of Japan), a June 1932 supplement of the magazine *Nihon kokumin*. Akiko devotes much of this ten-stanza *shintaishi* to praise for the Imperial Army in China, lauding the highly celebrated "human bomb" mission carried out by three Japanese soldiers near Shanghai on February 20 of that year. She honors the "patriotic heroes" *(resshi)* who charged into heavily fortified Chinese positions carrying explosives on their bodies, and she makes of this incident a rallying cry to exhort Japanese women on the home front to "redouble our own courage" in "unified devotion" to the "cause [of] the emperor's forces." It is a very different mission from the one she assigned in 1918 to Japanese women, whose "responsibility" in the face of "militarism" was, she wrote then, "to eradicate this barbaric thinking from our midst."[355]

"Citizens of Japan, A Morning Song"

Ah, the augustness of His Majesty's reign
That inspires people's hearts!
It is a time that ignites our sense of duty,
A time to unify in loyalty.

It is a time to cease empty arguments,
And smash sissified dreams of compromise.
Knowing their course to be just,
Our forces attack through sufferings a hundredfold.

Though his is the body of one soldier,
Carrying the demolition canisters,
He dances through the barbed wire,
And transforms that body into powder.

Though his is the body of one major,
He expects no mercy from the enemy,
And scatters that body, purer than a flower,
Giving life to a samurai's honor.

And these men are not alone.
Patriotic heroes with hearts like theirs
Rise to the challenge wherever the Emperor's forces go,
To the north and to the south.

And they are but one example.
For we, too, the people behind the guns,
Redouble our own courage many times over
And rally everyone to the cause.

Blood also courses in the eager hearts
Of our countrymen who are not soldiers.
They devote their lives day by day
To serve on the nation's behalf.

An example is this poem of mine
That speaks with the hearts of those men
Who, grasping the demolition canisters,
Ran to hurl themselves through barbed wire.

Even I, a powerless woman,
Am thus committed to our cause,
As are those people, superior among us,
Who carry out the esteemed ways of our peerless ancestors.

Ah, the augustness of His Majesty's reign
That inspires people's hearts!
It is a time that ignites our sense of duty,
A time to unify in loyalty.[356]

As Yamamoto Fujie points out, this poem reads rather like an imitation of the lyrics Tekkan composed a few months earlier for his widely popular *gunka* of the day, "Bakudan, san'yūshi."[357] If there is any continuity with "Kimi" in this poem, it is in the passion with which Akiko expresses a very different view of war. What perhaps most puts "Citizens of Japan, A Morning Song" at odds with Akiko's earlier work is that a poet admired for her innovative and unconventional use of language should rely so heavily on such slogans and buzzwords of the day as "a samurai's honor" (*bushi no meiyo*), "the esteemed ways of our peerless ancestors" (*fuso no bifū*) and "the people behind the guns" (*jūgo no tami*).

Yet the turnabout of Akiko and other women writers on the issue of war is hardly a phenomenon exclusive to Japan. During the first week of World War I suffragist leader Emmeline Pankhurst openly declared a truce in the British women's bitter struggle to gain the vote: "For the present at least our arms are grounded, for directly the threat of foreign war descended on our nation we declared a complete truce from militancy."[358] As in Japan two decades later, British women writers began turning out patriotic, prowar stories in which women were portrayed, as they are in "Citizens of Japan, A Morning Song," as passive supporters of their men at the front. In Florence L. Barclay's "My Heart's Right There," told from the viewpoint of a wife on the home front, the moral of the story is pronounced by her husband as he departs for war again after taking a leave back home to recover from wounds:

> "It's a righteous war, my girl; and every man who fears God and honours the King, should be up, and out; and ready to do his share; and every woman who loves her home, must be willing bravely to do her part, by letting her man go."[359]

Phrases like "righteous war," "doing our part," and "fighting bravely" also pervade the essays Akiko published in the early 1930s on the escalating hostilities in China and, later, her *tanka* on the early phase of the Pacific War. Her article "Tōshi-shō no mondai" (The Tungssu problem, 1931), which is filled with popular slogans, asserts the same view in prose that she expressed three years later in the poem "Rosy-Cheeked Death," that is, that Chinese are really pro-Japan, but that their military-clique government (*gunbatsu-seifu*) has misled them with anti-Japanese propaganda, which is to blame for the tragedy of the Manchurian Incident. She goes on in this piece to repeat the official rationale that, in China, Japan has only taken emergency measures as a policy of self-preservation (*hijō shudan no jiei-saku*) so that the Chinese people themselves (*Shina kokumin jishin*) can create an independent, peaceful new government (*dokuritsu shite heiwa na shin-seifu*) and restore good relations with Japan, "opening a secure path to coexistence and coprosperity [*kyōko na kyōson-kyōeki no michi o hiraku*]."

Similarly, in "Nisshin kokumin no shinwa" (Friendship between the citizens of Japan and China, 1932), she urges Japanese to be grateful to the Imperial Army and Navy for their great victory (*taishō*) in "mopping up [*sōtō*] a large Chinese force near Shanghai with unexpected swiftness, to the relief of Japanese and foreigners alike. . . . I celebrate the independence of Manchūkuo, which has initiated a reconciliation of thoroughgoing friendship between the Japanese and Chinese peoples." In an essay entitled "Inochi o kezuru" (Shortening their lives, 1932), she again urges people in Japan to

> be grateful, first, to the three brave warriors [*san'yūshi*, of the "suicide" mission near Shanghai], and to the officers and men of the Imperial Army and Navy, including the 4,000 casualties, who represent all of us Japanese. Beyond this, the actions of these men should inspire us all the more in each of our allotted peaceful labors.[360]

Her views came to be shared widely among intellectuals in Japan. Over the next few years, support for Japanese military policies in China was expressed by growing numbers of writers, including those who had recently written from a Marxist perspective. Many claimed, as did philosopher Miki Kiyoshi in 1936, that Japan was not fighting China's people but only the reactionary Chiang Kai-shek regime and his warlords. Political scientist Rōyama Masamichi, sinologist Ozaki Hotsumi, and economist Hosokawa Karoku joined Miki in supporting Japanese military policy, which, they wrote, aimed at liberating East Asia from Western imperialism. Miki later traveled with other writers to Japanese-occupied areas of Southeast Asia for the purpose of promoting the "superior qualities" of Japanese language and culture.[361]

At the start of the Pacific War, Akiko, now sixty-three, faced not only the worsening shortages of food and other necessities brought on by rationing but also painful, terminal illness. For a woman so active and productive, it must have been particularly difficult to be mostly bedridden from the time she suffered a brain hemorrhage in May 1940 until her death on May 29, 1942 following an attack of uremia. Still, throughout the ordeal of her final months, she continued gamely to entertain visits from friends and relatives, and to write poetry. Shortly after the attack on Pearl Harbor, she joined other Japanese poets as the only woman contributing poems to the January 1942 issue of *Tanka kenkyū* magazine's "Special Edition Marking the Imperial Declaration of War." That month the government proclaimed that the eighth day of every month thereafter be designated "Imperial Rescript Proclamation Day" (*taishō hōtaibi*), and on that day all newspapers subsequently reprinted the imperial war proclamation on their front pages.[362] The six *tanka* Akiko offered are somber and subdued compared with the more bombastic and vitriolic verses in what was one of many hastily assembled collections of exhortatory war poetry appearing over the next three years. Two of her poems refer with sorrow to the abruptly widened conflict:

mi-ikusa no shōsho no mae ni namida otsu yo wa kokkan ni iru shiwasu nite	Viewing the sacred war declaration, it is a time for falling tears as we enter the bitter cold of the twelfth lunar month.
hi no moto no ōsaishō mo yami ware mo onaji namida su ooki shōsho ni	Japan's prime minister and I, who am ill, cry the same tears over the august declaration of war.[363]

Akiko expresses similar sentiments in a *tanka* published the same month in the magazine *Tōhaku*:

ikusa aru Taiheiyō no seinan o omoite ware wa samuki yoru o naku	Thinking of the war in the Southwest Pacific, I weep through this cold night.[364]

These poems stand in sharp contrast to the outpouring of verses that celebrated the attack on Pearl Harbor and the declaration of war. Like *gunka* published in large quantities during the Sino-Japanese and Russo-Japanese Wars, these bellicose verses, including many composed by highly prominent poets, crudely vilified "wicked devil" nations in such lines as "The time has come to slaughter America and England; / Ah, how refreshing" and "The English villains, / The American villains."[365] Yet, if Akiko's *tanka* on the Pacific War are comparatively restrained, often sorrowful, she joined other poets to honor and encourage the Japanese forces in poems that continue to repeat catchphrases of the day:

tsuyoki kana ten o osorezu chi ni hajinu ikusa o su naru masuratake o wa	How strong! They fear not heaven nor feel shame on earth— our brave soldiers in battle.[366]
michi tose no kami no oshie ni sodaterare tsuyoshi higashi no ōyashima-bito	Raised with the teachings of three thousand years of the gods— the mighty people of the Eight Great Islands in the East.[367]

Among Akiko's poems in *Tanka kenkyū* on the troops are three that mention her son, recently promoted to lieutenant in the Imperial Navy, who was then serving on a battleship in the war zone. Two of these express her anxiety as she awaits reports from the front. The other, which urges him to fight courageously, was reprinted in a collection of exhortatory and celebratory war poems entitled *Daitōa sensō kashū* (Poetry of the Greater East Asia War) published by Tenri Jihōsha the year after her death (1943):

ko ga noreru mi-ikusabune no otonai o matsu ni mo arazu bu-un are kashi	Though I await news from the battleship with my son aboard, it does not come. Ah, may the fortunes of war be with him!

ko ga fune no Kuroshio koete tatakai wa hi mo kai nashi ya yamai suru haha	My son's ship crossed the Black Current and the battle has lasted for days. Is there still no outcome, his sick mother asks.[368]
suigun no tai-i to narite waga shirō mi-ikusa ni yuku takeku tatakae	Becoming a navy lieutenant, my fourth son goes now to the sacred war. Fight bravely![369]

Yamamoto Fujie touches on the inevitable comparison of this last poem to "Kimi shinitamō koto nakare" by noting the special affection Akiko had expressed for her fourth son. Yamamoto recalls that Akiko had dedicated the poem "Augyusuto" (Auguste, 1917) to him, having named him after the French sculptor Auguste Rodin (1840–1917), much admired in Japan, whom she had met in Paris seven years before its publication:

Augyusuto, Augyusuto, haha no somatsu no geijutsu nanka ga aa, nan ni narō? Watakushi wa omae ni yotte shiru koto ga dekita. Shinjitsu no chōkoku o shinjitsu no uta o shinjitsu no ongaku o, soshite shinjitsu no ai o.	Auguste, Auguste, Oh, what use is your mother's wretched art? From you I learned to know true sculpture, true poetry, true music, and true love.[370]

Yamamoto speculates that Akiko was recalling "Kimi," a plea for her brother not to give his life at Port Arthur, even as she composed a *tanka* exhorting her son to battle in the Pacific: "Perhaps she muttered to herself that each poem was 'true' [*shinjitsu*] for her in the context of each situation." Moreover, Yamamoto points out that Akiko wrote this poem during the first flush of Japanese military victories in the Pacific War, "when people in Japan could not possibly have imagined, even in their wildest dreams, the devastating defeat that loomed in the future."[371] Recalling Akiko's dispute with Keigetsu over "Kimi," in which she disavowed protest implications for that poem, it might be plausible that she considered the sufferings and losses of war regrettable but necessary during the Pacific War, if not during the Russo-Japanese War. Finally, Yamamoto's suggestion that Tekkan might have composed "Human Bombs: The Three Brave Warriors" at least in part for financial reward cannot be ruled out as one motivation for Akiko's publication of poetry and prose supporting war at a time of severely straitened circumstances for the Yosanos, with a large family to support, and for other Japanese.

Still, one cannot fail to be impressed with the distance Akiko had traveled since "Kimi." In 1904 she denounced armed conflict as the behavior of "beasts"; in 1918 she advocated pacifism, condemning militarism in Japan as "barbarian thinking [that] is the responsibility of us women to eradicate . . . from our midst."[372] By 1932 she was admonishing Japanese women to "cease empty arguments," "destroy sissified dreams of compromise," and "rally to the cause . . . behind the guns." She urged them to take an "example [from] those patriotic heroes in the imperial forces, purer than flowers, who scattered their bodies and gave life to the honor of warriors."[373] A decade later, in poetry she published shortly before her death, she exhorted her son to "fight bravely" in "the sacred war."[374] It is a remarkable journey about which very little has been written by the vast majority of postwar critics and biographers.

In recent years, as before 1945, Akiko's poetry and prose on war has often been explicated and evaluated within the context of prevailing political and philosophical currents of thought. Yūri Kaoru published one of the earliest postwar biographies of Akiko in 1948, during the third year of the seven-year Allied Occupation. Her 123-page paperback entitled *Akiko no shōgai* (The life of Akiko) opens with an introduction by Kawasaki Natsu honoring "a passionate poet," "a leader of the younger generation," and "a pioneer of women's liberation [*fujin kaihō no senkusha*]," who was also "a good wife and mother." Kawasaki could hardly have predicted the reputation Akiko gained abroad some two decades later through translations and studies of her work, so she notes with regret that "Akiko would have been a world-renowned artist had it not been for the disadvantageous restriction the Japanese language imposes internationally." She concludes by stating: "I am confident that this book is must reading for young Japanese women, who bear a heavy responsibility in the building of a new Japanese culture."[375] In subsequent chapters Yūri Kaoru continues in the same vein, portraying Akiko as, first, an eloquent advocate of peace (24) and "democratic freedom" (63); second, an impassioned opponent of "feudalistic tendencies" (58), "male domination" (63), and war (24); and third, "a conscientious wife and mother" (32–33).

References to "feudalistic" (*hōken-teki*) customs (18, 24) and "the building of a new Japanese culture" (*atarashii Nihon bunka no kensetsu*) (3) reflect Japan's postwar revulsion toward the recent conflict and the ideology that had supported it, a reversal that has been called an "inversion of values."[376] The press, which only a few months earlier had promoted Japan's imperial destiny and the traditional warrior ethic, was now filled with endorsements of "democracy" (*minshūshugi*) and condemnations of "feudalism" (*hōkenshugi*) and "militarism" (*gunkokushugi*), words sprinkled throughout Kawasaki's and Yūri's prose.[377] Considering Akiko's writings before 1928, it is understandable that she should have attracted attention at this time, becoming a heroic figure in early postwar Japan. In her chapter on "Kimi," subtitled "A Heart That Loved Peace" (Heiwa o ai suru kokoro), Yūri writes: "With the new Japan embarking as a peaceful nation, we Japanese can be proud that in our past we had a woman who so loved peace and advocated it so courageously."[378] Yūri adopts a less inflammatory reading of the passage thought by many to be critical of the emperor. "Akiko was in no way expressing antipathy toward the imperial family," she writes. "As one who loved the culture of the Heian imperial court from the time of her youth, Akiko naturally respected the imperial family" (25). While insisting that Akiko never intended to criticize the emperor, Yūri asserts that "the antiwar philosophy expressed in this poem and her hatred of military men and bureaucrats permeated her whole life" (23), and that "Akiko's abhorrence of feudalistic military men and bureaucrats continued for the rest of her life" (24). Clearly, such characterizations of Akiko's attitude toward war, in this and other studies after 1945, require reexamination in light of her complete oeuvre on this subject.

Unlike later postwar studies that also portray Akiko as one who opposed war and hated soldiers all her life, Yūri's biography, to its credit, does not entirely ignore poems Akiko published during the China and Pacific Wars. Her explications are highly selective, however, treating only certain lines that depict the sorrow of armed conflict and neglecting others that contradict her overall conclusions about Akiko's writing on war. She cites "Rosy-Cheeked Death" as "a poem lamenting the deaths of youthful Chinese soldiers at the time of the Shanghai Incident" (24–25) but fails to note that this work also praises the military superiority of "good neighbor Japan," a nation that, according to the poem, these "naive youths" have been "tricked" by "foolish" Chinese leaders into "resenting." In contrast, Yamamoto Fujie concedes that, "while at first glance this might be taken as an antiwar poem, on a second reading, one is troubled by these lines."[379] Of the poems Akiko wrote at the start of the Pacific War, Yūri mentions only the one quoted below, on future reconciliation, and ignores those couched in popular wartime slogans that lauded the strength of the Imperial Forces and exhorted Akiko's own son to battle:

ikusa no ato ni	When the war is over
taisetsu na no wa	everyone knows that

ai no kokoro to	what is important
dare mo shiru	is love in people's hearts.[380]

Yūri writes that "during the Pacific War not one person had the courage to speak out honestly [with the] antiwar philosophy Akiko expressed in 'Kimi.'" Higuchi Chiyoko also mentions World War II, quoting from Akiko's 1918 essays in which she denounced militarism as "barbarian thinking" and urged Japanese women to "eradicate it." Higuchi adds: "Akiko's words are equally applicable to our time. Her foresight evokes all the more admiration when we consider that these words were written twenty-five years before 'barbarian thinking' erupted into the disaster of World War II."[381]

Like Yūri's 1948 book, which promotes democracy and denounces feudalism, Higuchi's biography is written within the context of contemporary currents of thought in Japan, in this case from the early 1970s. It reflects the continuing advocacy of reducing armed conflict and, as its title suggests, renewed concern for the status of women. Thus, Higuchi understandably focuses on Akiko's writings that opposed war and the oppression of women, choosing to discuss her poems and essays that set important precedents for later writers and activists. Still, one wonders if, by dealing with the change in Akiko's writing on war after 1928, Higuchi might have shown how vulnerable such reformist ideas can be in the face of relentless official and popular pressures and, at the same time, given her readers a more accurate portrait of her subject. The same might also be said of the vast majority of postwar studies and biographies that deal at length with "Kimi" and its repercussions but that entirely ignore Akiko's later writings on war.

As already noted, there has been no shortage of postwar translations and explications of "Kimi" inside and outside Japan. Seventeen years before Higuchi's book, Maruyama Masao (b. 1914) criticized the poem in 1956, much as Kuroshima Denji had in 1929, for being "not so much an indictment of war as a simple expression of attachment to the primary group."[382] Also sharing Kuroshima's view, at least in part, was Okamoto Jun (1901–78) who agreed in 1969 that its articulation "within the confining petit-bourgeois outlook is a weak point." Okamoto did not hesitate to classify this poem as antiwar and chose the more inflammatory reading of the most controversial stanza, asserting that "it expresses sarcasm toward the emperor."[383] In a sweeping rejection, Katō Shūichi (b. 1919) dismisses whatever antiwar ideas "Kimi" might contain as invalid and unrealistic, criticizing it in 1963 as "sentimental pacifism":

> Compared with her brother's life, she wrote, it was not at all important whether Port Arthur fell or not. Of course, if Port Arthur had not fallen, Japan would have lost the war; if the war had been lost, there would have been no guarantee that the country would not have been occupied by Tsarist Russia. We do not know whether the poet was really prepared to accept all these possible results. She was against war, but she did not show any alternative to it.[384]

Among the mostly critical views of war in Japan since 1945, Katō expresses an ambivalence that has been especially conspicuous where Russia is concerned.[385] Maruyama, a leader in the movement against the U.S.-Japan Security Treaty, and Okamoto, a member of the Japan Communist Party, state opinions more closely associated with Marxist perspectives. Writing in 1976, Takenaga Yoshimasa agrees with Okamoto that Akiko criticizes the emperor in "Kimi," and calls this "an outrageous act [*taihen na koto*] for its time."[386] However, his overall evaluation of this work as "a genuine expression of what many Japanese women felt, [but] naive in its conception," sounds somewhat condescending.[387] Stating a similar view more respectfully, Kumasaka Taiko cautions readers that "Kimi" is an expression of one individual's hatred of war and love of family but "not an advocacy of individualism as a universal concept."[388]

Yano Hōjin writes in 1973 that, while Akiko's sentiments fell within the traditional pattern of a woman's concern for her family, she expressed them with a "modern boldness" that sets her apart from other poets of the time, both male and female. Yet Yano rejects the idea that "Kimi" is a pacifist or traitorous work, emphasizing that Akiko wrote it as a plea to her brother, which she had originally included in a letter to him. Yano calls Ōmachi Keigetsu's charges of treason "an overreaction," speculating that, if Keigetsu had printed his accusations in the West, Akiko could have sued him for libel.[389] Like Yano, Itsumi Kumi initially downplays philosophical implications in this poem, noting in 1969 that Akiko did not write her essays opposing war and militarism until fourteen years following its publication, after she had returned from a trip to Europe.[390] However, in 1975 when "women's liberation" (*josei kaihō*) was a recurring topic in the Japanese media, the same author credited this poem with "historical significance [for] planting the seeds of women's liberation in Japan [by] rejecting a submissive female role. . . . Akiko courageously affirms her love for Chūzaburō [and] her hatred of war."[391]

Considering the varied and sometimes contradictory explications of "Kimi" since 1945, one wonders how Akiko herself might have responded to postwar evaluations of it, especially to those that have been critical.

When reproached for writing "within the confining petit-bourgeois outlook," would she reply, as she did to Ōmachi Keigetsu's attack in 1905, that she was only expressing the feelings of women in Japan with loved ones at the front? Or would she defend "Kimi" in the context of her mid-Taishō essays that opposed war and militarism? How would she comment on the government's banning of "Kimi" during the Pacific War, especially in view of what she wrote herself about this conflict? What would she have to say, if anything, about the transformation in her writing on war after 1928? Would she explain, as Yamamoto Fujie speculated, that she considered the situation of her son heading for the Pacific War to be different from that of her brother at the (second) Battle of Port Arthur? Or, like poets Saitō Mokichi and Takamura Kōtarō, would she openly express regret for publishing poems that might have inspired young men to go to their deaths in a tragically misguided cause? Finally, how would she respond to the popularity of "Kimi" in recent years, and to portrayals of her in biographies since 1945 as a lifelong pacifist? If such questions are unanswerable, one hopes that asking them hypothetically can serve to caution future literary critics and biographers overly eager to portray a poet's life and work as a consistent expression of one particular philosophy or another, however widely such philosophy might be espoused and admired at the time.

6 Shimazaki Tōson: Internal Conflicts

Poet and novelist Shimazaki Tōson (1872–1943) depicted four wars in which Japan was involved during his long and prolific career. Unlike his friend, novelist Tayama Katai, Tōson never served in the military abroad or witnessed combat. However, he described the impact on Japan of conflicts with China (1894–95) and Russia (1904–5), penned firsthand accounts of hardships experienced during World War I by Europeans and resident Japanese in France, where he lived between 1913 and 1916, and wrote about the Pacific War. His writing on war includes fiction, prose reminiscences, and an extended narrative poem, "Nōfu" (The farmer, 1898), a work that has inspired literary critics in recent years to identify him as one of the first Japanese writers after the Meiji Restoration to express opposition to war by publishing antiwar poetry (*hansenshi*).[392] In this chapter I will discuss these works and the literary criticism in Japan that presents them as examples of antiwar literature.

Tōson was still distinguishing himself as a highly successful poet when he published the story "Utatane" (Restless sleep), set mostly during the Sino-Japanese War, in the November 1897 edition of the magazine *Shinshōsetsu* (New fiction). Although he had called this work an experiment, he was stung by scathing reviews and did not publish fiction again for four years.[393] While criticized for flaws in description and characterization, the story seems to have drawn its severest condemnation from those who strongly disapproved of its depiction of the sufferings and sacrifices of war.

Most of the narrative centers on Anegawa Koichi, the illness- and failure-prone son of Okuni and her husband, a career army officer who had been adopted into the family as a *yōshi*. Chapter one opens with the family at a performance of the Kabuki play "Ichinotani futaba gunki," based on a famous episode from *Heike monogatari*.[394] During a climactic scene when the Genji warrior Kumagai is poised with his sword to behead his own son, disguised as a Heike soldier, Major Anegawa looks on impassively while the women and Koichi are moved to tears. Later, as the play closes with Kumagai left alone on the *hanamichi,* overcome with grief for his son, Koichi cries again. This time he is scolded by his parents for this "unmanly" show of emotion, and he leaves the theater dejectedly for home.

Soon after this incident Koichi's long series of troubles begins. He fails in school and then runs away from the wholesaler in Yokohama where he has been contracted to work. For three years thereafter his family hears nothing from him until one day he suddenly returns home. He is sharply reprimanded by his father, now a lieutenant colonel, who urges Koichi to volunteer for the army despite the boy's chronic illnesses and fragile disposition. Even Okuni expresses doubts about her son's suitability for military life. Tōson consistently portrays him as highly sensitive and "womanlike," qualities that his father, with his stern military bearing, views as weaknesses in Koichi's character.[395]

Joining the army into which he might soon have been drafted anyway, Koichi manages to muddle through his training and, with the outbreak of hostilities, is ordered with his unit to Hiroshima for embarkation to China. Tōson dwells at length on Koichi's departure from Shinbashi Station in Tokyo, the first of many parting-for-war scenes he was to depict in his writing.[396] In this instance Okuni, crying inconsolably, nearly falls from the rickshaw she rides to the station. On his way to the front Koichi discovers that his best friend Tome, another contracted worker who had run away from the Yokohama hardware store, just happens to have been assigned to the same unit. It is one of the many coincidences and chance meetings Tōson sprinkles throughout the story. During the grueling passage aboard the troopship,[397] Tome is weakened by severe seasickness and dies shortly after their arrival in China. Now, for friendless Koichi, things go quickly from bad to worse.

His unit is ordered out on a dangerous forward patrol near Chinchou fortress. Before leaving, all the soldiers including Koichi pledge their willingness to die, but once underway he panics at the prospect of combat. He deserts his platoon as they pass the sentry line and runs off to hide in a field of withered reeds. When he crawls out three hours later, he feels acutely ashamed of himself for this and his past misdeeds and realizes he will probably be killed whether captured by enemy or "friendly" forces. He comes across a Chinese prisoner of war who has been tied to a tree. Feeling rather like a prisoner himself, Koichi strongly empathizes with this young man despite being unable to speak his language. He unties him and even gives him money before urging him, through hand signals, to run away.

Inevitably, Koichi is captured by his battalion, which, as the reader now learns, just happens to be commanded by his father.[398] The scene in which Colonel Anegawa, outwardly calm, shoots his son for desertion in front of the other soldiers is described from the viewpoint of Sankichi, a horrified former schoolmate of Koichi's who just happens to have been assigned as a military transport worker to this same battalion.[399] The narrative concentrates on the kind of tortured internal conflict that Tōson was to portray often thereafter in his writing on war:

> Sankichi watched Colonel Anegawa lift his rifle and aim it at Koichi. The colonel's face betrayed no hint of emotion, and his hands remained steady as he stood still and straight, his weapon poised. . . . Yet what pain he must have felt in his heart, what anguish! . . . When the gun fired with a sharp crack, the crowd surged forward. Sankichi stumbled after them, but by the time he got close enough to see, Colonel Anegawa had already gone. One soldier remained, swabbing the colonel's rifle with a piece of oilcloth.[400]

Now the viewpoint shifts to Colonel Anegawa and the conflict raging inside him. Although convinced he has performed his inescapable duty, he is deeply grieved at the death of his son, whom he sees in his dreams and as a ghost in his tortured imagination. The usually stoic colonel is even depicted seeking solace with his beloved horse, crying with his face buried in the animal's mane. Unable to escape his grief, Anegawa now throws himself into the heaviest fighting at the Battle of Itsu-shan, hoping that death in a clash of arms will spare him the further anguish of conflicting emotions. He suffers only a minor wound in the battle, however, and even when he is honored later during a victory parade after his return to Tokyo, he marches with "a sunburned face clouded by grief."[401]

The story's sorrowful conclusion is set in the Anegawa home following the victory parade. It is now revealed that Okuni suspects her husband of having lied about what happened at the front. She believes that the colonel, an adopted husband, has plotted to kill their son and her so he can seize all the family property for himself. Moaning that she cannot bear to live with such a man any longer, she reaches for a teapot containing water laced with arsenic as her husband comes into the room unexpectedly. His throat dry after drinking much sake, he demands "some water or tea." She drinks first "with a cold smile," then he snatches the cup from her and gulps down the remaining contents.[402] The couple soon die in an agony of vomiting and diarrhea, and in the story's final scene the three coffins of Koichi and his parents are carried from the house in a somber funeral procession.

For Tōson undoubtedly the most disheartening review of this work was coauthored by the prominent novelist Mori Ōgai (1862–1922) and published in the December 1897 issue of the literary magazine *Mezamashigusa* (The grasses of awakening), edited by Ōgai.[403] This review criticizes the numerous coincidences and chance meetings that set up dramatic confrontations in the story as more appropriate to old-fashioned storyplays than to contemporary fiction. It then proceeds to attack Tōson's characterizations as inconsistent or bizarre, his dialogue as unnatural, and much of his background description as inaccurate or unconvincing. It is not surprising that criticism in this review should focus particularly on Tōson's portrayals of the Sino-Japanese War and military life, considering that Ōgai served during the conflicts with China and Russia as a physician-officer in the medical corps and was promoted in 1907 to Surgeon General, the highest rank a doctor could attain in the Imperial Japanese Army.

But the review goes beyond objecting to inaccuracies in descriptions of military equipment, organization, and procedures to denounce such episodes as Okuni's near fall from the rickshaw on her way to Shinbashi Station, which the critics deem "no way to behave" for a Japanese mother sending her son off to war. Singled out for special condemnation is the scene in which Koichi releases the captured Chinese soldier, even giving him money to aid his escape. This episode is called unintentionally comical because, for one thing, according to Ōgai and the others, no prisoner of war would ever be left unguarded, tied to a tree. The reviewers wax their most sarcastic in berating Tōson for concocting this incident in his story to promote the dogmas (*daishisō*) of "cosmopolitanism" and "humanity," both words printed conspicuously and condescendingly in English.[404]

Recalling Mori Ōgai's stated determination to "strive for objectivity" in his own fiction that drew on historical events,[405] it is understandable that this review would criticize "Restless Sleep" for relying on chance meetings to move the narrative and such melodramatic effects as weather conditions that always seem to fit the mood of a particular scene. All the battles are fought after dark clouds have gathered, and Colonel Anegawa executes Koichi under a stormy sky. Moreover, descriptions of military life and the conflict itself lack a certain authenticity, reading rather like isolated lists of particulars such as gun smoke and trumpet calls. These could have been gleaned from newspaper articles that were themselves often more fancy than fact because reporters' movements were severely restricted at the front and their dispatches heavily censored by the Imperial Army (see chapter one, p. 27). In contrast, portrayals of departure scenes and victory celebrations in "Restless Sleep" are more convincing, perhaps because Tōson witnessed them firsthand.

Yet elements of fantasy condemned in this review as "old-fashioned" tend to enhance, rather than diminish, the evocative power of the story. Besides uncannily timed meetings and cloud formations, Tōson includes apparitions of the dead as well as the portentous performance of "Ichinotani" in chapter one. Although dismissed by the reviewers as artificial and unrealistic, such effects function at several points in "Restless Sleep" to heighten the dramatic intensity of events and sharpen the portrayal of characters' emotions in what is, after all, a work of fiction.[406] Moreover, the complaint that the story was written to promote particular dogmas seems misdirected. While Ōgai advocated a "literature of ideas,"[407] Tōson's poetry and fiction are virtually devoid of the author's political and philosophical pronouncements, concentrating rather on the depiction of internal conflicts that beset people under stress. On this point, one suspects that, as a career military officer at a time when Japan was celebrating battlefield triumphs in a purportedly "just war," Ōgai overreacted to a story that dwells on the individual suffering caused by armed conflict and portrays military men and their missions in this context. The period when this review appeared was also a time when intellectual and popular opinion in Japan was reacting strongly against currents of Western influence that had swept the nation during the earlier Meiji era and against the Triple Intervention of Russia, Germany, and France, which prevented Japan from acquiring the Liaotung Peninsula.

As noted above, more recent literary criticism in Japan also has focused on Tōson's depictions of war in his writing. The difference is that, since the end of World War II, his work has been praised for bearing the same kind of philosophical messages that Ōgai's review denounces. In recent years, Tōson's extended narrative poem "Nōfu" has been presented in excerpts at the beginning of anthologies, alongside "Senshisotsu" by Takeshima Hagoromo and "Ensentō" by Miyazaki Koshoshi, as one of the earliest examples of poetry opposing war to be composed in the "new-style verse form" (*shintaishi*) developed in the 1880s.[408] Like "Restless Sleep," these three works depicted events during the Sino-Japanese War and appeared in the decade before Yosano Akiko published her now much-celebrated *shintaishi* "Brother, Do Not Give Your Life" (see chapter five). Although it lacks the emotional intensity of either Akiko's "Brother, Do

Not Give Your Life" or Hagoromo's "A Fallen Soldier," Koshoshi's "Weary of War" has already been noted for its more explicit expression of pacifist philosophy, stated against a background of the bellicose fervor sweeping Japan during the Sino-Japanese War (see chapter three, p. 88):

Kachinu makenu to yo no naka no, nonoshiri-sawagu koe kiku wa, kozue o harau akikaze no, otozure yori mo nao tsurashi. Waga yo tanoshimu tami no tame, ikusa o yamuru sube araba.	The voices I hear all around us shouting of victory and defeat disturb me far more than the sound of the autumn wind blowing through the treetops. If only there were a way to abolish war for the sake of people who merely seek some happiness in their lives.
Mono-sawagashiki kono koro wa, sabishiki nobe mo kai arazu. Ashima o wataru kaze ni sae, odorokasaruru waga kokoro.	In this time of boisterousness, a lonely field gives no relief. Even the wind sweeping through the reeds stirs fear in my heart.[409]

In contrast, Japanese critics' recent inclusion of "The Farmer" in anthologies of poems identified as antiwar and the resulting portrayal of Tōson as a pioneer of modern antiwar literature in Japan are based, I believe, on a highly selective interpretation that has led to a mislabeling of this pivotal work. Such explication seems less concerned with analyzing a work of literature on its own terms than with reinterpreting literary history. During the years since World War II a number of literary critics and historians in Japan have sought evidence of opposition among Japanese writers before 1945 both to government policies of military expansion abroad and to popular opinion supporting these policies at home.[410]

To be sure, the term "antiwar literature," which has been applied in recent years to many works in many countries, eludes easy definition. Perhaps some of its clearest examples, discussed above, are such expository essays as Leo Tolstoy's *Bethink Yourselves!*, published at the height of the Russo-Japanese War, which expresses seething outrage at the "needless" resort to arms by the governments of Russia and Japan and unequivocally condemns all wars as "the universal stupefaction and brutalization of men."[411] In Japan, Kōtoku Shūsui courageously published essays vigorously opposing war and militarism following the dispatch of Japanese troops to China during the Boxer Rebellion of 1900,[412] as well as articles declaring "absolute opposition to war" shortly before and *even after* the outbreak of hostilities with Russia in February 1904.[413] Uchimura Kanzō, who openly converted to pacifism after initially supporting Japan's war against China in 1894–95, published a newspaper article in June 1903, when hostilities against Russia loomed, entitled "For the Abolishment of War," in which he denounced armed conflict as "nothing but an enormous crime."[414] Furthermore, as noted above, no country can claim a writer who expressed pacifist philosophy more fervently or consistently in his poetry and prose than Kinoshita Naoe (see chapter four). On March 25, 1904, six weeks after war was declared against Russia, Naoe wrote in *Mainichi shinbun* that "the loyalty and patriotism reporters now extol are nothing but cheap demagoguery and cannot be called true love of country." His *Pillar of Fire*, perhaps modern Japan's preeminent antiwar novel, is filled with statements by its protagonist denouncing the conflict with Russia as "a war between two governments each as tyrannical, as barbarous as the other. . . . The Emperor's name is invoked to justify every kind of crime."[415]

Applying the term "antiwar" becomes more problematic, however, when works of literature depict the death and suffering of armed conflict without criticizing a particular war or wars in general. Tōson movingly portrays war's devastating effects in "Restless Sleep" and in later works of prose, but he also acknowledges, in some of them, a necessity and inevitability for certain wars. Recent critics identify "The Farmer" as a trailblazing example of modern Japanese antiwar poetry and cite it to characterize Tōson as an author of antiwar literature. Yet this work, unlike "Weary of War," does not present a consistent viewpoint opposing armed conflict. Though labeled and anthologized as antiwar, it seems out of place among poems explicitly denouncing war that can be found even in the works of such writers as Yosano Tekkan and Mushanokōji Saneatsu,[416] who are better known for what they wrote at other times in support of Japan's military expansion. The problem is that, read as a whole, "The Farmer" is not a poem against war, even if it does portray a young draftee whose reluctance to report for induction sets him at odds with his parents. Nor is war a central concern in any of Tōson's other published poetry, though he describes its effects more extensively in his prose.

Known today more for the novels he produced after 1901, Tōson was a prime mover in the development of new verse forms in the Meiji period. His poems from the 1880s and 1890s, written in *shintaishi* and classical language, utilize rhetorical techniques and stanza structures from English poetry, along with allusions to English as well as classical Japanese literature. The results are more successful than Miyazaki Koshoshi's earlier odes to rural life, which are believed to have influenced Tōson, because Tōson's poems achieve greater emotional intensity and euphonious flow, particularly through the use of imagery from the natural environment and special auditory effects. If Koshoshi pioneered modern Japanese lyric poetry, Tōson refined it and, at the same time, made it appealing to a wider audience. Tōson's poetry is especially pleasing to the ear, and, although he borrowed on occasion from Western verse, he avoided the jarring foreign words that were used (and not infrequently misused) by early Meiji poets who wanted to sound "modern." The enduring popularity of Tōson's poetry is also due to the fact that the emotion he most often evoked was love. Love poems from *Wakana-shū* (Seedlings, 1897), perhaps his best-known collection, are still memorized regularly by young Japanese and have appeared abroad in several translations.[417]

The love between the young draftee and his fiancée that makes his departure for the front particularly anguishing is central to "The Farmer." This poem's length, probing characterizations, and dramatic structure mark it as a transitional work, which Tōson wrote at a time when he was moving away from lyric poetry and the fantasy-filled prose of "Restless Sleep" toward what is called "naturalist fiction" (*shizenshugi shōsetsu*) in Japan. Although it took many forms, Japanese naturalism is usually associated with meticulous evocations of daily life and psychological characterizations that are often rendered closely from events and personages in the authors' own lives.[418] In many instances naturalist fiction describes the impact on people in early twentieth-century Japan of such issues as war, poverty, disruption caused by rapid social change, sexual relationships outside marriage, and the anachronistically confining influences of the traditional family system. Tōson's novels after 1901 are often set in the context of such concerns, but, like "Restless Sleep," his later works concentrate on the internal conflicts within individual characters rather than the broad social implications of a particular situation.[419] "The Farmer" contains no such plea as Koshoshi's for war's abolishment, yet recent critics argue that Tōson has written a work opposing war by depicting the effects of the Sino-Japanese War on people in rural Japan.

The case for "The Farmer" as a poem against war relies heavily on information about the prevailing climate of public opinion in Japan and assumptions about what was going on in the poet's mind at the time of its writing. Critics who make this case emphasize that "The Farmer" was composed when the country was caught up in bellicose enthusiasm. Murata Masao asserts that it is especially significant as a "trailblazing" poem because it appeared when Japan was celebrating victory in a purportedly "just war."[420] Citing Tōson's recollection some thirty years later of "this time when the war seemed to be all around us," Itō Shinkichi concludes that "for Tōson, the Sino-Japanese War was a profound shock, leading him soon thereafter to a skepticism toward war." Itō notes that the poem depicts (1) a young man telling his parents he is reluctant to go to the front; (2) an emotional scene of parting between the man and his fiancée; and

(3) his postwar arrival back in his village, where he learns that tragedy has struck in his absence, a situation sharply contrasting with the triumphal returns and wild victory celebrations that were daily fare in the Japanese press. Yet these are not the only events portrayed in "The Farmer," and its overall concern is less with denouncing war than with exploring what Itō identifies as a secondary theme of this work: another kind of conflict that pits the desires and convictions of the individual against familial obligations and social pressures.[421] Tōson was to examine such conflicts, mostly as the internal struggles of his protagonists, repeatedly in the fiction he wrote after the turn of the century.

The efforts of such critics as Itō and Murata to present "The Farmer" as a poem against war reflect a tendency to rely too much at times on information about writers' lives when explicating their work. Considering certain aspects of Tōson's life, one can appreciate why this approach would seem especially attractive to those seeking to portray him as a writer of antiwar literature. As mentioned earlier, Tōson published prose reminiscences of both the Russo-Japanese War's impact on Japan and the disruption he witnessed with the outbreak of World War I in Europe. Moreover, his education and early literary associations might well have led him to advocate pacifism in his writing with references to Christianity and Western philosophy of the kind favored by Kinoshita Naoe and Miyazaki Koshoshi. Like them, he was trained in both, having been educated from 1887 to 1891 at Meiji Gakuin, a liberal arts college run by Presbyterian missionaries from Scotland and the United States. He was baptized in 1888 by Kimura Kumaji, a prominent Japanese Christian in whose house Tōson boarded as a student. At Meiji Gakuin he came to know and admire Christian-pacifist writer Kitamura Tōkoku (1868–94), who had a profound influence on many younger poets and novelists in the Meiji period. During his brief stint as a teacher at Meiji Women's College after graduation, Tōson preached to his students Tōkoku's spiritual ideals about love.[422]

Yet Tōson never embraced Christianity to the extent that Kinoshita, Tōkoku, or Koshoshi did, and his writing draws far more from literary texts in the West, particularly England, than from Western philosophy or religion.[423] Insofar as references to religion are found in "The Farmer," they are to the transience of worldly existence and the cycle of birth, death, and rebirth associated with Buddhism,[424] and not to the New Testament or to the God invoked by Koshoshi in "Overlooking My Hometown from Tashiro Hill," another of his poems condemning war.

Ana utate kami no tsukuri shi	How it saddens me!
hito wa mina onajiki mono o,	Created by God, all people are one.

kotonareru mono ni omoite,	Yet, thinking they are different,
hima naku zo hito wa arasou.	they fight on without respite.[425]

The religious figure of a Buddhist priest is included among the five central personae of "The Farmer," which is presented almost entirely as dialogues between the protagonist and his father, his mother, his fiancée, and the priest. Each dialogue takes place in a designated setting, such as a forest or a path between rice fields. These scenes serve to divide this extremely long poem of 870 lines into seven numbered sections, a form that also suggests that "The Farmer" represents a transition in Tōson's writing between poetry and fiction. Despite its length, Tōson maintains a *shintaishi* rhythm of lines with the seven-five syllable pattern throughout.

Even though the poem is presented as dialogues, what the speakers say is in noncolloquial classical language. Tōson preferred classical Japanese for poetry and did not join the tentative experiments begun by some Japanese poets at the end of the nineteenth century in the use of modern spoken language. This might have been a problem if he were seeking to convey the effect of contemporary conversations here as he did later in his fiction. Clearly he is not, and, although this poem is set in the Japan of 1894–95, its language enhances the timeless and universal quality of the farmer's dilemma and permits Tōson to insert references to classical Japanese poetry on war directly into the text of these poetic dialogues. British poet Wilfred Owen (1893–1918) achieves a similar effect by giving Latin titles to poems he wrote about men in combat during World War I.[426] Through Tōson's use of classical language and literary allusions, the personae in "The Farmer" seem to speak to the reader as well as to each other.

As a preface to "The Farmer" Tōson quotes from the first chapter of *Kōka shunjū* (Farming life), a didactic essay written in 1707 by agronomist Tsuchiya Matasaburō (1642–1719) and reprinted as a kind of farmers' almanac of practical homilies during the early Meiji era. Tsuchiya speaks in this section of the responsibilities, hardships, and rewards of farming. He warns that pleasures are few and the chores demanding, and emphasizes that "a good farmer works in harmony with what nature provides."[427] Tōson's poetry then opens with a brief introductory section (*jo*) praising the lush beauty of the banks of the Tone River, where the poem is set, although a precise location such as a village is never specified. In this section Tōson presents stanzas of varying length spoken by three alternating but unidentified "voices." These first dialogues among off-stage narrators serve to evoke the setting and to introduce the protagonist. The natural surroundings of the banks of the Tone River are noted especially for their powers to inspire. In contrast, human struggles to fulfill high hopes are said to amount to little more than "the crawling of insects," while people's joys and sorrows are likened to "drifting sands" in this "transient world of life and death." The section concludes with the introduction of the farmer as a man of good lineage, literally "without bad seeds" (*iyashiki tane narazu*), who is devoted to the cultivation of his fields from morning until night (149–50).

The farmer's lineage becomes a point at issue in section one of the poem's main text, entitled "Along a Path through the Rice Fields." The dialogue in this scene is between the protagonist and his father, who starts by expressing incredulity that his son, a dedicated farmer with a proud samurai heritage, should be reluctant to go to war:

Kono Morokoshi no ikusa ni zo	To this war in China
Nare wa yukaji to nageki kemu	You will not go, you moan.
Sono kokorone o hakarishi ga	I have tried to understand your feelings,
Waga utagai wa tokezariki	But my doubts are not dispelled.
Ima koso wa kaku Tonegawa no	Now you stand deep in the grasses
Kishibe no kusa ni uzumorete	Along the Tone River's banks
Ashita ni hoshi no kage o fumi	To carry on this humble calling.
Yūbe ni fukaki tsuyu o wake	You shoulder the plow and hoe,
Suki to kuwa to o kata ni shite	Walking over patches of morning starlight
Iyashiki waza wa itonamedo	And through the thick evening dew.
Moto homare aru mononofu no	But your lineage springs from
Takaki nagare o kumeru mi zo	A noble current of honored soldiers past.
Sugureshi uma ni muchiuchite	My father drove a fine horse with his whip
Kaze ni mayumi ni hikinarashi	And made bows ring in the wind.
Mune ni afururu masurao no	Manly honor brimmed in his heart
Homare wa umi no waku ga goto	Like swelling ocean tides,
Nozomi wa kumo no yuku ga goto	And his aspirations stretched
Ooshikarikeru waga chichi mo	Like moving clouds.
Kusaba no kage no yume ni dani	Should he, too, overhear your words,
Na ga koto no ha o morekikaba	Even as he dreams
Ikani hageshiki kurenai no	Beneath the shadow of grass and leaves,
Chishio no namida nagasuramu	How bitterly he would shed crimson tears of blood!
Ge ni nare wa shi mo waga ie no	Is your heart so fearful of battle
Takaki homare o sutsuru made	That you would cast down
Yo no kotowari mo wakanu made	The high honor of your family
Ikusa o ozuru kokoro ka ya	And disregard the rules that people live by? (151)

In admonishing the farmer, his father cites the proud heritage of their family, descended from warriors, and inviolable codes of social conduct (*kotowari*) rather than emperor-centered nationalism or the purportedly just cause of the Sino-Japanese War that were frequently invoked during this conflict. He thus shows himself to be a man whose values are firmly rooted in pre-Meiji Japan. For him, reluctance to go to war can only be seen as cowardice. His son insists there is another reason, and their dialogue continues:

<table>
<tr><td>Osore ya wa suru yoshi ya ima
Kokoro o ubau ikazuchi no
Furuu ga gotoku ōzutsu no
Manako no mae ni todoroku mo
Ware wa shizuka ni kuwa torite
Toshitsuki nareshi Tonegawa no
Kishibe ni idete oda utamu
Mata wa nagaruru tama tobite
Mimi no hotori o kasumu tomo
Tanare no suki o kata ni shite
Yūbe no uta o utaitsutsu
Ito hiyayaka ni kuwa no ki no
Hakage o fumite kaeru beshi</td><td>You ask, am I afraid?
If even now the cannon should roar
   before my eyes
With thunder that robs the senses,
I would quietly hoe the soil,
Tilling the rice field
   on the Tone River's banks
That I have come to know so well
   as years have passed.
And even if streaming shells
Should sail past my ear,
I would stroll homeward,
My familiar plow on my shoulder,
Treading unperturbed
Through the shade of mulberry leaves,
Singing the song of evening.</td></tr>
<tr><td>*Chichi*
Shikaraba tōki ikusa ni wa
Nadoka ideshi to nagekuramu</td><td>*Father*
If that is so, then why do you complain
Of going to distant battle?</td></tr>
<tr><td>*Nōfu*
Nagekazarame ya tatakai to
Nabete o omou waga mi nari
Tsurugi o toru mo hata utsu mo
Fukaki kejime wa arazaramu</td><td>*Farmer*
How can I not complain.
For when I think of war,
All in all I find no profound difference
Between taking up the sword
   and tilling the field.</td></tr>
<tr><td>Ware toki to shite hatanaka ni
Te ni motsu kuwa o nagesutete
Tagayashi suru mo hata utsu mo
Tsuchi o kaesu mo kusagiru mo
Ase mo abura mo orokashiku
Umare idetaru ware hito no
Munashiki inochi hitohi yori
Futahi ni tsunagu tame ka to zo
Omoeba mi o mo wasuretsutsu
Tatazumu koto mo ari shi nari</td><td>Sometimes
I toss my hoe down in the field
And stand lost in thought.
How foolish it all seems—
Tilling and plowing,
Turning soil and cutting weeds—
All the sweat and grime
That only sustains from day to day
The empty lives
We lead from birth.</td></tr>
</table>

Makoto no sama o tazunureba	When I seek the true state of things,
Tatakai tote mo mata onaji	War seems to be the same.
Nozue no kusa ni nagareyuku	How senseless it is
Ikeru chishio ya ika naran	To spill life's blood
Tsurugi no shimo ni horobiyuku	on the grass of distant plains!
Hito no sadame ya ika naran	How senseless it is for men to meet
Tare ka hi ni iru mushi no goto	their fate on frosty swords!
Ikeru inochi o horobishite	He who would destroy his life
Adashi honoho ni mi o yaku no	Like an insect plunging into fire,
Oroka no waza o manabu beki	And burn in the evanescent flames,
Aa tsuwamono no miru yume no	Must learn that such deeds are foolish.
Hana ya hito-toki haru yukaba	Ah, soldiers' dreams are fleeting as flowers;
Tsurugi mo hone mo fukakusa no	When spring departs,
Aoki shigemi ni umoruran	Their swords and bones lie buried
Ge ni susamajiki tatakai no	In thickets of tall grass.
Ato ni mo mashite utsushi yo ni	There is nothing sadder
Iya kanashiki wa arajikashi	In this world
	Than the aftermath
	Of dreadful battle. (152–53)

Tōson uses repetition to good effect throughout this poem, and in this passage it helps particularly to communicate the protagonist's emotion. The farmer's contention, carrying strongly Buddhist overtones, that much of human endeavor is but a series of mundane acts with little meaning beyond survival is emphasized by repetition of the particle *mo* in the lines *tagayashi suru mo hata utsu mo / tsuchi o kaesu mo / ase mo abura mo orokashiku*. Similarly, the intensity of the farmer's feeling about lives lost in war is firmly conveyed by repetition of the phrase *ika naran*.

What the farmer says about war also reverberates with echoes from classical Japanese literature. In associating soldiers' fleeting dreams with grass, Tōson is almost certainly alluding to Matsuo Bashō's (1644–94) famous poem from *Oku no hosomichi* (Narrow road to the deep north, 1689):

Natsukusa ya	Summer grass—
Tsuwamono domo ga	All that remains
Yume no ato	Of soldiers' dreams.

Carl Sandburg (1878–1967) also evokes the inexorable growth of grass to convey how the memories of soldiers' sacrifices tend to fade over time:

Pile the bodies high at Austerlitz and Waterloo.
Shovel them under and let me work—
I am the grass; I cover all.

And pile them high at Gettysburg
And pile them high at Ypres and Verdun,
Shovel them under and let me work.
Two years, ten years, and passengers ask the conductor:
What place is this?
Where are we now?

I am the grass.
Let me work.[428]

Tōson's comparison of a soldier who "destroy[s] his life" in war to "an insect plunging into fire" also has precedents in classical Japanese literature, including *Heike monogatari,* which was his source for the central motif of "Restless Sleep." Posed in "The Farmer," this comparison especially recalls *renga* poet Shinkei's (1406–77) "Mujō" (Evanescence, 1468), composed during the Ōnin War (1467–77). Shinkei, a Buddhist priest who was forced to flee his home during the conflict, invokes Buddhism's warning against delusions provoked by such desires as those for power and fame:

Natsumushi no	More absurd even
Hi odoru yori mo	than the summer moth dancing
Mononofu no	toward the fire—
Michi o omou wa	the mind that is inflamed
Oroka naruran	with the warrior's way.[429]

Evoking such echoes from Japan's literary past in lines that resonate with Buddhist overtones, the farmer thus pronounces war to be the ultimate in pointless human endeavors. This reply to his father, the closest thing to an expression of pacifist convictions by any speaker in this long poem of dialogues, is presented in its entirety as one of the excerpts from "The Farmer" selected for the anthology *Nihon hansenshi-shū* (Japanese antiwar poetry).[430] Yet the poem does not end here. Unimpressed by what he hears as shameless sophistry, the farmer's father severely chides his son for taking an attitude that defiles what the older man holds sacred. The next portion of their dialogue is not included in *Nihon hansenshi-shū:*

Chichi	*Father*
Orokashi ya sono kurigoto Yume miru hito no iu koto zo	"Ah, how foolish" is What idle dreamers often mutter.
Nōfu	*Farmer*
Sanari ukiyo no arasoi wa Izure ka yume ni arazaran	Yes, and are not the quarrels of this floating world All as in a dream?

Chichi	*Father*
Aa na ga mimi wa shiitareba	Alas, since your ears are deaf,
Ikani sugureshi mononofu no	The bell that honors such brave soldiers
Homare no kane mo hibiki nashi	Does not ring for you.
Nare ga manako wa shiitareba	Since your eyes are blind,
Ikani makoto no tarachio no	The flowering essence
Kotoba no hana mo iro zo naki	Of your father's words, however true,
Karisome naranu yo no waza	Has no color for you.
Azakeriwarau koto no ha wa	Words that scorn
Sawayaka naru ni nitaredomo	The labors of a fleeting world may sound eloquent,
Nonoshirikuruu masurao no	But when I see brave men
Mi no yukusue o nagamureba	Whom you malign so frantically,
Mina ochibure to namida nomi	I cannot but shed tears for all their ruined lives.
Aa waga mune wa kurushimi to	Alas, my heart overflows
Haji to ikari ni afuretari	With anguish, shame, and rage!
Kanashi asamashi yo no hito ni	And if your words should be overheard
Na ga koto no ha no more mo seba	By the people of this sad and wretched age,
Tsumetaki ase wa ame no goto	How my cold sweat would flow like rain,
Ikani nagarete ware o hitasan	Drenching me to the core.[431]

Repetitions of the interjection *aa* and the exclamatory *ikani* convey the intense outrage of the father who denounces his son's attitude toward war as clever rhetoric defiling the honor of soldiers. He is especially appalled because, from his perspective as a samurai's son, his own son is ridiculing men of the proud but declining samurai families of pre-Meiji Japan who have fallen on even harder times since the Restoration with the elimination of their ranks, stipends, and privileges. The enactment of universal male conscription in 1873, which ended the samurai monopoly on military skills and hardware, presaging the abolishment of Japan's warrior class, has the effect here of widening the gap between father and son. The farmer's father regrets the passing of an age when practicing warfare was the privilege of a proud elite, while his son is loath to take up arms as now required of him by law.

Not that the law was always obeyed. The notion of Japanese youth monolithically and enthusiastically heeding the call to arms after 1873 is belied by the Army Ministry's own Meiji-era surveys. Thousands of cases were recorded in which young men forged names, lied about their ages or family circumstances, faked adoptions, feigned illnesses, physically mutilated themselves, and fled as far away as America.[432] Tōson never explains how the farmer planned to avoid the military service his father viewed as an honor, but the immense generation gap evident here, a by-product of rapidly changing values and institutions in Meiji Japan, is probed in depth elsewhere by Tōson and other Japanese writers of his time.[433] In Tōson's case critics have often noted similarities between fathers depicted in his writing and his own father Masaki, a village headman with a hereditary title who taught Confucian classics to local children including his own and sought to maintain a stern samurai atmosphere at home. Tōson described his father as a severe and unapproachable man with whom he tried to avoid contact.[434] Like many others who lost their hereditary appointments and status after the Restoration, Masaki was economically and emotionally devastated by this experience. For him this led to acute depression, insanity, confinement, and finally death in 1886, a situation closely paralleling the protagonist's ordeal in Tōson's late novel *Yoakemae* (Before the dawn, 1935). The father who bitterly deplores the plight of former samurai in "The Farmer" bears certain resemblances to Masaki at a time when his opposition to the Meiji government's policies moved him to write several memorials to the emperor. Still, Tōson could not have depended entirely on him as a model for a father outraged at his son's reluctance to serve in a war that occurred eight years after Masaki's death.

In this poem the farmer's father is not the only parent urging him to go to war. Their dialogue is followed immediately by section two, which is set "Along the Same Narrow Path." Now his mother takes over in trying to convince him to change his mind. She appeals first to his sense of filial and social obligation:

Haha	*Mother*
Kakute mo nagaki natsu no hi ni o	Why do you spend
Hitori omoi ni shizumitsutsu	These long summer days
Midori no kage ni tatazumite	Lost in thought this way,
Iku sono toki o hetsuru zo ya	Lingering alone in the shade of green leaves?
Yume na urami so na ga chichi no	Do not hate your father,
Omoi amari shi kurogane no	Unable to contain himself,
Kobushi no ato wa murasaki ni	Though his iron fist
Fukaki itami o nokosu tomo	Will surely leave pain deep in purple bruises.
So wa arasoi no ato to shimo	These scars from quarreling
Omoeba sakoso urami are	Seem bound to make you bitter.
Itami wa ikani natsu no hi no	But even if the pain rises
Hageshiki sama ni nitari tomo	Like a summer day's fierce heat,
Na ga tarachio no akijimo no	Take to heart your father's lesson,
Oshie no hodo o omomiyo	Harsh as the autumn frost.
Mada itokenaki mukashi yori	From the books
Konomeru mama ni fumi mo yomi	You've liked to read
Mono no aware mo kotowari mo	Since the time when you were small,
Arakata wa shiru na ga mi nari	You have come to know life's certain sorrow

Tare ka konomite umeru ko ni
Wazawai are to negau beki
Shinobigataki o shinobitsutsu
Tōki ikusa ni yukine kashi

And the rules that we must live by.
Who would wish a beloved child
to meet with harm? And yet,
Enduring what is hard to bear,
You must go to distant battle.[435]

Tactile images of pain and temperature accentuate the dilemma of the mother sympathizing with her son even as she sides with his father. Like her husband, she speaks of "the rules we must live by" (*kotowari*). The farmer seems unconvinced at first, insisting again that those who seek honor in war are pursuing an illusion:

Nōfu

Makoto ya ware wa masurao no
Homare o shiranu kokoro yori
Tōki ikusa ni idetatsu o
Nageku mono ni wa arajiki kashi

Aa waga mune wa utsusu beki
Kotoba mo shiranu kanashimi o
Yado seshi hi yori hiru mo yo mo
Fukaki omoi ni shizumitsutsu
Mayoeru mushi no mado ni kite
Kanata konata ni tobu ga goto
Ame to tsuchi to ni mayou mi no
Oroka o kakotsu hoka araji
Kono kanashimi no chibusa yori
Ware samazama no chie o nomi
Nigaki yo no aji mono no ura
Hito no makoto mo itsuwari mo
Ajiwau mi to wa nari shi nari
Kono kanashimi wa ayashiku mo
Ware o izanai michibikite
Ki wa yo o ōu masurao no
Takaki homare mo yume to mise
Matsuri no yoru no tomoshibi ni
Tawaruru hito o kage to mise
Kuraki utena no utsushie ni
Mono no katachi no utsuru goto
Yo no samazama o miseshimeki
Kono kanashimi wa waga mune no
Fukaki soko yori wakiagari
Tōki ikusa ni yuku beki o
Hanataji to koso todomu nare

Farmer

In truth it is not from disregard
For the honor of brave men
That I complain of going
To distant battle.

Alas, since the day I found in my heart
A sadness words cannot express,
I have been lost deep in thought day and night.
And, like an insect gone astray
That flies to the window
And drifts this way and that,
Wandering between heaven and earth,
I can only curse my stupid fate.
From the breast of sadness
I drank of wisdom in many forms,
And have tasted life's bitterness,
Learning from the underside of things
About truth and falsehood among people.
This sadness has shown me strangely
That the lofty honor among brave men
Whose energies adorn this world
Is nothing but a dream;
That those who frolic in the torchlight
On festival night are only shadows;
That the varied ways of this world
Are as figures projected on a magic-lantern screen
hung over a darkened stage.
And though I should go to distant battle,
This sadness that wells up
From the depths of my heart
Stays with me no matter how hard
I try to break its hold. (154–55)

While maintaining his convictions about the futility of war, at least to this point in the poem, the farmer has now come to acknowledge his military obligation. Having apparently made some progress by appealing to filial and social responsibilities, his mother turns next to more practical concerns as she reminds him of the consequences that would likely result from his continued reluctance. She begins again by sympathizing with him:

Haha	*Mother*
Ge ni shigarami no seki tomete	How well I have known
Nagare mo aenu tanikawa no	Sadness
Sono kanashimi no arakata mo	Rising like a dam
Ware wa toku yori shireru nari	That stops the flow of mountain streams.
Sabare kaku made iiharite	Yet if you persist this way,
Ikusa no tabi o itoinaba	Loath to go to war,
Sono akatsuki ya ika naramu	What will dawn bring for you?
Omou mo kurushi tsumibito to	How it hurts me to think of you
Na nimo yobarete asa yūbe	Called a criminal day and night,
Kuraki hitoya no mado ni yori	Gazing at the starlight
Hoshi no hikari o miru no hoka	From a dark prison window
Mi ni sou kage mo arazaran	Without even a shadow
. . . .	to keep you company. (155)
	. . . .

The next time the farmer speaks, some 120 lines later, he has already decided to go to the front. Presenting this poem as a series of dialogues, Tōson never tells why the farmer changed his mind. Readers accustomed to more explicit delineations of a character's motivation are left to speculate on whether he relented to follow "the rules we must live by," to avoid further conflict with his father, to spare himself the dire consequences mentioned by his mother, or for some other reason. The dialogue structure of the poem also precludes Tōson from inserting comments on the farmer's decision that might have indicated whether or not the poet approves of it. This raises another problem for those who maintain that "The Farmer" is a poem opposing war. As for the editors of *Nihon hansenshi-shū*, their selective presentation of this work has the effect of concealing these ambiguities. For their concluding excerpt they have chosen to reprint a portion of section three in which the farmer's fiancée laments his impending departure, but they have left out the couple's final parting exchange, which follows immediately in section four. As in the earlier dialogue between father and son, this interruption of the text again gives the impression that the poet has made a philosophical statement when, in fact, he has only presented one side of a conversation. The anthology reprints the following two stanzas from the seven that comprise the fiancée's part of the dialogue in section three with no indication that two other stanzas in between have been left out:

Asu wa ikusa no kadode nari Tōki ikusa no kadode nari Semete wakare no namida o ba Nagori ni sen to negau kana	Tomorrow you leave home for war, For distant battle you set out. I ask only for tears of parting As a token of farewell.
Mune no omoi wa tsumoredomo Fubuki hageshiki koi nareba Kimi ga hikari ni terasarete Kieba ya to koso uramu nare	Thoughts of you gather deep in my heart, And in the raging snowstorm of our love, I glow with your light. Should this light go out, how bitter I would be![436]

Itō Shinkichi writes that these lines, which conclude the portion of "The Farmer" presented in *Nihon hansenshi-shū*, are "noteworthy in the history of modern verse for expressing the sorrow many women have endured seeing their loved ones off to war."[437] That sorrow is expressed in these excerpts cannot be denied. Still, readers of this anthology might be surprised to discover that Tōson's poem does not end here. The farmer and his fiancée have more to say about his departure for the front when they meet "In a Grove," the setting of section four:

Nōfu	*Farmer*
. . . . Haya kawagishi no kanata nite Rappa no hibiki kikoyuru wa Fune no yosooi totonoite Yobu ni ya aran aa saraba Tōki ikusa ni idetachite Inochi sadamenu mi naredomo Ikusa no kami no mimegumi ni Ware mo homare wa agenamu o	. . . . Already, from beyond the river bank, I hear the trumpet sound. Does it call to let me know the boat is ready? Ah, if summoned, then to distant battle I will go. And, though my life be uncertain, With the war god's blessing, I too will hoist my honor high. . . . .

Musume	*Girl*
. . . .	. . . .
Saraba futatabi kaerikite	Then, until you return
Ikusagatari o nasan made	To tell the stories of war,
Kuni kotonareru haruaki no	Take care of yourself through the wind and rain
Ame to kaze to o itoite yo	Of unfamiliar seasons in a foreign land.
Tsurugi no kage mo shimo saete	Though the frost be chilling in the shadow of swords,
Ikusa no nobe wa samuku tomo	Though the field of battle be cold,
Kano homare aru tsuwamono no	Do not prove unequal
Takeki waza ni wa otori so yo	To the brave deeds of other honored soldiers.[438]
. . . .	. . . .

This scene of their final meeting shows the couple sadly resigned to the farmer's departure, dictated by circumstances beyond their control. The war's effect on them as individuals is movingly portrayed. However, were Tōson seeking to express through their situation a more generalized opposition to war, it seems strange that the protagonist would place his faith in "the war god's blessing" and that the woman he loves would exhort him to "brave deeds," sounding rather like his father in section one.

The farmer mentions his father in the next dialogue, set "In the Shade of Green Trees," which takes place two years later, shortly after his return from China. Speaking to a local Buddhist priest, he is eager to tell of his wartime experiences:

Nōfu	*Farmer*
. . . .	. . . .
Kinshū-jō no aki fukaku Kagari no kage no kuraki yo wa Roei no shimo no samusa yori Mata Isu-zan no tatakai no Tama no arare no tabashirite Teru hi mo kuraki sama made o Waga natsukashiki furusato no Hito ni tsugenaba ikanaramu	From the chilling frost of bivouac At Chin-chou fortress in late autumn Where the night seemed darkest in the campfire's shadows, To the hail of bullets at the Battle of Itsu-shan Where even the shining sun went dark, I must tell it all To the people of my beloved village.
Yugao shiroki hanakage ni Iwai no sake o kumamu toki Kokoro ooshiki waga chichi wa Ikani manako o kiramekashi Shirakami nagaki waga oji wa Ikani mimi o ba sobadatete Waga toki izuru futatose no Ikusagatari o kiku naramu	My stouthearted father— How his eyes will sparkle As he drinks the wine of celebration In the shade of moonflowers! And my uncle with his long white hair— How his ears will prick up When he listens to my war stories of these past two years! (162)

Discussion of the recent conflict in China ends here as the protagonist looks forward to impressing family and friends with his war stories, his anticipation highlighted by the repetition of *ikani*. The mood of the poem changes abruptly a few lines later when the farmer learns from the priest that his fiancée has died of illness while he was away at the battlefront. There is, to be sure, a sorrowful irony in her death because she had feared the farmer would be killed in China. Still, it is difficult to find "antiwar significance" in this situation. The final three sections of the poem describe how the farmer considers seeking relief from despondency by becoming a wandering priest or even in death. Fortunately, he is able to overcome his grief by following the example of the girl's father, who has taken comfort in devotion to his job as a blacksmith. The farmer goes back to work in the fields, where he finds solace and renewed inspiration in the natural scenery of his "old home on the banks of the Tone River" (171–72).

Thus, the poem ends where it began, honoring the occupation of farming and praising the beauties of the Tone River landscape. The farmer's experience as a reluctant conscript sent to war remains largely undescribed and unexamined. Tōson seems far more concerned here, as in his later novels set against a background of troubles engendered in twentieth-century Japan by the traditional family system and lingering class distinctions, with probing the emotions of individuals under stress than with making philosophical or political statements. Though they may be well-intentioned, recent efforts by critics to create the impression of an antiwar poem by means of selective presentation distort Tōson's work just as surely as the deletions made during World War II by government censors, who sought to achieve the opposite effect by expurgating descriptions of extreme suffering, ruthless acts of Japanese soldiers, and war weariness from literature about the Sino-Japanese and Russo-Japanese Wars, while leaving references to patriotism and battlefield valor intact (see chapter three, p. 82, and conclusion, pp. 213–14).

After "The Farmer," Tōson went on to write about war and its aftermath, both in his prose reminiscences and his fiction. Poet and critic Okamoto Jun has even suggested that Tōson's decision to concentrate full-time on fiction after 1901 grew out of a desire to depict war more "realistically" than he could in his hitherto preferred medium of lyric poetry:

> Tōson's "The Farmer" is . . . as one might expect, elegiac and lyrical. However, when this lyric poet, best-known for his collection *Seedlings*, turned his attention to the relentless reality of war, he found that he could not describe it through his

accustomed lyricism. This can be seen as one motivation for his switching to fiction.[439]

Others have explained Tōson's shift to fiction as motivated less by artistic than economic concerns—that is, the need to support a growing family by selling short stories to magazines that paid him more than he could possibly earn from his poetry, even with its popularity among younger Japanese.[440] Whatever his reasons for changing his medium, Tōson's prose after 1901 contains several detailed descriptions of war's effects, particularly on his own career and personal life. A passage from his 1908 novel *Haru* (Spring) tells of the crowds that gathered in front of print shops in Japan during the Sino-Japanese War to look at *nishiki-e* paintings of the conflict that were often grotesquely insulting to Chinese:

> When he reached Fushimi-chō, there was a crowd of men and women before a print shop. Everybody was struggling to get a better look at the blood-thirsty war pictures. "On to Peking! On to Peking!" the eyes of the passersby seemed to say.[441]

In the preface to his first book of short stories, *Ryokuyō-shū* (Green leaf collection, 1907), Tōson again described the sad departures of young men for the front, this time from his recent memories of the conflict with Russia. Tōson had left Tokyo five years before the start of the Russo-Japanese War and was living with his wife and three daughters in Komoro, a small town in the Japan Alps some one hundred miles northwest of Tokyo. He taught English at a local school and grew vegetables, trying to make ends meet while he concentrated on his writing. From his account in *Green Leaf*'s preface, the war appears to have indirectly influenced his decision to begin his first novel, *Hakai* (The broken commandment, 1906), though this work deals not with war, but with the ordeal of its Burakumin protagonist, who decides to reveal his pariah-class origins and stop passing as an ordinary Japanese:

> After the Russo-Japanese War started, many of my acquaintances were drafted. Several of my fellow teachers left for military service, and two or three young men among my former students also went to the front. As a country schoolteacher, I often traveled to Komoro Station to see off people who were leaving for the war, and I witnessed many sorrowful partings of soldiers from their families. From my distant mountain retreat, I heard of friends in Tokyo who planned to observe the fighting, and I thought that I too would like to take my pen to the front. In the end I could not realize my ambition. As a result, I began the manuscript

> of *The Broken Commandment.* It occurred to me that life is a vast war, and that writers are simply war correspondents. I was comforted in the thought that I was performing the same service writing a novel as were my friends in the faraway fields of Manchuria.[442]

Critic and historian Ara Masahito (1913–79) maintained that this passage shows the influence on Tōson of opposition to war with Russia that was expressed in print by writers associated with the *Heimin shinbun* newspaper until its publication was suspended under government pressure in early 1905.[443] Tōson might have admired the Heiminsha authors, but his concluding remarks above can hardly support claims for him as an antiwar writer. As Ara conceded, Tōson states here a strict naturalist view, current in Japan at the time, of a writer as someone whose primary mission is to observe and record with cool precision.[444] Still, if he takes no explicit stand against the war with Russia as the Heiminsha writers did, Tōson later published highly personalized descriptions of its effects that go far beyond detached observations. In reminiscences of the years 1904–5, he elaborates further on conditions in Japan during the conflict and their impact on his own life:

> The endless rumors about the war that were everywhere, the almost daily shouts of "extra" by passing vendors—because of such things I could not quiet my heart even while staying in our thatched-roof house behind the Komoro riding grounds. One day a former student came to say good-bye before entering the army. The next day I went to Komoro Station to see off a close friend, our gym teacher, who had been drafted. I returned home with those sad and hearty shouts of men who risked their lives still ringing in my ears. What I saw of the war outside our house made it difficult to find the tranquility I needed to immerse myself in my writing. The longer the war lasted the more the town around us seemed gripped in an eerie stillness that disturbed me even more than the frenzy and confusion when the fighting started. The war's far-reaching effects invaded deep into our everyday lives, and I felt them acutely. I cannot forget that winter [of 1904–5] when I pressed on with the manuscript of *The Broken Commandment* in our thatched-roof house behind the riding grounds. . . . By now I had come to understand keenly the misery of war.[445]

Literary critics seeking to portray Tōson as a pioneer of modern antiwar literature in Japan quote at length from these recollections of the conflict with Russia. Yet, for some reason, they virtually ignore his fiction, which included a story depicting the psychological damage to a young man recently returned from the Russo-Japanese front. The ironically titled "Heiwa no hi" (Day of peace), first published in the August 1911 issue of the magazine *Taiyō,* is told from the viewpoint of Maki, who witnessed considerable death and destruction while serving in the field with the Imperial Army as a Chinese-language interpreter. He arrives back in Japan after the war, suffering from what might today be called post-traumatic stress syndrome, with continued feelings of anxiety and frequent delusions that strangers he encounters are trying to kill him. The narrative describes his journey by horse-drawn carriage and on foot to a small mountain village in the Kiso River Valley, where he pays a condolence call on the widow of a friend killed in battle. This work is most notable for contrasting Maki's deeply troubled state of mind with the postwar atmosphere of triumph and elation in Japan, exemplified by his fellow travelers, a sergeant who proudly displays his medals and an admiring young man who wishes that he too could have received military decorations and worn the uniform of a noncommissioned officer:

> When the young man asked if he had gotten any medals, the sergeant casually took out from his suitcase a small box with a metal clasp, opened it, and showed him the contents.
>
> "Hey, you really did! And two of them at that. Wow! Gold and silver. I'd sure like to wear some gold and silver." With that, the young man tried pressing the medals to his own chest. "You put them on," he then asked the sergeant. "So I can see what they're supposed to look like."
>
> "What's the point? You're a real nuisance, you know." But even as he protested, the sergeant showed the young man, placing the gleaming medals on the chest of his summer uniform.[446]

Sitting near them in the garden of a country inn, Maki is besieged with morbid recollections:

> As he listened to their conversation, Maki was remembering the war. The battlefield was still before his eyes—the unspeakable suffering of his service at the front, such as the constant struggle to survive the lack of sleep. How would these experiences affect the rest of his life? Among the soldiers attached to the First Army who went to the front, some had fallen ill and were sent back to the rear. He too had collapsed along the way. Left all alone, how many times he had trembled in panic and despair, urging his sick body forward and dragging his heavy legs until at last he made his way to the Red Cross field hospital.[447]

If Tōson portrays Maki's state of mind effectively, his descriptions of the battlefront in this work, like those in "Restless Sleep," remain rather unconvincing lists of particulars when compared, for example, with his friend Tayama Katai's graphic account of the Russo-Japanese War in the story *Ippeisotsu.*[448] Nevertheless, Tōson is successful in ironically juxtaposing the "peaceful day" of his story's title and setting with his protagonist's deeply disturbing ruminations about the war and its effects on those who fought it:

> The peaceful sunshine. How quiet it was. All the dreadful commotion of wartime—the tragic partings, the shouts of men going off to risk their lives—such things seemed to be hidden somewhere now. In this midday brightness it was as though social tranquility had been entirely restored and all the sorrow had been relieved. . . .
>
> Still, Maki could not forget the scene in that Red Cross field hospital. Visions crowded in on him—the window of his ward, the white futon smelling of the hospital, the many sick and wounded, the torsos of his fellow countrymen without arms, the gouged-out bullets, the bloodshed, and the death of a Russian prisoner of war. . . .
>
> He could not tell whether the noise of gunfire in his ears was what he had heard at the battlefront or an exploding sound inside his head. He felt the same wariness toward everything he saw around him now as he had at the front, and he was unable to relax, even for a moment. It exhausted him just to watch the sergeant and the local youth, his fellow travelers, though he had not exchanged a word with either of them. . . .
>
> Maki was not the only one unable to feel calm in this glorious climate of victory. He thought of a soldier he'd grown close to at the front who, shortly after returning to Japan in triumph, had been taken to a mental hospital. He remembered another friend who had made a lot of money transporting coal to ships at sea under heavy shelling, seemingly oblivious to the danger, but who, after peace came, had fallen unconscious at Shinbashi Station on his way home. There seemed to be a gnawing pain in the back of Maki's neck, and he was feeling slightly dizzy.[449]

While containing no explicit declarations of pacifist philosophy, "Day of Peace" depicts what Okamoto called war's "relentless" effects, which might have been more difficult to convey in the kind of poetry Tōson wrote before 1901. Yet Okamoto, Ara, and Itō do not mention this story in their studies of Tōson's writing on war, preferring to concentrate on "The Farmer" and his explicitly autobiographical prose. Itō cites several passages from Tōson's detailed firsthand accounts of conditions in France at the start of World War I. In these reminiscences Tōson portrays more of the sorrowful departure scenes endemic to armed conflict that he had described in "Restless Sleep," "The Farmer," "Day of Peace," and his earlier recollections of the Russo-Japanese War. Tōson himself departed Paris when the city was threatened by German invasion and moved to the French countryside for three months in 1914. Though never caught up in the fighting, he witnessed the panic and turmoil of a nation under attack, fearing at one point for his own safety. He recorded his experiences in a series of letters and dispatches, many of which were collected and published as *Sensō to Pari* (War and Paris, 1915). Below he describes the scene at two Paris railroad stations shortly after Germany had declared war on France:

> On August 1, [1914] I left my boarding house [with Mr. Kawata] and headed for Gare du Nord, where we were to see someone off for Belgium. On the way we stopped at Gare de l'Est. The sunlight at 1:00 on this unusually hot afternoon poured over the cobblestone streets. At Gare de l'Est we noticed that crowds of Germans and Austrians had gathered, ready to evacuate Paris. People sat amid their baggage directly on the concrete platform, legs outstretched, waiting for the train. I came face to face with a laborer who suddenly started to faint right in front of me. Making our way around the crush and confusion, we went on to Gare du Nord. But there, too, we encountered travelers with loads of baggage under their arms, people parting from one another reluctantly, and housewives with faces swollen from crying—all attesting to the emergency. We learned from a notice posted inside the station that all travel across the border between France and Germany had been suspended, and Kawata and I realized now that we faced a dangerous situation.[450]

Later, Tōson writes of more departures and their effect on people he knew in Paris:

> We began to hear often about Frenchmen who had been drafted. Mr. Kawata's French language teacher went to the front, and when a relative of the woman who ran my boarding house left for the army, her niece's face was swollen with tears. We also heard about the demolishing of shops that German merchants had left behind. Access to Paris was tightly controlled. Travel had become impossible and payment in foreign currency was absolutely forbidden. We began to feel as though the situation was forcing us to live marooned on some remote island. With service suspended on the Trans-Siberian Railroad, no correspondence reached us from Japan. (129)

Tōson's feelings of isolation in Paris might have led him to make unfavorable comparisons of France to Japan in wartime. Some of his letters appearing in *War and Paris* chide the French people generally for lacking unity of effort, and individuals for failing to observe a certain decorum Tōson associated with a nation mobilized. Such upbraidings also present problems for those seeking to portray Tōson as an antiwar writer:

> In this war the survival of France and the fate of its people were at stake. Seeing that even the Syndicalists were responding to the national crisis, we sensed that this was a struggle requiring a total effort. Hence, we thought it truly strange that, in such circumstances, runs on all the banks had begun and the citizens of Paris were hoarding food. At first we couldn't believe it since, for Japanese, it is impossible to imagine a state of mind in which people do not feel safe until all their money has been changed into gold coins and is held in their possession. Why were all the citizens in such a panic? . . . (132–33)
>
> Mr. Sawaki made an interesting observation that "in the West there is no such regard for social appearances [*sekentei*] as in Japan." We had seen a soldier in red trousers sitting legs outstretched on a grassy riverbank near Billancourt. He was bidding a reluctant farewell to a young country girl who appeared to be a housemaid. As we watched the easygoing, open manner of Westerners who are unconstrained even in wartime, we were reminded of how we were taught since childhood to be careful of social appearances in front of others. (146)

Although he expresses disapproval at the outpouring of emotion in this scene, one might ask why it did not remind Tōson of the episode from his story "Restless Sleep" in which Koichi's mother, weeping inconsolably, nearly falls from the rickshaw on the way to Shinbashi Station, where her son is to depart for the Sino-Japanese War. Still, if his observations here seem tinged with a mild chauvinism, Tōson appears to have second thoughts later when he reflects on the behavior of some Japanese during the war with Russia ten years before. He ends up wondering whether people in crisis might not tend to act much the same regardless of their nationality:

> Because the French government had adopted a policy of closing the banks instead of floating war bonds, we could not receive money orders from Japan. The banks refused to disperse any more than twenty francs per month even to the French. Along with emergency mobilization, the Army Ministry acted to requisition foodstuffs, and now Parisians began vying to lay in supplies of vegetables and other groceries. Hearing about this made

> me realize that such things could not simply be attributed to the individualism of Europeans. Rather, I came to appreciate the dreadful effects of economic panic. I could no longer listen indifferently to stories about people killing cats and mice for food during the Franco-Prussian War. Even now I recall a passage in Tayama Katai's eyewitness account from the Russo-Japanese War of battlefield correspondents fighting over rice balls. It frightened me to think that, if the day ever came when we were confined to the [Japanese] embassy, we too might find ourselves fighting over a rice ball. (140–41)

For Tōson that day never came. He left Paris in August 1914 for the comparative safety of the central French countryside and did not return to the city until November. The war was still grinding on when he ended his stay in France almost two years later. On his way home he stopped briefly in London during the summer of 1916, and reached Japan in July. In Tōson's absence, the nation's peripheral involvement in World War I on the side of the Allies had brought under Japanese control territory in China and the Pacific previously claimed by Germany, acquired by Japan after brief military operations in 1914 that resulted in few casualties. Although Japan had been almost entirely spared the trauma of "The Great War," people there joined those in Europe and America to celebrate Armistice Day in November 1918. Recalling his impressions seven years later, Tōson wrote that he had seen little that day to justify the mood of joy and optimism. In these recollections he maintains the role of a writer as witness and recorder of events, rather than as proselytizer against war and social injustice:

> On the night the return of peace was celebrated in Japan, I ran out to watch the long parade of lanterns. I also looked on amid the rice riots and other violent social disturbances that have occurred since 1918. I cannot say now that I was particularly moved by these events. Though it was a time when voices were raised high in calls for reform and freedom, I saw little that was inspiring.[451]

During the 1920s Tōson continued to produce fiction set against a background of conflicts and tensions in contemporary Japanese society, but with none of the ideological affirmations expressed by writers associated with Japan's proletarian literature movement, now reaching its height. His widely acclaimed short story "Arashi" (The storm, 1925), for example, takes place amid the social activism of the period but focuses on the troubled relations between a man in his forties and his four children. As in his description of war's effects a decade earlier, he writes as a keen observer, portraying people under stress—often with closely autobiographical parallels—at times of crisis and upheaval.

Tōson devoted much of his time between 1928 and 1935 to completing his large-scale novel *Before the Dawn*, noted above for a protagonist much resembling Tōson's father, who was devastated by the effects of the Meiji Restoration. Its publication brought Tōson the Asahi Culture Prize in 1936, thrusting him into the spotlight of celebrity. He attracted still wider attention in the press later that year by traveling to Europe and America as a member of Japan's delegation to the International PEN Club Conference. Upon his return he was appointed to the Imperial Arts Council, though he could take little part in its proceedings due to an attack of nephrosclerosis that kept him temporarily bedridden.

Tōson's activities and writings during the final years of his life, when Japan's military involvement widened steadily in Asia and the Pacific, can only seem discouraging to those who have proffered a case for him as an antiwar writer. To be sure, the public notoriety resulting from literary prizes and prestigious official appointments would have made it especially incumbent upon him to join the wartime associations of Japanese writers, hastily organized with government backing, that issued propaganda declarations in support of the war effort. At the same time, there is no evidence that he was coerced either to serve in 1942, at the age of seventy, as an honorary member of the Nihon Bungaku Hōkokukai (Japan Literary Patriotic Association), controlled by the Home Ministry, or to attend the Daitōa Bungakusha Taikai (Greater East Asia Writers Conference), the primary purpose of which was to proclaim the superiority of Japanese culture. In "My Hope for the Conference," he told the participants, including a number from other Asian nations, "Many of my fellow countrymen have been sent to the front. We fight not only for our own survival, but for the survival of the peoples of Greater East Asia. Whether on the battlefront or the home front, I want us to give meaning to the long struggle of our compatriots."[452]

Nor is it likely that Tōson was pressured into writing *Tōhō no mon* (Gate to the East), another ambitiously conceived novel set during the late-Tokugawa and early-Meiji periods. This work features several of the same characters and locations portrayed in *Before the Dawn*, suggesting that it was intended as a sequel, though its completion was prevented by Tōson's death in August 1943. Only the first four installments appeared serially in the magazine *Chūō kōron* between January and October of that year. Covering a period a decade beyond its predecessor, *Gate to the East* contains a didactic streak absent from *Before the Dawn* and is highly uncharacteristic of Tōson's work, which, as already indicated, is notably lacking in political and philosophical pronouncements. The author draws on his observations abroad to emphasize what he sees as essential differences between East and West and praises the "fierce tenacity" of the Japanese for resisting the penetration of alien culture, thereby preserving their "unique character." Such pronouncements, so atypical of Tōson's writing until that time, rang in close harmony with government declarations of Japan's wartime mission as leading and protecting Asian peoples against Western tyranny and corruption. This suggests that, like many other writers and intellectuals, Tōson had accepted official rationales for the war effort.[453] Furthermore, Tōson echoes other prominent Japanese writers of the time in extolling Japan's traditional warrior ethic, which he sees as revived by the Sino-Japanese War:

> With the coming of the Sino-Japanese War, the Meiji scene began to undergo a complete transformation. . . . People's spirits, which had been in great turmoil during the previous twenty years, and the soul of the nation [*kuni no mono no tamashii*], which had languished in a dark place, now began earnestly searching for something. After the war the people welcomed in a new day, rediscovering the true way of the warrior [*makoto no bushi no michi*] that had been hidden temporarily in an inconspicuous place.[454]

This is the same author who, thirteen years earlier, had movingly depicted "frenzy and confusion" during the conflict with Russia and "the misery of war." Yet it seems unfair to dwell on this last, unfinished work of a distinguished writer in his seventies whose health was failing. "Deconstructing" this novel and certain remarks in his prose reminiscences of Europe to show that Tōson was a militarist or an imperialist writer would be at least as misguided as presenting selected excerpts from "The Farmer" as evidence that he was an antiwar poet. More likely, he shared with writers everywhere a view of armed conflict that, over the course of his career, was neither static nor monolithic.

It would seem more fitting to conclude this discussion of war and the literary legacy of Shimazaki Tōson by considering the difficulty the Culture Section of Taisei Yokusankai (The Imperial Rule Assistance Association) must have encountered in choosing examples of his poetry for officially sponsored anthologies published between 1940 and 1944 that were intended to inspire Japanese to ever-greater toil and sacrifice in the war effort. Many prominent writers contributed poems composed especially for the occasion, bearing such titles as "Gunshin ni tsuzuke" (To the warrior gods), "Mi-ikusa no tame" (For the cause of the sacred war), and "Kanarazu katamu" (Victory is certain).[455] Tōson, however, had written little poetry for publication since the turn of the century. Hence, as with other important writers who had ceased to publish poetry or died, the authorities were obliged to choose earlier poems that seemed likely to stimulate patriotic fervor and support for the war even if they did not refer specifically to the current situation. In Tōson's case, they were evidently hard-pressed. The two poems they settled on, "Chikumagawa ryojō no uta" (Weary traveler along the Chikuma River) and "Tokiwagi" (Evergreen tree), are lyrical, if somber, evocations of rural terrain and foliage reprinted from Tōson's 1901 collection *Rakubai-shū* (Fallen plum blossoms).[456] One struggles to find some reason for their inclusion, beyond a desire to foster appreciation for Japan's natural scenery, that might enhance feelings of patriotism. Or could the compilers' attention have been attracted by Tōson's one-time personification of the stately subject of "Evergreen Tree" as an "emperor of the field" (*nobe no sumeragi*)? That this one isolated metaphor or the poem's rendering of a Japanese landscape could have led to its inclusion in an anthology of ultranationalistic and exhortative war poetry illustrates again how Tōson's work has at times been misapplied where war is concerned.

7 The "Democracy Poets" and the Pacific War

Shimazaki Tōson's poems seem out of place in wartime anthologies because so many writers turned out bellicose and vituperative verses after Pearl Harbor. That the Pacific War should have produced the largest number of conversions among poets who had previously written against war was, as noted above, partly the direct and indirect result of official pressures. Poets often lived on the income from their writings paid by magazines and publishing houses, which had come under the scrutiny of a government bureau that could close them down at any time.[457] Yet, while some might have written in support of the war out of economic necessity or for fear of falling under suspicion, the outpouring of jingoistic and derogatory verses seems for the most part to have been motivated by genuine feeling.[458] With the exception of Kinoshita Naoe, who died in 1937, this study focuses on poets who expressed views of war inconsistent with those articulated in their earlier writings. Yet it must be remembered that, as Donald Keene notes in his essay "Japanese Writers and the Greater East Asia War," when it came to turning out ultranationalistic exhortations after Pearl Harbor, "*almost everyone was involved.*"[459]

> The excitement and even relief with which writers greeted the news of Pearl Harbor are easily understandable. After a long period of inconclusive hostilities in China, the total war which most people had expected had at last begun, bringing a sense of relief that the uncertainties were over. For the relatively few writers of pronouncedly right-wing beliefs, the war represented a logical development in the sacred mission of the Japanese people; the more numerous left-wing writers could take comfort in the hope that the war would bring an end to colonialism and the influence of the white man in Asia.[460]

Some of the most striking turnabouts occurred among poets associated with the "Democracy Poetry" (*minshū shi*) movement, whose earlier writings had vigorously opposed war. "Democracy Poetry" developed in Japan shortly after World War I during the Taishō era (1912–25), when ideals of democracy (political and economic) and peaceful cooperation among nations were widely embraced in Japanese intellectual circles, as in Europe and America. Inspired by Tomita Saika's (1890–) translations of Edward Carpenter (1844–1929) and Walt Whitman (1819–92), Momota Sōji (1863–1955), Shirotori Seigo, and Fukuda Masao joined Saika to produce poetry and literary criticism on such themes as "art for freedom" (*kaihō no geijutsu*) and "art of the people" (*minshū geijutsu*). In keeping with their articulated philosophy, the poetic form favored by the "Democracy Poets" was free verse (*jiyū-shi*).

Shirotori Seigo has recently been singled out as "Japan's foremost antiwar poet" for works he published during the first half of the twentieth century.[461] These poems, reprinted many times in the early 1920s, appeared in anthologies of Japanese antiwar poetry published in the 1960s and 1970s.[462] Perhaps his best-known work among them is "Satsuriku no tendō" (The palace of slaughter, 1919), condemning war's glorification. Shirotori presents a critical description of the military museum Hall of the Honored (Yūshūkan), located on the grounds of Yasukuni Jinja, the shrine dedicated to deceased members of the Imperial Japanese Forces.[463] The poem is steeped in a tone of sorrowful irony:

> Come one, come all. Walk inside and look closely.
> Move along like fish, softly and smoothly.
> Do not to disturb
> The light and the dreams of souls shrouded silently in bitter grief.
>
> Inside this Hall of the Honored are shell fragments.
> And, from Japan and the countries of the world
>   are every sort of cannon and rifle,
> Weapons wearing the mindless cruel smiles that no hand can warm
>   or soften.
> Their natures unchanging,
> They have been passed on and on, tumbling bloodstained
>   from one age to the next,
>   from one place to another,
> To end up here, caught in a cavern of fate,
> Lying silently, motionlessly.
>
> I look further
> At the many swords forged by master artisans from ancient times,

At the splendid armor and the captured enemy booty,
At the portraits lining the walls of the many generals born of the
    history of Meiji wars.
From outside that distant realm of the dead,
Their resplendently colored uniforms and stern faces
Glitter emptily on display, like cast-off snake skins.

I look further,
    at the rows of countless small photographs of common soldiers
    who lost arms and legs,
    and whose artificial limbs
    are said to have been bestowed by Her Imperial Majesty, the Empress.
How are they getting along now?
And what has war done to their families?
"Just fight for the nation,"
"Consider your life as light as a feather," they were told.
Ah, it was off to the front for them, into the battle and the suffering.
Then, it was letters from home, the tedium of barracks life, crimes,
The deaths of fellow soldiers, looting the enemy camp, and
    exhaustion like mud.
Oh, experiences of blood, tears, and joy unfold and are buried
    without end.

And what of their warm, happy homes—young wives, aging parents,
    beloved brothers, sisters, and young children?
I think of them as I look at these soldiers;
And of the invisible shrapnel
That flies, thundering and roaring, through the sky;
Of the battle cries heard endlessly around the world,
    amid the bloodstains wrought by human ambitions so hard to restrain;
Of the smell of gunpowder,
And the call of the bugle to assault.

Oh, in the palace of slaughter
Souls inflicted with every possible wound
Are heaped one upon another.
The air of a quiet winter day is transparent like death,
And nothing moves.[464]

Shirotori's mention of the empress in connection with maimed soldiers has been read as a bold, if muted, challenge to the imperial family on the subject of war. Itō Shinkichi compares these lines to Yosano Akiko's highly controversial statement in "Brother, Do Not Give Your Life" that "the Emperor goes not himself into the battle."[465]

"Kōchi o ushinau hi" (The day they lost their farm fields) is another of Shirotori's poems to appear in recent anthologies of antiwar poetry.

Despite its classification today as a poem opposing war, this work seems to place more emphasis on economic and social inequities that are exacerbated by war, suggesting that it might be read, instead, as an early forerunner of the proletarian literature that flourished in Japan a few years after its publication. If it cannot be called antiwar, this poem expresses seething outrage: first, at the economic ruin, along with the loss of loved ones, suffered by family farmers whose sons died in the Russo-Japanese War; and, second, at wealthy speculators who exploited their deprivation:

> On the heels of the crop failure and famine in 1902
> Came the Russo-Japanese War in 1904.
> Told they must be ready to give their lives for the sake of the nation,
> all the men whose work in the fields supported their families
> were drafted.
>
> The poorest families
> Borrowed small sums from the wealthy.
> When their young sons died on the plains of Manchuria, longing for home,
> Slips of paper arrived at their impoverished houses announcing
> "a death in battle."
>
> With the whole nation at war, it was a time of grieving for small farmers,
> But landowners' pockets bulged ever fatter.
> The little money the farmers could not repay
> Grew to an enormous sum, and their lands were seized.
>
> Like iron filings pulled in by a magnet,
> Many fields were cunningly amassed by one landowner
> Until vast lands, as far as the eye could see, across whole
> neighborhoods and villages,
> Became his possession.
> Oh, these outrageous bloodsuckers
> Hide shamelessly behind white walls.
> For those at the front where shells rained down on them,
> For those who shed blood in the cause of justice,
> Oh, my country,
> You should know that some small medal or "certificate of merit"
> is no true compensation.
> Heard in the wind sweeping over green rice fields
> Are the lonely shouts of war
> And the rage at society's wrongs.
>
> Prisons exist not only under law,
> But also under the bright blue sky on endless fertile plains.
> For the people who have fallen to the status of tenant farmers,
> What once was their farmland is now a cruel prison.[466]

Also anthologized as an antiwar poem during the 1960s and 1970s is "Kaijō no yūutsu" (Gloom at sea), in which Shirotori denounces the expenditure of enormous sums, collected from high taxes, on military hardware:

> Dozens of warships float on the ocean,
>   forming a male nation of 20,000 sailors.
> The ships spew soot, smoke, noise,
>   and the smell of fuel oil oozing into the harbor.
> All the weapons aboard have been polished.
> Giant cannon muzzles burn hot in the sun,
> Packing shells that can strike five miles away.
>
> All of science's powers and a nation's wealth have been mustered,
> With the blood and sweat of masses of men,
>   to assemble this colossal spectacle.
>
> Ah, we roar with laughter at this monumental anachronism.
> Is it not a moral imperative to conclude an arms reduction pact?
> Who is it that itches to make war?
>
> Tension, nonsense, nothingness, brutality, waste,
> And hardships imposed on so many people trying to make a living—
>   How can these things bring us "peace?"
> On each warship, carrying 1,000 men,
> Almost as many gray shirts and pants are washed and dried.[467]

In these three works, published before 1930, Shirotori condemns war's glorification epitomized in the idolization of generals and the veneration of weapons. He deplores the devastating losses war inflicts on common soldiers and their families back home, along with the waste of national resources on armaments. Yet in poems Shirotori published during the Pacific War, when he was in his early fifties, he reverses position on all three of these issues by (1) celebrating the deification of nine submarine crewmen, posthumously designated "warrior gods," who died in the attack at Pearl Harbor,[468] (2) extolling the pride of their families back home on the farm, who "shed not one tear" for a son's "admirable . . . serv[ice] to the Empire," and (3) revering the artillery pieces used in the capture of Singapore by Imperial Japanese Forces commanded by a general now lionized.

Even the title of Shirotori's 1943 poem "Gunshin no fubo wa kyō mo tahata o tagayaseri" (Today, too, parents of the warrior god plow their fields) seems to contradict the message in "The Day They Lost Their Farm Fields," his poem on farmers whose sons died in the Russo-Japanese War:

Even on this day
The parents of the warrior god
Silently plow their fields.

Hearing of the death in war of their beloved child,
Not one tear do they shed,
But say "How admirable! He served the Empire."
At the Buddhist altar they quietly offer a votive candle,
Clasping their hands prayerfully before his photograph
in gallant uniform.

The Nine Brave Warriors—
All were born in simple country homes
Among graceful mountains and rivers,
Where they roamed over the black earth
And under crystal stars.
First taught loyalty and filial piety,
They were raised to honor the gods and Buddha.

Ah, in this time of national crisis,
How the hearts of the Japanese bloom like flowers!
The Nine Warrior Gods, with daily practice and precise planning,
Infiltrated deep into Pearl Harbor,
Making themselves into explosives;
And, in the spirit of unwavering loyalty,
Instantly sank the enemy warships,
prided throughout the world as "unsinkable,"
Just as if they had been wooden boats.[469]
. . . .

The parents who "shed . . . not one tear" for the loss of a son, admiring his sacrifice as a "warrior god" for "the Empire" as they bow before his photograph, appear in sharp contrast to the "aging parents" evoked sympathetically in "The Palace of Slaughter." In his earlier poem Shirotori "look[ed] at . . . small photographs" on the museum's walls, showing sons with artificial limbs, and lamented "the suffering [of] common soldiers" who were told to "fight for the nation" and to "consider [their lives] as light as a feather." Here he extols their "unwavering loyalty" and "the hearts of Japanese that bloom like flowers . . . in this time of national crisis."

Laurence Binyon (1869–1943) expresses similar sentiments evoking parents, tears, and a "royal" cause in his 1914 poem "For the Fallen (September 1914)" on British youths dying in World War I. The young men who live on as "warrior gods" for Shirotori have become "immortal" for Binyon:

With proud thanksgiving, a mother for her children,
England mourns for her dead across the sea.
Flesh of her flesh, they were, spirit of her spirit,
Fallen in the cause of the free.

Solemn the drums trill: Death august and royal
Sings sorrow up in immortal spheres.
There is music in the midst of desolation
And a glory that shines upon our tears.[470]

In "Yamashita shōgun" (General Yamashita, 1942) Shirotori presents a heroic portrayal of the man who led the Imperial Japanese Forces' successful attack on Singapore. His veneration of General Yamashita in this poem clashes conspicuously with the ridicule he aimed two decades before at the adulation of generals in "The Palace of Slaughter." He portrays "cannons" with "giant barrels" as awe-inspiring objects, in sharp contrast to his earlier denunciation in "Gloom at Sea" of a noisy, smelly warship and its "giant cannon muzzles" as "brutality, waste" and a "monumental anachronism":

In the distant sky, black smoke drifts over the open sea.
It is Singapore's last moments.
The giant barrels of cannons poised in the jungle
Come to life as the bombardment proceeds.
Under raining shells, tree leaves scatter.
Amid the cannons' smoke and the rain of shells,
He crouches impassively, calmly opening a map,
And plans strategy with his staff officers—General Yamashita.
. . . .[471]

These poems that Shirotori published during the Pacific War are very rarely mentioned by biographers and critics and almost never reprinted today. Literary histories and biographical encyclopedias of modern Japanese writers usually omit them from his list of works.[472]

Fukuda Masao, Shirotori's somewhat better-known colleague among the "Democracy Poets," has also retained the reputation of a poet who wrote against armed conflict, despite poems he published during the Pacific War celebrating military victories and praising the "warrior gods." However, these later poems, though rarely reprinted,[473] receive passing reference in biographical encyclopedias, and one literary historian has discussed Fukuda's about-face in his poetry on war.

In a book provocatively titled *Kindai shi no haiboku: shijin to sensō sekinin* (The defeat of modern poetry: poets and war responsibility, 1980)

Abe Takeshi writes that Fukuda's early poems on the sufferings and sacrifices of rural Japanese in wartime convey "humanism," though they are not explicitly pacifistic. Abe quotes Fukuda's most famous poem on war, "Hitotsu no ressha to hankechi" (Handkerchiefs waving from a train, 1922), which portrays the departure of Japanese soldiers for the front in the Siberian Intervention of 1918–22.[474] The government eventually mobilized over 73,000 troops in this ill-fated venture, undertaken to claim Japan's "special position" in the area and to protect the South Manchuria Railway. The Siberian Intervention was launched initially with French, British, American, and Canadian as well as Japanese troops, ostensibly to rescue a unit of Czech soldiers trapped at the end of World War I, but really in the hopes of rolling back the Russian Revolution. Japan's prolonged involvement in the Shiberia Shuppei, which came to be known sarcastically as the Shiberia Shippai (Siberian Failure), met with growing opposition at home and abroad, compelling the Japanese government to withdraw forces that it had hoped would secure its interests in northern Manchuria. They were the last to leave, in October 1922, after suffering casualties in a number of battles with local troops.[475] In Fukuda's poem, the benumbed reaction of onlookers to a passing troop train seems to reflect the widespread skepticism in Japan toward this military misadventure:

> They board the train
> With shouts of banzai welling up in a startling outburst—
> The soldiers dispatched to Siberia.
> In that moment as the train passes,
>
> Handkerchiefs wave from its windows, as though competing for attention,
> While people stand in bewilderment along the tracks to see the soldiers off.
> Only one old rickshaw man
> Yells banzai and tips his hat.
>
> At first I am shocked to the depths of my soul.
> How tragic!
> Their shouts are like cries of despair.
> They are going to their deaths. To their deaths.
> What a tragedy for our people!
>
> From this emotion welling up in me,
> I was seized unexpectedly with a deep sorrow that raised
> goose bumps on my skin.
> Then came tears that filled my eyes.
> Oh, you men, I know too much to yell banzai.
> Forgive me. I will send you off with tears.[476]

Evoking a scene of striking similarity, Wilfred Owen described British soldiers departing by train for World War I in "The Send-Off." This poem, which also includes "dull" porters and troops with faces "grimly gay," concludes on a tragically prophetic note, as Owen died at the front in 1918.

> Down the close darkening lanes they sang their way
> To the siding-shed,
> And lined the train with faces grimly gay.
>
> Their breasts were stuck all white with wreath and spray
> As men's are, dead.
>
> Dull porters watched them, and a casual tramp
> Stood staring hard,
> Sorry to miss them from the upland camp.
>
> Then, unmoved, signals nodded, and a lamp
> Winked to the guard.
>
> So secretly, like wrongs hushed-up, they went.
> They were not ours;
> We never heard to which front these were sent;
>
> Nor there if they yet mock what women meant
> Who gave them flowers.
>
> Shall they return to beating of great bells
> In wild train-loads?
> A few, a few, too few for drums and yells,
>
> May creep back, silent, to village wells,
> Up half-known roads.[477]

One of the few published poems to protest the Siberian Intervention, "Handkerchiefs Waving from a Train," like "The Send-Off," effectively conveys the confusion of emotions typical in scenes of soldiers departing for the front. Yet in expressing his own feelings, Fukuda veers off into bathos ("How tragic!") and self-righteous polemics ("I know too much to yell banzai"), tendencies that occasionally mar antiwar poetry in Japan and elsewhere. Abe Takeshi also quotes from "Aozameta inaka" (The pale countryside, 1924) in which Fukuda writes, as Shirotori had, on the hardships of farming in Japan, which were exacerbated by conscription:

> The land tax is high,
> The eldest son is drafted,

And the second son runs off, lured by the city.
The air in the country is lonely, unsettled,
And the soil, smelling of decay, has become infertile.[478]

The skepticism in Japan about the Siberian Intervention contrasted sharply with the popular enthusiasm that swept the nation during other conflicts, from the Sino-Japanese War of 1894–95 to the Pacific War of 1941–45. The national Diet had rallied unanimously behind the war effort in both the Sino-Japanese and Russo-Japanese Wars, but the dispatch of troops to Siberia in the summer of 1918 was, from the beginning, the focus of heated parliamentary debate. The lack of support was evident outside as well as inside parliament's walls and reflected less a distaste for continental expansion as such (a policy that had been popular at the turn of the century and would be again in the 1930s) than a shift of priorities. Imperial troops embarked for Vladivostok in August 1918 at the same time Japan erupted in a nationwide protest over the exorbitant price of rice. The rapid growth of the economy during World War I had, in other words, shifted the focus of attention away from the further expansion of Japanese power on the continent to more immediate concerns at home. Major demonstrations for price stability, labor reform, and universal manhood suffrage marked the first few months of the Intervention and signified that the popular concern was for reform at home, not for additional territorial gains abroad. Nor did it help the cause of the army that over 100,000 troops were mobilized against the Japanese people to suppress the rice riots.[479] As Fukuda's poetry suggests, the shouts of banzai that echoed from the large crowds who saw departing soldiers off from Japan's railroad stations to the Sino-Japanese and Russo-Japanese Wars were rarely heard during the Siberian Intervention.

Then, as Abe Takeshi notes, "during the [Pacific] war the 'Democracy Poets,' too, turned out verses like those everyone else was writing."[480] In a jolting reversal of metaphor, Japan's soil, which Fukuda described in "The Pale Countryside" as rendered infertile by conscription and high taxes, becomes, in 1944, "the soil of our nation," and those conscripted become "the warriors of our Empire's land, / Unremittingly giving life to the soil [that] produce[s] the strength . . . to strike down those who do not revere His Majesty":

"Tsuchi ni ikuru uta" (The song that lives in our soil, 1944)

Get angry,   still more angry,   angry at the enemy!
Shoot and shoot again
Until you strike down those who do not revere His Majesty.

This is true loyalty.
    Together with the soil of our nation,   be still angrier.
    Work together to keep increasing production. . . .

Oh, soil, produce even more, produce the strength
To strike down, with abundant power,
Those who do not revere His Majesty.
Double the strength of His Majesty's people,
Volunteers of the soil who are building a new world. . . .

Oh, plow,   ever deeper,   and cultivate
To build His Majesty's Imperial Reign.
Shoot and shoot again
Those who do not revere His Majesty.
    The Way of Cultivation that makes the crops abundant
    Is His Majesty's greatly cherished joy. . . .

Be proud,   still more proud,   proud of the honor!
Take pride in your unending resolve to shoot
Those who do not revere His Majesty.
    We are the warriors of our Empire's land,
Unremittingly giving life to the soil.[481]

Fukuda's portrayal of wartime life in Japan also undergoes a striking transformation in his poem "Kansha" (Gratitude, 1942), which he dedicates to the Japanese soldiers victorious in the Dutch East Indies and to the people supporting them back home whose "joy" it is to endure hardships for the "great cause" of the war effort:

Filled to overflowing with the mood of spring
Is the burning fervor of the nation where gentle breezes blow.
In this morning's warm sky of thin clouds,
Today, too, with the light of the gods shining,
The images of the warrior spirits soar powerfully,
And appear majestically in my eyes wet with tears.

Ah, following upon the victory song with the surrender of all
    Dutch East Indies forces,
Yesterday was Army Commemoration Day with its sweetly
    plum-scented memories.
Tomorrow we celebrate the second great victory.
Hear her spirited voice—the wife of the neighborhood association chief
As she comes carrying the eggs and ration pails.
How grateful we are for the glory we are living.

I have persevered over the long road of honest poverty.
Sick in body, I worshipped the gods for purification,

Living for poetry. Now,
Since the Imperial Proclamation of War ignited my fervor,
I have found joy in devoting myself to this great cause.
These have all been days of tears, days of gratitude.
. . . .[482]

The tears of "joy" and "gratitude" in this poem to the "glory" of war are shed by the same poet who sent Japanese soldiers off "with tears" to the Siberian Intervention, which he called "a tragedy for our people." Yet such eulogizing of war in poetry is hardly exclusive to Japan. Though sounding pompous and grandiloquent when read today, Fukuda's "Kansha" could plausibly have generated inspiration for the war effort when it was first published in 1942. By contrast, it is hard to see how Robert Nichols' flat and cliché-ridden "Invocation," a poem eulogizing England's entrance into World War I that also applies celestial metaphor, could have inspired anything but unintended humor:

Begin, O guns, and when ye have begun
Lift up your voices louder and proclaim
The sick moon set, arisen the strong sun,
Filling our skies with new and noble flame.
The soldier and the Poet now are one
And Heroic more than mere name.[483]

Fukuda draws again on natural phenomena symbolizing war for his laudation "Shinju-wan no gunshin kyuchū—kaigun tokubetsu kōgekitai o utau" (The nine warrior gods of Pearl Harbor—a poem in honor of the navy special attack force, 1942). This description of sailors who leave for their mission facing death "with a smile" comes from the same poet who expressed his "deep sorrow" over the departure twenty-three years earlier of soldiers bound for death and suffering in Siberia:

Prepared to lay down their lives on a fiery road to eternity,
In their mission they built shining pillars of divinity—
As we hear of their exploits on this day, the many branches of cherry trees,
    too, are again budding with the burning fervor of the nation.
Oh, in this fine weather, so beautifully mild,on the Empress's birthday,
I bow down in profound reverence and weep.
They will never return. The heroism of the Nine Warrior Gods of
    the Pearl Harbor Special Attack Force!

With a plan unparalleled in times past,
    they set out on their mission with a smile,
And uttered one phrase, "I'm on my way,"
That filled the depths of their finely trained spirits.

They advanced under minefields, with total concentration,
    at the extreme moment between life and death,
and awaited the dawn from the bottom of the bay,
    like fish in the moonlight,
With the enemy warships etched in silhouette.
. . . .

Oh, sea and air forces together launched the deadly combined assault!
Heroic deeds became pillars of fire, pillars of water . . . . .
    oh, pillars of human sacrifice.
The results they achieved, which make the flesh dance,
Were reported calmly from a boat radio, "The attack has succeeded,"
    followed by the sound of raging waves
And the eternal song of the Pacific Ocean,
    praising this unparalleled deed of honor.

Their bodies in watery graves—Iwasa, Yokoyama, Furuno, Hiroo,
    Yokoyama, Sasaki, Ueda, Katayama, Inagaki: the Nine Warrior Gods—
How deeply I am moved, looking up at the image of those gods in the
    sky above, with the light reflecting in my tearstains, as they
    soar through the vast blue of their accomplished mission.
The eternal spirits of Yamato convey their loyalty.
The eternal enlightened way of Greater East Asia is to be praised forever.[484]

Again, Fukuda's tears shed for the "tragedy" of soldiers departing for Siberia become, two decades later, tears of "profound reverence" for Japanese who died in "the achieve[ment of] . . . this unparalleled deed of honor." Laurence Binyon's "For the Fallen (September 1914)" glorifies "death august and royal" in strikingly similar metaphor:

They went with songs to the battle, they were young,
Straight of limb, true of eye, steady and aglow.
They were staunch to the end against odds uncounted,
They fell with their faces to the foe.

They shall grow not old, as we that are left grow old:
Age shall not weary them, nor tears condemn.
At the going down of the sun and in the morning
We will remember them.

They mingle not with their laughing comrades again;
They sit no more at familiar tables of home;
They have no lot in our labour of the day-time;
They sleep beyond England's foam.

But where our desires are and our hopes profound,
Felt as a well-spring that is hidden from sight,

To the innermost heart of their own land they are known
As the stars are known to the Night;

As the stars that shall be bright when we are dust,
Moving in marches upon the heavenly plain,
As the stars that are starry in the time of our darkness,
To the end, to the end, they remain.

It would be difficult to determine the precise motivations of Fukuda, Shirotori, and others among the "Democracy Poets" for writing poems with views of war that differ so drastically from those expressed in their earlier poetry. Even with the mood of enthusiasm that brims from these works, the possibility that these men might have felt official or popular pressures, directly or indirectly, cannot be ruled out, especially since they had been associated with a movement profoundly influenced by British and American poetry. Fukuda Masao's daughter Misuzu, also a free-verse poet, recalls that during the last years of World War II, their home was visited every week by officers of the Special Higher Police (*tokkō*). But she also remembers that her father expressed pleasure at the Japanese military victories he read about in the morning newspaper, and that he served as president of the local neighborhood association (*tonari-gumi*) during the Pacific War. Having suffered partial paralysis ever since a stroke in 1937, he writes in "Kansha" of seeking relief for a "sick . . . body" in performing Shinto rituals of "purification" (*misogi*), and finding "joy" in "devoting myself" to the war effort, "this great cause." For him, as for many Japanese, the attack on the naval base at Pearl Harbor was an act of self-preservation for a nation that was being denied essential raw materials in an embargo imposed by England and the United States. Yet Fukuda was also a victim of the Pacific War, in which he lost a son in the Philippines, a brother in Indochina, and his home in Tokyo to firebombing. Misuzu recalls that her father, who joined practices with bamboo spears to defend against the expected enemy invasion, had already resigned himself to the nation's defeat by the spring of 1945.[485] His 1946 novel *Hai-sen chokugo* (Just after the defeat)[486] is a moving account of the poverty and disruption at war's end.

As we look back on the Pacific War, it also seems reasonable that, having espoused the philosophy of popular sovereignty, "Democracy Poets" might have been particularly impressed, at least initially, with its official rationale as a conflict being waged by Japan to liberate the peoples of Asia from Western colonialism.[487] Thus, they wrote about soldiers dying in this conflict who had, in Laurence Binyon's words, "fallen in the cause of the free." Government justifications for the war were reiterated daily in the press, and historians busily compiled new textbooks portraying Japan as the champion of East Asia from ancient times. Toyotomi Hideyoshi, a subject of ridicule among intellectuals during the Taishō era for his failed attempt to invade China through Korea at the end of the sixteenth century, was now recast as heroic pioneer of the Greater East Asia Co-Prosperity Sphere.[488]

In the poems quoted above written in support of the war, Shirotori and Fukuda celebrate Japanese victories over British forces in Singapore, then a colony of England, and over Holland's army in the Dutch East Indies. Furthermore, advocates of democracy would likely have shared widespread resentment that lingered in Japan over European refusal to include in the League of Nations' charter a racial equality clause supported by Japanese delegates to the 1919 Versailles conference of World War I allies; and over such immigration and naturalization laws in the United States as the "Gentlemen's Agreement" of 1908 and the Quota Law of 1924, which severely discriminated against Japanese.[489] Ben-Ami Shillony has compared the intellectual climate in Japan during the Pacific War with that of the Russo-Japanese War:

> The intellectuals' support of the Pacific War contrasted with the critical attitude adopted by a group of writers and scholars towards the Russo-Japanese War some forty years earlier, when Kōtoku Shūsui, Yosano Akiko, and others expressed their . . . views. There were several reasons for this difference. At the beginning of the century, intellectuals were few and their education was Western. The war was fought because of an immediate threat, and there was as yet no precedent of a military victory over a Western power. Moreover, the war was not an ideological one: in 1904 Japan did not champion the cause of oppressed peoples, and Asia was the spoil to be won rather than an area to be freed. However, by the 1940s there were more intellectuals and they had all received a nationalistic education, in which the 1905 victory over Russia was already depicted as the shining example of Japan's spiritual superiority. The Pacific War had been preceded by a decade of growing militarization, resentment against the West, and gradual suppression of speech and writing. Asia was no longer a backward continent from which Japan wished to dissociate herself, but the oppressed brother waiting to be liberated. During both wars the intellectuals regarded themselves as teachers of the masses, with a mission to lead the people in times of confusion. This principle of the social responsibility of the scholar, deriving from both Confucianism and Marxism, was shared during the war by many intellectuals, nationalists, liberals, and socialists alike. . . . Men of letters were rediscovering their Asian roots.[490]

With this prevailing intellectual environment, public excitement over the war at a feverish pitch, and the press strictly censored in Japan, the question remains today as to whether poets and other writers could or should have suspected that the actual result of Japan's military conquests was to replace one form of colonialism with another, and that the tragically misguided war effort was doomed to catastrophic failure costing millions of lives. Unfortunately, it is a question explored only rarely in postwar Japan, unlike in Germany, where the history of wartime aggression and atrocities is taught extensively in the schools and the issue of widespread support among writers and the public for wartime government policies has been examined in depth.[491] Poet Kaneko Mitsuharu expressed concern that many in Japan seemed to want only to forget the "grotesque" excesses of the 1930s and 1940s. Too often, he said, when the subject of the war is raised, "people make a sour face and look away in silence, as if one is trying to tear open old wounds."[492]

What the small number of studies in Japan and elsewhere show is that Japanese poets supported the war for philosophical, personal, and professional reasons that often overlapped (see chapter eight). Few opted to remain silent, and still fewer decided to risk publishing even highly veiled criticism of the war effort.[493] The vast majority who cooperated, often with enthusiasm, faced very different kinds of pressures after 1945.

8 Takamura Kōtarō and Saitō Mokichi: War and Repentance

Among poets who wrote in support of the Pacific War, feelings of embarrassment and charges, such as those made by Abe Takeshi, that Japanese writers shared in "war responsibility" (*sensō sekinin*) led many to omit their wartime poems from postwar collections, including editions purporting to be their "complete works."[494] Two prominent poets, however, whose output of prowar writings had been particularly copious and fanatical, openly described the shock of defeat and their belated recognition of the delusion in Japan's wartime ideology. Takamura Kōtarō and Saitō Mokichi expressed regret for publishing exhortative, bellicose verses that might have encouraged young Japanese to go to their deaths.

In Takamura's case, biographers have speculated that his despondency following the death in 1938 of his wife Chieko, who had spent her last years in a psychiatric hospital, led him to seek relief in wartime emotionalism.[495] It is also possible that, after an initial infatuation with the West during his youthful travels between 1906 and 1909, the prejudice and alienation he experienced as a Japanese in Europe and America might have sharpened his feelings of antipathy toward "enemy nations" during the Pacific War and rendered him more susceptible to government propaganda depicting Japan as liberator and leader of Asia.[496]

His earliest writings on his journey abroad radiate a joyful infatuation with Europe and even include unfavorable comparisons to Japan. The son of a famous sculptor, Takamura always considered his own work in that medium more important than his poetry.[497] He left Japan for New York in 1906 to study sculpture there and in England and France. A tone of adoration bordering on sycophancy permeates a poem he addressed to Bernard Leach, the potter he befriended in London where they were both art students in 1907:

"Yorokobi o tsugu" (Announcing my joy, 1914)
—TO B. LEACH—

My friend of the Anglo-Saxon race I respect and love!
My friend of the race
That produced Shakespeare and Blake,
Newton and Darwin,
Turner and Beardsley,
And now has produced Augustus John![498]
. . . .

Though he calls Leach a "friend," Takamura evokes his fellow student as a kind of racial exemplar. In another poem Takamura recalls Leach nostalgically, again as a representative of "the Anglo-Saxon race I respect and love":

"Haitaisha yori—Baanaado Riichi-kun ni tei su"
(From a reprobate—offered to Bernard Leach, 1914)

Generous and serious friend!
My friend of the Anglo-Saxon race I respect and love!
When I think of your warm friendship I all but want to weep.
I remember that day when, as a rare evening shower
Fell on Chelsea, raising white smoke,
I first shook your hand.[499]

Similarly, Takamura's retrospective poetry on his stay in Paris during 1908 and 1909 shows an idealization of European culture, which is compared favorably with that of Japan:

"Pari" (Paris, 1947)

I became an adult in Paris.
In Paris too I first touched the opposite sex,
And in Paris first found a liberation of my soul.
Paris accommodates every species of human being
With an air of taking for granted. . . .
The modern age began in Paris;
Beauty was born and blossomed in Paris.
My eyes were opened to the truths of poetry;
I observed what culture meant
In each of the common people I encountered,
I became aware of an incomparable gap:
Even amid my nostalgia for the things and ways of Japan
I rejected them all.[500]

These initial expressions of rapture notwithstanding, anger emerges in Takamura's poetry and prose composed shortly after his stay abroad. He wrote then of intense feelings of alienation, self-doubt, and hostility that resulted in part from prejudice he encountered. He of course resented being called a "Jap," but was also annoyed at what he called "the peculiarly religious, good-willed pressure"[501] of Christian missionaries in the United States whose attentions made him feel smothered and patronized. His sentiments recall Uchimura Kanzō's earlier observations on such "unchristian features of Christendom" in America as "strong racial prejudice" and the "mission show."[502] Takamura writes from the unusual vantage point of a caged animal at the Bronx Zoo in the poem "Shirokuma" (Polar bear, 1925):

> . . . .
> The polar bear is not to be tamed;
> Alone he breathes Arctic air outside New York.
>
> A contemptible, instructive friendliness pervades his
> surroundings;
> A wonderful Christian materialism that all but chokes him
> Attempts to kill a dreamer-Jap.
> . . . .[503]

Takamura's nostalgic recollection that in Paris he "first touched the opposite sex" contrasts sharply with intense feelings of alienation and antipathy he expressed in 1910, focusing particularly on his relationships with French women. He noted: "Paris filled me with infinite loneliness. The joyous shouts in Paris streets are about to plunge me into a bottomless pit of melancholy."[504] It is not surprising that such feelings would give rise to hostile impulses.

> That is why, even amid the shouts of joy of Paris, I suffer every day an anguish that is bone-deep. The white people always say of orientals that they are inscrutable. The white race is also an insoluble riddle. I cannot comprehend even the little movements of their fingers. Even while I am embracing a white woman I cannot help wondering if I am not embracing a stone, hugging a corpse. I have often longed to drive a knife deep into a pure-white waxen breast.[505]

Then, after Pearl Harbor, Takamura's negative experiences in Europe and America might well have caused him to feel antipathy toward "enemy nations" more acutely, and to accept more readily official rationalizations of Japan's "sacred war" as leading Asia's liberation from

Western colonialism. His poetry during the Pacific War combines castigation of Western nations for their "tyranny in the East" with a kind of righteous joy that Japan was winning military victories over countries where Japanese had encountered discrimination, personally and officially. His work echoes ideas and slogans from "The Basic Principles of a New World Order," drafted by philosopher Nishida Kitarō for the Great East Asia Declaration issued by the Japanese government in December 1943, which reads in part:

> The Great East Asia War is a sacred war because it is the culmination of the historical progress of Asia. For a long time, the Anglo-Saxon imperialists have oppressed the peoples of East Asia and exploited their resources. . . . Japan will win this war because her people are determined to sacrifice their lives for it. . . . Japan's victory will save Asia and will offer a new hope for mankind.[506]

Biographer Yoshimoto Takaaki notes that Takamura, with his embrace of the war effort, seemed to find release from previously ambivalent feelings about places where, in fact, he had met with pleasant as well as unpleasant experiences: "The war provided him with his first opportunity to free himself from the tragic conflict in his heart that went back to his student days in Europe and America."[507] Along with this emotional transformation, Takamura's poems on the China and Pacific Wars, like those of Yosano Akiko and the "Democracy Poets," reveal a sharp philosophical departure from his earlier writings. Makoto Ueda observes:

> There is . . . the problem of Kōtarō's anti-British and anti-American poems. Until the late 1930s, he was known as a humanist poet and a member of the idealistic White Birch group, composed of writers and artists who had a profound faith in the basic goodness of human nature and advocated respect for individuality, love of all mankind, and freedom from all forms of hatred and violence. Like other members of the group, he ardently admired idealistic humanists of the West such as Tolstoy and Romain Rolland; indeed, he was the first person ever to undertake a Japanese translation of Rolland's masterpiece, *Jean Christophe*. Yet when the war broke out he became one of the most outspoken poets supporting the militaristic government. Before then he had published only two books of poetry, *The Journey* (1914) and *Chieko Poems* (1941). Suddenly he began producing many poems in praise of the war, filling three anthologies: *These Great Days* (*Ōinaru hi ni*, 1942), *Uncle's Poems* (*Ojisan no shi*, 1943), and *The Records* (*Kiroku*, 1944).[508]

At the center of Takamura's wartime philosophy was his devotion to the emperor, who represented divine authority on earth and the source of life to whom no sacrifice was too great. In the title of one work from *Uncle's Poems*, he characterized Japanese war dead as "those who return to the source" (*minamoto ni ki suru mono*):

> Throughout the millennium the Great Deity has reigned.
> Those who know the source of life gain a strength
> that enables them to do deeds out of proportion to their stature.
> Those oppressed with self-doubt
> are in utter darkness, with no knowledge of the great cause.
> But those who simply return to the source
> can see the bright sun and moon;
> without questioning living or dying,
> they respond to His will with all they have.
> Winter, spring, summer, and autumn have passed,
> and December 8 is here again.
> Soldiers killed in the war are not dead:
> their life shining brightly, they guide us.
> Now is the time to serve the country with dedication and courage.
> Let all of us, each in his way,
> return to the source of life.
> Powerful are those who return to the source![509]

In his "Jūnigatsu yōka" (December eighth), published a year earlier, Takamura also proclaimed the emperor's divinity and celebrated the attack on Pearl Harbor as a lesson to those who had held Japan in low esteem:

> Remember December eighth!
> On this day the history of the world was changed.
> The Anglo-Saxon powers
> On this day were repulsed on Asian land and sea.
> It was their *Japan* which repulsed them,
> A tiny country in the Eastern Sea,
> Nippon, the Land of the Gods
> Ruled over by a living god.[510]

In another of his poems celebrating the attack on Pearl Harbor, Takamura affirms official justifications for the war as a struggle against Western colonialism that would liberate and unify Asia:

> We are standing for justice and life,
> While they are standing for profits.
> We are defending justice,
> While they are attacking for profits.

They raise their heads in arrogance,
While we are constructing the Great East Asia family.[511]

Many of Takamura's poems specifically echoed government propaganda and predictions of success in the war effort. In "Chinshi seyo Shō-sensei!" (Mr. Chiang, reflect on this! 1940), he chides the Chinese Nationalist leader for siding with Britain and the United States against Japan in what he warns will be a losing cause:

My country, Japan, is not destroying yours, sir;
We're only destroying anti-Japanese thought.
If you, sir, persist in your anti-Japanism, you will also perish.
My country, Japan, has now attacked America and England.
America and England have been rejected by the Heaven and Earth of East Asia.
Their allies will be crushed.
Does this bode good or ill for your country, sir?
Reflect, sir, reflect![512]

"Shingapōru kanraku" (The fall of Singapore) and "Karera o utsu" (We strike them), both published in 1942, also suggest how enthusiastically Takamura had embraced official justifications for the war effort. In the first poem, "the Anglo-Saxon race" for which Takamura had declared his "respect and love" in 1914 now becomes "the arrogant Anglo-Saxons" and "the savage poisonous snakes." Meanwhile, in conquering Singapore Japan has become the "power that has thrown down power" to "sever the linchpin" of the British Empire. Japanese soldiers are "our neighbors who spill their blood" and "give their lives in a righteous cause" to "smash the fangs and claws" of an enemy that "covets profits" and has "encircled us for two centuries, . . . emasculating the people of East Asia."[513]

In these poems Takamura reiterates the officially proclaimed cause for the Greater East Asia War, summarizing the effects of Western colonialism and proclaiming Japan's mission to end it. He downgrades the power of profits and weapons that Western nations used to colonize East Asia and exalts Japan's spiritual power derived from national unity of purpose, a willingness to sacrifice for a just cause, and the emperor's "august virtue," asserting that "the victory of our forces is certain." Novelist Shiga Naoya echoed these views in observing after the fall of Singapore that "the Americans are boasting of their economic power and huge military budgets. . . . But how much poorer they are in spiritual power compared with Japan."[514] Assertions that the war's successful outcome was assured by Japanese spiritual superiority went beyond poets and novelists and was expressed routinely by such Japanese government and military leaders as Prime Minister Tōjō Hideki and General Kawabe Masakazu. In November 1942, eight months after the fall of Singapore and five months after the Battle of Midway, Reserve Army General Suzuki Teiichi, president of the Wartime Planning Board, explained to reporters:

> The key to final victory lies not in the material fighting strength of the nation, but in the spirit which infuses strength in all directions. There are some who are rather pessimistic in view of the enormous national resources of the U.S. However, material wealth does not decide the outcome of war. . . . The side with a great productive power can be compared to a bulky adversary in a duel. . . . It is not difficult to recognize a difference in spirit between the Anglo-Americans and the Japanese. They have been brought up with the ideology of individualism and democracy, while we, the Japanese, have been raised with sacred spiritual ideas. . . . Should we be determined to sink every enemy ship, then we have nothing to fear, regardless of the great number of enemy warships. . . . The mightier the enemy forces are, the greater Japan's victory will be.[515]

Even when America's material superiority began to take its toll and the tide of war was turning against Japanese forces after their initial succession of victories, Takamura and other poets continued to produce bellicose and exhortatory verses appealing to the "courage" and "unity" of the nation's youth. By now he was head of the poetry section in the Japan Literary Patriotic Association (Nihon Bungaku Hōkokukai), established in May 1942 under the sponsorship of the government's Cabinet Information Bureau, which also oversaw censorship. Although membership in the Association was not required, some three thousand writers joined to express their patriotism or to avoid risking their publishing prospects. Ben-Ami Shillony observes: "In a country like Japan, where the group values of loyalty and harmony were still considered very important, there was far less need for coercion in order to line up the intellectuals, the writers, and the artists behind the nation in arms."[516]

One of the Japan Literary Patriotic Association's first actions was to fund the collection and publication of classical Japanese poetry valorizing war and soldiers. Fujiwara Teika's (1162–1241) famous *Ogura hyakunin isshu* (Ogura collection by one hundred poets), featuring poems on love and nature, has been used for centuries as material for a popular New Year's card game. However, it was superseded for three years starting in 1942 by *Aikoku hyakunin isshu* (Patriotic poems by one hundred poets), containing martial poetry from *Man'yōshū* and by such Tokugawa-period nationalists as Hirata Atsutane. In January 1943 the Association's *haiku* section began dispatching poets to battlefronts and factories, where it was hoped that poetry would be good for the morale of soldiers and workers.[517]

The Association's members also included distinguished novelists Shiga Naoya and Tanizaki Jun'ichirō, who ran afoul of the censors for his 1943 novel *Sasameyuki* (The Makioka sisters). After its first two installments appeared in the January and March issues of *Chūō kōron*, the magazine suspended its publication and printed an announcement in the June issue citing "the possibility that this novel might exert an undesirable influence, in view of present exigencies." Although by no means an antiwar novel, this engrossing family drama baring the intimate details of a declining Osaka household beset with scandal was considered by the military to be dangerously distracting and a threat to national morale in "this time of emergency."[518]

Takamura's poems, by contrast, had begun to read like recruiting posters in verse. He dedicated "Boku mo tobu" (I, too, will fly, November 1944) to the young men of the Youth Corps Fliers, and "Zengakuto tatsu" (All students are rising to the cause, 1944) to students, previously receiving draft deferments, who were conscripted starting in late 1943.[519] "Boku mo tobu" tells of a boy whose "heart beats faster" as he hears the "cheerful buzzing" of airplanes that seem to call to him as they pass over his roof. He longs to defend "Greater East Asia, / Striking down the enemy planes!" The poem concludes with his plea for his parents to let him become a Youth Corps Flier. "Zengakuto tatsu" tells of students who are "honored with the call to arms," and praises "the power that forges school caps into steel," which adds "a vital and vigorous component to the Emperor's invincible forces."[520]

Donald Keene has written that Takamura, looking back in retrospect after the war, "was especially tortured by the fear that his wartime poetry might have inspired men to go to their deaths for a cause that now appeared to have been misguided."[521] This is the subject of his poem "Wa ga shi o yomite hito shi ni tsukeri" (Men, having read my poems, went to their deaths, 1948):

> . . . .
> To save myself from the fear of death
> I became desperate about "desperate times" and wrote.
> My countrymen at the front lines read these poems.
> Men read them and went to their deaths.

The submarine captain who wrote his family
That he reread my poems each day soon afterward went down with
his ship.[522]

Other poems from this period express regret for swallowing wartime ideology and for writing poetry in support of it:

"Shūsen" (The end of the war, 1947)

. . . .
We were saved from starvation by the Occupation Army.
And barely escaped with our lives.
At that time the Emperor himself came forward
And explained he was not a living god.
With the passage of time
The beam has been removed from my eye;
Before I knew it a heavy weight of sixty years had melted away.
. . . .[523]

And in his self-deprecatory "Shō-sensei ni zansha su" (Apology in shame to Mr. Chiang, 1948), Takamura repudiates the "imbecility" of his earlier, derisive view of the nationalist leader stated in "Mr. Chiang, Reflect on This!" (see pp. 8, 196).[524]

Like Takamura, *tanka* poet Saitō Mokichi pursued a dual career and spent time in Europe. A medical doctor specializing in psychiatry, Mokichi studied neuropsychiatry in Vienna and Munich between 1921 and 1925 and had at least one disturbing encounter with anti-Japanese sentiment. In 1923 eminent German psychiatrist Emil Kraepelin, whose work Mokichi had long admired, refused to shake his hand when they met in Munich. Mokichi also found that his considerable accomplishments and experience in the field were not sufficiently acknowledged by his colleagues in Munich, and that he was not treated there with the respect he felt he had earned.[525] Yet, like Takamura, Mokichi also had good relationships with Europeans, including his immediate supervisor Walter Spielmeyer, who, Amy Vladeck Heinrich writes, "was warm toward Japanese students."[526] Mokichi appears to have shared Takamura's early propensity to idealize Europeans, eulogizing great scholars in poems Heinrich calls "saccharine in their worshipful tone."[527]

With his mixed experiences abroad and his deeply rooted patriotism, perhaps it should not be surprising that, two decades after his return, Mokichi wrote in his diary on the Pearl Harbor attack that "the Empire yesterday opened war on America and England. My aged blood danced.

. . . In the afternoon I worshipped at the Meiji Shrine. I met Prime Minister Tōjō and the Naval Minister."[528] By this time Mokichi had already composed poetry in support of Japanese forces fighting in the China War. Among five of his verses that were broadcast on the radio throughout Japan shortly after the Marco Polo Bridge Incident of 1937 are these three:

kurogane no kabuto kamurite idetatamu Ōkimi no tame oya no kuni no tame	Let us put on our helmets of steel and go forth in the cause of our sovereign, in the cause of the fatherland!
Shanhaisen no butai omoeba honōdatsu kokoro to narite koyoi nemurezu	When I think of the corps at the battleground of Shanghai, my heart is ablaze with rising flames, and tonight I cannot sleep.
obitadashiki gunba jōriku no sama o mite watakushi no akatsuki namida sekiaezu	Looking on as the legion of chargers is going ashore, my own hot tears flow unrestrained.[529]

Heinrich observes that Mokichi's support of the war was rooted in a strong sense of duty, rather than in a particular ideology:

> Mokichi's support was not merely a matter of course; it was enthusiastic: war stirred his blood. He was a patriot in the Meiji mold, and firmly believed it his duty to follow, not question, the Emperor and through him the nation. His responsibility was to serve, not to judge. The roots of this patriotism were firmly planted in his childhood, in his war games, and his prayers for his soldier brothers who fought in Manchuria. They were nurtured in his manhood as well, in his study of the *Man'yōshū* and his association of himself with Hitomaro. . . . He considered the *Man'yōshū* not only a poetic model but a spiritual one, and he valued the obedience to the imperial will expressed in the Frontier Guard poems.[530]

Mokichi's embracing of the Frontier Guard poems as a "spiritual model" recalls Yosano Tekkan's advocacy in 1895 of the "manliness" (*masuraoburi*) he found in martial poems from *Man'yōshū* as a standard for Japanese poetry. Mokichi's patriotic poetry, like Tekkan's, is said to fail as literature,[531] but his war poems never fell to Tekkan's level of bloodthirstiness and vituperation. The absence of political philosophy in Mokichi's war poems also puts him at odds with Takamura, who, as we have seen, often wrote versifications of Japanese government propaganda. Heinrich has noted that "Mokichi was not ignorant of political theory . . . however, he was looking at the visible reality of newsreels, and not at the underlying causes for the activities. . . . Mokichi believed in the ideal; he had no political acumen and no interest in politics."[532]

Mokichi's many wartime poems[533] include three published in 1943 on the Japanese navy's sinking of the two British battleships *Repulse* and *Prince of Wales* in December 1941. John Dower recalls that "Churchill described this as his greatest shock of the war." In Japan it was hailed as the latest in a string of military successes that would culminate two months later in the invasion and occupation of Singapore. On the demise of the "unsinkable" warships, Dower writes:

> These two British battleships were dispatched to Singapore in the fall of 1941 upon Churchill's insistence that this meager show of sea power, combined with the U.S. military presence in the Philippines, would deter Japan from advancing south. Two days after the Japanese called this feeble bluff by attacking Pearl Harbor and the Philippines, they sank the two great vessels in the South China Sea with astonishing ease, losing only three planes in the process, . . . by a succession of perfectly executed air attacks launched from Japanese carriers.[534]

Mokichi's *tanka* celebrating the destruction of both battleships was anthologized two years later in *Daitōa sensō kashū* (Collected poems of the Greater East Asia War):

"Gōchin" no atarashiki go yo tsukuzuku to hōsha shi kuru mono o ai shi mitsu	A new word, "instant sinking," radiates deeply within us, and we cherish it.
Reparusu wa shunmoku no ma ni shizumiyuki Purinsu obu Weruzu wa sakei shitsutsu sukoshi nigu	The *Repulse* went down in an instant. The *Prince of Wales* heeled over to the port side, and fled a short distance.[535]

Several months after Japan's forces began to suffer setbacks in the conflict, Mokichi continued to turn out exhortative poems. Two in the series "Kami no mi-gun" (The army of His Divine Majesty) are dedicated to the more than two thousand Japanese soldiers, an entire garrison, who died in May 1943 fighting an American force five times as numerous at the Battle of Attu in the Aleutian Islands.[536] Following this battle, the term *gyoku-sai*, literally "shattering the jewel" but denoting in this case "the choice of an honorable death against insurmountable enemy forces," came into popular spoken and printed usage. Two years later, in the spring of 1945 when U.S. saturation bombing wreaked massive death and destruction on Japan's cities, the term became *ichioku gyokusai*, "the honorable death of all one hundred million Japanese," a call for national extermination as preferable to surrender.[537]

"Attsu-tō no chūkon ni sasagu" (To the loyal spirits of Attu Island, 1943)

hitori-dani ikinokoraji to uttae shi sumera mi-gun no tamashii zo kore	Having fought to the very last man, these are the spirits of His Majesty's Forces.
kanashisa wa sugu ni hitotsu naru kokoro nite ima koso wa yobe waga otakebi o	The sadness truly unites our hearts. Now let us raise our war cries.[538]

Heinrich observes that Mokichi "had seen enough of the aftermath of defeat in Europe in the early 1920s to believe that victory must be attained no matter what the cost."[539] Then, after Japan's defeat, in a poem from his 1949 collection *Shirokiyama* (White mountains) he conveyed the sentiments of many Japanese who felt they had been deceived by the government as to both the war's aims and its prospects:

gunbatsu to iu koto sae mo shirazarishi ware o omoeba namida shi nagaru	When I think that I did not even know of such a thing as military cliques, my tears flow forth.[540]

Noting that Mokichi's book of commentary *Man'yō shūka* (The best poems of the *Man'yō*) had been "carried into battle by thousands of young soldiers," Heinrich identifies another *tanka* from *White Mountains* as a poem "concern[ing] a burdensome sense of responsibility for his collaboration with the war effort"[541]:

michi no be ni hima no hana saki- tarishi koto nani ka tsumi fukaki kanji no gotoku	Beside the road the flowers of the *hima* plant were blossoming: like my feeling of some kind of heavy crime.

Such expressions of remorse by Mokichi and Takamura contrast sharply with the reluctance of other poets to discuss, or even to acknowledge, their wartime writings. Lest one assume that such retrospective regret is a phenomenon exclusive to Japan, it is important to remember that Siegfried Sassoon was not the only poet in the West to pen verses in support of war that he later found embarrassing. If World War I produced some of the finest English poetry on war, it also inspired verses Bernard Bergonzi calls "feeble," "deplorable," and "pathetic."[542] He notes the "bogus toughness" of "The Bayonet" by distinguished Georgian poet Wilfrid Gibson:

> This bloody steel
>   Has killed a man.
> I heard him squeal.
>   As on I ran. (60)

Unlike Sassoon, Gibson produced all of his poetry on World War I as a civilian observing from the "home front." Yet even men who saw the war firsthand published poetry about it that critic Douglas Goldring found to be "valueless as literature" (62). It is hard to imagine that in more ordinary times this effort by Geoffrey Johnson, a student enlistee trying his hand at verse, would have found its way into print:

> "Without Shedding of Blood"
>
> Malvern men must die and kill,
> That wind may blow on Malvern Hill;
> Devonshire blood must fall like dew,
> That Devon's bays may yet be blue;
> London must spill out lives like wine,
> That London's lights may ever shine. (62)

Johnson's call for human sacrifices in war might be compared to Takamura's praise of "our neighbors who spill their blood" in "The Fall of Singapore." If anything, however, Takamura's phrase, though clichéd, seems at least to convey a certain dignity, while the demand of Johnson that "London must spill out lives like wine" is expressed in a simile that strikes the reader as maudlin, even comical. Writing in a similar vein, Robert Nichols, who served briefly on active duty in World War I, produced "The Assault," a venture into free verse atypical of his usually formal and sedate style (64). It concludes:

> Bullets. Mud. Stumbling and skating.
> My voice's strangled shout:
> "*Steady pace, boys!*"
> The still light: gladness.
> Ha! Ha! Bunched figures waiting.
> Revolver leveled quick!
> Flick! Flick!
> Red as blood.
> Germans. Germans.
> Good! O good!
> Cool madness. (64)

Of this poem Douglas Goldring wrote:

> It was characteristic of our wartime criticism that this masterpiece of drivel, instead of exciting derision, was hailed as a work of genius with avidity. . . . Lying about in every smart London drawing-room you would find the latest little volume, and at every fashionable bookshop the half-crown war poets were among the "best selling lines." . . . An atmosphere was quickly and easily created favourable to the sale of verse, and the always gullible English public, flattered by the remarks in the Press about its "revived interest in poetry," disbursed its shillings with lavishness only equaled by its lack of discrimination. (64, 61)

Still, at least some critics, such as Harold Monro who edited *Poetry and Drama*, maintained their standards:

> The war poetry that has appeared in the press does not seem to have represented an exalted, a natural, or even a valuable form of patriotism. . . . We get an impression of verse-writers excitedly gathering to *do something* for their flag, and as soon as they begin to rack their brains how that something may be done in verse, a hundred old phrases for patriotic moments float into their minds, which they reel into verse or fit into sonnets—and the press is delighted to publish them.[543]

It is a situation, in some respects, not unlike that which prevailed in Japan during the Pacific War, when such a distinguished poet as Fukuda Masao could write:

> Get angry, still more angry, angry at the enemy!
> Shoot and shoot again
> Until you strike down those who do not revere His Majesty.
> This is true loyalty.[544]

Fukuda, Takamura, Gibson, and Nichols all might have done well to heed the words of essayist Hirata Takuboku (1873–1943), written in 1894 during the conflict with China that inspired the first deluge of war poems in post-Restoration Japan:

> At the present time, the mention of war literature is the very quintessence of foolishness. . . . What the litterateurs now call war literature or new-style military poetry is, as [Kōda] Rohan [novelist, 1867–1947] has said, nothing but the uninteresting husks of poetry, the abortive work of poets with rather dubious goals. Though they may, thanks to mass hysteria, be popular for a time, there is not one particle of eternal poetic values in their work.[545]

As noted above, critics also condemned writers ten years later, at the height of the conflict with Russia, who were thought to be capitalizing on "the war craze" to sell their work. The magazine *Jidai shichō* called them "claptrap dealers" who turned out "shallow, phony junk"[546]; and Takizawa Shūgyō accused them of "kowtowing to the war gods in search of profits."[547] Poet and critic Hiraide Shū preceded Douglas Goldring by ten years in expressing disdain for the pen-wielding profiteers of war: "Lacking the slightest trace of an idea, such claptrap feeds the bottomless appetites of booksellers and panders to popular fads."[548]

Thus poets in many countries have found themselves embarrassed for penning exhortative war poems of the kind that Goldring and Hiraide have called "valueless as literature." Yet, unlike most of their contemporaries in Japan, Takamura and Saitō, whose poems seem less obnoxious than the many vituperative and racist wartime verses, openly expressed regret for writing poetry in support of what they later recognized to have been a tragically misguided cause. Their postwar statements contrast with other writers' efforts to conceal or "revise" wartime works and with the refusals of some to acknowledge that the war had been a mistake. Such reluctance can also be found among writers who supported the Axis cause in Europe. John Updike observes, "It *is* disappointing: the bulk of right-wing intellectuals and artists from fascism's thirties heyday—Pound, Hamsun, Céline, Heidegger, most notoriously—did not publicly express much repentance." Updike notes that Romanian writer Norman Manea "rightly regrets that so little honest testimony has emerged from the fellow-travelers of fascism."[549] Manea could be speaking for writers both in Europe and Japan when he advocates that, with more such honesty, "we could probably not only understand more thoroughly the past but also have a better idea of the future of humanity."[550]

Conclusion: Postwar Reflections and the Antiwar Revival

Literary critics' scathing denunciations of wartime verse produced in Europe and Japan raise the question as to whether literature written in support of war can ever be artistically successful. Is the term "war poetry" an oxymoron? In "On Being Asked for a War Poem," W. B. Yeats (1865–1939) wrote during World War I, "I think it better in times like these / A poet's mouth be silent."[551] Nobel Peace Prize recipient Elie Wiesel's best-known writings document the Holocaust, which was finally ended by the Allied invasion of Europe. Yet he has cautioned against "glorify[ing] war" and advised writers, "Don't make poetry out of murder, out of bloodshed." He points out that the most bellicose portion of the Bible, the Book of Joshua, is devoid of poetry.[552]

Since the poems on armed conflict that are most often praised as literature are overwhelmingly those that condemn war, one might conclude that poetry against war is of inherently higher literary quality than that which supports it. Perhaps because poetry denouncing the death and suffering of war usually focuses on individual experience to which readers can connect, it is likely to be more highly evaluated than that which appeals to broad, collective causes in rationalizing such losses and anguish, or which poses them in the context of heroism. Famous war poems are plentiful in English, ranging from "The Charge of the Light Brigade," in which Alfred Lord Tennyson (1809–92) eulogizes the "honour" and "glory" of "noble" British soldiers killed in the Crimean War,[553] to "The Battle Hymn of the Republic," in which Julia Ward Howe (1819–1910) deifies the Union Army as "the coming of the Lord" with "His terrible swift sword."[554] Yet such poems are rarely included in anthologies of what compilers consider the "canon" of exemplary poetry in English. King Henry the Fifth's exhortation to his men in Shakespeare's play named for this wartime monarch is perhaps the most famous literary call to arms in the English language, but it hardly represents the bard at his best:

> Once more unto the breach, dear friends, once more,
> Or close the wall up with our English dead!
> In peace there's nothing so becomes a man
> As modest stillness and humility;
> But when the blast of war blows in our ears,
> Then imitate the action of the tiger:
> Stiffen the sinews, summon up the blood.[555]

However, opposing war does not necessarily guarantee good poetry. In literature East and West, poems classified as antiwar abound that rely for their impact on slogans and didactic pronouncements or that depict war's victims with a melodrama that quickly descends into bathos. Uchimura Kanzō, a distinguished Christian writer and orator, had initially supported the 1894–95 conflict with China as what he called a "righteous war." He accepted the official rationale that Japanese forces were "protecting" Korea from the Chinese government's "backward" policies, and he proclaimed that the "sacred right of neighborhood compels us to interfere on [Korea's] behalf."

Uchimura later said he felt betrayed when he became convinced that the government's motives had been something less than "chivalric." In a letter to a friend dated May 22, 1895, one month after the signing of the peace treaty at Shimonoseki, Uchimura employed biblical language to describe himself as a foolish prophet for supporting "a righteous war [that] has changed into a *piratic* war."[556] In "Jisei no kansatsu" (Observations on the times), an article he published in the August 15, 1896 issue of the magazine *Kokumin no tomo*, he wrote: "[Japanese] think of killing Chinese soldiers as a wild boar hunt."[557]

> Now that we stand in the position of victors we forget our chief aim, independence of our neighbor; the attention of the entire nation has been stolen by such things as the carving out of new territory and the expansion of new markets. They are preoccupied with trying to garner more than enough profit and war gains.[558]

The following year he published an article in English addressed to an international readership in which he specified his objections to the war:

> Japan acted hypocritically . . . because the righteous war was concluded unrighteously. . . . The money we exacted as the price of the blood we shed for "the salvation of our weakly

> neighbor" was not spent—no, not a single cent of it—for the elevation and consolidation of the said helpless neighbor, but wholly for the increase of our own armament.[559]

Uchimura cited his disillusionment with the Sino-Japanese War as ultimately leading him to embrace pacifism ten years later on the eve of the war with Russia. His articles opposing Japan's entry into this conflict, published even after it was well under way, stand as courageous expressions of dissent in the face of heightened government censorship and widespread public support for the war effort (see chapters five and six). His essays condemning both wars inspire readers to share his seething outrage. However, he had less success late in 1896 when he decided to convey his feelings in poetry. "Yamome no joya" (A widow's New Year's eve) is composed for the most part in the *shintaishi* form, from the viewpoint of a woman whose husband died at the Battle of Weihaiwei.

Tsuki kiyoshi, hoshi shiroshi, shimo fukashi, yoru samushi, ie mazushi, tomo sukoshi, toshi tsukite hito kaerazu.	The moon is clear, the stars are white, and frost is deep on this cold night. My home is poor and friends I lack. The year ends, but he's still not back.
Omoi wa hashiru nishi no umi, namida wa kōru ikaiwan, minami no shima ni funade seshi, koishiki hito no ato yukashi.	My thoughts turn to the western sea, to the bay of frozen tears at Weihaiwei. I want to follow my beloved's trail, to where his boat for South Island set sail.
Hito ni wa haru no haregomoro, ikusa isao no iwaizake, ware ni wa kari no wabizumai, hitori tamukuru aka no mizu.	While others don bright New Year's dress and drink toasts to the exploits of war, I remain secluded in temporary lodgings where, alone, I offer holy water.
Ware munashū shite hito michi, ware otoroete kuni sakayu, tei o meido no tsuma ni tsukushi, setsu o sengo no kuni ni mattō su.	I face emptiness while others' lives are full. I decline while the nation prospers. I shall always be faithful to my husband in the netherworld, as I pass my days in this triumphant nation.
Tsuki kiyoshi, hoshi shiroshi shimo fukashi, yoru samushi ie mazushi, tomo sukoshi toshi tsukite hito kaerazu.	The moon is clear, the stars are white, and frost is deep on this cold night. My home is poor and friends I lack. The year ends, but he's still not back.[560]

With all the obnoxious prowar verses generated by the conflict with China, this poem demonstrates that an antiwar viewpoint does not assure a good poem. Uchimura conveys the stark contrast between a war widow's prospects for a lifetime of "emptiness" and "others' lives," which seem "full" as they celebrate "the exploits of war" in "this triumphal nation," but his repetition of rhyming sequences ending with the syllable *shi* creates a sing-song effect highly inappropriate to the mood of the poem's speaker. Such refrains work well when the mood is satirical, as in Kinoshita Naoe's "Song of the Banging Drum" (see chapter four, pp. 103–4), but seem here to trivialize the widow's sorrow, making it sound rather like childish self-pity.

That opposition to war does not necessarily produce good poetry was demonstrated again in Japan half a century later. The outpouring of poems classified as antiwar after 1945 followed another period when prowar verses had been copiously produced. In his "1967-nen Nihon no natsu" (Japan's summer of 1967), published in *Nihon hansenshi-shū*, Yoshida Kin'ichi draws a parallel between the Pacific War and U.S. intervention in Vietnam, calling—rhetorically one assumes—for racial retribution:

> In that August of twenty-two years ago it was not on Berlin or Rome
> in the countries of white skin that the atomic bomb was dropped,
> But on Hiroshima where it was sure to be yellow skin
> that burned to a dangling scar.
> . . . .
>
> Japanese and Vietnamese are people of the same color.
> Yesterday's keloid scars were from the atomic bomb.
> Today they are from napalm.
> When Asian people, gaunt and weary, cry out for peace,
> Others, fat and greasy, escalate the war.
>
> In Vietnam, cluster bombs pierce yellow skin,
> Lean yellow skin, riddling it like a honeycomb.
>
> Shoot those cluster bombs at America!
> Those "parent" bombs holding the 2,000 "children" bombs—
> Let them pierce white skin, riddling it like a honeycomb.[561]

One might question whether a poem that calls, even rhetorically, for shooting cluster bombs at people should be classified as antiwar. Furthermore, Yoshida's assertion of racial comradery between Vietnam and Japan might be hard to accept for Vietnamese who remember that two million people in Vietnam starved to death under wartime Japanese occupation, when much of the local rice crop was confiscated to feed Japanese soldiers and civilians.[562] Yoshida's pronouncement that atomic bombs would not have been dropped on "the countries of white skin" ignores the history of nuclear weapons. Japanese and American historians justifiably question the decision to use them in 1945, but the United States began development some five years earlier because Nazi scientists were thought to be on the verge of producing an atomic bomb. The first U.S. prototypes, planned with Germany as their hypothetical target, were not completed before Germany surrendered in May 1945.

In a more purposeful distortion of history, Katagiri Yuzuru sarcastically paraphrases Japanese government propaganda of the 1940s to denounce U.S. military intrusion in Southeast Asia. His poem, translated here in part, has also been classified as antiwar:

> Tōjō called America savage and said we had to guard the peace in Asia.
> Now we even think maybe Tōjō was right,
> For it is certain that America savagely disturbs the peace in Asia.[563]

By evoking, even sarcastically, wartime hate propaganda as a protest against U.S. intervention in Southeast Asia, Katagiri seems to confirm the view that, in postwar Japan, impassioned opposition to U.S. military policies has at times abetted the tendency to distort or ignore Japan's history of wartime aggression and atrocities.[564] Nevertheless, while such poems as Katagiri's take perhaps too much "poetic license" with history and are less than distinguished as literature, they succeed in conveying the horror felt in Japan, a recent target of air attacks, toward U.S. bombings in Southeast Asia.

The losses, outrages, and inequities of war have been lamented elsewhere in poetry long on sorrow and anger but short on literary quality. Among British poems condemning the death and suffering of World War I, those by Ford Madox Ford (1873–1939) have been characterized by Bernard Bergonzi as "rhythmically inert, with lax, intermittently rhyming lines, and little interest in the verbal texture."[565] Like Uchimura's "A Widow's New Year's Eve," Ford's "Antwerp," from his *Collected Poems* of 1914, depicts the suffering war imposes on women:

> This is Charing Cross;
> It is midnight;
> There is a great crowd
> And no light.
> A great crowd, all black that hardly whispers aloud.
> Surely, that is a dead woman—a dead mother!
> She has a dead face;
> She is dressed all in black,
> She wanders to the bookstall and back
> At the back of the crowd;
> And back again and again back,
> She sways and wanders.[566]

Bergonzi describes Ford's poems from *On Heaven* (1918), lamenting the deaths of British soldiers in World War I, as "loosely meditative," "sentimental," and "anachronistic," composed in a sporadically rhyming form of "semi-free verse" Bergonzi calls "a maddening vehicle"[567]:

> Poor little Arnott—poor little lad . . .
> And poor old Knapp,
> Of whom once I borrowed a map—and never returned it,
> And Morris and Jones and all the rest of the Welch,
> So many gone in the twenty-four hours of a day. . . .[568]

American poets, like their British and Japanese counterparts, have produced poems opposing war that read more like manifestos or melodramas than poetry. In "The Philippine Conquest" (1900), Edgar Lee Masters denounces U.S. motives in the Spanish-American War as selfish and hypocritical:

> It is the army of an empire and not a republic,
> Our soldiers in the Philippines
> are not fighting for any principle.
> They are not defending their homes.
> They are not staying aggression.
> They are not repelling an attack upon liberty.
> There is no sentiment in the struggle.
> There is no conscience in the fight.
> It is of no consequence to our soldiers
> whether they win or lose,
> except as a matter of honor, advancement and money.
> For these they are there to conquer,
> as the Arabs were in Spain,
> as Spain was in Peru and Mexico,
> and as Great Britain is in South Africa.
> To conquer for spoils not for themselves,
> because they are only hired men,
> but for the trusts at home—
> as the Spanish regulars fought for gold
> for the sovereign,
> as the Englishman is fighting for the banks of London.[569]

Like much of Japan's proletarian literature, such works convey more philosophical specificity than poetic subtlety. However, there are poems in Japan, as elsewhere, that carry a philosophical ambiguity that has made them the subject of controversy as to whether they oppose or support war. While read initially as honoring battlefield sacrifices and inspiring home-front efforts in wartime, these works were later singled out as examples of poems against war. As noted above, Siegfried Sassoon had initially written "Kiss," a childish tribute to the weapons of war, as an expression of sincere bellicose enthusiasm on the eve of his service in World War I, but he later presented it as antiwar satire after his horrifying battlefield experiences.

Perhaps the best-known poem in Japan to receive such conflicting readings is "Yuki no shingun" (Marching through the snow, 1895), by Nagai Kenshi (1865–1940), commander of the Imperial Japanese Army Band and a prolific composer of *gunka*. The poem generates a sardonic, and occasionally black, humor typical of soldiers' ditties everywhere. Although it was a popular marching song for Japanese troops who faced particular hardships ill-equipped and underclothed for winter on the Chinese continent, the fourth stanza of this work was expurgated in reprintings after 1937, when full-scale war erupted again with China. Later, the entire poem was banned during the Pacific War because the current government, apparently failing to see the humor, alleged that it was "filled with a feeling of hopelessness among soldiers, which depresses their fighting spirit"[570]:

yuki no shingun	Marching through the snow,
kōri o funde	tramping over ice,
dore ga kawa yara	we cannot even tell
michi sae shirezu	the river from the road.
uma wa taoreru	How can we leave behind
sutete mo okezu	our horses when they fall?
koko wa izuku zo	Wherever we go,
mina teki no kuni	it is enemy country.
mamayo daitan	Lighting up,
ippuku yareba	we take a smoke,
tanomi sukuna ya	but find little solace
tabako ga nihon	in two cigarettes.
yakanu himono ni	We survive, but barely,
hannie meshi ni	eating cold, dried fish
namaji inochi no	and half-cooked rice
aru sono uchi wa	'round a campfire
koraekirenai	in the unbearable chill.
samusa no takibi	Smoke
kemui hazu da yo	surrounds us
namaki ga iburu	from the smoldering green wood.
shibui kao shite	Wearing grim faces,
kōmyōbanashi	we talk of glorious deeds,
sui to iu wa	and taste the sourness
umeboshi hitotsu	of one pickled plum.
Ki nomi ki no mama	How free and easy it is
kiraku na fushido	to sleep in the clothes we wear
hainō makura ni	with knapsacks for pillows

gaitō kaburya
sena no nukumi de
yuki tokekakaru
yagu no kibigara
shippori nurete
musubikanetaru
roei no yume o
tsuki wa tsumetaku
kao nozokikomu

and raincoats for covers,
and the warmth from our backs
melting the snow.
Our blankets are stalks of millet and grain,
all soaking wet.
On bivouac we dream
of what cannot be
while the moon peers down coldly
on our faces.

inochi sasagete
dete kita mi yue
shinuru kakugo de
tokkan suredo
buun tsutanaku
uchijini seneba
giri ni karameta
juppei mawata
sorori sorori to
kubishimekakaru
dōse ikashite
kaesanu tsumori

We came
to give our lives.
Resolved to die,
we raise the battle cry.
If the fate of war
does not decree our deaths,
The cotton clothing we are sent,
twined with duty,
will slowly suffocate us,
Since we are not intended
to return home
alive.[571]

Government expurgations of this poem and of fiction that graphically depicted the suffering of Japanese soldiers at the front cast doubt on the assertion of Ruth Benedict in *The Chrysanthemum and the Sword* that an account of "the sacrifices and suffering of war . . . is enough for the Japanese audience. . . . The people [portrayed] have repaid *on* [obligation] with everything that was in them, and [serve as] propaganda of the militarists."[572] If they were originally intended to inspire dedication and sacrifice, such works as "Marching through the Snow" were later viewed by government censors as a danger to wartime morale. Reading this poem today, one would not be surprised to find it in an anthology of antiwar poetry alongside Wilfred Owen's "Exposure," a poem that evokes winter at the (World War I) front through circumstances, mood, and imagery that are strikingly similar:

> Our brains ache, in the merciless iced east winds that knive us . . .
> Wearied we keep awake because the night is silent . . .
> Low, drooping flares confuse our memory of the salient . . .
> Worried by silence, sentries whisper, curious, nervous,
> But nothing happens.
>
> . . . .
> The poignant misery of dawn begins to grow . . .
> We only know war lasts, rain soaks, and clouds sag stormy,

. . . .
But nothing happens.

Pale flakes with fingering stealth come feeling for our faces—
We cringe in holes, back on forgotten dreams, and stare, snow-dazed,
Deep into grassier ditches. So we drowse, sun-dozed,
Littered with blossoms trickling where the blackbird fusses,
—Is it that we are dying?[573]

Interpretations and evaluations of war literature in Japan changed perhaps most markedly after World War II. Not only were poems once condemned as "treasonous" and later censored now held in high esteem, but even works by such writers as Hino Ashihei (1907–60), who supported Japanese military expansion and wrote detailed accounts of the conflict in China, are read by many in Japan today as documenting the tragic results of a misguided policy, an interpretation Hino could hardly have intended.[574] Some writers claimed that poems written during the war that appeared to support it were, in fact, protests against it, camouflaged in popular wartime slogans that were intended satirically to convey double meanings as a way of circumventing government censors.

If such *ex post facto* readings are difficult to verify, the recent outpouring in Japan of literature opposing war, the extensive searches by Japanese scholars for antiwar poetry written before 1945, and their efforts, sometimes based on selective or erroneous information, to make pacifist heroes of writers who produced such poetry, are all manifestations of the widespread revulsion in Japan against armed conflict after 1945. This revulsion also explains in large part why poetry that was written in support of war is now generally held in such low esteem, and why many writers who produced such poems during World War II prefer not to mention these works and to delete them from reprinted collections today. Still, in addition to Takamura and Mokichi, who published poetry after 1945 that expressed regret for their wartime verses, other Japanese poets have written on the misguided wartime policies and ideologies that had enjoyed wide popular support but led the nation to ultimate catastrophe.

Until recently Kaneko Mitsuharu was widely regarded as one of the very few Japanese writers to maintain an antiwar position throughout the conflicts in China and the Pacific. His poems on Japan's militarization in the 1930s, on the emperor system, and on the war in China have been hailed as landmarks of literary dissent. Then, in January 1976, Sakuramoto Tomio published an article entitled "Kaneko Mitsuharu-ron no kyomō chitai" (A zone of falsehood in studies of Kaneko Mitsuharu) in the magazine

Bungei tenbō,[575] noting that, while several of Kaneko's poems from the mid-1930s are justifiably admired as monuments of protest, some of his poems identified as antiwar and printed in his postwar collections were partially revised from their original versions published in the later 1930s. Sakuramoto suggests that the revisions were made to conceal what was, according to him, Kaneko's later "cooperation" in the war effort. This article sparked a vigorous rebuttal (*hanron*) from a number of poets and literary critics.[576] The poet's defenders maintained that Sakuramoto was reading too much into the revised passages and pointed out that poets often polish earlier works when they are to be reissued. The situation is further complicated by Kaneko's comments in his autobiography indicating that he had deliberately camouflaged the protest in his poetry during the war to mislead the authorities.[577] Much of the debate turns on whether Kaneko intended the popular wartime slogans appearing in the original versions of these poems to be read satirically or not. Kaneko himself was never able to respond to the charges in Sakuramoto's article because it was published the year after the poet's death.

According to his autobiography, Kaneko composed a series of poems toward the end of the war, between 1943 and 1945, while he lived in a small village near Mount Fuji, having evacuated Tokyo to escape Allied bombings.[578] In "Kanbō" (Bird's-eye view), which he dates to April 17, 1944 but which was not published until 1947,[579] Kaneko denounces the aggression of Imperial Forces and the hypocrisy of wartime ideology:

> "Soldiers of the gods" presiding over "peace in the Orient"
> Raped and plundered all within their reach.
> Then they acquired the murderous weapons of modern "civilization."
>
> The faded dream of the "Co-Prosperity Sphere,"
> more battered and warped than an old discarded shoe.[580]

In an allusion to Dante's *Inferno*, Kaneko published "Jigoku ni tsuite no nōto" (Notes on hell) in 1948,[581] which describes the extreme hardships and deprivations of the immediate postwar period as one result of the excesses of wartime ideology. This poem also expresses skepticism toward the Occupation's idealistic pronouncements about "democracy" and "reform," which are characterized as the substitution of one religion for another:

> Japan has been roasted in hell's fire.
> Still, none of the people here can see
> that the nation's fall was their own.

This hell was recently the parade ground of the gods,
    where now large-sized boots with steel hobnails saunter to and fro.
America—she can only litter the place with chewing gum.

The dead sleep on concrete station platforms.
    Gaunt faces of corpses.
Even the wind is lonely. The end of the world seems near.
Inside the transparent head of their God,
    can there really be a plan
    for a more wonderful world?[582]

Many Japanese poets have written movingly on the tragedy of World War II, though few mention, as Kaneko does, the mistakes that led the nation into ever-widening armed conflict. The majority of poems in Japan on the war in retrospect describe victims of massive U.S. air raids on Japanese cities, and the atomic bombings of Hiroshima and Nagasaki in particular. Many historians now consider the nuclear attacks to have been unnecessary for ending the war and regard them as the worst of many atrocities committed by Allied Forces during the conflict.[583] The following are two of the most effective and enduring of the "atomic bomb poems" (*genbaku-shi*). The first voices the horror and chaos of the event, while the second evokes the cataclysm in retrospect:

"MIZU O KUDASAI" (Give me water, 1946) by Hara Tamiki (1905–51)

GIVE ME water
AH GIVE ME water
LET ME DRINK
Death WOULD BE BETTER THAN THIS
Death WOULD BE
AAH
HELP HELP
Water . . .
Water . . .
SOMEHOW PLEASE
SOMEONE
    OHOHOHOH
    OHOHOHOH
THE heavens ARE split asunder
THE city HAS disappeared
THE river
IS FLOWING
    OHOHOHOH
    OHOHOHOH
Night IS COMING

Night IS COMING
IN BURNT DRY eyes
ON FESTERING lips
BLISTERING hot
THIS STAGGERING DISTORTED
Face's
GROAN IS THAT OF A HUMAN BEING
OF A HUMAN BEING.[584]

"Hachigatsu muika" (August 6, 1951) by Tōge Sankichi (1917–53)

That brilliant flash—who can forget it?
In a split second, 30,000 in the streets vanished;
the screams of 50,000 pinned under in pitch black
died away.

The churning yellow smoke thinned to reveal Hiroshima:
buildings split, bridges fallen,
packed streetcars burned,
an endless heap of rubble and embers.
Soon a procession of the naked, crying, walking in bunches,
trampling on brain matter:
charred clothes about waists,
skin hanging like rags
from arms raised to breasts.

Corpses at the Parade Ground, scattered about like stone statues;
at the river's edge, too, fallen in a heap, a group that had crawled
    toward a tethered raft,
turning gradually, under the burning rays of the sun, into corpses;
in the glare of the flames piercing the night sky,
the area where Mother and Brother were pinned under alive—
it too went up in flames.
In the feces and urine on the floor of the arsenal
a group of schoolgirls who had fled lay fallen;
bellies swollen like drums, blinded in one eye,
    skin half-gone, hairless, impossible to tell
    one from the other—
by the time the rays of the morning sun picked them out,
they had all stopped moving;
amid the stench, the only sound:
the flies buzzing about metal washbasins.

The stillness that reigned over the city of 300,000:
who can forget it?
In that hush

the white eyes of dead women and children
sent us
a soul-rending appeal:
who can forget it?[585]

John Whittier Treat has noted that literary representations of the nuclear attacks, like those of the Holocaust, "expose . . . the fundamental challenge posed literature by modern violence, namely whether or not anything, including the assumption of intelligibility, remains whole in the wake of total power to eliminate all vestiges of culture."[586] Quoting one "historian of battle," George Feifer has written that "war's horror exists partly because outsiders can't know it. . . . [It] is too little related to 'anything recognizably human or natural.'"[587] Faced with these challenges, some poets in Japan have chosen to evoke the unprecedented devastation of World War II from a minimalist perspective, placing the destructive power of bombs and bullets in the context of daily life more familiar to readers who did not experience this conflict. Such poems on the war in retrospect include these two works by women. Ibaragi Noriko (1926–) writes on how war stole a girl's youth in a poem that is now assigned in Japanese public schools to provide students, most of whose parents have no memory of the war, with some idea of what the times were like:

"Watashi ga ichiban kirei datta toki" (When I was at my prettiest)

When I was at my prettiest,
cities collapsed with a rumbling
and the blue sky could be seen in absurd places.

When I was at my prettiest,
many of the people around me died—
in factories, at sea, and on nameless islands.
I lost my chances to dress up.
When I was at my prettiest,
no one gave me sweet gifts.
Men knew only how to salute,
then off they all went, leaving behind nothing but memories
of their handsome eyes.

When I was at my prettiest,
my head was empty
and my heart was hardened.
Only my hands and feet shone chestnut color.

When I was at my prettiest,
my country lost a war—

What idiocy!
Rolling up the sleeves of my blouse, I walked defiantly
through the mean streets of town.

When I was at my prettiest,
jazz poured out of the radio,
and, feeling giddy as if I had just broken a no-smoking ban,
I reveled in a foreign country's sweet music.

When I was at my prettiest,
I was extremely unhappy.
I felt entirely out of place.
I was terribly lonely.

So I have decided to live a long life, if I can,
like Georges Rouault in France,
who painted beautiful pictures when he was old.[588]

By dismissing the "lost . . . war" as "idiocy," Ibaragi avoids the question of how the Japanese public could have given such widespread support for so long to the government's policy of military expansion. Had she written more about the war than its direct effects on one woman's life, perhaps this poem would not have been approved by the Ministry of Education for reading in public schools (see introduction, p. 8). Still, it is a powerful evocation of personal hardships in wartime and early-postwar Japan, ending on a note of hope.

Ibaragi's reference to a postwar infatuation with jazz recalls that the music of "enemy nations" had been banned in wartime Japan by the Information Bureau on January 2, 1942, a policy that was often erroneously applied to the works of German composers Ludwig van Beethoven and Richard Wagner.[589] Early postwar hedonism, described by novelists as well as poets,[590] has been attributed to feelings of relief at the end of a long and devastating conflict, release from the many wartime constraints and deprivations, and profound disillusionment with moral authority represented by the wartime Japanese government. Allied Occupation policies, though often well-intentioned, also engendered a certain amount of resentment and exasperation because they seemed at times to be contradictory and unrealistic. Despite the official espousing of women's rights and other egalitarian ideals, Japanese-organized recruitment of prostitutes for G.I. clientele was unofficially sanctioned, and people living in cities were forced to deal on the black market for foodstuffs that Occupation rationing and pricing regulations made unobtainable legally.[591] American technical and material aid and U.S. government purchases in Japan during the Korean War helped initially to launch the "economic miracle," nurtured effectively, if not always equitably, for four decades by government, business, and the work force. The Japanese are now among the world's most affluent people, and the nation has become a leading economic power.

Looking at Japan today, it is hard to imagine what conditions were like there during the early postwar period, a time when, with memories still fresh of the recent conflict, some of the best antiwar poetry was written. In the poem "Ibo: nyūsu eiga kara" (Wart: on seeing a newsreel), which links the sorrow of Japanese and American war widows, Murai Takeko succeeds in universalizing their loss, despite vast differences in their economic circumstances, by describing the memories and feelings stirred in Japan by a newsreel report on the Korean War:

. . . .

Her two children, Rose and Jenny,
too young to understand when told their father had died,
appeared with a smiling innocence
no different from Japanese children.

. . . .

All at once I began to weep
at the horror of war
for us in poverty
and for sweet American children with beautiful toys.
From a close-up on the screen, the wart above the eyebrow of this new
widow loomed disturbingly over the audience in that crowded theater.[592]

"Wart," like "When I Was at My Prettiest," reads like straightforward narrative, lacking the allusive and metaphorical qualities often associated with poetry. Yet, since there are no hard and fast rules on what makes a poem, Murai can pose the irony of differing economic circumstances in lines that effectively convey shared sorrow with Americans who lost loved ones in armed conflict. Her poem is a notable contrast to angry denunciations of the "Amerika" represented by the vast U.S. military presence in Japan, anthologized more recently as antiwar poetry.

Poets have condemned U.S. military actions in Asia and the Japanese government's cooperation in them, as well as the continued stationing of some fifty thousand American troops over a network of bases, three-quarters of which are concentrated on less than one percent of Japan's land in the small island prefecture of Okinawa. One of the earliest poems criticizing the prolonged U.S. occupation and military presence in Okinawa was written a few years after the Pacific War by Yamanokuchi Baku, born and raised in Naha, capital of the prefecture that was devastated by the worst battle of this conflict and subjected to a "postwar" period of political and economic deprivation that, in the view of many local residents, continues to this day. Yamanokuchi writes of the seizures of farmland by U.S. occupation authorities for the construction of military bases. His poem's title, "Fuchin bokan Okinawa" (Unsinkable aircraft carrier Okinawa, 1964), took on special irony twenty years after its first publication when Prime Minister Nakasone Yasuhiro used the same phrase to extol Japan's role within the "Western Alliance" in a speech supporting continuation of the U.S.-Japan Security Treaty. Yamanokuchi's poem reads:

> . . . .
> We struggled to our feet from the devastating tragedy of war,
> dragging our bodies covered with wounds,
> and survived somehow in Okinawa
> that has now become an unsinkable aircraft carrier
> where 800,000 wretched lives
> have been driven into a corner of the deck
> with no way to grow rice
> on the steel and concrete.
> . . . .[593]

Poems from Okinawa continue to protest shortages of land, disruptions of daily life from low-flying aircraft and frequent war games, and G.I. crime, which reached a peak in the late-1960s but still accounts for fatal traffic accidents and, occasionally, rape and murder.[594] Shiro Yū (b. 1932) first published "Okinawa" in 1972, the year Japanese sovereignty was restored after nearly three decades of U.S. military occupation. He draws a connection between the ordeal of people who crowded into caves attempting to survive the 1945 battle, in which more than 147,000 Okinawans died, and the dangers and disruptions people there faced during U.S. involvement in Vietnam, when the island was used as a training ground and staging area for U.S. forces deployed to Southeast Asia[595]:

> After all these years
> we are still in a cave
> that has no exit.
> . . . .
> I remember my sister,
> screaming in terror as she tried to stay alive.
> Her bones have long been buried here,
> but still we cannot leave.
> Out in the countryside
> where we should hear waves breaking on the rocks

and turtledoves calling from trees grown thick,
our eardrums are assaulted
with the clatter of tanks and bulldozers
crawling over the earth,
with the roar of jets climbing and diving,
followed by the bursts of napalm bombs.
(Yes, war goes on as before.)
And, much like twenty-six years ago,
we huddle together
in this cave with no exit,
our heads lowered,
our arms embracing,
face to face,
. . . .
no longer able to cry.[596]

Shiro's more recent "Soshite sengo" (Then came "postwar," 1982) voices protest themes common in Okinawa since reversion—the island's continuing militarization and the apparent insensitivity of many who visit from the mainland as consumers of vacation pleasures and souvenirs. This poem describes mainland honeymooners frolicking in front of Shirayuri Shrine, dedicated to local high school girls who were conscripted in 1945 by the Japanese military as battlefield nurses and died in the Battle of Okinawa[597]:

Ten years after the reversion pact
Okinawa has changed, they say.
In Naha new buildings
and hotels that line the streets
tower over people walking by;
and now highways circling the island
are nicely paved, they say.
. . . .
Thousands from the mainland
come each year
to buy postcards, drink the local rice liquor,
and gaze at traditional fabrics and dyes.
They pick up sea shells
while sipping Coca-Cola
and toss away the empty cans.

Happy honeymooners,
arriving at the beach,
pull off their clothes.
Then, after breathless embraces,
they board buses to tour the battle sites

and take turns posing for snapshots
in front of Shirayuri Shrine,
laughing all the while.

Yes, Okinawa has surely changed
these past ten years.
A generation that never saw the war
and knows it only through words printed and spoken
has swelled in numbers,
while those who lived through it
are decreasing day by day.

But on the U.S. air base at Kadena
F-4s and F-15s still stand ready day and night
to fly off and make war
anywhere on earth.
And from their bases at Ginowan
the latest weapons of mass-murder
reach up with muzzles poised, awaiting orders.

What has changed with the reversion pact
is that now Japan's Self-Defense Forces
proudly guard America's bases
with P-2J sub-spotter planes they fly around the clock,
keeping watch over the vast Pacific's waves.
Because in all these "postwar" years
one thing has never changed:
The Pentagon still runs this island.[598]

Japanese retrospectives on World War II, with the notable exception of many in Okinawa, are justifiably criticized for too often presenting their country only as a victim of war, while ignoring the nation's role as aggressor in a catastrophe that cost more than twenty million lives, half of them Chinese.[599] Nevertheless, even if they were supporters of the war while it was being waged, many in Japan who remember the grievous losses suffered in this long, devastating conflict[600] and how they felt after the surrender in August 1945 still speak of a profound sense of betrayal by a government that had deceived them both as to the war's aims and its prospects. This powerful skepticism toward government on the issue of war and the military, expressed in such poems as "Then Came 'Postwar,'" has proven to be deeply rooted and enduring in Japan. Opposition is widespread to proposed revisions of the "no-war clause" in the Japanese Constitution and to government efforts to expand the budget and the role of Japan's Self-Defense Forces (S.D.F.), whose formation in the early 1950s, at the urging of the United States during the Cold War, has been challenged as unconstitutional.[601]

Kazuko Watanabe, professor of women's studies at Kyōto Sangyō University, notes that "prior to the Gulf War, thousands of women demonstrated in Tokyo against sending 'defensive' personnel to the gulf, and against the proposal permitting the first post-World War II dispatch of troops overseas."[602] On the debate over Japanese participation in the Gulf War, journalist Nakanishi Terumasa wrote:

> The reluctance of most Japanese to accept [an overseas role for the S.D.F.] is motivated by a . . . fear . . . that any small step toward dispatching S.D.F. units might open a crack in the dike, leading inevitably to full-fledged rearmament and the use of military power for egoistic objectives. Since echoes of this fear can be heard from Japan's Asian neighbors, it has a compelling power. Another factor is the "military allergy" of many Japanese. World War II caused reflexive feelings of antipathy toward anything and everything militaristic to become deeply rooted in the national psyche. . . . The intensity of antiwar sentiment among the Japanese is remarkable. There may be religious sects that are even more pacifistic, but there probably are few or no other modern countries whose citizens are equally firm in their opposition to war. . . . Perhaps the gulf war will initiate a change in attitudes. Or perhaps domestic factors, such as the replacement of the older generations by youngsters now coming of age, will weaken the military allergy. As long as the general public remains adamantly opposed to military involvement in the world's trouble spots, the Japanese government will have its hands full.[603]

Amid much controversy, the government eventually contributed some thirteen billion dollars to support "Operation Desert Storm," and in April 1991 sent twenty-nine minesweepers and ten support vessels, with S.D.F. crews, to assist other nations in removing mines from the Persian Gulf. In the summer of 1992, after long and bitter debate in the Diet over S.D.F. deployment to Cambodia with a United Nations Peace-Keeping Operation (PKO), a contingent of unarmed Japanese forces was sent as "noncombatant" participants amid large protest demonstrations in several cities. Government officials insisted that the S.D.F. would be stationed in areas of Cambodia separated from hostilities and would engage only in the building and repairing of bridges and roads. Nevertheless, wives and children of the soldiers deployed seemed little reassured by such pronouncements as they stood on the tarmac at Komaki Air Base near Nagoya bidding tearful farewells with pleas of "hurry back" and "return safely."[604] Steven R. Weisman wrote in *The New York Times*:

> The one area of public affairs where the tradition of consensus and acceptance of official decisions has broken down is

> the area tied to Japan's militaristic past. [In June 1992] the Parliament approved legislation permitting Tokyo to have unarmed forces join United Nations peacekeeping efforts. After an agonizing and angry debate, the Government was forced by the opposition parties to back away from its proposal to allow such forces to participate in quasi-combat operations, even under the aegis of the United Nations. The Japanese public, it seems, is still too distrustful of its leaders on matters of basic security to allow such a thing to happen.
>
> This distrust is significant, and seems to be a product of the way Japanese learn their history. Schools teach the young that the disasters of World War II were brought on by a militarist elite that hijacked an unwilling nation and took it to war. Most Western historians regard this as oversimplified, but it is a lesson the Japanese have learned well.[605]

As for the possibility of future involvement in war, today the media in both Japan and the United States tend to describe the current trade disputes in military terms—"economic Pearl Harbor," "trade war," and "market capture."[606] An imagined war between the two countries has been portrayed in widely read fiction and sensationalist journalism.[607] Yet few seriously contemplate the possibility that trade disagreements will lead to another conflict of arms, especially considering the many shared interests of the two nations and prevailing Japanese attitudes toward war and the military. With an international economy that relies heavily on the orderly exchange of goods and services, no nation would have more to lose in a war than Japan. It seems most unlikely that, despite the recently reported rise of negative feelings toward the United States (*ken-Bei*), the kind of ultranationalistic, exhortative, and vituperative war poems produced periodically in Japan between 1894 and 1945 would capture the public fancy again any time soon.[608] Nevertheless, during periods of tension and crisis, some of the invective and racial stereotyping found in such poetry has reemerged.[609] We have noted this tendency in poetry classified in Japan as "antiwar," which protests U.S. military policies and the continuing presence of American forces and bases in the country. In Katagiri Yuzuru's poem, quoted above, opposing U.S. intervention in Southeast Asia, he states, presumably with tongue in cheek, that "Tōjō was right [when he] called America savage." And Yoshida Kin'ichi urges, in rhetorical overkill, that Asians "shoot those cluster bombs at America! / . . . / Let them pierce white skin." In more explicit racial caricature, Arakawa Akira describes U.S. soldiers in Okinawa as "menacing white wolves" in his poem "Yūshoku jinshu" (The colored race). In a heavy-handed response, U.S. authorities moved in 1956 to impose a temporary ban on the literary magazine *Ryūdai bungaku*, which published this poem, while Okinawa was still under the U.S. military occupation that dragged on for twenty years after the Allied Occupation of mainland Japan ended in 1952.[610] One stanza of Arakawa's poem reads:

> The whites,
> The flabby, hairy whites
> Bring missiles to our island,
> Strut around arrogantly,
> And act like our masters,
> Calling us yellow.[611]

One hopes that, if the U.S. military presence in Asia diminishes with the end of the Cold War, comparatively recent verses of this kind will, like the vituperative war songs of the past, retain interest only historically as examples of the changing views of war in modern poetry.[612] Yet it is important, I believe, to study the old war songs, however anachronistic they seem today, and to examine the radical transformations that have occurred in the writings of poets on the issue of armed conflict. These poems, produced in many cases by poets who had previously written in opposition to war, demonstrate not only how long-standing prejudices, stereotypes, and animosities can easily resurface at times of international tension, but also how vulnerable humanitarian and artistic ideals can be in the face of relentless popular pressures and government coercion. The danger of ignoring or covering up such writings is that, once people who remember World War II have passed on, the insidious psychological and cultural effects of armed conflict, as well as its physical horrors, will be trivialized, romanticized, or forgotten.

Notes

Notes to Introduction (pp. 1–19)

1. Siegfried Sassoon, *Siegfried's Journey, 1916-1920* (New York: The Viking Press, 1946), 25. See the discussion of Sassoon's changing views of war in Bernard Bergonzi, *Heroes' Twilight: A Study of Literature of the Great War*, 2d ed. (London and Basingstoke: Macmillan, 1980), 92–108.
2. "Absolution" (1915) in Siegfried Sassoon, *The War Poems of Siegfried Sassoon*, edited by Rupert Hart-Davis (London: Faber and Faber, 1983), 15. The first stanza is quoted with commentary in Bergonzi, *Heroes' Twilight*, 93.
3. Sassoon, *War Poems*, 29.
4. Graves's remarks are cited in Bergonzi, *Heroes' Twilight*, 94.
5. From "Suicide in the Trenches" (1918), in Sassoon, *War Poems*, 119.
6. From "Counter-Attack" (1917), in Sassoon, *War Poems*, 105.
7. Siegfried Sassoon, *Memoirs of an Infantry Officer* (London: Faber and Faber, 1930), 308. Also see Arthur E. Lane, *An Adequate Response: The War Poetry of Wilfred Owen and Siegfried Sassoon* (Detroit: Wayne State University Press, 1972), 90.
8. Sassoon, *War Poems*, 96.
9. Bergonzi, *Heroes' Twilight*, 108.
10. In Bergonzi, *Heroes' Twilight*, 108. This work is not included in Sassoon, *War Poems*, though it had been written forty-three years before this collection was published. As we shall see, poems supporting war have also been omitted from the collected works of Japanese poets.
11. In Bergonzi, *Heroes' Twilight*, 101.
12. Ian Hamilton, "Spender's Lives," *The New Yorker* (February 28, 1994), 72. Hamilton describes a second conversion by Spender, who, like many European and American intellectuals, had briefly joined the Communist Party in the 1930s: "Spender [later] contributed to the much-discussed 1949 anthology 'The God That Failed,' a collection of contrite essays by six of Europe's most prominent ex-Communists" (p. 79). According to Hamilton, Spender also agreed in 1953 to edit the literary section of *Encounter*, an anti-Communist

monthly magazine funded by a supposedly independent Fairfield Foundation. In the mid-1960s many writers became suspicious when the magazine refused to publish criticism of the U.S. Vietnam involvement or of other dubious ventures in American foreign policy. Undergoing yet another conversion, Spender expressed public outrage in 1967, when, to the surprise of few, it was disclosed that the money for *Encounter* had for many years been coming from the C.I.A. (p. 83). This agency's methods, which also included the funding of selected student publications, represent another example of a government's effort to control the press in wartime.

13. See especially the widely read book by H. C. Engelbrecht and F. C. Hanighen, *Merchants of Death: A Study of the International Armament Industry* (New York: Dodd, Mead and Company, 1934).
14. Bergonzi, *Heroes' Twilight*, 213. Referring to the profusion and quality of poetry produced on World War I, Paul Fussell remarked, "Oh What a Literary War." See Paul Fussell, *The Great War and Modern Memory* (New York: Oxford University Press, 1975), xi.
15. See, for example, Sam Hanson and Lucille Harten, eds., *The "Good War" in Retrospect: Memories of World War II* (Pocatello, ID: Idaho State University Press, 1987). Studs Terkel's characterization of this conflict as "the last good war" is quoted on p. 1.
16. Harry Whitten, "From Pacifist to Participant," in Hanson and Harten, *The "Good War,"* 97.
17. See "The Beat Goes On," quoted in chapter four, p. 104.
18. The U.S. military enforced tight controls on reporters covering the Gulf War, which required them to travel in "media pools" escorted by public relations officers. This meant that television audiences saw this conflict as a "video-game war" through officially provided video tapes of missiles swooping down from American aircraft to explode on "enemy targets" with apparent precision. Only after the fighting ended was it reported in the mainstream American press that U.S. air raids had killed thousands of Iraqi civilians, mistakenly targeting apartment houses, hospitals, and municipal government buildings. In sharp contrast, television coverage of the Vietnam War included graphic footage of burning villages, as well as wounded Vietnamese civilians and American soldiers. The Gulf War also produced its share of slogans. Saddam Hussein declared that Americans would "swim in their own blood" in "the mother of all battles," while George Bush vowed to "kick ass." American opponents of the war chanted "no blood for oil" at protest rallies. Viewing the Gulf War within the context of U.S. support for Saddam Hussein that continued virtually until the day of the Kuwait invasion, a *New Yorker* editorial remarked: "How strange that the United States, in a region crucial to its interests and those of the entire industrialized world, would follow policies that were by turns reckless, erratic, and amateurish, and that ended in an unnecessary war" (August 17, 1992, p. 21).
19. Published in *Hato yo!* (Oh dove!), May 1991. Translation by John Solt.
20. Following the Satsuma Rebellion (1877), a major military uprising against the Meiji government, conflicts abroad included the Sino-Japanese War (1894–95), the Boxer Rebellion (1900), the Russo-Japanese War (1904–5), the Siberian Intervention (1918–22), the Shantung Deployments (1927 and 1928), the

Manchurian Incident (1931), the Shanghai Incident (1932), the China War (1937–45), the Nomonhan Incident (1939), and the Pacific War (1941–45).

21. See Donald Keene, *Appreciations of Japanese Culture* (Tokyo: Kodansha International, 1981), 262–67.
22. Ibid., 267–89.
23. Dramatic re-creations of battles from the Revolutionary War, replete with firing muskets and "dead" soldiers, are still staged at several locations in the United States to commemorate the Fourth of July and other holidays. President Harry S. Truman shortened the original name of "Victory over Japan Day," which marked Imperial Japan's surrender on August 14, 1945, and officially designated it Victory Day in 1946. This was subsequently declared a legal holiday in several states to commemorate the end of World War II. However, by 1975 all states observing this holiday had abolished it, except Rhode Island, where it is still popularly called "V-J Day" in print and spoken word. Incidents of anti-Asian harassment and violence in Rhode Island that occur around the time of the holiday (the second Monday in August) have been attributed to its designation, but heavy-handed pressure from the American Legion and the Veterans of Foreign Wars has led to the defeat in the state legislature of four bills proposing to change the name.
24. See the fiction "Yobihei" (The reservist, 1894) and "Biwa-den" (Tale of the lute, 1896) by Izumi Kyōka; and the poems "Tsuru ga buji" (Tsuru is safe, 1895) and "Ensentō" (Weary of war, 1897) by Miyazaki Koshoshi (both works discussed in chapter three).
25. See John Whitney Hall, *Japan: From Prehistory to Modern Times* (New York: Delacorte Press, 1970), 303–4.
26. Ibid., 304.
27. See Akiyama Kiyoshi, Itō Shinkichi, and Okamoto Jun, eds., *Nihon hansenshi-shū* (Tokyo: Taihei Shuppansha, 1979), 37–38. This is the eleventh printing of this popular anthology since its first publication in 1969.
28. For translation and commentary on "Hitotsu no ressha to hankechi" (1922) see chapter seven.
29. See "Etajima kenji no uta" (Song of Etajima's stalwart youth, 1921) by Jindai Takeo, "Rikugun shikan gakkō kōka" (The army officer's school anthem, 1921) by Teranishi Tamiya, and "Kansen kinmu" (Battleship duty, 1924) by Ōwada Tateki and Sasaki Nobutsuna. Collected in Nagata Gyōji, ed., *Nihon gunka meikyoku hyakusen* (Tokyo: Nobarasha, 1975), 72, 91, and 97, respectively.
30. Janet E. Hunter, comp., *Concise Dictionary of Modern Japanese History* (Berkeley, CA: University of California Press, 1984), 196–97.
31. "Santō e yatta tegami" (Letter sent to Shantung) is written from the viewpoint of a Japanese draftee who speaks of his "bloody hands" after following orders to invade China and kill Chinese soldiers, even though he doesn't believe China is Japan's enemy. Partially reprinted in Akiyama, Itō, and Okamoto, *Nihon hansenshi-shū,* 53–54.
32. William Tyler calls Ishikawa Jun's "Marusu no uta" (The song of the war god) "one of the rare instances of resistance literature written in Japan during the crucial years before the Pacific War" (Ishikawa Jun, *The Bodhisattva, or Samantabhadra: A Novel,* translated from the Japanese with an introduction and critical essay by William Jefferson Tyler [New York: Columbia University Press, 1990], xi).

33. Samuel Hynes (*A War Imagined: The First World War and English Culture* [New York: Atheneum, 1991], 25–29) describes what, in some respects, was a similar deluge in England after August 5, 1914, when over 3,000 poems were produced on World War I by 2,225 poets:

> From that day on there were almost daily war poems in *The Times*, by Poet Laureate Robert Bridges, Kipling, Maurice Hewlett, Edmund Gosse, Laurence Binyon and William Watson, and many less-known and never-to-be known poets. During August 1914 as many as a hundred poems a day arrived at *The Times*, and though the number declined somewhat thereafter, several thousand had been received by the following August.

34. In early September 1914 the British government created a new Department of Information, characterized by Samuel Hynes as a ministry "of British propaganda." Appointed its director, C. F. G. Masterman "summoned a number of writers to the department offices at Wellington 'for the organization of public statements of the strength of the British case and principles in the war by well-known men of letters.'" This meeting on September 2, 1914 is thought to have inspired Thomas Hardy to write his famous war poem, "Men Who March Away," dated September 5, 1914 (Hynes, *A War Imagined*, 26). Wartime censorship of the arts, which has recently been documented and studied extensively in Japan, has also occurred in the United States, where the antiwar film "War Brides" was banned during World War I by the Committee on Public Information because "the philosophy of the picture is so easily misunderstood by unthinking people."
35. It is estimated that, after the outbreak of the China War in 1937, 3.1 million Japanese lost their lives, including 800,000 civilians (Hall, *Japan*, 349).
36. Schneider also writes:

> Not much credit for [knowledge of recent German history] goes to [students'] families. From what I could ascertain, grandfathers tell their grandchildren the same things they told us, their children, 30 years ago: stories of the terrors of expulsion from eastern countries, the horrors of nightly bombing raids, of executions and rapes. In short, their focus is always on the suffering of Germans, not on the sufferings inflicted by Germans on others.

See Peter Schneider, "The Sins of the Grandfathers: How German Teenagers Confront the Holocaust, and How They Don't," translated by Joel Agee, *The New York Times Magazine* (December 3, 1995), 75.
37. In Yoshimoto Takaaki, *Takamura Kōtarō* (Tokyo: Shunjūsha, 1977), 147–48.
38. From a 1947 poem translated by Donald Keene in *Dawn to the West: Japanese Literature of the Modern Era* (New York: Holt, Rinehart and Winston, 1984), 2:307. See also chapter eight.
39. From his 1960 poem "Amerika no shinfoni" (American symphony), translated by Tsuruoka Yoshihisa in Ōoka Makoto and Thomas Fitzsimmons, eds., *A Play of Mirrors: Eight Major Poets of Modern Japan* (Rochester, MI: Katydid Books, 1987), 111–12.

40. See Kurihara Sadako, *Kuroi tamago: senryō ken'etsu to hansen-genbaku shikashū* (Kyoto: Jinbun Shoin, 1983); Kurihara Sadako, *Black Eggs*, translated by Richard H. Minear (Ann Arbor, MI: Center for Japanese Studies, The University of Michigan, 1994); and Akiyama, Itō, and Okamoto, *Nihon hansenshi-shū,* 141–59, 219–20. The U.S. Occupation of Japan strictly enforced a policy of prepublication censorship, officially termed a "Press Code," which banned from print (1) supportive references to pre-surrender ideology exalting the military or the nation's imperial destiny, (2) statements thought to connote criticism of Occupation policies, and (3) even the republication of existing plays, legends, and children's stories containing revenge motifs. See Jay Rubin, "From Wholesomeness to Decadence: The Censorship of Literature under the Allied Occupation," *Journal of Japanese Studies* 11.1 (Winter 1985): 72–103.
41. See Meera Viswanathan, "Poetry, Play and the Court in *Tosa Nikki,*" *Comparative Literature Studies* 28.2 (1991): 425–31.
42. Historian Ben-Ami Shillony writes, "On the eve of the Pacific War Japan possessed one of the most sophisticated mass media networks in the world. Books, magazines, and newspapers were printed by the million, distributed to every corner of the country, and read by an inquisitive and literate public." Shillony puts the number of newspapers in Japan at 848 before the government began encouraging mergers after 1940 in order to facilitate wartime censorship and conserve newsprint. See Ben-Ami Shillony, *Politics and Culture in Wartime Japan* (New York: Oxford University Press, 1981), 91–92.
43. See Keene, *Appreciations*, 300–2.
44. Ibid., 302–19.
45. Ibid., 301. See also Keene, *Dawn to the West*, 2:333 and "The Barren Years: Japanese War Literature," *Monumenta Nipponica* 33.1 (Spring 1978): 100, as well as Ienaga Saburō, *The Pacific War: 1931-1945*, translated by Frank Baldwin (New York: Pantheon, 1978), 204–6.
46. "Ōshō" first appeared in *Kokumin shisen* (Selected poems of the citizenry). All translations are by the author unless otherwise cited. The publisher of this anthology could not be determined, but a photograph of its cover and a partial list of poems included appears in Sakuramoto Tomio, *Shijin to sekinin* (Tokyo: Kobayashi Insatsu, 1978), 52–54. Literary historians theorize that government censors, mostly military officers who knew little about poetry, failed to apprehend the pointed irony in this poem. "Ōshō" is reprinted in Yamanokuchi Baku, *Yamanokuchi Baku zenshū* (Tokyo: Shichōsha, 1975), 1:377–78. Born and raised in Naha, Okinawa Prefecture, Yamanokuchi Baku spent most of his adult life in Tokyo. Poet and critic Iijima Kōichi called this "a daring poem" for its grim depiction of wartime mobilization. His commentary appears in Itō Shinkichi, et al., eds., *Nihon no shiika* (Tokyo: Chūō Kōronsha, 1967–70), 20:376–77. "Drafted" bears a remarkable similarity in tone and imagery to the first four lines of Siegfried Sassoon's "Conscripts" (1917) on England mobilized during World War I:

> Fall in that awkward squad and strike no more
> Attractive attitudes! Dress by the right!
> The luminous rich colors that you wore
> Have changed to hueless khaki in the night.

47. "War and Poetry," *Times Literary Supplement* (October 8, 1914), 448; in Hynes, *A War Imagined*, 30.
48. Ryusaku Tsunoda, Wm. Theodore de Bary, and Donald Keene, comps., *Sources of Japanese Tradition* (New York: Columbia University Press, 1964), 2:198–99.
49. From an interview published in *The Defense Monitor* (Newsletter of the Center for Defense Information) 23.4 (1994): 2.
50. See Keene, *Appreciations*, 305. Among the widely read studies of the high value placed in Japan on obligations to others are Ruth Benedict, *The Chrysanthemum and the Sword: Patterns of Japanese Culture* (Boston: Houghton Mifflin Company, 1946); Chie Nakane, *Japanese Society*, rev. ed. (Harmondsworth, Middlesex: Penguin, 1973); and Minami Hiroshi, *Nihonjin no shinri* (Tokyo: Iwanami Shoten, 1960). In *Japanese Patterns of Behavior* (Honolulu: University of Hawaii Press, 1976), Takie Sugiyama Lebra describes Japanese society, using such terms as "social preoccupation," "collectivism," and "sociocult," and emphasizes the importance of "establishing identity by [group] belongingness." More recently, Francis Fukuyama has characterized Japan as a "soft authoritarian" society based on "communitarian" rather than "individualistic" principles ("Threat to Democracy May Come from Asia," *The Daily Yomiuri*, February 25, 1992). Shimazaki Tōson extols the "true way of the warrior" in *Tōhō no mon* (1943), in *Shimazaki Tōson zenshū* (Tokyo: Chikuma Shobō, 1981–83), 2 (1981): 311 (passage translated in chapter six, p. 173). Yet, as we shall see, there are notable examples of individual writers in Japan who took considerable personal and professional risks expressing dissent in wartime. Furthermore, since the 1980s more young people, sometimes called *shinjinrui* (the new breed), seem to be questioning traditional "communitarian" values. They prefer to support themselves working independently or as freelancers (*furī arubaitā*), instead of joining large companies that provide generous security and benefits but demand loyalty in the form of long overtime hours and attendance at frequent company social functions.
51. "Bakudan san'yūshi" is quoted in Yamamoto Fujie, *Kogane no kugi o utta hito: kajin Yosano Akiko no shōgai* (Tokyo: Kōdansha, 1985), 707–8. See chapter two, pp. 73–74.
52. Samuel A. Ward is the composer credited on the sheet music (Chicago: Calumet Music Company, 1942).
53. Many Americans have objected that a song with such bellicose lyrics ("the rockets' red glare, the bombs bursting in air") and a melody of such wildly sweeping range that it is notoriously difficult to sing should continue to be the national anthem. (In Japan it would be classified as a *gunka* or "military song.") John Philip Sousa's "The Stars and Stripes Forever" has frequently been suggested as a more suitable alternative. Visitors from Japan are often surprised by the ritual of American athletes and spectators standing *en masse* for the playing of *The Star-Spangled Banner* before many sporting events. In Japan *Kimi ga yo* (The reign of our emperor), sung for the most part only at major ceremonies and such events as the final day of the six annual professional sumo tournaments, is the subject of lively and sometimes bitter controversy for its associations with wartime and prewar ideology.
54. In George Cary Eggleston, ed., *American War Ballads and Lyrics* (New York and London: G.P. Putnam's Sons, 1889), 1:119.

55. Ibid., 2:30–34.
56. Mrs. Longfellow's comments are quoted in Henry Wadsworth Longfellow, *The Poetical Works of Longfellow* (Boston: Houghton Mifflin Company, 1975), 56. Her husband's remarks are quoted with commentary in Aaron Kramer, ed., *On Freedom's Side: An Anthology of American Poems of Protest* (New York: Macmillan, 1972), 62.
57. Kramer, *On Freedom's Side*, 62.
58. Eggleston, *American War Ballads*, 37. More recent anthologies and collections of American poetry tend to include "The Arsenal at Springfield," but to exclude "The 'Cumberland'" (see, for example, Henry Wadsworth Longfellow, *Henry Wadsworth Longfellow: Selected Poems*, edited by Lawrence Buell [New York: Penguin Books, 1988] and Norman Foerster, ed., *American Poetry and Prose* [Boston: Houghton Mifflin, 1934]). The one exception I found was Louis Untermeyer, ed., *American Poetry: From the Beginning to Whitman* (New York: Harcourt, Brace and Company, 1931), which contains "The 'Cumberland,'" but not "The Arsenal at Springfield." Like Tekkan's "Three Brave Warriors," "The 'Cumberland'" was set to music as a war song during the conflict it depicted. Composer Francis Booth (1813–1904) published his score in 1863 at the height of the American Civil War (Boston: Oliver Ditson and Company). As noted above, the later tendency to include the antiwar poetry and exclude the "prowar" poems of famous poets can also be seen in Japan, where the wartime poems of established writers have been routinely excluded from collections published after World War II, even those identified as their "complete works."
59. Hynes, *A War Imagined*, 26, 29.
60. See Richard H. Mitchell, *Thought Control in Prewar Japan* (Ithaca, NY: Cornell University Press, 1976); Shillony, *Politics and Culture*; and Jay Rubin, *Injurious to Public Morals: Writers and the Meiji State* (Seattle: University of Washington Press, 1984).
61. Masaoka Shiki (1867–1902), Yosano Tekkan, Takeshima Hagoromo (1872–1967), Miyazaki Koshoshi, Kinoshita Naoe (1869–1937), Yosano Akiko, Shimazaki Tōson (1872–1943), Shirotori Seigo, Fukuda Masao, Takamura Kōtarō, and Saitō Mokichi.

Notes to Chapter 1 (pp. 20–45)

62. See W. G. Beasley, *The Modern History of Japan*, 3d rev. ed. (New York: St. Martin's Press, 1981) and Fujii Kimiaki, "Nippon," in Hisamatsu Sen'ichi, et al., eds. *Gendai Nihon bungaku daijiten* (Tokyo: Meiji Shoin, 1972).
63. In Oka Yasuo, "Nisshin sensō to bundan," *Kokubungaku kaishaku to kanshō* 9 (October 1964): 14; portions translated by Donald Keene in Keene, *Appreciations*, 64. Also see Janine Beichman, *Masaoka Shiki* (Boston: Twayne Publishers, 1982), 19–22.
64. Robert Brower, "Masaoka Shiki and Tanka Reform," in *Tradition and Modernization in Japanese Culture*, edited by Donald Shively (Princeton, NJ: Princeton University Press, 1971), 413–14.
65. In Beichman, *Masaoka Shiki*, 14.

66. Brower, "Masaoka Shiki," 385.
67. Both authors are quoted in Oka, "Nisshin sensō to bundan," 13.
68. In ibid., 14.
69. In ibid., 15.
70. Masaoka Shiki, *Shiki zenshū*, edited by Masaoka Chūsaburō et al. (Tokyo: Kōdansha, 1975–78), 13:359. Translated in Beichman, *Masaoka Shiki*, 20.
71. In Oka, "Nisshin sensō to bundan," 14.
72. In Gamachi Fumio, "Masaoka Shiki," *Kokubungaku kaishaku to kanshō* 37.10 (August 1972): 93.
73. Masaoka, *Shiki zenshū* (1975–78), 12:154–71.
74. Beichman, *Masaoka Shiki*, 2–3.
75. Masaoka, *Shiki zenshū* (1975–78), 12:154.
76. See Edward J. Drea, "In the Army Barracks of Imperial Japan," *Armed Forces and Society* 15.3 (Spring 1989): 343–44.
77. Masaoka, *Shiki zenshū* (1975–78), 12:155–56.
78. In Oka, "Nisshin sensō to bundan," 15.
79. In Gamachi, "Masaoka Shiki," 93. Strict censorship and limited access to information explains in part why reporters often sent back highly embroidered dispatches or fanciful "war stories," which boosted the circulation of their newspapers but perpetuated misconceptions about the war and stereotypes about Chinese.
80. Ibid.
81. Masaoka, *Shiki zenshū* (1975–78), 12:97.
82. Gamachi, "Masaoka Shiki," 94.
83. Tsunoda, de Bary, and Keene, *Sources of Japanese Tradition*, 2:199–200.
84. Masaoka, *Shiki zenshū* (1975–78), 12:165.
85. Hirano Ken, et al., eds., *Sensō bungaku zenshū* (Tokyo: Asahi Shinbunsha, 1972), supplement, 217.
86. Masaoka, *Shiki zenshū* (1975–78), 12:84.
87. See Hino Ashihei, *Mugi to heitai* (Tokyo: Kaizōsha, 1938) and *Tsuchi to heitai* (Tokyo: Kaizōsha, 1938).
88. Ariyoshi Sawako, *Hishoku* (Tokyo: Kadokawa Shoten, 1967), 347–49. Yasukuni Jinja is a Shinto shrine dedicated to Japanese who have died in wars since the Meiji Restoration. Visits there by recent prime ministers have sparked controversy in Japan and abroad because the names of men designated as war criminals by the Tokyo War Crimes Tribunal are commemorated there, and because Japan's postwar constitution prohibits state support of religion.
89. Masaoka, *Shiki zenshū* (1975–78), 12:86.
90. Ibid., 87.
91. Both poems quoted in Oka, "Nisshin sensō to bundan," 14. Translation of second poem is by Donald Keene (Keene, *Appreciations*, 264).
92. Hirano, *Sensō bungaku zenshū,* 218.
93. Masaoka Shiki, *Shiki zenshū,* edited by Kawahigashi Hekigotō et al. (Tokyo: Kaizōsha, 1929–31), 337.
94. Translated in Makoto Ueda, *Matsuo Bashō* (Boston: Twayne Publishers, 1970), 125.
95. In Fussell, *The Great War*, 261.
96. Bergonzi, *Heroes' Twilight*, 58.

97. Cleanth Brooks, R. W. B. Lewis, and Robert Penn Warren, eds., *American Literature: The Makers and the Making* (New York: St. Martin's Press, 1973), 2:2664. Tate's poem recalls Bashō's later and more famous *haiku* included in his *Oku no hosomichi* (Narrow road to the deep north, 1689):

natsukusa ya	Summer grass—
tsuwamono domo ga	all that remains
yume no ato	of soldiers' dreams.

98. Masaoka, *Shiki zenshū* (1975–78), 12:95–96.
99. Masaoka, *Shiki zenshū* (1929–31), 7:336.
100. The title refers to a band of traveling Chinese musicians, separated from home like the Japanese soldiers, who play a piece described in the poem as having an especially sorrowful melody.
101. Ibid., 340–41.
102. *Man'yōshū,* 20:4408–12; translated in Nippon Gakujutsu Shinkōkai, eds. and trans., *The Manyōshū* (New York: Columbia University Press, 1965), 177–78.
103. Masaoka, *Shiki zenshū* (1929–31), 7:337–39.
104. In Furukawa Gen, "Kyōiku kenkyū hōkōki IV" (Ambles in educational research IV), *Sōbun* 107 (April 1972): 18-21. Translated in Lebra, *Japanese Patterns of Behavior*, 56.
105. Masaoka, *Shiki zenshū* (1929–31), 7:118–19.
106. See Ivan Morris, *The Nobility of Failure: Tragic Heroes in the History of Japan* (New York: Holt, Rinehart and Winston, 1975).
107. Masaoka, *Shiki zenshū* (1929–31), 7:377.
108. Ibid.
109. Oka, "Nisshin sensō to bundan," 15.
110. Masaoka, *Shiki zenshū* (1929–31), 7:385.
111. Gamachi, "Masaoka Shiki," 94 and Oka, "Nisshin sensō to bundan," 16.
112. Masaoka, *Shiki zenshū* (1929–31), 7: 387.
113. Masaoka, *Shiki zenshū* (1929–31), 6:13; translated in Brower, "Masaoka Shiki," 392.
114. Brower, "Masaoka Shiki," 397.
115. Masaoka, *Shiki zenshū* (1975–78), 7:37; translated in Beichman, *Masaoka Shiki*, 86.
116. Masaoka, *Shiki zenshū* (1975–78), 7:40; translated in Beichman, *Masaoka Shiki*, 86.

Notes to Chapter 2 (pp. 46–76)

117. The two *tanka* were published in *Waseda bungaku* 67 (August 1894).
118. 1894 poems in Yano Hōjin, *Tekkan-Akiko to sono jidai* (Tokyo: Yayoi Shobō, 1973), 50–51.
119. Noda Utarō, ed., *Yosano Tekkan Yosano Akiko shū,* in vol. 51 of *Meiji bungaku zenshū* (1968), 40.
120. Keene, *Dawn to the West*, 2:15.
121. Ibid., 19–20.

122. Edwin A. Cranston calls it "Byronic posing" in "Young Akiko: The Literary Debut of Yosano Akiko (1878–1942)," *Literature East and West* 18.1 (March 1974): 23.
123. Itsumi Kumi, *Hyōden: Yosano Tekkan, Akiko* (Tokyo: Yagi Shoten, 1975), 92.
124. Keene, *Dawn to the West*, 15.
125. In Itsumi, *Hyōden*, 92.
126. Yano, *Tekkan-Akiko*, 50.
127. Noda, *Yosano Tekkan*, 19; translation in Keene, *Dawn to the West*, 16.
128. From poem in *Tōzai nanboku* (1896), quoted and translated in Itsumi, *Hyōden*, 72.
129. Itsumi, *Hyōden*, 96.
130. Father of poet Horiguchi Daigaku (1892–1981).
131. The judgment of the trial resulting from the inquiry is translated in F. A. McKenzie, *The Tragedy of Korea* (London: Hodder and Stoughton, 1908), 263–68.
132. Denis Warner and Peggy Warner, *The Tide at Sunrise: A History of the Russo-Japanese War, 1904–1905* (New York: Charter House, 1974), 93.
133. McKenzie, *The Tragedy of Korea*, 52–53.
134. Printed serially over four issues in the second incarnation of the magazine *Myōjō* (1925), and quoted at length in Itsumi, *Hyōden*, 51, 63, 65, 67, 95, 97, 98, 100–8, 113, 121, 123, 126, 568, and 570.
135. Ibid., 95.
136. Noda, *Yosano Tekkan*, 18.
137. Ibid., 30–31.
138. Ibid., 12. Just as Queen Min had represented to many Japanese what was wrong in Korea, her murder came to represent for Koreans the prolonged intrusion of Japan into their nation's affairs. Ironically, with all the criticism the queen's assassination brought upon Japan in Korea and abroad, the success of the October 1895 coup was very short-lived. In February 1896 another coup, organized this time by Russian diplomats, gave their country temporary preeminence in Korean politics. Rivalry between Japan and Russia for influence in Korea, involving railway and commercial rights as well as military and political considerations, persisted until the issue was decided by Japan's victory in the Russo-Japanese War. Beyond professed concerns for Korean "independence," the Japanese government had long maintained that, because of Korea's proximity, instability there posed a threat to Japan. In 1910 the government took ultimate control of the situation by formally annexing Korea as a colony. Many internal and external factors can be cited to explain the long ordeal of Korea's struggle for unity and independence, an ordeal that continues to this day. China and Russia had also resorted to treacherous and violent means seeking economic, political, and military advantages there during the last two decades of the nineteenth century. And, though their presence was much smaller, the United States and European nations had pursued diplomatic and commercial interests with little regard for Korean sovereignty. But Japanese actions during this period and nearly forty years of brutal colonial rule, when Japanese occupiers tried to suppress Korean language and culture even to the extent of requiring Koreans to change to Japanese names, left a legacy of bitterness among Koreans that persists

today. These feelings have not been alleviated recently by Japanese government officials' reluctance and belatedness in acknowledging that, during the war, hundreds of thousands of Koreans were brought to Japan forcibly for dangerous and debilitating labor, and that many young Korean women were compelled to work as prostitutes for Japanese soldiers at the front. Koreans have been particularly outraged by efforts in Japan to revise public school history textbooks in a way that would downplay Japanese aggression, and by the recent assertions of former education minister Fujio Masayuki that Japanese occupation had benefited Korea.

139. Ibid. Translation in Keene, *Dawn to the West*, 16.
140. In Itsumi, *Hyōden*, 98.
141. Ibid., 96–97.
142. From "Sajō no kotoba" in ibid., 99.
143. As for what actually took place, General Miura Gorō, who had recently replaced Inoue Kaoru as minister in Seoul, and his first secretary, Sugimura Fukashi, are generally believed to have organized the coup. They reportedly recruited Japanese (perhaps including Tekkan and Kaien) and Korean supporters of the pro-Japanese faction and directed the bloody operation. The ring leaders decided to act on October 8 because the royal palace was guarded that day only by Japanese troops and unarmed Koreans. Ten Japanese dressed in uniforms seized from Korean policemen forced their way into the palace with help from the "guards." Once inside, they hunted down the queen in her chambers, leaving a trail of sword-slashed dead and dying among her aides, many of whom steadfastly denied knowledge of her whereabouts. The queen, too, was cut down by swords, then dragged—possibly still alive—to a park near the palace where her body was doused in cooking oil and burned. This fire, as Denis and Peggy Warner (*The Tide at Sunrise*, 94) have noted, "will never be fully extinguished . . . in the hearts of the Korean people." Besides the Warners' work, I have drawn on accounts in Hillary Conroy, *The Japanese Seizure of Korea: 1868–1910, A Study of Realism and Idealism in International Relations* (Philadelphia: University of Pennsylvania Press, 1960), 261–382, and Sohn Pow-key, Kim Chol-choon, and Hong Yi-sup, *The History of Korea* (Seoul: Korean National Commission for UNESCO, 1982), 215–18.

From its actions and statements in the fall of 1895, however, it is clear that the Japanese government was more concerned about Western reaction to the assassination of Queen Min than with resentment in Korea. At first General Miura denied any Japanese responsibility, blaming it all on Koreans. When it became obvious that Japanese were involved, Miura maintained that they must have been "ruffians, vagabonds, marplots, and troublemakers, who could be hired to commit almost any crime by anybody. Japan has done much for Korea," he added. "It has fought a war to secure Korea's independence, it has loaned money, and has for years sent advisors here to aid in reforming and uplifting the country." (His remarks, translated in McKenzie, *The Tragedy of Korea*, 68, sound like those that are thought to have led to Fujio Masayuki's resignation as education minister a century later.) After an unsuccessful attempt by Japanese authorities in Seoul to prevent details of the incident from reaching the press abroad, Prime Minister Itō Hirobumi soon felt compelled to take action that today might be called "damage control" to stem the tide of condemnation in foreign capitals. He promised a full inquiry, denying that the Japanese government in Tokyo had any knowledge of the affair, and vowed to "seek out and punish, if possible, every unworthy son of Japan connected with this crime. . . . Not to do so would be to condemn Japan in the eyes of the world" (ibid).

If General Miura's claim of innocence was quickly exposed, Prime Minister Itō is thought to have been speaking truthfully when he denied the involvement of high government officials in the assassination, which, from all available evidence, was organized locally by Japanese diplomats in Seoul (Conroy, *The Japanese Seizure of Korea*, 312). In fact, General Miura's predecessor, Inoue Kaoru, was a cautious and experienced diplomat who had enjoyed comparatively good relations with the Korean court. When news of the assassination reached the government in Tokyo, barely one month after Miura had assumed his post, a secret message was sent to the legation in Seoul ordering the General's recall and punishment for acting "in complete disobedience to his instructions" (ibid., 311). Miura and his top aides were then brought back to Japan along with other Japanese suspected of involvement. Miura was stripped of his military rank and honors and placed on trial with forty-five others at the courthouse in Hiroshima.

144. From "Sajō no kotoba" in Itsumi, *Hyōden*, 98.
145. Noda, *Yosano Tekkan*, 8.
146. In Itsumi, *Hyōden*, 98.
147. Noda, *Yosano Tekkan*, 8. Tekkan was not alone in his sympathies. The suspects were welcomed back to Japan as conquering heroes by large and enthusiastic crowds as described by Kikuchi Kenjō, a reporter for the *Kokumin shinbun*:

> The Japanese felt an intensely deep sympathy. Welcomers from all over the country were gathered when the defendants arrived at Ujina pier. They formed a line along the route the defendants took and gave them a rousing and supportive reception. People who came to visit the prison and pay their respects filled the inns at Hiroshima. It was a spectacle much like the welcoming home of a victorious army. (Itsumi, *Hyōden*, 99)

148. Warner and Warner, *The Tide at Sunrise*, 94.
149. Yamabe Kentarō, "On the Ŭlmi Incident, Development of Japan-Korea Relations," *International Politics* 2:69–81, quoted in Sohn, Kim, and Hong, *The History of Korea*, 217. F. A. McKenzie (*The Tragedy of Korea*, 72), a contemporary British observer, called the verdict "an amazing finding . . . probably unequaled in judicial annals." What seems most astonishing about the trial is that the official transcript of the judgment, though spotted with condemnatory references to Queen Min and the Korean court, records in great detail the plotting and preparations for the assassination—naming Japanese conspirators. It then describes what had occurred on October 8, 1895 right up to the point when "the whole party entered the palace through the Kuang-hua Gate, and at once proceeded to the inner chambers" (ibid., 267). What comes next, however, reads like a non sequitur. "Notwithstanding these facts, there is no sufficient

evidence to prove that any of the accused actually committed the crime originally meditated by them. . . . The accused, each and all . . . are hereby released from confinement" (ibid., 267–68). Also see Carter J. Eckert, et al., *Korea Old and New: A History* (Seoul: Ilchokak Publishers, for Korea Institute, Harvard University, 1990), 229.

The verdict was widely celebrated in Japan. Another British observer remarked that Miura Gorō had become "the idol of the hour" who was "visited by high officials at Hiroshima and honored at a great banquet" (from *The Far East* 1 [February 1896]: 20 in McKenzie, *The Tragedy of Korea*, 74). The Japanese government immediately restored to the general his former rank and honors.

150. From "Sajō no kotoba" in Itsumi, *Hyōden*, 101.
151. In Itsumi, *Hyōden*, 102–3.
152. From *Tōzai nanboku*, in Noda, *Yosano Tekkan*, 32.
153. Once again Korean royalty played a key role in the carefully planned action, which began in the morning with the king escaping in a closed sedan chair, ordinarily used by women, from the palace, where he had been living under considerable threat of assassination. The Russian legation had been well prepared to receive him, and he quickly set up court there, issuing orders and proclamations. He decreed that a new government be formed immediately and that members of the former cabinet be hunted down and beheaded. Within a few hours a pro-Russian cabinet was in place, and Korean soldiers, accompanied by large crowds of exuberant civilians, went hunting for former cabinet ministers (McKenzie, *The Tragedy of Korea*, 77–81).
154. From "Sajō no kotoba" in Itsumi, *Hyōden*, 104.
155. In this later attempt, Korean officers had apparently sought help from Japanese officials in their effort but had been flatly turned down at a time when rivalry between Japan and Russia in Korea was being played out at the bargaining table rather than in the streets of Seoul. See George Alexander Lensen, *Balance of Intrigue: International Rivalry in Korea and Manchuria, 1884–1899* (Tallahassee, FL: University Presses of Florida, 1982), 2:640–41. In the 1882 coup, Japanese and Koreans of the pro-Japanese faction had started a fire during a state banquet in the royal palace, which was taken over by Japanese troops amid the ensuing confusion. Messengers were then sent to summon government ministers, each of whom was assassinated as he arrived. The results of this coup were to set the pattern for things to come. A pro-Japanese cabinet was installed that soon switched its allegiance to the pro-Chinese faction when the extent of Japanese involvement came to light (Warner and Warner, *The Tide at Sunrise*, 89–90 and Eckert et al., *Korea Old and New*, 210–11).
156. From "Sajō no kotoba" in Itsumi, *Hyōden*, 104.
157. Lensen, *Balance of Intrigue*, 622–23.
158. Itsumi, *Hyōden*, 105.
159. In Itō et al., *Nihon no shiika*, 4:17.
160. In ibid., 22.
161. Keene, *Dawn to the West*, 18.
162. Noda, *Yosano Tekkan*, 32.

163. Okina Kumi (evidently author's name was Okina before marriage), "Kimi shinitamō koto nakare," *Nihon kindai bungaku* 10 (May 1969): 20–21.
164. Noda, *Yosano Tekkan*, 41.
165. See Koshoshi's "Tsuru ga buji," discussed in chapter three, and Kyōka's "Gaisensai" (Victory parade, 1897).
166. Reprinted in Jon Stallworthy, comp. and ed., *The Oxford Book of War Poetry* (New York: Oxford University Press, 1984), 68–69.
167. Noda, *Yosano Tekkan*, 39–40.
168. In Itsumi, *Hyōden*, 107.
169. From an article by Tekkan in *Yomiuri shinbun* (November 24–25, 1987), in ibid., 108–9.
170. Ibid.
171. Itsumi, *Hyōden*, 110.
172. From "Sajō no kotoba" in ibid., 122.
173. Ibid., 99.
174. Noda, *Yosano Tekkan*, 116.
175. From "Desert Flowers" (1943) by Keith Douglas and "Break of Day in the Trenches" (1916) by Isaac Rosenberg, in Fussell, *The Great War*, 253 and 251, respectively.
176. See Okina, "Kimi shinitamō koto nakare," 22 and Itsumi, *Hyōden*, 226. Her poem is discussed in chapter five.
177. Itsumi, *Hyōden*, 226.
178. Noda, *Yosano Tekkan*, 86–87.
179. Translated by Robert Lowell, *Imitations* (New York: Farrar, Straus, and Giroux, 1961); reprinted in Stallworthy, *Oxford Book of War Poetry*, 141.
180. Noda, *Yosano Tekkan*, 119.
181. Stallworthy, *Oxford Book of War Poetry*, 91.
182. From Tekkan's 1901 collection *Murasaki* (Purple) in Noda, *Yosano Tekkan*, 137.
183. Noda, *Yosano Tekkan*, 137.
184. Tekkan departs from historical fact when he implies, in the last line of this poem, that Japanese were not involved in the rampage. Japanese soldiers were reported to have seized three million taels of silver from the Chinese government's treasury as well as official stores of rice and silk.
185. Noda, *Yosano Tekkan*, 137.
186. See Itsumi, *Hyōden*, 225–28; and Itō et al., *Nihon no shiika*, 4:21–22, 44–50.
187. In Okina, "Kimi shinitamō koto nakare," 13.
188. Noda, *Yosano Tekkan*, 200–1.
189. Ibid., 201-2.
190. Itsumi, *Hyōden*, 343 and Okina, "Kimi shinitamō koto nakare," 13.
191. In Itsumi, *Hyōden*, 343.
192. Itsumi ignores it in studies cited above. Neither Tekkan's two war poems in *Dokugusa* nor his *gunka* on the "suicide" mission near Shanghai are included in Itō et al., *Nihon no shiika*. In 1905 Tekkan stopped using this pen name he had assumed in 1890 and wrote again under his given name, Hiroshi.
193. Yamamoto, *Kogane no kugi o utta hito*, 701–2.

194. Ueno Hidenobu, *Tennō Heika banzai: Bakudan San'yūshi josetsu* (Tokyo: Chikuma Shobō, 1989).
195. See Yamamoto, *Kogane no kugi o utta hito*, 705–8; Komota Nobuo, et al., eds., *Nihon ryūkōka-shi* (Tokyo: Shakai Shisōsha, 1981), 1:111 and 294; and Nagata, *Nihon gunka meikyoku hyakusen*, 95–96, which includes words and music. See also chapter five, pp. 138–39.
196. In Yamamoto, *Kogane no kugi o utta hito*, 707–8.
197. In Eggleston, *American War Ballads and Lyrics*, 2:33.
198. Yamamoto, *Kogane no kugi o utta hito*, 708–9.
199. In ibid., 706.
200. Sunaga Asahiko, *Tekkan to Akiko* (Tokyo: Kinokuniya Shinsho, 1971), 186–87.

Notes to Chapter 3 (pp. 77–89)

201. Murata Masao, "Nihon hansenshi shōshi: Nisshin sensō kara taiheiyō sensō made," in *Sensō to wa nanika: hansenshi-shū,* edited by Murata Masao and Noguchi Masayoshi (Tokyo: Gendai Shokan, 1969), 271.
202. Although they often recount the battlefield exploits of famous military leaders, the *gunki monogatari*, which were produced mostly during the Kamakura period (1192–1333), also contain numerous poignant accounts of the suffering caused by armed conflict that are cited today as early examples of antiwar literature in Japan. *Heike monogatari* is especially noted for its depiction of the sorrow war brings.
203. Reprinted in Akiyama, Itō, and Okamoto, *Nihon hansenshi-shū,* 271.
204. Stallworthy, *Oxford Book of War Poetry*, 169.
205. The song "The Oath of Ōtomo" is quoted in the poem numbered *Man'yōshū* 18:4094–97 by Ōtomo no Yakamochi (d. 785), translated as "A poem in celebration of the imperial rescript on the discovery of gold in Michinoku Province," in Edwin A. Cranston, *A Waka Anthology, Volume One: The Gem-Glistening Cup* (Stanford, CA: Stanford University Press, 1993), 458–59. The lines of Yakamochi's poem containing the song with the phrase *kusamasu kabane* read:

Umi yukaba	"If we go on the sea,
Mitsuku kabane	Our dead are sodden in water;
Yama yukaba	If we go on the mountains,
Kusamasu kabane	Our dead are grown over with grass.
Ōkimi no	We shall die
He ni koso shiname	By the side of our lord,
Kaerimi wa	We shall never
Seji to kotodate	Look back." So they proclaimed,
Masurao no	They who passed down
Kiyoki sono na o	From the ancient time till now,
Inishie yo	In our present day
Ima no otsutsu ni	That pure name of valiant men,
Nagasaeru	They the fathers
Oya no kodomo so	Of the sons we are . . .

206. Murata, "Nihon hansenshi shōshi," 272.
207. Ibid.
208. See ibid. and Akiyama, Itō, and Okamoto, *Nihon hansenshi-shū,* 17.
209. See Keene, *Dawn to the West,* 2:202, and Sasabuchi Tomoichi, *Rōmanshugi no tanjō* (Tokyo: Meiji Shoin, 1958), 787.
210. Many leading Japanese Christians initially supported this conflict as a "just war," but some later changed their views. Uchimura Kanzō, perhaps the most prominent among them, complained that the government had misled the Japanese people and was seeking only the spoils of war. Uchimura thereafter embraced pacifism.
211. Kunikida Doppo, *Aitei tsūshin* (Letters to my dear brother, 1894–95) (Tokyo: Sakuryō Shobō, 1908) and Tayama Katai, *Ippeisotsu* (One soldier), in *Waseda bungaku* (January 1908).
212. Donald Keene, comp. and ed., *Modern Japanese Literature: From 1868 to the Present,* vol. 2 of *Anthology of Japanese Literature* (New York: Grove Press, 1956), 142.
213. See especially the novel *Kisei* (Homecoming, 1890).
214. Hunter, *Concise Dictionary of Modern Japanese History,* 24.
215. *Kokumin shinbun* (August 9, 1894).
216. *Kokumin no tomo* (January 1895), 44–64. This magazine was published by Min'yūsha.
217. See Donald Keene, "The Sino-Japanese War of 1894–95 and Its Cultural Effects in Japan," in Keene, *Appreciations,* 259–99.
218. *Kokumin no tomo,* 52. An Imperial Army training manual published in 1908 compared the barracks to a family in which the company commander is the father. See Drea, "In the Army Barracks of Imperial Japan," 335.
219. In Shimazaki Tōson's early story "Utatane" (1897), the protagonist's father, a career army officer, expresses similar aversion to his son's "sensitive and womanlike" qualities and is pleased at the transformation he perceives after the boy joins the army. See chapter six.
220. *Kokumin no tomo,* 56. Her statement suggests a biblical allusion to "He is brought as a lamb to the slaughter" (Isaiah 53:7).
221. *Kokumin no tomo,* 59.
222. See the introduction, n. 22.
223. Nishida Masaru, "Kindai Nihon ni okeru sensō to bungakusha," in Nishida Masaru, ed., *Sensō to bungakusha* (Tokyo: San'ichi Shobō, 1983), 10.
224. Ibid.
225. Reprinted in Sasabuchi, *Rōmanshugi no tanjō,* 824–25.
226. Reprinted in Akiyama, Itō, and Okamoto, *Nihon hansenshi-shū,* 17.
227. Tsuboi, ed., *Nihon no Teikō-shi* (1974), 41.
228. Sasabuchi, *Rōmanshugi no tanjō,* 798.

Notes to Chapter 4 (pp. 90–106)

229. From "Zange" (1906). See Okano Yukie, "Kinoshita Naoe: Nisshin Nichiro tsuranuku hansen" (Kinoshita Naoe: antiwar throughout the Sino-Japanese and Russo-Japanese Wars), in Nishida, *Sensō to bungakusha,* 77. *Kokutai* is

variously translated as "national polity," "national structure," and "fundamental national character." The term was often cited before 1945 as central to the concept of the Japanese nation, and it is much-discussed today as an expression of emperor-centered nationalism, exclusivism, imperialism, and a totalitarianism that encouraged the suppression of dissent.

230. See Masaoka Shiki's poem ridiculing the return of Liaotung (chapter one, p. 42).

231. Naoe's opposition to the Japanese government's return of Liaotung is discussed in Okano, "Kinoshita Naoe," 81; in Yamagiwa Keiji, *Hyōden Kinoshita Naoe* (Tokyo: Sanseidō, 1977), 63; and in translator Kenneth Strong's introduction to Naoe's 1904 novel *Hi no hashira* (Pillar of fire) (Kenneth Strong, trans., *Pillar of Fire* by Kinoshita Naoe [London: Allan and Unwin, 1972], 23). The phrase quoted from Naoe's speech is translated by Strong.

232. Though completed in 1897, this work remained unpublished until it appeared posthumously in the July 1955 issue of *Bungaku* magazine.

233. In addition, after returning troops brought the disease home with them, some 30,000 Japanese died of cholera in 1895.

234. Okano, "Kinoshita Naoe," 80. See especially "Biwa-den" by Izumi Kyōka and "Shichi ki ochi" (Seven fallen cavalrymen, 1897) by Hirotsu Ryūrō. Okano's praise for Kyōka's "realism" puts him at odds with other literary critics and historians. Charles Shirō Inouye has characterized Kyōka's use of "traditional literary modes" found especially in "picture-centered *gesaku* texts of the nineteenth century" as a reaction against "the discourse of realism [that was] imported from the West [and] came to exert more and more influence on Japanese writers." See "Notes on Three Tales" in Inouye, *Three Tales of Mystery and Imagination: Japanese Gothic by Izumi Kyōka* (Kanazawa, Japan: Takuwa Bijutsu Insatsu, Ltd., 1992), 129–60, also cited in chapter six, n. 406.

235. See "Keizaiteki shinpō to waga kokumin shisō" (Economic progress and the philosophy of our citizens) in *Jitsugyō no tomo* (January-February 1897); "'Chūkun aikoku' no gimon" (The problems with "loyalty and patriotism") in *Mainichi shinbun* (May 22, 1902); "Kakumei no jomaku" (Prelude to a revolution) in *Mainichi shinbun* (March 16, 1902); and "Higunbi-ron" (On disarmament) in *Mainichi shinbun* (May 19, 1903). Portions of these articles are quoted in Okano, "Kinoshita Naoe," 82–84.

236. Shūichi Katō, *A History of Japanese Literature*, translated by Don Sanderson (Tokyo: Kodansha International, 1983), 2:156.

237. Okano, "Kinoshita Naoe," 93.

238. His essay is entitled "Sensō jinshu" (A warlike people). See Strong, *Pillar of Fire*, 26.

239. Ibid., 27.

240. The article is entitled "Gunkoku jidai no genron" (The press in an age of militarism), in Itsumi, *Hyōden*, 352–53.

241. Strong, *Pillar of Fire*, 5.

242. Ibid., 9.

243. Katō, *A History of Japanese Literature*, 156.

244. Strong, *Pillar of Fire*, 6–7.

245. Naoe's feeble, secondhand characterization of these workers bears out Strong's criticism of an "elitist aura" in *Pillar of Fire* (p. 7).

246. For a partial list see Rubin, *Injurious to Public Morals*, 281.
247. See reviews in *Shinkōron* of March 1904 and *Teikoku bungaku* of July 1904, portions of which are quoted in Okano, "Kinoshita Naoe," 90.
248. Takenaga Yoshimasa, *Nihon kindai sensō bungaku-shi* (Tokyo: Kasama Shoin, 1976), 69.
249. In mid-Taishō, a time when many poets were writing about peace and democracy, Mushanokōji published the poem "Sensō wa yokunai" (War is wrong). Two decades later, however, he joined the many Japanese writers who wrote in support of the Pacific War, and he denounced President Roosevelt as "ignorant" for being "unaware of the danger of taking on Japan as an enemy." See Keene, *Appreciations*, 300–21.
250. Okano, "Kinoshita Naoe," 90–93.
251. Translation by Strong, *Pillar of Fire*, 27. Original in Yamagiwa, *Hyōden Kinoshita Naoe*, 157.
252. Bergonzi, *Heroes' Twilight*, 104–5.
253. Akiyama, Itō, and Okamoto, *Nihon hansenshi-shū,* 28.
254. Stallworthy, *Oxford Book of War Poetry*, 310–11.
255. Akiyama, Itō, and Okamoto, *Nihon hansenshi-shū,* 28.
256. Ibid., 28–29.
257. In Tsuboi Shigeji, ed., *Nihon no teikō-shi* (Tokyo: Kōwadō, 1974), 58.
258. In ibid., 57–58.
259. Merle Travis, "Sixteen Tons" (American Music, Inc., 1947).
260. Sonny Bono, "The Beat Goes On" (Coalition Music, Inc. & Chris-Marc Music, 1967).
261. Strong, *Pillar of Fire*, 39–41.
262. Naoe's devotion to Zen meditation in no way meant that he had rejected Christianity. Like other Japanese Christians, Naoe advocated teachings and practices from both Christianity and Buddhism.
263. Translation and commentary on this passage in Strong, *Pillar of Fire*, 48–49. Criticizing contemporary trends and policies by alluding to legendary or actual events in former times is a technique used by Japanese writers that can be traced back at least as far as some of the "historical" Kabuki plays and *gesaku* fiction of the mid-Tokugawa period.
264. In Yamagiwa, *Hyōden Kinoshita Naoe*, 311.

Notes to Chapter 5 (pp. 107–143)

265. Some recent translations, full and partial, include David Titus in Masao Maruyama, *Thought and Behaviour in Modern Japanese Politics*, edited by Ivan Morris (London: Oxford University Press, 1963), 154–56; Sharon Rhoads in Higuchi Chiyoko, *Her Place in the Sun: Women Who Shaped Modern Japan* (Tokyo: The East Publications, 1973), 172–74; James Kirkup in A. R. Davis, ed., *Modern Japanese Poetry* (St. Lucia, Queensland, Australia: University of Queensland Press, 1978), 5–6; Atsumi Ikuko and Graeme Wilson, "The Poetry of Yosano Akiko," *Japan Quarterly* 21.1 (January-March 1974): 184; Dorothy Robins-Mowry, *The Hidden Sun: Women of Modern Japan* (Boulder, CO: Westview Press, 1983), 36; and Rubin, *Injurious to Public Morals*, 56–57.

266. See Rubin, *Injurious to Public Morals*, 57. Japanese casualties in this battle are given as 72,008 in Shumpei Okamoto, *The Japanese Oligarchy and the Russo-Japanese War* (New York: Columbia University Press, 1970), 108.
267. Full text with commentary in Irie Haruyuki, *Yosano Akiko no bungaku* (Tokyo: Ōfūsha, 1983), 56–59.
268. See Robins-Mowry, *The Hidden Sun*, 36 and Rubin, *Injurious to Public Morals*, 56–59.
269. See "Hansen bungaku-ron" (On antiwar literature) by novelist and essayist Kuroshima Denji (1898–1943) in *Puroretariya geijutsu kyōtei* (Tokyo: Sekaisha, 1929), 119–21. Okamoto Jun (1901–78) repeats this criticism forty years later in his essay "Nihon hansenshi no rekishiteki haikei" (The historical background of Japanese antiwar poetry) in Akiyama, Itō, and Okamoto, *Nihon hansenshi-shū*, 239–40.
270. Robbins-Mowry, *The Hidden Sun*, 36.
271. Poetry opposing the Russo-Japanese War is discussed in chapters four and seven. See "Kōchi o ushinau hi" (The day they lost their farm fields, 1904) by Shirotori Seigo, "Shōshū-hei" (Draftee, 1904) by Kinoshita Naoe, and "Ranchō gekiin" (Frenzied cadences of discord, 1904) by Nakazato Kaizan, all of which are quoted with commentary in Irie, *Yosano Akiko no bungaku*, 42–46. For examples of poetry on the Sino-Japanese War of 1894–95, see chapters one through three.
272. Quoted with commentary in Irie, *Yosano Akiko no bungaku*, 41–42. Widely known as "Naoko," the poet's given name was Kusuoko. She began her literary career as a novelist and also tried her hand at translating Russian and German fiction. Although her most famous poem today is the *shintaishi* "O-hyaku-do mōde," she usually composed in *tanka* form. Critic Yano Hōjin describes her from a photograph as an extremely beautiful woman, and he notes that Natsume Sōseki is said to have admired her and to have depicted his impressions of her in female characters in his fiction and poetry. See Yano, *Tekkan-Akiko to sono jidai*, 222–26.
273. Yano, *Tekkan-Akiko to sono jidai*, 222.
274. Honma Hisao, "Akiko to Naoko," in *Zoku Meiji bungaku-shi* (Tokyo: Tōkyōdō, 1964), 46–47.
275. Takenaga, *Nihon kindai sensō bungaku-shi*, 82–84.
276. *Taiyō* 10.8 (June 1904): 144–45.
277. I learned of "Song of the Attack" at a seminar on war literature taught by Professor Nishida Masaru at Hōsei University in the summer of 1983.
278. Susan J. Pharr, *Political Women in Japan: The Search for a Place in Political Life* (Berkeley, CA: University of California Press, 1981), 18.
279. Higuchi, *Her Place in the Sun*, 160–61.
280. Her lack of interest in these courses did not seem to handicap her in successfully raising eleven children, one of whom became a physician, and another, chairman of the Olympic Committee for the 1964 Tokyo Games.
281. Cranston, "Young Akiko." I owe my initial interest in Yosano Akiko to this article.
282. Yūri Kaoru, *Akiko no shōgai* (Tokyo: Saika Shobō, 1948), 7.
283. Ibid., 8.
284. Cranston, "Young Akiko," 20.

285. Ibid., 31–32.
286. Higuchi, *Her Place in the Sun*, 166–67; and Cranston, "Young Akiko," 39.
287. Translated by Sharon Rhoads in Higuchi, *Her Place in the Sun*, 182–83. See Akiko's essays published between 1918 and 1928, collected in Shinma Shin'ichi, ed., *Yosano Akiko zenshū* (Tokyo: Bunsendō, 1972), volumes 10 and 11. In "Mirai no fujin to nare" (Become women of the future, 1918), reprinted in 10:5–21, she tells women not to accept men's glorified pronouncements about war and to speak out on the sacrifices and suffering war brings to women and their families. In "Heiwa shisō no mirai" (The future of a philosophy of peace, 1918), in 10:56–58, she asks why civilizations that have produced such technological marvels as the airplane have failed to find a method for avoiding war, and she urges greater efforts to achieve peace in the world. In "Shuppei to fujin no kōsatsu" (Women's viewpoint on the Siberian Intervention, 1918), in 10:87–91, she denounces "militarism" (*kyōheishugi*) in Japan and those who "advocate aggression" (*shinryaku-shugi*) in pursuit of "territorial ambitions" (*ryōdo-teki yashin*), following the dictum of "might makes right." She encourages Japanese women to speak out against the excessive size and influence of the military establishment. In other essays Akiko uses language with surprising currency today to criticize "men's treatment of women as objects" (*danshi ga joshi o "mono" to shite toriatsukau koto*) and to advocate that women "stop being victims and move toward greater independence" (*gisei yori dokuritsu e*). She also supports the abolishment of prostitution and the adoption of status-neutral terms of address, such as *anata*, by men toward their wives, instead of the more common *omae*, connoting lower status for the woman.
288. See Drea, "In the Army Barracks of Imperial Japan," 330.
289. In Tsunoda, De Bary, and Keene, *Sources of Japanese Tradition*, 2:199.
290. In Rubin, *Injurious to Public Morals*, 58.
291. Despite the Japanese government's repeated claims that it was "protecting the independence of Korea," Japanese intrusion there greatly accelerated after the Sino-Japanese and Russo-Japanese Wars, leading to outright annexation in 1910 and brutal colonial rule that lasted until 1945 (see Andrew C. Nahm, ed., *Korea under Japanese Colonial Rule* [Kalamazoo, MI: Center for Korean Studies, Western Michigan University, 1973]).
292. Okamoto, *The Japanese Oligarchy*, 41–102; and Rubin, *Injurious to Public Morals*, 55.
293. Okamoto, *The Japanese Oligarchy*, 105–223; and Beasley, *The Modern History of Japan*, 172–73.
294. Rubin, *Injurious to Public Morals*, 55-56.
295. Shumpei Okamoto (*The Japanese Oligarchy*, 140) characterizes *Heimin shinbun* writers as "intellectuals [who] were more interested in propagating their usually academic ideals than cultivating the support of the people. In the face of the torrent of popular enthusiasm for the war, their valiant efforts were ineffective." Of Akiko and Naoko, Okamoto writes: "It was perhaps only through their emotional appeals that the anti-war advocates reached the Japanese people. . . . But although such poets and the anti-war forces in general exerted a strong emotional appeal, they were unable to have any real influence on public opinion at this time." Okamoto also mentions Ōtsuka

Naoko's "vehemently chauvinistic" poem "Shingeki no uta" in a footnote on p. 273.

296. Portions of "Gunkoku jidai no genron" (The press in this age of militarism) are quoted and discussed in Itsumi, *Hyōden*, 352–53. See pp. 92–93 and n. 240.
297. Furukawa Kiyohiko, "Meiji bungaku to Nichi-Ro sensō," *Hon no techō* 5.6 (August 1965): 13–21.
298. Quoted in Itsumi, *Hyōden*, 352–53.
299. Quoted in ibid., 353.
300. Stallworthy, *Oxford Book of War Poetry*, 97.
301. Itsumi, *Hyōden*, 354.
302. Leo Tolstoy, *Bethink Yourselves!*, translated by V. Tchertkoff (Boston: Ginn and Company, 1904), 1.
303. This statement also recalls the line in Kinoshita Naoe's poem, quoted on p. 100, in which a Japanese youth drafted reluctantly into the same war vows: "I will kill no 'enemy,' I swear it."
304. To indicate points of similarity, I have added all italics in the translated portions of Tolstoy's and Akiko's works presented in this and subsequent paragraphs.
305. Honma, "Akiko to Naoko," 46; and Fred G. Notehelfer, *Kōtoku Shūsui: Portrait of a Japanese Radical* (Cambridge, England: Cambridge University Press, 1971), 101.
306. Itsumi, *Hyōden*, 353–54.
307. Notehelfer, *Kōtoku Shūsui*, 107.
308. Ibid., 97.
309. Atsumi and Wilson, "The Poetry of Yosano Akiko," 181; and Higuchi, *Her Place in the Sun*, 176.
310. Higuchi, *Her Place in the Sun*, 176. Even among the mostly exhortative poems on the Russo-Japanese War attributed to Emperor Meiji are some that refer to hardships. Below are Curtis Page's translations of three poems attributed to the emperor, which are included in Page's anthology *Japanese Poetry* (Boston: Houghton Mifflin, 1923), 166.

> Strike down the foeman, as thy country's foe,
> With all thy might and skill.
> But even while thou strikest, thou must know
> He is a fellowman, and love him still.
>
> Thousand-sword-swift-brandishing
> Gods of ancient Yamato
> How your noble hearts must glow
> To see my joyous people bring
> All their lives for offering.
>
> My children all are gone
> To battle-gardens, and old men
> Must till the mountain-fields.

311. Higuchi, *Her Place in the Sun*, 176.

312. Keigetsu's comments are translated in Rubin, *Injurious to Public Morals*, 57.
313. In Yano, *Tekkan-Akiko to sono jidai*, 225.
314. Rubin, *Injurious to Public Morals*, 57.
315. Yano, *Tekkan-Akiko to sono jidai*, 206–7.
316. *Myōjō* (November 1904): 98–100. Her "Open Letter" is discussed in Rubin, *Injurious to Public Morals*, 57–58.
317. *Myōjō* (November 1904): 98–100. Rubin, *Injurious to Public Morals*, 57–58.
318. In Itsumi, *Hyōden*, 349–50. See also Yano, *Tekkan-Akiko to sono jidai*, 204–9.
319. Rubin, *Injurious to Public Morals*, 58.
320. Ibid., 58–59.
321. In Itsumi, *Hyōden*, 351.
322. Ibid.
323. See n. 287.
324. Some of the best-known works of proletarian literature, such as Hayama Yoshiki's (1894–1945) *Umi ni ikuru hitobito* (Men who live at sea, 1926) and Kobayashi Takiji's (1903–33) *Kani kōsen* (The cannery boat, 1929), might be recognized more widely today as literary masterpieces except for *de rigueur* doctrinal debates among their characters and polemic intrusions of their authors.
325. Keene, *Modern Japanese Literature*, 27. *The Cannery Boat* appears on pp. 333–38 and is listed as "translated anonymously."
326. See poet Kaneko Mitsuharu's (1895–1975) account of "domination" by proletarian writers and critics in literary circles during the mid-1920s, and of their influence over what was published and reviewed, in *Ninpinin-den* (Brute's journal) (Tokyo: Daikōsha, 1971), 221–22.
327. Critic Miyamoto Kenji's (1908–) well-known 1929 essay "Haiboku no bungaku" (The Literature of Defeat) portrays the fiction writer Akutagawa Ryūnosuke (1892–1927) as representing an age of bourgeois excess.
328. George Tyson Shea, *Left-Wing Literature in Japan* (Tokyo: Hōsei University Press, 1964), 176.
329. After Kuroshima led other writers out of the group associated with the magazine *Bunsen* (Literary vanguard), they immediately formed the *Bunsen* Datō Dōmei (The League to Overthrow *Bunsen*). Two months later, seven writers from *Bunsen*, including Hayama Yoshiki and Maedakō Hiroichirō (1888–1957), signed a statement denouncing Kuroshima in the magazine's January 1931 issue (volume 8, number 1, p. 199). See Shea, *Left-Wing Literature*, 182–86.
330. Kuroshima, *Puroretariya geijutsu kyōtei*, 119–32. The text of this essay is frequently interrupted by *fuseji* marks ("X") of the kind that were inserted by publishers concerned that certain words or phrases, even in a work of literature or literary criticism, would lead to its banning by the Home Ministry. However, as noted below, Kuroshima indicates that, at least in one instance, he has inserted these marks himself. For an excellent account of how publishers used *fuseji* to avoid censorship, see Rubin, *Injurious to Public Morals*, 29-31.
331. Kuroshima, *Puroretariya geijutsu kyōtei*, 119, 127.
332. Ibid., 127.
333. Shillony, *Politics and Culture*, 111.
334. Kuroshima, *Puroretariya geijutsu kyōtei*, 119–20.

335. Ibid., 120.
336. Ibid., 120–21.
337. Ibid., 121.
338. The third example of "bourgeois antiwar literature" Kuroshima cites is Mushanokōji Saneatsu's (1921–) novel *Aru seinen no yume* (A young man's dream, 1916–17), which Kuroshima criticizes for failing to identify the perpetrators of the "egoism" Mushanokōji blames in this work for causing wars.
339. In Yūri, *Akiko no shōgai*, 99. Akiko's poems from *Man-Mō yūki* are collected in Shinma, *Yosano Akiko zenshū*, vol. 4. The comparison suggested here between weeping and the moaning sound (*musebu ne*) of falling sand recalls similar comparisons in classical *tanka* between weeping and the groaning sound (*musebu ne*) of ice buckling in winter.
340. Ienaga, *The Pacific War*, 58–65. Ienaga goes on to describe how, three years later on September 18, 1931, such a plot succeeded when Japanese troops detonated another explosion, which they blamed on the Chinese army, destroying a section of the railway in the notorious Manchurian Incident. This time there was no opposition from the government in Tokyo when the Japanese army occupied all of Manchuria, installed a puppet emperor, and declared the new "nation" of Manchukuo.
341. See Yūri, *Akiko no shōgai*, 99–101; Irie, *Yosano Akiko no bungaku*, 185–86, 200–2; and Ienaga, *The Pacific War*, 59.
342. Yamamoto, *Kogane no kugi o utta hito*, 688. Because the vast majority of literary critics and historians in Japan and America have ignored Akiko's later writing on war, I am greatly indebted to Yamamoto's presentation, with valuable commentary, of the poetry and prose on war Akiko published after 1928.
343. Ibid., 688.
344. Ienaga, *The Pacific War*, 59; and Yamamoto, *Kogane no kugi o utta hito*, 689.
345. Yamamoto, *Kogane no kugi o utta hito*, 689.
346. Ibid.
347. Ienaga, *The Pacific War*, 63–66.
348. Beasley, *The Modern History of Japan*, 202.
349. First appeared in the April 1932 issue of the magazine *Tōhaku* (Winter oak). Reprinted in Shinma, *Yosano Akiko zenshū*, 8:272–75; quoted with commentary in Yamamoto, *Kogane no kugi o utta hito*, 709–11.
350. Reports and editorial opinion from Japanese newspapers on the situation in China are translated extensively in the English-language magazine *The Japan Weekly Chronicle*. See especially the issues from February 18 through March 30, 1932, which include accounts of the "human bomb" mission carried out by three Japanese soldiers on the outskirts of Shanghai and commentary on its implications for the home front. Novelists also produced stories supportive of Japanese military policies in China. Naoki Sanjūgo (1891–1934), for whom a prize was named that is still awarded semiannually to writers of popular fiction, published *Nippon no senritsu* (Japan arises) in 1932. Its main character, closely resembling the author in the events and circumstances of his life, proclaims:

> China is a country that is hardly aware as to whether she possesses territory or not. The authority of the Nanking government extends over

> only a part of the whole country, nor is the Canton dialect used in Nanking, any more than is the Japanese language. . . . For the Japanese to develop the lands of China, in the interest of both the Chinese and the Japanese, is indeed a blessing to humanity.

The translation is from *Introduction to Modern Japanese Literature* (Tokyo: Kokusai Bunka Shinkōkai, 1970), 2:xvi-xvii.

351. Aono's comments are quoted in Kaneko Mitsuharu, *Kaneko Mitsuharu zenshū* (Tokyo: Shōrinsha, 1974), 5:409.
352. Louise Young examined the role of Japan's press in building public support for the government's military policies in her lecture "An Empire of the Masses: Japan and Manchukuo 1932–1945," delivered at Harvard University on November 13, 1992.
353. Tsuboi Shigeji, then editor of the magazine *Taiko* (Drum), was interrogated and reprimanded by the *kenpeitai* for publishing Kaneko's poem "Ka" (Mosquitoes, 1935), an unflattering caricature of Imperial Army soldiers. Kaneko's extended narrative poem "Awa" (Bubbles, 1935) is an unsparing portrayal of death and suffering at the battlefront in China. Novelist Ishikawa Tatsuzō was arrested and brought to trial in 1938 for depicting atrocities committed in China by Japanese soldiers in his story "Ikite iru heitai" (Living soldiers). The March 1938 issue of the magazine *Chūō kōron*, in which it first appeared, was banned.
354. See Higuchi, *Her Place in the Sun*, 182–83, and Akiko's 1918 essays "Mirai no josei to nare" and "Shuppei to fujin no kōsatsu" in Shinma, *Yosano Akiko zenshū*, 10:5–21, 87–91 (portions summarized in n. 287).
355. Yamamoto, *Kogane no kugi o utta hito*, 711–14.
356. While Akiko characterizes herself in this poem as a "powerless woman" (*muryoku no onna*), some scholars have argued recently that women gained confidence and self-esteem in times of war after the Meiji Restoration because in modern Japan *all* Japanese were expected to contribute to the war effort, not just men of the samurai class. Women were praised both as workers after national mobilization and as mothers who produced future soldiers. See Kazume Yoshi, "Images of Japanese Women in U.S. Writings and Scholarly Works, 1860–1990: Formation and Transformation of Stereotypes," *U.S.-Japan Women's Journal* 1 (1991): 28–29. Others maintain, however, that, while women's roles changed in wartime, their status did not improve significantly. Facing a labor shortage late in the Pacific War, for example, the government established the Women's Volunteer Labor Corps (Joshi Rōdō Teishintai) in January 1944 to bring single women into such war industries as aircraft maintenance. Although this was a considerable break with the past, it represented something less than a major step toward equality for women in Japanese society. Many single women were harassed by local neighborhood associations into "volunteering." Others were urged into marriage, which automatically exempted them, or were excused if their families depended on them for household chores and child care. The Labor Ministry estimated in March 1945 that 472,000 women were employed through the "corps," but this number included those who had already been working before it was established. Those who were assigned jobs in war industries often faced harsh working

conditions not unlike those endured by women contracted to textile factories in the 1920s. See Thomas R. H. Havens, *Valley of Darkness: The Japanese People and World War Two* (New York: Norton and Company, 1978), 106–13.

357. In Tekkan's version of this *shintaishi* set to music by Tsuji Junji, the seventh and ninth verses closely parallel portions of Akiko's poem:

toki naki mama ni tenka shite	Swiftly igniting the fuses
idakiaitaru hakaitō	To the demolition canisters they carry,
tetsujōmō ni itaritsuki	They reach the barbed wire
waga mi morotomo mae ni nagu	And, with the explosives, hurl their bodies forward.
. . . .	. . . .
sakete chiru mi o hana to nashi	Bodies torn and scattered become like flowers
Jingi no gun ni sasagetaru	Offered to the army of humanity and justice.

Full text of the version set to music is in Nagata, *Nihon gunka meikyoku hyakusen*, 95–96. An earlier text, published in the newspaper, is quoted with commentary in Yamamoto, *Kogane no kugi o utta hito*, 706–9. See translation and discussion of this version in chapter two, pp. 73–74.

358. Emmeline Pankhurst, *My Own Story* (London: Eveleigh Nash, 1914), 363. Quoted in Hynes, *A War Imagined*, 88.

359. Florence L. Barclay, *My Heart's Right There* (London, 1914), 58. Quoted in Hynes, *A War Imagined*, 92.

360. These essays were published in a collection of her prose and poetry entitled "Yūshōsha to nare" (Let's be the victors, 1934), portions of which are quoted with commentary in Yamamoto, *Kogane no kugi o utta hito*, 714–15. Items from this collection are reprinted in Shinma, *Yosano Akiko zenshū*, 11:339–466.

361. Shillony, *Politics and Culture*, 112.

362. Ibid., 99.

363. Two other poems from the same collection read:

Rūzuberuto Daitōryō o atarashiki sekai no menzen ni uchinomesu beshi	With this new world before our eyes, we must strike down President Roosevelt!
	Toki Zenmaro
Ajia no teki jinrui no teki Bei-Ei o ima koso ute to kami norashitari	Enemies of Asia, enemies of humanity— Now is the time to strike America and England, the god has proclaimed.
	Sōma Gyofū

In Yamamoto, *Kogane no kugi o utta hito*, 745–47.

364. In ibid., 747–48.

365. Translation and commentary on these poems, by Saitō Ryū and Kawata Jun, respectively, are provided in Keene, *Appreciations*, 304–5.

366. From the January 1942 issue of *Tanka kenkyū*, quoted in Yamamoto, *Kogane no kugi o utta hito*, 746.
367. From the January 1942 issue of *Tōhaku*, quoted in ibid., 748.
368. These two poems are from the January 1942 issue of *Tanka kenkyū,* quoted with other selections in ibid., 746–47.
369. Quoted with other selections from this anthology in Sakuramoto Tomio, *Shijin to sekinin*, 17–19.
370. In Yamamoto, *Kogane no kugi o utta hito*, 747. The colloquial, free-verse style of this poem is unusual for Akiko's work. Augyusuto changed his name to Iku in 1933.
371. Ibid., 747–48.
372. See Shinma, *Yosano Akiko zenshū,* 10:56–58, 87–91; and Higuchi, *Her Place in the Sun*, 183.
373. Phrases from "Citizens of Japan, A Morning Song," translated on pp. 133–34.
374. Phrases from poems published in January 1942 , translated on p. 138.
375. Yūri, *Akiko no shōgai*, 3.
376. See Keene, "The Barren Years," 68. Funahashi Seiichi refers to *kachi no tentō* in his article "Kokugo mondai to minzoku no shōrai" (The Japanese language question and the future of our people), *Chūō kōron* (May 1961): 48–56.
377. The authors' views are expressed with the ring of strong conviction, but it must also be noted that, during this time, the U.S. Occupation was enforcing strict prepublication censorship, which banned from print supportive references to pre-1945 ideology exalting the military or the nation's imperial destiny. See Rubin, "From Wholesomeness to Decadence," 72–103.
378. Yūri, *Akiko no shōgai*, 25.
379. Yamamoto, *Kogane no kugi o utta hito*, 711.
380. In Yūri, *Akiko no shōgai*, 24–25.
381. Higuchi, *Her Place in the Sun*, 183.
382. Maruyama, *Thought and Behavior in Modern Japanese Politics*, 147.
383. Okamoto Jun, "Nihon hansenshi no rekishiteki haikei" (The historical background of Japanese antiwar poetry), in Akiyama, Itō, and Okamoto, *Nihon hansenshi-shū,* 239–40.
384. Shūichi Katō, "Japanese Writers and Modernization," in Marius Jansen, ed., *Changing Japanese Attitudes toward Modernization* (Princeton, NJ: Princeton University Press, 1965), 429.
385. A distinguished novelist, poet, and essayist, Katō's views are somewhat out of character for an advocate of many liberal, idealistic, and internationalist causes and the author of *Aru hareta hi* (One clear day, 1945–50), a novel effectively depicting brutalization and repression in late wartime Japan, and the sense of release when the war finally ended.

    Antipathy toward the Soviet Union in Japan after 1945 was aggravated by the Soviet forces' brutal invasion of Manchuria at the end of the war, by lengthy detainment of thousands of Japanese as prisoners at hard labor in Siberia after the war, and by continued Russian occupation of four islands northeast of Hokkaido. In a sense, this hostile view of the Soviet Union is consistent with pre-1945 views of this nation, going back to the late nineteenth century when Russia was widely perceived as a threat to Japan's security and interests.

386. Takenaga, *Nihon kindai sensō bungaku-shi,* 79.
387. Ibid., 81.
388. In ibid., 84.
389. Yano, *Tekkan-Akiko to sono jidai,* 198–99, 213, 226.
390. Okina, "Kimi shinitamō koto nakare," 26. Later bibliographical reference in Irie, *Yosano Akiko no bungaku,* 219, identifies the author of this article as Itsumi Kumi, her name after marriage.
391. Itsumi, *Hyōden,* 352.

Notes to Chapter 6 (pp. 144–174)

392. See Akiyama, Itō, and Okamoto, *Nihon hansenshi-shū,* 17–19. Originally published in 1969, this is the eleventh printing of the anthology. Also see Murata Masao and Noguchi Masayoshi, eds., *Sensō to wa nanika: hansenshi-shū* (Tokyo: Gendai Shokan, 1969), 274–75.
393. Itō Kazuo, ed., *Shimazaki Tōson jiten* (Tokyo: Meiji Shoin, 1982), 45.
394. This is one of several Kabuki and Noh plays inspired by events and personages from the Genpei Wars of the twelfth century. It is a rendering for the stage of events surrounding the Battle of Ichinotani much as they are portrayed in *Heike monogatari.*
395. The story appears in Shimazaki Tōson, *Shimazaki Tōson zenshū* (Tokyo: Chikuma Shobō, 1966–71), 16:418–84.
396. Such departure scenes are frequently portrayed in Japanese literature and film on war. As recently as September 1992, when units of the Japan Self-Defense Forces left for "peace-keeping operations" in Cambodia amid widespread public opposition to their deployment abroad, television coverage dwelled at length on the openly tearful good-byes and pleas for a safe return of wives and children. The departing troops' families did not seem reassured by government pledges that Japanese forces would assume "noncombat" roles in areas separated from hostilities, where they would limit their activities to building or repairing bridges and roads for the transport of relief supplies and the resumption of commerce. See p. 225.
397. For poet Masaoka Shiki's firsthand account of conditions aboard Japanese troopships bound for China, see chapter one, pp. 23–26.
398. This particular coincidence, though highly improbable in, for example, the U. S. Army of World War I, was at least conceivable in the Imperial Japanese Army, which organized most units around soldiers from the same local areas. See Drea, "In the Army Barracks of Imperial Japan."
399. Ibid.
400. Shimazaki, *Shimazaki Tōson zenshū* (1967–71), 16:467.
401. Ibid., 477.
402. Ibid., 482.
403. Ozaki Kōyō (1867–1903) and Kōda Rohan (1867–1947) are listed with Mori Ōgai as co-contributors to *Mezamashi-gusa* 42 (December 1897): 18–19.
404. Mori, *Mezamashi-gusa,* 18-19. In his writings Ōgai often used terms from European languages, mostly German, to identify political, philosophical, and

aesthetic concepts. In this passage, however, the insertion of English words heightens its derisive tone.

405. See Richard John Bowring, *Mori Ōgai and the Modernization of Japanese Culture* (Cambridge, England: Cambridge University Press, 1979), 217.

406. Charles Shirō Inouye examines Izumi Kyōka's successful application in his early twentieth-century fiction of "traditional narrative modes" found especially in "picture-centered *gesaku* texts of the nineteenth century." Inouye notes that, in utilizing melodrama and richly evocative imagery, Kyōka was bucking the trend in Japan "at the time when the discourse of realism, imported from the West, came to exert more and more influence on Japanese writers," particularly "the naturalists." See "Notes on Three Tales" in Inouye, *Three Tales of Mystery and Imagination*, 129–60. Ironically, Tōson became known as a leading naturalist when he resumed writing fiction after the turn of the century. See p. 148.

407. Inouye, *Three Tales of Mystery and Imagination*, 129–60.

408. See anthologies cited in n. 392, and chapter three, which examines Hagoromo's and Koshoshi's writing on war.

409. Reprinted in Akiyama, Itō, and Okamoto, *Nihon hansenshi-shū,* 17, and Murata and Noguchi, *Sensō to wa nanika*, 272.

410. See, for example, Ienaga, *The Pacific War*, 203–28; Ara Masahito, "Senjika no 'geijutsu teikōha,'" *Kokubungaku kaishaku to kyōzai no kenkyū* (June 1965); Tsuboi, *Nihon no teikō-shi*; Ishii Kenji, "Meiji bungaku to heiwa e no michi," in *Kindai Nihon bungakushi kenkyū* (Tokyo: Miraisha, 1965); and "Nisshin, Nichi-Ro sengo no bungaku," special issue of *Kokubungaku kaishaku to kanshō* (August 1972).

411. Tolstoy, *Bethink Yourselves!,* first published in Japanese translation as "Nanjira, kuiaratameyo" in the August 7, 1904 issue of *Heimin shinbun*. See chapter five, pp. 117–20.

412. Kōtoku Shūsui, "Hi-sensō shugi," *Yorozu chōhō* (August 7, 1900).

413. In the newspaper *Heimin shinbun*, which he coedited with Sakai Toshihiko. See especially the issues from January 17, 1904 until the newspaper's demise, under relentless government pressure, with its final issue on January 29, 1905.

414. Uchimura Kanzō, "Sensō haishi ron," *Yorozu chōhō* (June 30, 1903).

415. Kinoshita, *Hi no hashira*; translated in Strong, *Pillar of Fire*, 185–86. Aside from *Pillar of Fire*, Kinoshita Naoe published poetry in 1903–4 denouncing war, which appears in Akiyama, Itō, and Okamoto, *Nihon hansenshi-shū,* 28-29 and in translation in Strong, *Pillar of Fire*, 27. See chapter four.

416. See chapter two on changing views of war in Yosano Tekkan's poetry. Novelist, poet, and essayist Mushanokōji Saneatsu had been a prominent member of the Shirakaba-ha (White Birch Society), writers who advocated humanism, pacifism, and shared communal resources. Mushanokōji led efforts to build "ideal villages" in the countryside modeled on Tolstoyan principles (see Shillony, *Politics and Culture in Wartime Japan*, 113). He declared in his early-Taishō poem entitled "Sensō wa yoku nai" (War is wrong), reprinted in Murata and Noguchi, *Sensō to wa nanika*, 26: "I oppose war" (*sensō ni hantai suru*). But two decades later he celebrated the outbreak of hostilities with America

and England as a struggle against Western imperialism, denouncing Roosevelt (see n. 249). Also see Mushanokōji's poem "Daitōa sensō daini-nen no haru o mukaete" (Welcoming in spring of the second year of the Greater East Asia War) in volume 2 of *Nihon shishū* magazine (1943).

417. This collection's popularity among Japanese youth is noted in Edwin McClellan, *Two Japanese Novelists* (Chicago: University of Chicago Press, 1969), 75–76. See translations by Donald Keene in Keene, *Dawn to the West*, 2:210–11, and by James Kirkup in Davis, *Modern Japanese Poetry*, 1–3.

418. See William F. Sibley, "Naturalism in Japanese Literature," *Harvard Journal of Asiatic Studies* 28 (1968): 157–69.

419. See especially *Hakai* (The broken commandment, 1906), *Ie* (The family, 1911), and *Shinsei* (A new life, 1918–19).

420. Murata, "Nihon hansenshi shōshi," 275. Murata concedes that, as a lyricist, Tōson did not protest "vigorously" (*sekkyokuteki* [*ni*]) in "The Farmer," but he maintains that this work "is of great historical significance because Tōson was one of the earliest modern poets to evoke war weariness [*ensen*] and the misery of war [*sensō no hisan*]."

421. Itō et al., *Nihon no shiika*, 1:266–86. Tōson's retrospective comment appears in his essay of reminiscences entitled "Machi ni arite" (Around town, 1930), full text in Shimazaki, *Shimazaki Tōson zenshū* (1981–83), 11:165–268. While acknowledging that "Tōson does not speak about it in his writings," Itō contends that

> this shock developed soon thereafter into a skepticism toward war [*sensō no kaigi*] [which is] a principal theme [*jūyō na shudai*] of "The Farmer." . . . Amid the rising [bellicose] sentiment popular in Japan at the time, such skepticism toward war did not stop at skepticism alone but was imbued with significance as a critical [*hihan-teki*] view of war. War weariness [*ensen*] did not stop at war weariness alone but was imbued with war renouncing [*hisen*] and antiwar [*hansen*] significance.

Itō's overeagerness to find such messages in "The Farmer" is, it must be said, highly uncharacteristic of a distinguished literary critic whose sensitive and illuminating commentaries on the work of several modern poets, including Tōson, are notable for their close textual analysis. He has played a crucial role in making post-Meiji poetry, once thought by many Japanese to be incomprehensibly abstract and complex, accessible to a wide readership.

422. Janet Walker, *The Japanese Novel of the Meiji Period and the Ideal of Individualism* (Princeton, NJ: Princeton University Press, 1979), 134–35.

423. Ibid., 130–31.

424. Buddhism, of course, also contains a pacifist strain Tōson might have emphasized had he been writing an antiwar poem.

425. *Kokumin no tomo* magazine (February 1895).

426. See "Apologia Pro Poemate Meo" (1917) and "Dulce Et Decorum Est" (1917).

427. "The Farmer" is the concluding work in Tōson's collection *Natsukusa* (Summer grass, 1898). Passages in this chapter are quoted from Shimazaki, *Shimazaki Tōson zenshū* (1981–83), 1:148–72.

428. Carl Sandburg, "Grass," *The Complete Poems of Carl Sandburg, Revised and Expanded Edition* (New York: Harcourt Brace Jovanovich, 1970), 136.
429. "Mujō" (Evanescence), poem number 79 from *Gondai-sōzu Shinkei shū* (Poetry collection of Priest Shinkei, 1468). Translation by Esperanza Ramirez-Christensen in *Heart's Flower: The Life and Poetry of Shinkei* (Stanford, CA: Stanford University Press, 1994), 112.
430. See n. 392.
431. Shimazaki, *Shimazaki Tōson zenshū* (1981–83), 1:153.
432. See Takashi Fujitani, "Kindai Nihon ni okeru kenryoku no tekunorojii: guntai, 'chihō,' shintai," translated by Umemori Naoyuki, *Shisō* 845 (November 1994).
433. See Tōson's novels *Hakai* and *Yoake-mae* (Before the dawn, 1935), as well as *Kokoro* (1914) by Natsume Sōseki (1867–1916).
434. Walker, *The Japanese Novel*, 126.
435. Shimazaki, *Shimazaki Tōson zenshū* (1981–83), 1:153–54.
436. Akiyama, Itō, and Okamoto, *Nihon hansenshi-shū*, 19.
437. Itō et al., *Nihon no shiika*, 1:274–75.
438. Shimazaki, *Shimazaki Tōson zenshū* (1981–83), 1:161.
439. Okamoto Jun, "Nihon hansenshi no rekishiteki haikei" in Akiyama, Itō, and Okamoto, *Nihon hansenshi-shū*, 238.
440. This is the opinion of novelist Masamune Hakuchō (1879–1962) quoted in Keene, *Dawn to the West*, 1:254–55.
441. Translated by Donald Keene in Keene, *Appreciations*, 269.
442. Shimazaki, *Shimazaki Tōson zenshū* (1981–83), 2:195.
443. Ara Masahito, "Sensō to bungaku," *Hon no techō* 5.6 (August 1965): 9.
444. Ibid.
445. From "Machi ni arite" (1930), quoted in Shimazaki, *Shimazaki Tōson zenshū* (1981–83), 11:229–30.
446. Ibid., 4:367–68.
447. Ibid., 366.
448. Tōson praised "Tayama-kun" for his depictions of war. This passage suggests that Tōson might have particularly admired Tayama's moving portrayal in *Ippeisotsu* of an enlisted man suffering from beriberi at the Russo-Japanese front.
449. Shimazaki, *Shimazaki Tōson zenshū* (1981–83), 4:367–68.
450. Shimazaki, *Shimazaki Tōson zenshū* (1967–71), 13:123.
451. From recollections in "Haru o machitsutsu" (Waiting for spring, 1925), quoted in Itō et al., *Nihon no shiika*, 1:297–98. Full text is in Shimazaki, *Shimazaki Tōson zenshū* (1981–83), 11:85–163.
452. "Taikai e no kibō," a message published in *Asahi shinbun*, November 3, 1942. Reprinted in Shimazaki, *Shimazaki Tōson zenshū* (1981–83), 12:457–59. Ironically, the proceedings of the conference were held in English because, although its usage had been banned in February 1942 as "an enemy language," English was the only common vehicle for communication among the delegates from several Asian countries. This situation was reported to be especially troubling for Prime Minister Tōjō, who served as conference chairman. See Shillony, *Politics and Culture in Wartime Japan*, 150.

    In early September 1914, one month after England's entry into World War I, the British government created a new Department of Information (or "of

British propaganda" as Samuel Hynes called it). Attending meetings organized by the Department chief, C. F. G. Masterman, fifty writers issued the following "Authors' Declaration," published September 18, 1914 in both *The London Times* and *The New York Times*:

> The undersigned writers, comprising amongst them men and women of the most divergent political and social views, some of them having been for years ardent champions of good will towards Germany, and many of them extreme advocates of peace, are nevertheless agreed that Great Britain could not without dishonour have refused to take part in the present war. . . . [T]he undersigned feel bound to support the cause of the Allies with all their strength, and with a full conviction of its righteousness, and with a deep sense of its vital import to the future of the world.

See Hynes, *A War Imagined*, 27.

453. See discussion of this novel in William E. Naff's "Introduction" to his translation of Tōson's *Before the Dawn* (Honolulu: University of Hawaii Press, 1987), xxxii; in Keene, *Dawn to the West*, 2:270; and Ino Kenji, "Shimazaki Tōson," in Hisamatsu et al., *Gendai Nihon bungaku daijiten*, 528.
454. Shimazaki, *Shimazaki Tōson zenshū* (1981–83), 2:311.
455. By Kubota Utsubo (1877–1967), Kawata Jun (1882–1966), and Saitō Mokichi (1882–1953), respectively. These poems appeared in a six-volume series published by the Association in 1941–43.
456. Included in volumes 1 and 2 of the above series, published in July 1941 and March 1942, respectively. Contents of the first four volumes are listed in Sakuramoto Tomio, *Shijin to sensō* (Tokyo: Kobayashi Insatsu, 1978), 70–76.

Notes to Chapter 7 (pp. 175–190)

457. The Cabinet Information Bureau (Naikaku Jōhō Kyoku). See Keene, *Appreciations*, 301; and Rubin, *Injurious to Public Morals*, 256–78.
458. Keene, *Appreciations*, 302.
459. Ibid.
460. Ibid.
461. Itō Shinkichi, "Kindai ni okeru 'sensō to shijin' ni tsuite" (On "war and poets" in recent times), in Akiyama, Itō, and Okamoto, *Nihon hansenshi-shū*, 255.
462. In Akiyama, Itō, and Okamoto, *Nihon hansenshi-shū*, 31–32 and 43–45, and Murata, "Nihon hansenshi shōshi," 26.
463. The name of this museum was changed after World War II to Hōmotsu Ihinkan (Treasury of Articles Left by the Deceased). Since 1945 Yasukuni Jinja, where the enshrined include Tōjō Hideki and other military leaders convicted in the Tokyo War Crimes Trials, has become the center of controversy focusing on a number of issues. Visits there by prime ministers on August 15, End of the War Day (*Shūsen kinenbi*), in recent years have been criticized as violating the constitutional separation of state and religion and as insulting the victims in Japan and abroad of the nation's past military aggression.
464. In Akiyama, Itō, and Okamoto, *Nihon hansenshi-shū*, 44–45; and Koumi Eiji, ed., *Gendai-shi no kaishaku to kanshō jiten* (Tokyo: Ōbunsha, 1979), 254–55.

465. Itō, "Kindai ni okeru 'sensō to shijin' ni tsuite," in Akiyama, Itō, and Okamoto, *Nihon hansenshi-shū*, 256. See chapter five, pp. 120–21.
466. Reprinted fully in Akiyama, Itō, and Okamoto, *Nihon hansenshi-shū*, 31–32, and partially in Koumi, *Gendai-shi*, 257, in which commentary by poet Asao Tadao (1932–) identifies this poem as *sensō hihan* (criticism of war).
467. In Akiyama, Itō, and Okamoto, *Nihon hansenshi-shū*, 43–44.
468. Actually there were ten who did not return, but canonization was denied to Ensign Sakamaki Kazuo, who survived and was captured by U.S. forces. See John Deane Potter, *Yamamoto: The Man Who Menaced America* (New York: The Viking Press, 1965), 115.
469. In Sakuramoto, *Shijin to sekinin*, 355–56.
470. Stallworthy, *Oxford Book of War Poetry*, 209.
471. In Sakuramoto, *Shijin to sekinin*, 36.
472. Sakuramoto's book, cited above, in which they are collected was not printed by a standard book publisher, but by a local printing press. Shirotori's wartime poems are listed in Abe Takeshi, *Kindai-shi no haiboku: Shijin no sensō sekinin* (Tokyo: Ohara Shinseisha, 1980), 107. Otsukotsu Akio writes in Odagiri Susumu, et al., eds., *Nihon kindai bungaku daijiten* (Tokyo: Kōdansha, 1984), 766, that Shirotori "composed comparatively little poetry during the war."
473. A few are included in Fukuda Masao, *Fukuda Masao zen-shishū* (Tokyo: Kyōiku Shuppan Sentaa, 1984), 646–55.
474. Abe, *Kindai-shi no haiboku*, 99–100.
475. See Hunter, *Concise Dictionary of Modern Japanese History*, 205. Also see John Albert White, *The Siberian Intervention* (Princeton, NJ: Princeton University Press, 1950); James W. Morley, *The Japanese Thrust into Siberia, 1918* (New York: Columbia University Press, 1957); John K. Fairbank, Edwin O. Reischauer, and Albert M. Craig, *East Asia: The Modern Transformation* (Boston: Houghton Mifflin, 1965), 567–68; and Eckert et al., *Korea Old and New*, 333.
476. Fukuda, *Fukuda Masao zen-shishū*, 192.
477. Stallworthy, *Oxford Book of War Poetry*, 192–93.
478. Abe, *Kindai-shi no haiboku*, 102.
479. I owe this explanation of the lack of public enthusiasm for the Siberian Intervention to a paper given by Frederick Dickinson for the Japan Forum at Harvard University on April 8, 1994. For a more detailed analysis of the increasing importance in Japan after 1917 of domestic over international concerns, and the resulting effect on the authoritarian and militarist agenda of the established elite, see Frederick Dickinson, "World War I and Japan: The Dissipation of Consensual Continentalism, 1914–1919" (Ph.D. dissertation, Yale University, 1993), chapter four.
480. Abe, *Kindai-shi no haiboku*, 106.
481. Fukuda, *Fukuda Masao zen-shishū*, 652–53.
482. Ibid., 646.
483. Quoted from Nichols's first collection, *Invocation: War Poems and Others* (London, 1915), in Bergonzi, *Heroes' Twilight*, 63.
484. In Sakuramoto, *Shijin to sekinin*, 354. This work does not appear in Fukuda's "complete poems."
485. Fukuda Misuzu, interview by the author, recorded at her home in Yokohama, June 5, 1997.

486. Fukuda Masao, *Haisen Chokugo* (Tokyo: Ikkeisha, 1946).
487. See Keene, *Appreciations*, 302. In what might be called today a blow for "political correctness," the Japanese government announced on December 15, 1941 that it was banning "the obnoxious word Far East . . . derived from the conception of the British that England was the center of the world" (Shillony, *Politics and Culture in Wartime Japan*, 141).
488. Shillony, *Politics and Culture in Wartime Japan*, 113.
489. See Akira Iriye, *Pacific Estrangement* (Cambridge, MA: Harvard University Press, 1972), 183, 187, 210–11, 233–34.
490. Shillony, *Politics and Culture in Wartime Japan*, 114–15, 117–18.
491. More open and thorough discussion of wartime events in Germany has not prevented the outbreak of lethal "neo-Nazi" violence, directed especially against recent immigrants, after the nation's reunification in 1990. Right-wing groups in Japan have also committed violent acts recently, including the murder of a newspaper reporter and the serious injury of Mayor Motoshima Hitoshi of Nagasaki in an assassination attempted because he had said that the emperor shared in responsibility for the war.
492. From an interview recorded in 1971.
493. See Iijima's commentary on "Ōshō" in Itō et al., *Nihon no shiika*, 20:376–77. Ienaga Saburō cites novelists Tanizaki Jun'ichirō and Kawabata Yasunari as examples of writers who represent a kind of "passive resistance" because their works of the 1930s and early 1940s ignored the war almost entirely (Ienaga, *The Pacific War*, 205–6). Poet Nishiwaki Junzaburō (1894–1982) is sometimes noted for "maintaining silence" during the years of the Pacific War, but convincing evidence is lacking that this was a deliberate act of defiance or protest (Hara Shirō, "Nishiwaki Junzaburō," in Odagiri et al., *Nihon kindai bungaku daijiten*, 1129).

Notes to Chapter 8 (pp. 191–206)

494. See Keene, *Appreciations*, 300–1.
495. J. Thomas Rimer, *A Reader's Guide to Japanese Literature* (Tokyo: Kodansha International, 1988), 126.
496. Steve Rabson, "'Occidentalism' and Self-Reflection: Western Personae in the Work of Modern Japanese Poets," in *The Walls Within: Images of Westerners and Images of the Japanese Abroad* (Vancouver, BC: Institute of Asian Research, The University of British Columbia, 1989), 98–99, 103.
497. Makoto Ueda, *Modern Japanese Poets and the Nature of Literature* (Stanford, CA: Stanford University Press, 1983), 233.
498. Translation by Donald Keene in Keene, *Dawn to the West*, 2:301. Original in Itō et al., *Nihon no shiika*, 10:54–57.
499. Translation by Donald Keene in Keene, *Dawn to the West*, 2:301. Original in Itō et al., *Nihon no shiika*, 10:23–28.
500. Translation by Donald Keene in Keene, *Dawn to the West*, 2:302–3. Original in Itō et al., *Nihon no shiika*, 10:349–50.
501. Translation of Takamura's reminiscences by Donald Keene in Keene, *Dawn to the West*, 2:301. Original in Itō et al., *Nihon no shiika*, 10:148–49.

502. Uchimura Kanzō, *How I Became a Christian* (Tokyo, 1895), 103–4. Quoted in Shunsuke Kamei, "The Sacred Land of Liberty: Images of America in Nineteenth Century Japan," in Akira Iriye, ed., *Mutual Images: Essays in American-Japanese Relations* (Cambridge, MA: Harvard University Press, 1975), 70.
503. Translated by Donald Keene in Keene, *Dawn to the West*, 2:300. Original in Itō et al., *Nihon no shiika*, 10:146–49.
504. In Yoshimoto, *Takamura Kōtarō*, 15. Partial translation by Donald Keene in Keene, *Dawn to the West*, 2:303.
505. Keene, *Dawn to the West*, 2:303.
506. Translation in Shillony, *Politics and Culture in Wartime Japan*, 112.
507. Yoshimoto, *Takamura Kōtarō*, 128. Translation by Donald Keene in Keene, *Dawn to the West*, 2:305–6.
508. Ueda, *Modern Japanese Poets*, 232–33.
509. Translation in ibid., 247–48.
510. In Serizawa Shunsuke, *Takamura Kōtarō* (Tokyo: Chikuma Shobō, 1982), 206–7. Translation by Donald Keene in Keene, *Appreciations*, 304.
511. First published in *Yomiuri shinbun* and reprinted in the collection *Kiroku* (Tokyo: Ryūseikaku, 1944). Translation by Ben-Ami Shillony in Shillony, *Politics and Culture in Wartime Japan*, 142.
512. In Yoshimoto, *Takamura Kōtarō*, 129. Translation by Donald Keene in Keene, *Dawn to the West*, 2:306. See Takamura's postwar "Apology in shame to Mr. Chiang," in the introduction, p. 8.
513. For this language, see Sakuramoto, *Shijin to sekinin*, 29–31, and Sakuramoto, *Shijin to sensō*, 10. For other examples from the outpouring of poems on the fall of Singapore, see Keene, "The Barren Years," 90–91. Citing his father's elimination of some wartime poems from postwar collections, Takamura Tadashi declined requests for permission to publish full translations of "The Fall of Singapore," "We Strike Them," "I, Too, Will Fly," and "All Students Are Rising to the Cause."
514. From the collection of essays "Shoshun" (Early spring), in Shiga Naoya, *Shiga Naoya zenshū* (Tokyo: Iwanami Shoten, 1973–74), 7:306–7. Translated by Ben-Ami Shillony in Shillony, *Politics and Culture in Wartime Japan*, 134. Claims that spiritual and moral superiority outweigh material considerations in war are by no means exclusive to Japan. British literary critic Clutton Brock outlined his criteria for poets writing in support of the British cause at the start of World War I. Like Takamura, he speaks of "the spirit," the "triumph of an idea," and the "eternal" life of those who die in battle:

> [T]hough they are far more aware than they used to be of the ugly and stupid side of war, they will still, and quite rightly, for the most part pass all that by and insist that for them the thing that matters in war is not the waste and loss of the body and the goods of the body, but the escape of the spirit into that eternal world in which bodily death is as nothing compared with the triumph of an idea. (Hynes, *A War Imagined*, 30)

515. Translated by Ben-Ami Shillony in Shillony, *Politics and Culture in Wartime Japan*, 134–35.
516. Ibid., 120.

517. Ibid., 116, 118.
518. Keene, *Appreciations*, 313. During World War I the British government took broad powers of censorship under the Defence of the Realm Act, which gave it the authority "to prevent the spread of reports likely to cause disaffection or alarm." Samuel Hynes notes that the Act led to the imposing of "restraints" on art and culture and was applied by magistrates who ordered playscripts destroyed and writers jailed for distributing pacifist literature. Under its provisions His Majesty's government also "assumed control over a citizen's right to . . . open a pub, treat a friend to a drink, or consort with a prostitute" (Hynes, *A War Imagined*, 79–81).
519. See Havens, *Valley of Darkness*, 138–42. Science students were initially exempted from conscription, indicating that, despite their public statements about the decisiveness of spiritual superiority, Japan's government leaders appreciated the value of science and technology in modern warfare (Shillony, *Politics and Culture in Wartime Japan*, 139).
520. From *Hikō-shishū tsubasa* (Tokyo: Tōkyō Shuppan Kabushiki-gaisha, 1944), quoted in Sakuramoto, *Shijin to sekinin*, 174–75; and from *Kiroku*, quoted in Sakuramoto, *Shijin to sekinin*, 253–54.
521. Keene, *Dawn to the West*, 2:307.
522. Translated by Donald Keene in Keene, *Dawn to the West*, 2:307. Quoted in Yoshimoto, *Takamura Kōtarō*, 147.
523. Translation by Donald Keene in Keene, *Dawn to the West*, 2:307. Quoted in Itō et al., *Nihon no shiika*, 10:364–65.
524. In Yoshimoto, *Takamura Kōtarō*, 147–48. See introduction, p. 8.
525. See Amy Vladeck Heinrich, *Fragments of Rainbows: The Life and Poetry of Saitō Mokichi, 1882–1953* (New York: Columbia University Press, 1983), 46–47. The author writes that Kraepelin

> was particularly angered by the fact that some Japanese students who fled Europe at the outbreak of [World War I] later sought restitution for belongings they had left behind. His resentment over the exclusion of German and Austrian scholars from international organizations was directed against Japan in particular: perhaps he felt, as many Germans did, that Japan had been ungrateful and betrayed the country that had provided guidance for Japanese scientific progress during the Meiji period.

For her illuminating study of this poet, Heinrich makes judicious use of several biographical sources on Mokichi and gives a compelling account of how historical events affected his work.

526. Ibid., 47.
527. Ibid., 49.
528. Translation by Donald Keene in Keene, *Appreciations*, 305.
529. From his collection *Kan'un* (1940). Translated in Heinrich, *Fragments of Rainbows*, 65–66, who writes that *Kan'un* "was characterized by poems glorifying war. In it Mokichi progressed from a poet of love to a poet of patriotism."
530. Ibid., 67–68.
531. Ibid., 69.
532. Ibid., 68.

533. See Sakuramoto, *Shijin to sensō,* 73, and Hirano et al., *Sensō bungaku zenshū,* supplement, 180–88.
534. John W. Dower, *War without Mercy: Race and Power in the Pacific War* (New York: Pantheon Books, 1986), 101–2.
535. Sakuramoto, *Shijin to sekinin,* 17.
536. Dower, *War without Mercy,* 231.
537. Ibid., 232–33.
538. Sakuramoto, *Shijin to sekinin,* 417.
539. Heinrich, *Fragments of Rainbows,* 68.
540. Ibid.
541. Ibid., 67, 71.
542. Bergonzi, *Heroes' Twilight,* 60–62.
543. Quoted from "Varia," *Poetry and Drama* 2 (September 1914): 251 in Hynes, *A War Imagined,* 29.
544. See chapter seven, pp. 184–85.
545. From Kōsaka Masaaki, *Japanese Thought in the Meiji Era,* translated by David Abosch (Tokyo: Pan-Pacific Press, 1958), 266–67.
546. From an editorial in the August 1904 issue.
547. In the April 1904 issue of *Myōjō,* quoted in Furukawa, "Meiji bungaku to Nichi-Ro sensō."
548. In the June issue of *Myōjō.* Quoted in Itsumi, *Hyōden,* 352–53.
549. John Updike, "Of Sickened Times," *The New Yorker* (November 16, 1992): 137.
550. In ibid., 138.

Notes to Conclusion (pp. 207–227)

551. In Stallworthy, *Oxford Book of War Poetry,* 171.
552. Comments in an interview with journalist Bill Moyers on a television program entitled "Bill Moyers: Facing Hate with Elie Wiesel," broadcast August 26, 1992.
553. British school children were required to memorize this poem. Reprinted in Stallworthy, *Oxford Book of War Poetry,* 115.
554. Reprinted in ibid., 135.
555. *King Henry V,* act 3, scene 1.
556. Uchimura's remarks are quoted in John F. Howes, "Uchimura Kanzō: The Bible and War," in Nobuya Bamba and John F. Howes, eds., *Pacifism in Japan: The Christian and Socialist Tradition* (Vancouver, BC: University of British Columbia Press, 1978), 101–2.
557. Partial translation in Bamba and Howes, *Pacifism in Japan,* 102.
558. In Kōsaka, *Japanese Thought in the Meiji Era,* 348.
559. "A Retrospect" in *Yorozu chōhō* (December 14–16, 1897). Portions quoted in Bamba and Howes, *Pacifism in Japan,* 102.
560. First published in *Fukuin shinpō* (December 25, 1896). In Uchimura, *Uchimura Kanzō zenshū,* 21:26. For another translation, see Bamba and Howes, *Pacifism in Japan,* 102–3.
561. In Akiyama, Itō, and Okamoto, *Nihon hansenshi-shū,* 182–84.
562. Editorial, *The New York Times* (July 12, 1992), section 4, p. 20.

563. From "Subete no ningen wa byōdō ni tsukurareta?" (Are all men created equal?), in Akiyama, Itō, and Okamoto, *Nihon hansenshi-shū*, 170–71.
564. Panel presentation on war and remembrance at the Association for Asian Studies annual meeting held in Boston, Massachusetts on March 27, 1994.
565. Bergonzi, *Heroes' Twilight*, 79.
566. In ibid., 80.
567. Ibid., 80.
568. In ibid.
569. In Kramer, *On Freedom's Side*, 80–81.
570. Nagata, *Nihon gunka meikyoku hyakusen*, 18.
571. In ibid., 18–19. As a U.S. Army draftee in 1966, I marched to songs with a similar sardonic humor expressed in such lines as "Hup, two, three, whirl. / Forget about home 'cause Jodie's got your girl" and "Cover your ass with that poncho, Sam. / It gets mighty cold in North Vietnam."
572. Benedict, *The Chrysanthemum and the Sword*, 193–94.
573. Stallworthy, *Oxford Book of War Poetry*, 189–90.
574. See especially his trilogy *Mugi to heitai* (Wheat and soldiers, 1938), *Tsuchi to heitai* (Earth and soldiers, 1938), and *Hana to heitai* (Flowers and soldiers, 1939).
575. Reprinted in Sakuramoto, *Shijin to sensō*, 205–38.
576. Their views are summarized with reasonable fidelity in Sakuramoto's *han-hanron*, published in Sakuramoto, *Shijin to sensō*, 239–64.
577. Kaneko Mitsuharu, *Shijin: Kaneko Mitsuharu jiden* (Tokyo: Heibonsha, 1957), 195–96.
578. See ibid., 214–15. Sakuramoto complains in "A Zone of Falsehood in Studies of Kaneko Mitsuharu" that the composition dates (ranging from October 1943 to July 1945) appended to these poems when they were first published in 1947 and 1948 cannot be confirmed. He suggests that they could have been written after the war rather than during it (see Sakuramoto, *Shijin to sensō*, 205–38).
579. In *Masu* (Trout) (March 1947).
580. Kaneko, *Kaneko Mitsuharu zenshū*, 2:194–95.
581. In his collection *Rakkasan* (Parachute) (Tokyo: Nihon Mirai-ha, 1948).
582. Kaneko, *Kaneko Mitsuharu zenshū*, 4:153. Three lines from Kaneko's poem "Fuji" had been censored by Occupation authorities before it was first published in 1947. "America put on her clodhoppers / and, using Fuji as a guide, / arrived in Japan from the sky." In one sense, at least, the censorship enforced under the Occupation's Press Code was more thorough than that carried out earlier by the Japanese Home Ministry. Even the fact of censorship was censored under the Occupation so that entire pages had to be reprinted to omit offending passages, while it was sufficient under the earlier regulations to replace prohibited words and phrases with *fuseji* marks ("X").

    The publication of "Notes on Hell" suggests that, in some cases, Occupation censors were more lenient than the Home Ministry had been when it came to the content of literary works. See Rubin, "From Wholesomeness to Decadence," 71–103.
583. See Dower, *War without Mercy*, 33–73, 300; and Ienaga, *The Pacific War*, 201–2.

584. Translation by John Whittier Treat in his "Early Hiroshima Poetry," *Journal of the Association of Teachers of Japanese* 20.2 (November 1986): 224–25.
585. Translation by Richard H. Minear in his *Hiroshima: Three Witnesses* (Princeton, NJ: Princeton University Press, 1990), 306–7.
586. Treat, "Early Hiroshima Poetry," 209–10.
587. George Feifer, *Tennozan: The Battle of Okinawa and the Atomic Bomb* (New York: Ticknor and Fields, 1992), xiv. Feifer does not identify the "historian of battle" he quotes.
588. In Akiyama, Itō, and Okamoto, *Nihon hansenshi-shū,* 126–27. Rouault (1871–1958) continued to produce paintings of women until his death at age eighty-seven.
589. In support of the ban, the Nippon Music Culture Association, the Nippon Record Music Culture Association, and the Musicians' Association issued a joint statement in January 1943 resolving to "weed Japan of the influence of American jazz," which they conceded had become pervasive. In practice, the police lacked the knowledge or inclination to enforce distinctions between, for example, a Franz Schubert symphony and a Billy Strayhorn ballad, and many coffee shops went back to playing jazz recordings, though at lowered volume, a few weeks after the ban was announced (see Shillony, *Politics and Culture in Wartime Japan*, 144). Another effort at patriotic music banning was tried unsuccessfully twenty years earlier in England during World War I. Symphony conductor Thomas Beecham presented twenty-five of what were announced as "No-German" concerts, excluding the work of German composers, for the Promenade series of May and June 1915. Beecham's series, conceived without government encouragement or coercion, attracted only lukewarm interest, however, and music by Brahms, Mozart, Bach, and Wagner was restored to the Promenade series of autumn 1915 (see Hynes, *A War Imagined*, 76–77).
590. See especially Osaragi Jirō, *Kikyō* (Homecoming, 1948); and Mishima Yukio, *Kinjiki* (1951), translated by Alfred H. Marks as *Forbidden Colors* (New York: Alfred A. Knopf, 1968).
591. See Ienaga, *The Pacific War*, 236–37.
592. In Akiyama, Itō, and Okamoto, *Nihon hansenshi-shū*, 165–66.
593. First published in Yamanokuchi Baku, *Yamanokuchi Baku shishū* (Tokyo: Hara Shobō, 1964), 82–83.
594. See *Shima kūkan kara '85: Okinawa, han-kaku, hansen ansorojī* (From the island space Okinawa '85: an antinuclear and antiwar anthology) (Naha: Akebono Insatsu, 1985).
595. Steve Rabson, trans., *Okinawa: Two Postwar Novellas by Ōshiro Tatsuhiro and Higashi Mineo* (Berkeley, CA: Institute of East Asian Studies, University of California, Berkeley, 1989; reprinted 1996), 132.
596. Author's translation slightly revised from ibid., 132–33.
597. Ibid., 133.
598. Shiro Yū, "Soshite sengo" (Then came "postwar") in *Shijin kaigi* (Poets' Conference) 20.5 (May 1982): 26–27. Translation in Rabson, *Okinawa*, 134–35.
599. Each year local newspapers in Okinawa give far greater prominence than the mainland press to anniversaries of such events as the Pearl Harbor attack and the Nanking Massacre. Okinawan authors have also published numerous

accounts of the extreme cruelties imposed on local residents by Imperial Japanese Forces. During the Battle of Okinawa, soldiers from the mainland shot thousands of Okinawans so they could grab shelter from enemy fire for themselves in overcrowded caves, and they ordered mass suicides to stretch dwindling food supplies. Memories of such atrocities explain in part why opposition to the growing number of Self-Defense Forces in Okinawa has been particularly intense. See Rabson, *Okinawa*, 1–2, 29; and Shinzato Keiji, Taminato Tomoaki, and Kinjō Seitoku, *Okinawa-ken no rekishi* (Tokyo: Yamakawa, 1980), 214–15. A mainland historian also describes atrocities and outrageous sacrifices imposed on Okinawans by Imperial Forces in Ienaga, *The Pacific War*, 198–99.

Two Japanese prime ministers made statements in 1992 and 1993 expressing regret in the most explicit terms yet for wartime actions and policies. In January of 1992 documentary evidence was provided by Yoshimi Yoshiaki of Chūō University linking the Japanese government to the forced labor of "comfort women" as prostitutes for Imperial Japanese forces. A few days later, during a previously scheduled visit to South Korea, Prime Minister Miyazawa Kiichi offered an apology to Korean women forced into prostitution. The next year, after the Liberal Democratic Party was defeated in national elections and more documentary evidence was discovered by American historian Grant Goodman, new Prime Minister Hosokawa Morihiro made an unprecedented apology for Japan's "past aggressive acts and colonial rule" in his opening speech before parliament. Subsequently, the word "crimes" has been used by Japanese diplomats abroad to describe wartime military actions in Asian countries.

600. The number of Japanese who lost their lives after the outbreak of the China War in 1937 is estimated at 3.1 million, 800,000 of them civilians (Hall, *Japan*, 349).

601. Article Nine stipulates:

> Aspiring sincerely to an international peace based on justice and order, the Japanese people forever renounce war as a sovereign right of the nation and the threat or use of force as a means of settling international disputes.
>
> In order to accomplish the aim of the proceeding paragraph, land, sea, and air forces, as well as other war potential, will never be maintained. The right of belligerency of the state will not be recognized.

The preamble to the Constitution states: "We, the Japanese people, [are] resolved that never again shall we be visited with the horrors of war through the action of government."

Although written under the supervision of U.S. Occupation authorities, the 1946 Constitution, and especially its antiwar clauses, have been widely supported in Japan as expressing the will of the people. Four years after its promulgation, when General MacArthur ordered the creation of a "National Police Reserve" to replace American troops who were being hurriedly transferred to battlefields in Korea, many Japanese protested that this violated the Constitution. Since the Occupation ended in April 1952, similar protests have arisen each time the Japanese government, with strong encouragement from Washington, has expanded the scale and role of the military, from the establishment of a "National Security Force" in 1952 and the "Self-Defense Forces" in 1954 to the more recent deployment of troops abroad for "peace-keeping operations" in Cambodia.

602. Kazuko Watanabe, "The New Cold War with Japan: How Are Women Paying for It?" *Ms.* (November-December 1991), 21.

603. Nakanishi Terumasa, "To War in the Gulf," *Japan Echo* 18.1 (Spring 1991): 7. Other contemporary historians have noted changing attitudes toward the military in Japan. In a lecture at Brown University on April 28, 1993, William Steele cited the generation gap and the lack of information in public schools about Japan's role in World War II as factors that have weakened both public support for Article Nine and opposition to further expansion of the Japanese military.

604. See "1992-nen nyūsu hairaito," N.H.K. television, December 1992. On April 8, 1993, Nakata Atsuhiko, a civilian volunteer from Osaka, and his Cambodian interpreter were shot and killed in what is generally believed to have been a Khmer Rouge ambush in north central Kompong Thom Province.

605. Steven R. Weisman, "An American in Tokyo," *The New York Times Magazine* (July 26, 1992), 38.

606. During tensions over currency revaluation in 1987, the *Sankei shinbun* wrote:

> In a few months the yen soared from 245 to the dollar to 200. This was the equivalent of Japan's loss of four aircraft carriers at Midway. Washington's final objective is probably an exchange rate of 100 yen to the dollar. That represents Japan's total defeat and General Douglas MacArthur's triumphant entry into Tokyo. We must not lose the Pacific War twice.

Translated in Thomas L. Friedman, "Trade War Isn't So Swell Either," *The New York Times* (Sunday, March 6, 1994), section 4, p. 4.

607. See especially George Friedman, *The Coming War with Japan* (New York: St. Martin's Press, 1992), in which the author even predicts on p. 403 that "the second U.S.-Japanese war . . . will not be the last."

608. Friedman ("Trade War Isn't So Swell Either," 4) writes that the

> difference between trade wars and real wars [is that] in trade wars almost every sword is double-edged. That is, because of the degree to which the Japanese and American economies are intertwined—$155 billion a year in merchandise trade between the two—it is very hard for the United States to hit Japan with sanctions without hurting American consumers, retailers or manufacturers, who depend on Japanese products, and vice versa. That is why Paul R. Krugman, professor of economics at M.I.T., likes to say: "A trade war is a conflict in which each side uses most of its ammunition to shoot itself in the foot."

609. See Dower, *War without Mercy*, 13; and John G. Russell, "Narratives of Denial: Racial Chauvinism and the Black Other in Japan," *Japan Quarterly* 38.4 (October-December 1991): 416–28.

610. As noted above, approximately 75 percent of the U.S. military presence in all of Japan is concentrated in Okinawa. Some 30,000 American and 6,000 Japanese military personnel are stationed there on bases that occupy one-fifth of the island's land area.

611. Akiyama, Itō, and Okamoto, *Nihon hansenshi-shū*, 219–20. Hostile stereotyping and racist caricatures of Japanese can be found in the recent writing of Americans, too, though rarely in poetry. Michael Crichton's popular novel *Rising Sun* (New York: Alfred A. Knopf, 1992), made into a film in 1993, refers to the "Japanese threat" (p. 295) and describes Japanese as "irritating" (p. 15) and "masters of indirect action. It's their instinctual way to proceed" (p. 245).

612. At this writing, prospects for substantial reduction of U.S. forces in Asia are not encouraging. Former President George Bush asserted that retaining large numbers of land-based American troops in countries abroad is necessary for avoiding "instability" in his vaguely defined "new world order." Though promising major reductions of troops in Europe, President Clinton has announced plans to maintain 100,000 U.S. forces in East Asia. Many American policy makers believe that, despite public opposition to U.S. bases in Japan, South Korea, and the Philippines (where the government ordered their removal), the continuing presence of the U.S. military in the area "serves as a sort of neutral arbiter, keeping a number of would-be regional powers in balance" and preventing "historical animosities" from "explod[ing]" (see Thomas L. Friedman, "America's Japan Policy: Fractured Vision," *The New York Times Magazine* [June 28, 1992], 52). In a dissenting opinion, the Center for Defense Information, a military research institute staffed largely by retired U.S. generals and admirals, stated in its regular newsletter (*The Defense Monitor* 21.3 [1993]: 7) that Japan's

> Self-Defense Forces are quite capable and formidable. Concern about a resurgence of militarism in Japan would at the present time appear unwarranted. *The majority of Japanese are adamantly opposed to militarism.* . . . [South Korea] spends about twice as much [as North Korea] on its substantially more modern military and has twice as large a population from which to draw troops. South Korea does not need U.S. garrison forces to defend itself.

Bibliography

Abe Takeshi. *Kindai-shi no haiboku: Shijin no sensō sekinin* Tokyo: Ohara Shinseisha, 1980.

Abrams, M. H., ed. *The Norton Anthology of English Literature*, vol. 2. New York: W. W. Norton and Company, 1986.

Akiyama Kiyoshi, Itō Shinkichi, and Okamoto Jun, eds. *Nihon hansenshi-shū* (Anthology of Japanese antiwar poetry). Tokyo: Taihei Shuppansha, 1979.

Ara Masahito. "Senjika no 'geijutsu teikōha'" ("Artistic resistance" during the war). *Kokubungaku kaishaku to kyōzai no kenkyū* (June 1965).

———. "Sensō to bungaku" (War and literature). *Hon no techō* 5.6 (August 1956): 9.

Ariyoshi Sawako. *Hishoku* (Beyond color). Tokyo: Kadokawa Shoten, 1967.

Atsumi Ikuko and Graeme Wilson. "The Poetry of Yosano Akiko." *Japan Quarterly* 21.1 (January-March 1974): 181–87.

Bamba, Nobuya and John F. Howes, eds. *Pacifism in Japan: The Christian and Socialist Tradition*. Vancouver, BC: University of British Columbia Press, 1978.

Barclay, Florence L. *My Heart's Right There*. London, 1914.

Beasley, W. G. *The Modern History of Japan*. 3d rev. ed. New York: St. Martin's Press, 1981.

Beichman, Janine. *Masaoka Shiki*. Boston: Twayne Publishers, 1982.

Benedict, Ruth. *The Chrysanthemum and the Sword: Patterns of Japanese Culture*. Boston: Houghton Mifflin Company, 1946.

Bergonzi, Bernard. *Heroes' Twilight: A Study of Literature of the Great War*. 2d ed. London and Basingstoke: Macmillan, 1980.

Bowring, Richard John. *Mori Ōgai and the Modernization of Japanese Culture*. Cambridge, England: Cambridge University Press, 1979.

Brooks, Cleanth, R. W. B. Lewis, and Robert Penn Warren, eds. *American Literature: The Makers and the Making*, vol. 2. New York: St. Martin's Press, 1973.

Brower, Robert. "Masaoka Shiki and Tanka Reform." In *Tradition and Modernization in Japanese Culture*, Donald Shively, ed. Princeton, N.J: Princeton University Press, 1971.

Conroy, Hilary. *The Japanese Seizure of Korea: 1868–1910, A Study of Realism and Idealism in International Relations*. Philadelphia: University of Pennsylvania Press, 1960.

Cranston, Edwin A. *A Waka Anthology, Volume One: The Gem-Glistening Cup*. Stanford, CA: Stanford University Press, 1993.

———. "Young Akiko: The Literary Debut of Yosano Akiko (1878–1942)." *Literature East and West* 18.1 (March 1974): 19–45.

Davis, A. R., ed. *Modern Japanese Poetry*. St. Lucia, Queensland, Australia: University of Queensland Press, 1978.

Dickinson, Frederick. "World War I and Japan: The Dissipation of Consensual Continentalism, 1914–1919." Ph.D. dissertation, Yale University, 1993.

Dower, John W. *War without Mercy: Race and Power in the Pacific War*. New York: Pantheon Books, 1986.

Drea, Edward J. "In the Army Barracks of Imperial Japan." *Armed Forces and Society* 15.3 (Spring 1989): 329–48.

Eckert, Carter J., et al. *Korea Old and New: A History*. Seoul: Ilchokak Publishers, for Korea Institute, Harvard University, 1990.

Eggleston, George Cary, ed. *American War Ballads and Lyrics*. 2 vols. New York and London: G. P. Putnam's Sons, 1889.

Engelbrecht, H. C., and F. C. Hanighen. *Merchants of Death: A Study of the International Armament Industry*. New York: Dodd, Mead and Company, 1934.

Fairbank, John K., Edwin O. Reischauer, and Albert M. Craig. *East Asia: The Modern Transformation*. Boston: Houghton Mifflin, 1965.

Feifer, George. *Tennozan: The Battle of Okinawa and the Atomic Bomb*. New York: Ticknor and Fields, 1992.

Foerster, Norman, ed. *American Poetry and Prose*. Boston: Houghton Mifflin, 1934.

Friedman, Thomas L. "Trade War Isn't So Swell Either." *The New York Times* (Sunday, March 6, 1994), section 4, p. 4.

Fujitani Takashi. "Kindai Nihon ni okeru kenryoku no tekunorojii: guntai, 'chihō,' shintai" (Technologies of power in modern Japan: the military, the "local," the body). *Shisō* 845 (November 1994): 163–76.

Fukuda Masao. *Fukuda Masao zen-shishū* (The complete poems of Fukuda Masao). Tokyo: Kyōiku Shuppan Sentaa, 1984.

———. *Haisen chokugo* (Just after the defeat). Tokyo: Ikkeisha, 1946.

Funahashi Seiichi. "Kokugo mondai to minzoku no sho¤rai" (The Japanese language question and the future of our people). *Chūō kōron* (May 1961): 48–56.

Furukawa Gen. "Kyōiku kenkyū hōkōki IV" (Ambles in educational research IV). *Sōbun* 107 (April 1972): 18-21.

Furukawa Kiyohiko. "Meiji bungaku to Nichi-Ro sensō" (Meiji literature and the Russo-Japanese War). *Hon no techō* 5.6 (August 1965): 13–21.

Fussell, Paul. *The Great War and Modern Memory*. New York: Oxford University Press, 1975.

Gamachi Fumio. "Masaoka Shiki." *Kokubungaku kaishaku to kanshō* 37.10 (August 1972): 92–95.

Hall, John Whitney. *Japan: From Prehistory to Modern Times*. New York: Delacorte, 1970.

Hanson, Sam, and Lucille Harten, eds. *The "Good War" in Retrospect: Memories of World War II*. Pocatello, ID: Idaho State University Press, 1987.

Havens, Thomas R. H. *Valley of Darkness: The Japanese People and World War Two*. New York: W. W. Norton and Company, 1978.

Heike monogatari (The tale of the Heike). 2 vols. Edited by Ichiko Teiji. *Nihon koten bungaku zenshū* 29 and 30. Tokyo: Shōgakkan, 1973.

Heinrich, Amy Vladeck. *Fragments of Rainbows: The Life and Poetry of Saitō Mokichi, 1882–1953*. New York: Columbia University Press, 1983.

Higuchi Chiyoko. *Her Place in the Sun: Women Who Shaped Japan*, English version by Sharon Rhoads. Tokyo: The East Publications, 1973.

Hikō-shishū tsubasa (Aviation poems: wings). Tokyo: Tōkyō Shuppan Kabushiki-gaisha, 1944.

Hino Ashihei. *Mugi to heitai* (Wheat and soldiers). Tokyo: Kaizōsha, 1938.

_____. *Tsuchi to heitai* (Earth and soldiers). Tokyo: Kaizōsha, 1938.

Hirano Ken, et al., eds. *Sensō bungaku zenshū* (Collected war literature). 7 vols. Tokyo: Asahi Shinbunsha, 1972.

Hisamatsu Sen'ichi, et al., eds. *Gendai Nihon bungaku daijiten*. Tokyo: Meiji Shoin, 1972.

Honma Hisao. "Akiko to Naoko." In *Zoku Meiji bungaku-shi*. Tokyo: Tōkyōdō, 1964.

Howes, John F. "Uchimura Kanzō: The Bible and War." In Nobuya Bamba and John F. Howes, eds., *Pacifism in Japan: The Christian and Socialist Tradition*. Vancouver, BC: University of British Columbia Press, 1978.

Hunter, Janet E., comp. *Concise Dictionary of Modern Japanese History*. Berkeley, CA: University of California Press, 1984.

Hynes, Samuel. *A War Imagined: The First World War and English Culture*. New York: Atheneum, 1991.

Ienaga Saburō. *The Pacific War: 1931–1945*. Translated by Frank Baldwin. New York: Pantheon, 1978.

Inouye, Charles Shirō. *Three Tales of Mystery and Imagination: Japanese Gothic by Izumi Kyōka*. Kanazawa, Japan: Takuwa Bijutsu Insatsu, Ltd., 1992.

Irie Haruyuki. *Yosano Akiko no bungaku* (The literature of Yosano Akiko). Tokyo: Ōfūsha, 1983.

Iriye, Akira. *Pacific Estrangement*. Cambridge, MA: Harvard University Press, 1972.

_____, ed. *Mutual Images: Essays in American-Japanese Relations*. Cambridge, MA: Harvard University Press, 1975.

Ishii Kenji. "Meiji bungaku to heiwa e no michi" (Meiji literature and the road to peace). In *Kindai Nihon bungakushi kenkyū*. Tokyo: Miraisha, 1965.

Ishikawa Jun. *The Bodhisattva, or Samantabhadra: A Novel*. Translated from the Japanese with an introduction and critical essay by William Jefferson Tyler. New York: Columbia University Press, 1990.

Itō Kazuo, ed. *Shimazaki Tōson jiten* (Shimazaki Tōson dictionary). Tokyo: Meiji Shoin, 1982.

Itō Shinkichi. "Kindai ni okeru 'sensō to shijin' ni tsuite" (On "war and poets" in recent times). In Akiyama Kiyoshi, Itō Shinkichi, and Okamoto Jun, eds., *Nihon hansenshi-shū* (Anthology of Japanese antiwar poetry). Tokyo: Taihei Shuppansha, 1979.

——, Itō Sei, Inoue Yasushi, and Yamamoto Kenkichi, eds. *Nihon no shiika* (Anthology of Japanese poetry). 26 vols. Tokyo: Chūō Kōronsha, 1967–70.

Itsumi Kumi. *Hyōden: Yosano Tekkan, Akiko* (A critical biography of Yosano Tekkan and Akiko). Tokyo: Yagi Shoten, 1975.

Kaneko Mitsuharu. *Kaneko Mitsuharu zenshū* (The complete works of Kaneko Mitsuharu). 5 vols. Tokyo: Shōrinsha, 1974.

——. *Ninpinin-den* (Brute's journal). Tokyo: Daikōsha, 1971.

——. *Rakkasan* (Parachute). Tokyo: Nihon Mirai-ha, 1948.

——. *Shijin: Kaneko Mitsuharu jiden* (Poet: autobiography of Kaneko Mitsuharu). Tokyo: Heibonsha, 1957.

Katō, Shūichi. *A History of Japanese Literature*. 3 vols. Translated by Don Sanderson. Tokyo: Kodansha International, 1983.

Keene, Donald. *Appreciations of Japanese Culture*. Tokyo: Kodansha International, 1981.

——. "The Barren Years: Japanese War Literature." *Monumenta Nipponica* 33.1 (Spring 1978): 67–112.

——. *Dawn to the West: Japanese Literature of the Modern Era*. 2 vols. New York: Holt, Rinehart and Winston, 1984.

——, comp. and ed. *Modern Japanese Literature: From 1868 to the Present*. Vol. 2 of *Anthology of Japanese Literature*. New York: Grove Press, 1956.

Kinoshita Naoe. *Hi no hashira*. Tokyo: Mainichi Shinbun, 1904.

Kiroku (Chronicle). Tokyo: Ryūseikaku, 1944.

Komota Nobuo, Shimada Yoshifumi, Yazawa Tamotsu, and Yokozawa Chiaki, eds. *Nihon ryūkōka-shi* (A history of Japanese popular songs). 2 vols. Tokyo: Shakai Shisōsha, 1981.

Kōsaka Masaaki. *Japanese Thought in the Meiji Era*. Translated by David Abosch. Tokyo: Pan-Pacific Press, 1958.

Kōtoku Shūsui. "Hi-sensō shugi" (Opposition to war). *Yorozu chōhō* (August 7, 1900).

Koumi Eiji, ed. *Gendai-shi no kaishaku to kanshō jiten* (Dictionary for the interpretation and appreciation of contemporary poetry). Tokyo: Ōbunsha, 1979.

Kramer, Aaron, ed. *On Freedom's Side: An Anthology of American Poems of Protest*. New York: Macmillan, 1972.

Kunikida Doppo. *Aitei tsūshin* (Letters to my dear brother). Tokyo: Sakuryō Shobō, 1908.

Kurihara Sadako. *Black Eggs*. Translated by Richard Minear. Ann Arbor, MI: Center for Japanese Studies, The University of Michigan, 1994.

——. *Kuroi tamago: senryō ken'etsu to hansen-genbaku shikashū* (Black eggs: Occupation censorship and collected antiwar and atomic bomb poetry). Kyoto: Jinbun Shoin, 1983.

Kuroshima Denji. *Puroretariya geijutsu kyōtei* (Studies of proletarian art). Tokyo: Sekaisha, 1929.

Lane, Arthur E. *An Adequate Response: The War Poetry of Wilfred Owen and Siegfried Sassoon.* Detroit, MI: Wayne State University Press, 1972.

Lebra, Takie Sugiyama. *Japanese Patterns of Behavior.* Honolulu: University of Hawaii Press, 1976.

Lensen, George Alexander. *Balance of Intrigue: International Rivalry in Korea and Manchuria, 1884–1889.* 2 vols. Tallahassee, FL: University Presses of Florida, 1982.

Longfellow, Henry Wadsworth. *Henry Wadsworth Longfellow: Selected Poems.* Edited by Lawrence Buell. New York: Penguin Books, 1988.

——. *The Poetical Works of Longfellow.* Boston: Houghton Mifflin Company, 1975.

Lowell, Robert. *Imitations.* New York: Farrar, Straus and Giroux, 1961.

Man'yōshū. 4 vols. Edited by Akiyama Ken et al. *Nihon koten bungaku zenshū* 1–4. Tokyo: Shōgakkan, 1980.

Maruyama, Masao. *Thought and Behaviour in Modern Japanese Politics*, edited by Ivan Morris. London: Oxford University Press, 1963.

Masaoka Shiki. *Shiki zenshū* (The complete works of Masaoka Shiki). 22 vols. Edited by Kawahigashi Hekigotō et al. Tokyo: Kaizōsha, 1929–31.

——. *Shiki zenshū* (The complete works of Masaoka Shiki). 22 vols. Edited by Masaoka Chūsaburō, et al. Tokyo: Kōdansha, 1975–78.

McClellan, Edwin. *Two Japanese Novelists.* Chicago: University of Chicago Press, 1969.

McKenzie, F. A. *The Tragedy of Korea.* London: Hodder and Stoughton, 1908.

Minami Hiroshi. *Nihonjin no shinri* (The psychology of the Japanese). Tokyo: Iwanami Shoten, 1960.

Minear, Richard H., ed. and trans. *Hiroshima: Three Witnesses.* Princeton, NJ: Princeton University Press, 1990.

——, trans. *Black Eggs,* by Kurihara Sadako. Ann Arbor, MI: Center for Japanese Studies, The University of Michigan, 1994.

Mitchell, Richard H. *Thought Control in Prewar Japan.* Ithaca, NY: Cornell University Press, 1976.

Miyazaki Koshoshi. *Kisei* (Homecoming). Tokyo: Min'yūsha, 1890.

Mori Ōgai, ed. *Mezamashi-gusa* 42 (December 1897): 10–20.

Morley, James W. *The Japanese Thrust into Siberia, 1918.* New York: Columbia University Press, 1957.

Morris, Ivan. *The Nobility of Failure: Tragic Heroes in the History of Japan.* New York: Holt, Rinehart and Winston, 1975.

Murata Masao. "Nihon hansenshi shōshi: Nisshin sensō kara taiheiyō sensō made" (A short history of Japanese antiwar poetry: from the Sino-Japanese War of 1894–95 to the Pacific War). In *Sensō to wa nanika: hansenshi-shū*, edited by Murata Masao and Noguchi Masayoshi. Tokyo: Gendai Shokan, 1969.

Murata Masao and Noguchi Masayoshi, eds. *Sensō to wa nanika: hansenshi-shū.* Tokyo: Gendai Shokan, 1969.

Nagata Gyōji, ed. *Nihon gunka meikyoku hyakusen* (100 famous Japanese military songs). Tokyo: Nobarasha, 1975.

Nahm, Andrew C., ed. *Korea under Japanese Colonial Rule*. Kalamazoo, MI: Center for Korean Studies, Western Michigan University, 1973.

Nakane, Chie. *Japanese Society*. Rev. ed. Harmondsworth, Middlesex: Penguin, 1973.

Nichols, Robert. *Invocation: War Poems and Others*. London, 1915.

Nippon Gakujutsu Shinkōkai, eds. and trans. *The Manyōshū*. New York: Columbia University Press, 1965.

Nishida Masaru, ed. *Sensō to bungakusha* (War and writers). Tokyo: San'ichi Shobō, 1983.

"Nisshin, Nichi-Ro sengo no bungaku" (Literature following the Sino-Japanese and Russo-Japanese Wars). Special issue of *Kokubungaku kaishaku to kanshō* (August 1972).

Noda Utarō, ed. *Yosano Tekkan Yosano Akiko shū*. Vol 51 of *Meiji bungaku zenshū*. 1968.

Notehelfer, Fred G. *Kōtoku Shūsui: Portrait of a Japanese Radical*. Cambridge, England: Cambridge University Press, 1971.

Odagiri Susumu, et al., eds. *Nihon kindai bungaku daijiten* (Dictionary of Japanese modern literature). Tokyo: Kōdansha, 1984.

Oka Yasuo. "Nisshin sensō to bundan" (The Sino-Japanese War and literary circles). *Kokubungaku kaishaku to kanshō* 9 (October 1964): 12–16.

Okamoto, Shumpei. *The Japanese Oligarchy and the Russo-Japanese War*. New York: Columbia University Press, 1970.

Okano Yukie. "Kinoshita Naoe: Nisshin Nichiro tsuranuku hansen" (Kinoshita Naoe: antiwar throughout the Sino-Japanese and Russo-Japanese Wars). In Nishida Masaru, ed., *Sensō to bungakusha* (War and writers). Tokyo: San'ichi Shobō, 1983.

Okina Kumi. "Kimi shinitamō koto nakare" (Brother, do not give your life). *Nihon kindai bungaku* 10 (May 1969).

Ōoka Makoto and Thomas Fitzsimmons, eds. *A Play of Mirrors: Eight Major Poets of Modern Japan*. Rochester, MI: Katydid Books, 1987.

Page, Curtis, ed. *Japanese Poetry*. Boston: Houghton Mifflin, 1923.

Pankhurst, Emmeline. *My Own Story*. London: Eveleigh Nash, 1914.

Pharr, Susan J. *Political Women in Japan: The Search for a Place in Political Life*. Berkeley, CA: University of California Press, 1981.

Potter, John Deane. *Yamamoto: The Man Who Menaced America*. New York: Viking Press, 1965.

Rabson, Steve. "'Occidentalism' and Self-Reflection: Western Personae in the Work of Modern Japanese Poets." In Kinya Tsuruta, ed., *The Walls Within: Images of Westerners and Images of Japanese Abroad*. Vancouver, BC: Institute of Asian Research, The University of British Columbia, 1989.

——, trans. *Okinawa: Two Postwar Novellas by Ōshiro Tatsuhiro and Higashi Mineo*. Berkeley, CA: Institute of East Asian Studies, University of California, Berkeley, 1989.

Ramirez-Christensen, Esperanza. *Heart's Flower: The Life and Poetry of Shinkei.* Stanford, CA: Stanford University Press, 1994.

Rimer, J. Thomas. *A Reader's Guide to Japanese Literature.* Tokyo: Kodansha International, 1988.

Robins-Mowry, Dorothy. *The Hidden Sun: Women in Modern Japan.* Boulder, CO: Westview Press, 1983.

Rubin, Jay. "From Wholesomeness to Decadence: The Censorship of Literature under the Allied Occupation." *Journal of Japanese Studies* 11.1 (Winter 1985): 72–103.

——. *Injurious to Public Morals: Writers and the Meiji State.* Seattle: University of Washington Press, 1984.

Russell, John G. "Narratives of Denial: Racial Chauvinism and the Black Other in Japan." *Japan Quarterly* 38.4 (October-December 1991): 416–28.

Saitō Mokichi. *Saitō Mokichi zenshū* (The complete works of Saitō Mokichi). 36 vols. Tokyo: Iwanami Shoten, 1973–75.

Sakuramoto Tomio. *Shijin to sekinin* (Poets and responsibility). Tokyo: Kobayashi Insatsu, 1978.

——. *Shijin to sensō* (Poets and war). Tokyo: Kobayashi Insatsu, 1978.

Sasabuchi Tomoichi. *Rōmanshugi no tanjō* (The birth of romanticism). Tokyo: Meiji Shoin, 1958.

Sassoon, Siegfried. *Memoirs of an Infantry Officer.* London: Faber and Faber, 1930.

——. *Siegfried's Journey, 1916–1920.* New York: Viking Press, 1946.

——. *The War Poems of Siegfried Sassoon.* Edited by Rupert Hart-Davis. London: Faber and Faber, 1983.

Serizawa Shunsuke. *Takamura Kōtarō.* Tokyo: Chikuma Shobō, 1982.

Shea, George Tyson. *Left-Wing Literature in Japan.* Tokyo: Hōsei University Press, 1964.

Shiga Naoya. *Shiga Naoya zenshū* (The complete works of Shiga Naoya). 15 vols. Tokyo: Iwanami Shoten, 1973–74.

Shillony, Ben-Ami. *Politics and Culture in Wartime Japan.* New York: Oxford University Press, 1981.

Shima kūkan kara '85: Okinawa, han-kaku, hansen ansorojii (From the island space Okinawa '85: an antinuclear and antiwar anthology). Naha: Akebono Insatsu, 1985.

Shimazaki Tōson. *Before the Dawn,* translated by William E. Naff. Honolulu: University of Hawaii Press, 1987.

——. *Shimazaki Tōson zenshū* (The complete works of Shimazaki Tōson). 18 vols. Tokyo: Chikuma Shobō, 1966–71.

——. *Shimazaki Tōson zenshū* (The complete works of Shimazaki Tōson). 13 vols. Tokyo: Chikuma Shobō, 1981–83.

——. *Yoake-mae* (Before the dawn). Tokyo: Shinchōsha, 1935.

Shinma Shin'ichi, ed. *Yosano Akiko zenshū* (The complete works of Yosano Akiko). 14 vols. Tokyo: Bunsendō, 1972.

Shinzato Keiji, Taminato Tomoaki, and Kinjō Seitoku. *Okinawa-ken no rekishi* (The history of Okinawa Prefecture). Tokyo: Yamakawa, 1980.

Sibley, William F. "Naturalism in Japanese Literature." *Harvard Journal of Asiatic Studies* 28 (1968): 157–69.

Sohn Pow-key, Kim Chol-choon, and Hong Yi-sup. *The History of Korea*. Seoul: Korean National Commission for UNESCO, 1982.

Stallworthy, Jon, comp. and ed. *The Oxford Book of War Poetry*. New York: Oxford University Press, 1984.

Strong, Kenneth, trans. *Pillar of Fire* by Kinoshita Naoe. London: Allen & Unwin, 1972.

Sunaga Asahiko. *Tekkan to Akiko*. Tokyo: Kinokuniya Shinsho, 1971.

Takamura Kōtarō. *Takamura Kōtarō zenshū* (The complete works of Takamura Kōtarō). 18 vols. Tokyo: Chikuma Shobō, 1982.

Takenaga Yoshimasa. *Nihon kindai sensō bungaku-shi* (A history of modern Japanese war literature). Tokyo: Kasama Shoin, 1976.

Tayama Katai. *Ippeisotsu* (One soldier). In *Waseda bungaku* (January 1908).

Tolstoy, Leo. *Bethink Yourselves!* Translated by V. Tchertkoff. Boston: Ginn and Company, 1904.

Treat, John Whittier. "Early Hiroshima Poetry." *Journal of the Association of Teachers of Japanese* 20.2 (November 1986): 209–31.

Tsuboi Shigeji, ed. *Nihon no teikō-shi* (Japan's poetry of protest). Tokyo: Kōwadō, 1974.

Tsunoda, Ryusaku, Wm. Theodore de Bary, and Donald Keene, comps. *Sources of Japanese Tradition*. 2 vols. New York: Columbia University Press, 1964.

Uchimura Kanzō. *How I Became a Christian*. Tokyo, 1895.

——. "Sensō haishi ron" (For the abolishment of war). *Yorozu chōhō* (June 30, 1903), and in *Uchimura Kanzō zenshū*, vol. 21, p. 27.

——. *Uchimura Kanzō zenshū* (The complete works of Uchimura Kanzō). 25 vols. Edited by Yamamoto Taijirō. Tokyo: Kyōbunkan, 1960–65.

Ueda, Makoto. *Matsuo Bashō*. Boston: Twayne Publishers, 1970.

——. *Modern Japanese Poets and the Nature of Literature*. Stanford, CA: Stanford University Press, 1983.

Ueno Eishin. *Tennō Heika banzai: Bakudan San'yūshi josetsu*. Tokyo: Chikuma Shobō, 1989.

Untermeyer, Louis, ed. *American Poetry: From the Beginning to Whitman*. New York: Harcourt, Brace and Company, 1931.

Updike, John. "Of Sickened Times." *The New Yorker* (November 16, 1992).

Van Devanter, Lynda, and Joan A. Furey, eds. *Visions of War, Dreams of Peace: Writings of Women in the Vietnam War*. New York: Warner Books, 1991.

Viswanathan, Meera. "Poetry, Play and the Court in *Tosa Nikki*." *Comparative Literature Studies* 28.2 (1991): 425–31.

Walker, Janet. *The Japanese Novel of the Meiji Period and the Ideal of Individualism*. Princeton, NJ: Princeton University Press, 1979.

Warner, Denis, and Peggy Warner. *The Tide at Sunrise: A History of the Russo-Japanese War, 1904–1905*. New York: Charter House, 1974.

White, John Albert. *The Siberian Intervention*. Princeton, NJ: Princeton University Press, 1950.

Yamagiwa Keiji. *Hyōden Kinoshita Naoe* (A critical biography of Kinoshita Naoe). Tokyo: Sanseidō, 1977.

——. *Kinoshita Naoe*. Tokyo: Rironsha, 1955.

Yamamoto Fujie. *Kogane no kugi o utta hito: kajin Yosano Akiko no shōgai* (Driver of golden nails: the life of the poet Yosano Akiko). Tokyo: Kōdansha, 1985.

Yamanokuchi Baku. *Yamanokuchi Baku shishū*. Tokyo: Hara Shobō, 1964.

——. *Yamanokuchi Baku zenshū* (The complete works of Yamanokuchi Baku). 4 vols. Tokyo: Shinchōsha, 1975.

Yano Hōjin. *Tekkan-Akiko to sono jidai* (Tekkan and Akiko: their lives and times). Tokyo: Yayoi Shobō, 1973.

Yoshi, Kazume. "Images of Japanese Women in U.S. Writings and Scholarly Works, 1860–1990: Formation and Transformation of Stereotypes." *U.S.-Japan Women's Journal* 1 (1991): 28–29.

Yoshimoto Takaaki. *Takamura Kōtarō*. Tokyo: Shunjūsha, 1977.

Yūri Kaoru. *Akiko no shōgai* (The life of Akiko). Tokyo: Saika Shobō, 1948.

Index

Abe Isoo, 95
Abe Takeshi, 181, 184, 191; and *Kindai shi no haiboku: shijin to sensō sekinin* (The defeat of modern poetry: poets and war responsibility), 181–82, 184
Abosch, David, 263n.545
Aikoku hyakunin isshu (Patriotic poems by one hundred poets), 197
Akutagawa Ryūnosuke, 249n.327
Allied Occupation, 9, 139, 199, 216–17, 220, 227, 232n.40, 253n.377, 264n.582, 266n.601
Andō Kensuke, 53
Andō Satoru, 130
antiwar poetry, 8, 11, 67, 77, 78, 80, 81, 88, 89, 108, 117, 121, 123, 125–27, 140, 144, 149, 150, 151–52, 157, 161–62, 166, 170, 172, 173, 176, 177–78, 183, 207–13, 210, 214–15, 221–24, 226, 230n.31, 246n.269, 250n.338, 255nn.415, 416, 256nn.420, 421, 259n.466
Aono Suekichi, 132
Ara Masahito, 166, 168
Arakawa Akira, and "Yūshoku jinshu" (The colored race), 226–27
Arima Ryōkitsu, 68
Ariyoshi Sawako, 31; and *Hishoku* (Beyond color), 31
Asahi shinbun, 72–73
Asao Tadao, 259n.466
"Authors' Declaration," 258n.452
Ayukai Kaien, 49, 52, 53

"Bakudan san'yūshi" (Human bombs: the three brave warriors), 7, 133, 135, 250n.350
Barclay, Florence L., 134; and "My Heart's Right There," 134–35
Bates, Katherine Lee, and "America the Beautiful," 13
Battle of Attu, 202
Battle of Okinawa, 222–23
"The Beat Goes On," 104
Beethoven, Ludwig van, 220
Benedict, Ruth, and *The Chrysanthemum and the Sword,* 214
Bergonzi, Bernard, 3, 203, 211, 212
Binyon, Laurence, 180, 187; and "For the Fallen," 180–81, 187–88
Blunden, Edward, 33
Bono, Sonny, and "The Beat Goes On," 104
Booth, Francis, 234n.58
Boxer Rebellion, 5, 61, 66, 149, 229n.20
Brock, Clutton, 11; and "War and Poetry," 261n.514
Browning, Robert, and "Incident of the French Camp," 65
Buddhism and Buddhists, 10–11, 25, 28, 48, 118, 130, 152, 153, 156, 157, 163, 164, 180, 245n.262, 256n.424
Bungei sensen, 125

Bungei tenbō, 216
Bunsen, 249n.329
Bunsen Datō Dōmei, 249n.329
Burakumin, 72, 165
Bush, George, 229n.18, 268n.612
Byron, Lord, 117

Cambodia, 267n.601
Canada, 82
Carpenter, Edward, 176
censorship, 5, 9, 10, 16, 17, 92, 93, 96, 98, 115, 120, 143, 148, 175, 188, 190, 213–14, 215, 220, 226–27, 229n.18, 231n.34, 232n.40, 232n.46, 235n.79, 249n.330, 251n.353, 253n.377, 255n.413, 262n.518, 264n.582
Central Intelligence Agency (U.S.), 229n.12
Chang Tso-lin, 128–29
cherry blossoms, 31, 32, 35, 36, 69, 101
Chiang Kai-shek, 6, 8, 129, 136, 199
Chikuhaku-en, 110
China and the Chinese, 5, 6, 7, 8, 12, 16, 17, 26–43, 46, 62, 66, 67, 69, 83, 90, 92, 106, 109, 127–36, 140, 145, 147, 149, 163, 165, 171, 175, 189, 194, 196, 200, 208, 213, 215, 224, 235n.79, 236n.100, 237n.138, 241n.184, 250n.340, 250–51n.350, 251n.353
China War (1937–45), 7, 12–13, 17, 31, 69, 106, 109, 175, 194, 196, 200, 215, 231n.35, 251n.353, 266n.600
Chin-chou, 22, 25, 26, 29, 30, 31, 32, 34, 35, 36, 38, 145, 163, 235n.79
Christianity and Christians, 82, 92, 94, 98, 118, 119, 152, 193, 208, 243n.210, 245n.262
Chūō kōron, 172, 198, 251n.353, 253n.376
Civil War (U.S.), 13–14, 15, 74–75, 207
Clinton, Bill, 268n.612
Cranston, Edwin A., 237n.122
Crichton, Michael, 268n.611

Daitōa Bungakusha Taikai (Greater East Asia Writers Conference), 172
Daitōa sensō kashū (Collected poems of the Greater East Asia War), 137–38
democracy, 127, 139, 140, 141, 176
"Democracy Poets," 7, 175–90, 194
Dickinson, Frederick, 259n.479
Dokugusa (Poison herbs), 68, 69, 71, 76, 224n.192
Douglas, Keith, 62
Dower, John, 201

Encounter, 228–29n.12
End of the War Day *(Shūsen kinenbi),* 258n.463
England and the British, 1–3, 5, 6, 11, 12, 15, 33, 69, 74, 85, 101, 130, 134, 137, 150, 152, 182, 188, 189, 191, 196, 197, 199, 201, 203, 207, 208, 211, 212, 231n.33, 231n.34, 232n.46, 255n.404, 256n.416, 257–58n.452, 260n.487, 262n.518, 263n.553

Feifer, George, 219, 265n.587
Ford, Ford Maddox, 211–12; and "Antwerp," 211; and *On Heaven,* 212
France and the French, 5, 90, 102, 115, 144, 148, 168–71, 182, 191, 192, 193
Franco-Prussian War, 64, 71
free verse, 4, 9, 176, 188
Friedman, George, 267n.607
Friedman, Thomas L., 267n.608
Fujio Masayuki, 238nn.138, 143
Fujiwara Teika, and *Ogura hyakunin isshu* (Ogura Collection by one hundred poets), 197
Fujo zasshi, 110
Fukuda Masao, 6, 7, 176, 181–88, 189, 204; and "Aozameta inaka" (The pale countryside), 183–84; and *Haisen chokugo* (Just after the defeat), 188; and "Hitotsu no ressha to hankechi" (Handkerchiefs waving from a train), 6, 182–83; and "Kansha" (Gratitude), 185–86, 188; and "Shinju-wan no gunshin kyuchū—kaigun tokubetsu kōgekitai o utau" (The nine warrior gods of Pearl Harbor—a poem in honor of the navy special attack force), 186–87; and "Tsuchi ni ikuru uta"

(The song that lives in our soil), 184–85, 205
Fukuda Misuzu, 188
Fukuoka nichi-nichi shinbun, 85
Fukuyama, Francis, 233n.50
fuseji ("X" deletion marks), 249n.330, 264n.582

ganshin shōtan (bitter struggle for vengeance), 115
genbaku-shi (atomic bomb poems), 217–19
Genji monogatari, 113
Germany and the Germans, 5, 8, 90, 115, 148, 169, 171, 190, 199, 211, 231n.36, 246n.272, 254n.404, 258n.452, 260n.491, 262n.525
Gibson, Wilfrid, 205; and "The Bayonet," 203
Goldring, Douglas, 203, 205
Goodman, Grant, 266n.599
Graves, Robert, 2
Gulf War, 4–5, 225, 229n.18
gunka (war song), 6, 12, 59, 67, 69, 72, 73, 76, 81, 85, 109, 110, 136, 213, 233n.53
gunshin (warrior god), 68, 69, 101, 179–80, 181, 259n.468

haiku, 9, 20, 22, 29, 31, 42, 71, 113, 198
Hall of the Honored (Yūshūkan), 176. *See also* Hōmotsu Ihinkan
Hamilton, Ian, 3; and "Spender's Lives," 228–29n.12
Hana-momiji (Flowers and red leaves), 78
Hara Tamiki, and "MIZU O KUDASAI" (Give me water), 217–18
Hayama Yoshiki, 249nn.324, 329
Heike monogatari, 145, 157, 242n.202, 254n.394
Heiminsha, 99, 166
Heimin shinbun, 92, 93, 95, 115–16, 119, 120, 122, 166, 255nn.411, 413
Heinrich, Amy Vladeck, 199, 201, 202, 262nn.525, 529
Higuchi Ichiyō, 113
Hino Ashihei, 215, 264n.574
Hiraide Shū, 116, 122–23, 205
Hirata Atsutane, 198
Hirata Takuboku, 205
Hiratsuka Raichō, 114
Hirose Takeo, 69–71
Hiroshima, 23, 26, 29, 32, 51, 53, 54, 145, 210, 217–19
Hirotsu Ryūrō, 81
Hōmotsu Ihinkan (Treasury of Articles Left by the Deceased), 258n.463. *See also* Hall of the Honored
Hosokawa Karoku, 136
Hosokawa Morihiro, 266n.599
Howe, Julia Ward, and "The Battle Hymn of the Republic," 207
Hussein, Saddam, 4
Hynes, Samuel, 231n.33, 258n.452, 262n.518

Ibaragi Noriko, and "Watashi ga ichiban kirei datta toki" (When I was at my prettiest), 219–20
"Ichinotani futaba gunki," 144, 148
Ienaga Saburō, 250n.340, 260n.493
Iijima Kōichi, 9, 232n.46, 260n.493
Imperial Japanese Army and Navy, 6, 7, 11, 12, 16, 22, 23, 24, 25, 26, 27, 29, 30, 34–37, 38, 40–43, 44, 71, 72, 94, 106, 107, 110–12, 114, 115, 124, 128, 130, 133, 135, 137, 140, 147, 148, 167, 176–77, 179, 184, 186–87, 200, 213, 216, 238n.143, 241n.184, 250n.340, 251n.353, 266n.599
Imperial Rescript to Soldiers and Sailors (Gunjin chokuyu), 11–12, 28, 114
Inoue Kaoru, 238–39n.143
Inouye, Charles Shirō, 244n.234, 254n.406
Ishikawa Jun, 7; and "Marusu no uta" (The song of the war god), 230n.32
Ishikawa Tatsuzō, 7, 132, 251n.353
Itō Hirobumi, 94, 238–39n.143
Itō Shinkichi, 151–52, 162, 168
Itsumi Kumi (Okina Kumi), 48, 50, 53, 58, 60, 63, 71, 76, 142, 241n.192, 254n.390
Itsu-shan, 146, 163
Izumi Kyōka, 5, 59, 87, 255n.406

The Japan Weekly Chronicle, 250n.350
Jidai shichō, 116, 205
Johnson, Geoffrey, and "Without Shedding of Blood," 203
Jojō shishū, (Lyric Poetry), 82

Kabuki, 144, 245n.263, 254n.394
kachi no tentō (inversion of values), 253n.376
Kakuda Kin'ichirō (Kennan), 122
Kaneko Mitsuharu, 132, 190, 215–17, 249n.326; and "Awa" (Bubbles), 251n.353; and "Fuji" (Mount Fuji), 264n.582; and "Jigoku ni tsuite no nōto" (Notes on hell), 2–17; and "Ka" (Mosquitoes), 251n.353; and "Kanbō" (Bird's-eye view), 216
Katō Shūichi, 92, 93–94, 99, 106, 141–42, 253n.385
Katagiri Yuzuru, 211
Kawabata Yasunari, 260n.493
Kawabe Masakazu, 197
Kawai Suimei, 48
Kawasaki Natsu, 139–40
Kawata Jun, and "Mi-ikusa no tame," 174, 258n.455
Keene, Donald, 58, 123–24, 175, 198
Key, Francis Scott, and "The Star-Spangled Banner," 13, 233n.53
Kikuchi Kenjō, 239n.147
"Kimi ga yo" (The reign of our emperor), 42, 233n.53
Kimura Kumaji, 152
Kinoshita Naoe, 82, 90–106, 109, 116, 150, 210; and "Aoyama bochi nite" (At Aoyama cemetery), 101–2; and "Byōchū-gin" (Writing while ill), 106; and *Hi no hashira* (Pillar of fire), 91–99, 105, 115, 150, 152, 175, 244n.245, 255n.414; and "Ichiya no karine" (One night's rest), 90, 97, 100; and *Kami, ningen, jiyū* (God, man, and freedom), 105; and "Ponpoku uta" (Song of the banging drum), 103–4, 210; and *Ryōjin no jihaku* (Confessions of a husband), 99; and "Sekai heiwa ni tai suru Nihon kokumin no sekinin" (The Japanese people's responsibility toward world peace), 92; and "Sensō no uta" (Songs of war), 101; and "Shin-taishō" (The new generals), 102–3; and "Shōshū-hei" (Draftee), 103, 248n.303
Kitamura Tōkoku, 152
Kobayashi Masaharu, 72, 75
Kobayashi Takiji, 15–16; and *Kani kōsen* (The cannery boat), 249n.324
Kōda Rohan, 113, 205, 254n.403
Kokinshū, 21
Kokoro no hana, 114
Kokumin no tomo, 83, 87, 208
Kokumin shinbun, 83
kokutai (national polity), 90, 243–44n.229
Komura Jutarō, 53, 55, 57
Konoe Division, 23, 26, 27
Korea and the Koreans, 5, 6, 8, 43, 47, 48, 49–63, 66, 69, 72, 83, 84, 85, 115, 189, 208, 237–38n.138, 238–39n.143, 239–40n.149, 240nn.153, 155, 247n.291, 266n.599, 268n.612
Korean War, 8, 221, 266n.601
Kōtoku Shūsui, 92, 95, 115, 116, 120, 122, 149, 189
Kubota Utsubo, and "Gunshin ni tsuzuke" (To the warrior gods), 174
Kunikida Doppo, 82
Kuroshima Denji, 124–27, 141, 249n.329, 249n.330, 250n.338; and *Puroretariya geijutsu kyōtei* (Principles of proletarian art), 125, 249n.330

Liaotung Peninsula, 5, 42, 43, 44, 90–91, 128, 148, 244n.230
Longfellow, Henry Wadsworth, 14–15; and "The Arsenal at Springfield," 14; and "The Cumberland," 14–15
London Times, 117

MacArthur, Douglas, 266n.601
MacLeish, Archibald, and "Memorial Rain," 102
Maedakō Hiroichirō, 349n.329
Mainichi shinbun, 92, 93, 95, 99, 100, 116, 150

Manchuria, 109, 115, 118, 126, 128–29, 135, 166, 178, 182, 200, 250n.340, 253n.385
Manchurian Incident, 15, 135, 230n.20, 250n.340
Manea, Norman, 205–6
Man'yōshū, 21, 34, 36–37, 47–48, 65, 78, 198, 200, 202, 242n.205
Marco Polo Bridge Incident, 7, 200
Maruyama Masao, 141, 142
Masaoka Shiki, 20–45, 47, 57, 62, 78, 83, 254n.397; and "Akiya" (Abandoned house), 38; "Gunkan haken" (Battleship deployed), 43; and *Jinchū nikki* (Diary at the front), 27, 30, 31, 32, 34; and *Jūgun kiji* (Record of my journey with the army), 23–29, 41, 43; and "Jūgun kishō" (War medal), 40–41; and *Kinshū zasshi* (Miscellaneous poems on Chin-chou), 29, 32, 33, 34, 35, 37–38; and "Kūson" (Deserted village), 38; and *Meiji 29,* 29; and "Nisshin jōyaku" (Sino-Japanese Treaty), 41–42; and "Shin-jin ni kawarite kokorozashi o nobu" (Stating a man of China's resolve), 39–40; and "Shōkin shūyō" (Accepting the indemnity), 42; and *Waga yamai* (My illness), 21; and "Wakana" (Young greens), 38
Masterman, C. F. G., 258n.452
Masters, Edgar Lee, and "The Philippine Conquest," 212
Matsuo Bashō, 53, 156; and *Nozarashi kikō* (Records of a weather-beaten skeleton), 33; and *Oku no hosomichi* (Narrow road to the deep north), 236n.97
McKenzie, F. A., 239n.149
Mexican War, 14
Miki Kiyoshi, 136
Ministry of Education (Monbushō), 8
Min'yūsha, 82
Miura Gorō, 53, 54, 55, 238–39n.143, 240n.149
Miyamoto Kenji, 249n.327
Miyazaki Koshoshi, 5, 16, 57, 59, 67, 77, 81–89, 148, 149, 150, 152, 255n.408; and "Bushi-damashii" (Warrior spirit), 83; and "Ensentō" (Weary of war), 81, 82, 87, 88, 148, 149, 150; and "Kaisen-shi" (News that the war has begun), 83; and "Shukushō-ka" (Victory song), 83; and "Tashiro-zaka yori kokyō mioroshite yomeru chōka" (Overlooking my hometown from Tashiro Hill), 87, 152–53; and "Tsuru ga buji" (Tsuru is safe), 83–87
Miyazawa Kiichi, 266n.599
Miyoshi Jūrō, 6; and "Santō e yatta tegami" (Letter sent to Shantung), 230n.31
Momota Sōji, 176
Mongolia, 109, 128
Moore, Thomas, 82
Mori Ōgai, 18, 57, 60, 147, 148, 254nn.403, 404
Motoshima Hitoshi, 260n.491
Mukden, 127, 128–29, 130
Mukden Incident, 127, 128
Munro, Harold, 204
Murai Takeko, and "Ibo: nyūsu eiga kara" (Wart: on seeing a newsreel), 221
Murata Masao, 81, 151, 152, 256n.420
Mushanokōji Saneatsu, 99, 150, 255–56n.416; and *Aru seinen no yume* (A young man's dream), 250n.338; and "Sensō wa yokunai" (War is wrong), 245n.249
Myōjō, 61, 67, 71, 107, 109, 116, 120, 121, 122–23
Myōjō-ha, 110

Nagai Kenshi, 213; and "Yuki no shingun" (Marching through the snow), 213–14
Naitō Meisetsu, 71
Nakamura Fusetsu, 22
Nakanishi Terumasa, 225
Nakasone Yasuhiro, 222
Nakata Atsuhiko, 267n.604
Naoki Sanjūgo, 250n.350
Napoleonic Wars, 117

Natsume Sōseki, 246n.272
naturalism *(shizenshugi),* 126, 151, 166, 255n.406
The New Yorker, 229n.18
The New York Times, 225–26
Nichols, Robert, 204, 205; and "The Assault," 204; and "Invocation," 186
Nihon Bungaku Hōkokukai (Japan Literary Patriotic Association), 172, 197
Nihon hansenshi-shū (Japanese anti-war poetry), 157, 161–62, 210, 230n.27
Nihon josei, 133
Nihon kokumin, 133
Nihon Sayoku Bungeika Sōrengō, 124
19th Route Army, 130–31
Nippon, 20, 21, 22, 27, 43
Niroku shinpō, 48, 54
Nishida Kitarō, "The Basic Principles of a New World Order," 194
Nishida Masaru, 87, 246n.277
Nishiwaki Junzaburō, 10, 260n.493
Noh, 30, 254n.394
Nomonhan Incident, 230n.20
"no-war clause" (Constitution of Japan, 1947), 224, 266n.601, 267n.603
nuclear attacks, 8, 217–19

Ochiai Naobumi, 48, 49, 54, 57, 59, 60, 78
Oda Sugao, 113
Okada Tarajirō, 105
Okamoto Jun 141, 142, 164–65, 168. *See also Nihon hansenshi-shū*
Okamoto, Shumpei, 247–48n.295
Okano Yukie, 91, 92, 99, 106, 244n.234
Okina Kumi. *See* Itsumi Kumi
Okinawa, 8, 221–24, 226–27, 232n.46, 265n.599, 268n.610
Okura Kihachirō, 94
Omachi Keigetsu, 57, 77, 78, 108, 121–23, 138, 142, 143
Onin War, 157
Otsuka Naoko, 16, 109–12, 114, 121, 246n.272; and "Obohei" (Enlisted soldier), 110; and "O-hyaku-do mōde" (A hundred visits to the shrine), 109–10, 121; and "Shingeki no uta" (Song of the assault), 110–12, 246n.277, 247–48n.295; and "Waka-goke" (Young widow), 110
Otsukotsu Akio, 259n.472
Owen, Wilfrid, 153, 183, 214; and "Exposure," 214–15; and "The Send-Off," 183
Ozaki Hotsumi, 136
Ozaki Kōyō, 113, 254n.403

Pacific War, 7, 12, 16, 17, 69, 109, 136, 137, 138, 140, 141, 143, 144, 168, 172, 175–76, 179–81, 184, 188, 189, 191, 194, 204, 210, 213, 215–20, 221–23, 245n.249, 251n.356, 255–56n.416
pacifism and pacifists, 18, 90, 94, 95, 99, 100, 103, 104, 105, 109, 115, 125, 127, 139, 141, 142, 143, 150, 152, 182, 215, 225, 256n.424, 262n.518
Pankhurst, Emmeline, 134
Pearl Harbor, 7, 12, 69, 136, 137, 180, 186, 188, 193, 195–96, 199–200, 201, 226, 265n.599
Poetry and Drama, 204
Port Arthur, 5, 6, 12, 16, 17, 22, 26, 29, 30, 68–71, 85, 86, 90, 107, 111, 118, 121, 128, 131, 142, 143
Prince of Wales, 201
Proletarian Literature, 15, 94, 106, 108, 123–27, 171, 178, 212, 249nn.324, 326, 327, 329
Puroretariya geijutsu kyōtei (Principles of proletarian art), 125

Queen Min, 50, 51, 52, 62, 237n.138, 238–39n.143, 239–40n.149

renga, 57, 157
Repulse, 201
Revolutionary War (U.S.), 230n.23
Rimbaud, Arthur, and "Evil," 64–65
Rodin, Auguste, 138
Roosevelt, Franklin, 245n.249
Rosenberg, Isaac, 62
Rouault, Georges, 220, 265n.588
Rōyama Masamichi, 136
Rubin, Jay, 122

Russia and the Russians, 5, 6, 17, 50, 55–57, 66, 68–71, 72, 90, 110, 115, 117–20, 124, 142, 148, 149, 168, 237n.138, 240n.155, 246n.272, 253n.385

Russo-Japanese War, 6, 12, 27, 52, 67, 68–71, 77, 92–99, 107, 108, 109, 110–12, 115, 116, 117–23, 126, 131, 137, 138, 144, 147, 149, 150, 152, 164, 165–68, 169, 170–71, 173, 178, 179, 184, 189, 205, 209, 237n.138, 246n.271, 247nn.291, 295, 257n.448

Ryūdai bungaku, 226–27

Saitō Mokichi, 7, 17, 143, 199–203, 205, 215, 262nn.525, 529; and "Attsu-tō chūkon ni sasagu" (To the loyal spirits of Attu Island), 202; and *Daitōa sensō kashū* (Collected poems on the Greater East Asia War), 201; and "Kami no mi-gun" (The army of His Divine Majesty), 202; and "Kanarazu katamu" (Victory is certain), 174; and *Kan'un* (Cold clouds), 262n.529; and *Shirokiyama* (White mountains), 202–3

Sakai Toshihiko, 92, 115, 120, 122, 255n.413

Sakamaki Kazuo, 259n.468

Sakuramoto Tomio, and "Kaneko Mitsuharu-ron no kyomō chitai" (A zone of falsehood in studies of Kaneko Mitsuharu), 215–16, 264n.578

Sandburg, Carl, and "Grass," 156–57

Sasaki Nobutsuna, 110, 114, 230n.29

Sassoon, Siegfried, 1–3, 16, 203, 213; and "Absolution," 1; and "Conscripts," 232n.46; and "Counter-Attack," 2; and "Fight to a Finish," 2–3; and "Kiss," 1–2, 213; and "Silent Service," 3; and "Suicide in the Trenches," 2; and "To Any Dead Officer," 100–1

Satsuma Rebellion, 229n.20

Schneider, Peter, 8, 231n.36

Scott, John (of Anwell), "The Drum," 59

Seitō (Blue stockings), 114

Self-Defense Forces (Japan), 224–26, 254n.396, 266n.599, 266–67n.601, 268n.612

Senki, 125

senryū, 9

Sensō ni tai suru sensō (War against war), 124, 125

Shakaishugi no shi (Socialist poetry), 103

Shakespeare, William, 207–8

Shanghai, 12–13, 69, 72–74, 130–32, 133–34, 135, 140, 241n.192, 250n.350

Shanghai Incident, 130–32, 135, 140

Shantung Deployments, 229n.20

shasei (realistic depiction), 22, 28

Shiga Naoya, 196, 198

Shillony, Ben-Ami, 125, 197, 232n.42

Shimazaki Tōson, 18, 67, 81, 89, 144–74, 257n.448; and "Arashi" (The storm), 171–72; and "Chikumagawa rojō no uta" (Weary traveler along the Chikuma River), 174; and *Hakai* (The broken commandment), 165, 166; and *Haru* (Spring), 165; and "Heiwa no hi" (Days of peace), 167–69; and "Nōfu" (The farmer), 89, 144, 148–49, 150, 151–52, 153–165, 168, 169, 173, 256nn.421, 427; and *Rakubai-shū* (Fallen plum blossoms), 174; and *Ryokuyō-shū* (Green leaf collection), 165; and *Sensō to Pari* (War and Paris), 169–71; and "Taikai e no kibō" (My hope for the conference), 172; and *Tōhō no mon* (Gate to the east), 172–73; and "Tokiwagi"(Evergreen tree), 174; and "Utatane" (Restless sleep), 144–48, 150, 151, 156, 168, 169, 170, 243n.219; and *Wakana-shū* (Seedlings), 151, 164; and *Yoake-mae* (Before the dawn), 159, 172

Shina-ron (Theories on China), 132

Shinji Kiyoshi, 80

Shinkei, and "Mujō" (Evanescence), 157

Shinsei, 123

Shinshōsetsu, 144

shintaishi (new-style poetry), 29, 35, 40, 46, 48, 57, 58, 59, 62, 66, 67, 68, 69, 72, 73, 77, 78, 81, 89, 101, 107, 109, 126, 127, 133, 148, 150, 153, 209, 246n.272, 252n.357
Shinto, 10, 25, 28, 101, 188, 235n.88
Shioi Ukō, 78
Shirakaba-ha (White Birch Society), 255n.416
Shiro Yū, and "Okinawa," 222–23; and "Soshite sengo" (Then came "postwar"), 223–24
Shirotori Seigo, 7, 176–81, 183, 188, 189, 246n.271, 259n.472; and "Gunshin no fubo wa kyō mo tahata o tagayaseri" (Today, too, parents of the warrior god plow their fields), 179–80; and "Kaijō no yūutsu" (Gloom at sea), 179; and "Kōchi o ushinau hi" (The day they lost their farm fields), 177–78, 179, 246n.271; and "Satsuriku no tendō" (The palace of slaughter), 176–77, 180, 181; and "Yamashita shōgun" (General Yamashita), 181
Siberian Intervention (Shiberia Shuppei), 6, 124, 182–83, 184, 186, 187, 229n.20, 259n.479
Sino-Japanese War (1894–95), 5, 21, 22, 23, 24, 26, 27, 28–42, 43, 45, 46–47, 48, 49, 50, 53, 57, 58, 61, 65, 72, 77, 80, 81, 83–89, 90–91, 97, 109, 110, 137, 144, 147, 148, 149, 151, 154–55, 159, 162–64, 165, 170, 173, 184, 205, 208, 209, 213, 229n.20, 235n.79, 246n.271, 247n.291
"Sixteen Tons," 104
Socialism and socialists, 92, 94, 95, 98, 99, 104, 105, 124–27, 125, 189
Sōma Gyofū, 252n.363
Sorley, Charles, 33
Sousa, John Philip, and "The Stars and Stripes Forever," 233n.53
South Manchurian Railway Company, 127–28, 182
Spanish-American War, 212
Spencer, Herbert, 22
Spender, Stephen, 3
Steele, William, 267n.603
Stevens, Wallace, and "The Death of a Soldier," 80
Strong, Kenneth, 93, 94, 99, 100, 106, 244n.245
Sugimura Fukashi, 53, 238n.143
Sun Yat-sen, 130, 131
Sunaga Asahiko, 76
Suzuki Jōzō, 56
Suzuki Shigesaburō, 105
Suzuki Teiichi, 197

Taisei Yokusankai (The Imperial Rule Assistance Association), 173
Taiyō, 109, 121, 122, 167
Takamura Kōtarō, 7, 8, 9, 17, 143, 191–99, 201, 205, 215, 261n.513, 261n.514; and "Boku mo tobu" (I, too, will fly), 198; and "Chinshi seyo Shō-sensei!" (Mr. Chiang, reflect on this!), 196; and "Haitaisha yori—Baanaado Riichi-kun ni tei su (From a reprobate—offered to Bernard Leach), 192; and "Jūnigatsu yōka" (December eighth), 195; and "Karera o utsu" (We strike them), 196; and "Minamoto ni ki suru mono" (Those who return to the source), 195; and "Pari" (Paris), 192; and "Shingapōru kanraku" (The fall of Singapore), 196, 203; and "Shirokuma" (Polar bear), 193; and "Shō-sensei ni zansha su" (Apology in shame to Mr. Chiang), 8, 199; and "Shūsen" (The end of the war), 199; and "Wa ga shi o yomite hito shi ni tsukeri" (Men, having read my poems, went to their deaths), 198–99; and "Yorokobi o tsugu" (Announcing my joy), 192; and "Zengakuto tatsu" (All students are rising to the cause), 198
Takamura Tadashi, 261n.513
Takayama Chogyū, 22, 77, 81
Takeda Takako, 108
Takeshima Hagoromo, 67, 77–81, 82, 89, 148, 149; and "Senshi-sotsu" (A fallen soldier), 77, 78–81, 88, 148, 149

Takizawa Shūgyō, 116, 205
Tamano Hanako, 117
Tanikawa Shuntarō, and "Patience," 4
Tanizaki Jun'ichirō, 198, 260n.493; and *Sasameyuki* (The Makioka sisters), 198
tanka, 12, 16, 17, 40, 43, 44, 46, 47, 48, 50, 54, 57, 58, 61, 62, 83, 113, 114, 116, 117, 127, 128, 132, 135, 136, 138, 201, 202, 246n.272, 250n.339
Tanka kenkyū, 127, 136
Taoism, 82
Tayama Katai, 82, 126, 144, 168, 171, 257n.448; and *Ippeisotsu* (One soldier), 82, 126, 168, 257n.448
Teikoku bungaku, 78
Tennyson, Alfred Lord, and "The Charge of the Light Brigade," 207
Tenri Jihōsha, 137
Terkel, Studs, 229n.15
Tōge Sankichi, and "Hachigatsu muika" (August 6, 1951), 218–19
Tōgi Rihō, 80
Tōhaku, 136–37
Tōjō Hideki, 197, 211, 257n.452, 258n.463
Tōkai Sanshi, and *Kajin no kigu* (Strange encounters with beautiful women), 94
Toki Zenmaro, 252n.363
Tōkyō nichi-nichi shinbun, 72, 73
Tokyo War Crimes Tribunal, 235n.88
Tolstoy, Leo, "Bethink Youselves!" (Nanjira, kuiaratameyo) (Nichi-Ro sensō ron), 117–20, 122, 149, 248n.304, 255n.416
Tomita Seika, 176
Toyotomi Hideyoshi, 66, 189
Travis, Merle. *See* "Sixteen Tons"
Treat, John Whittier, 219
Treaty of Portsmouth, 115
Triple Intervention, 5, 24, 42, 43, 51, 81, 90, 115, 148
Truman, Harry S., 230n.23
Ts'ai T'ing-k'ai, 130, 131
Tsuboi Shigeji, 88, 103, 251n.353
Tsuchiya Matasaburō, and *Kōka shunjū* (Farming life), 153
Tsuji Junji, 69, 73, 252n.357
Tu Fu, 62; and "A Spring View," 34
Tyler, William, 230n.32

Uchimura Kanzō, 28, 90, 116, 149–50, 193, 208–10; and "Jisei no kansatsu" (Observations on the times), 208; and "Sensō haishi ron" (For the abolishment of war), 150; and "Yamome no joya" (A widow's New Year's eve), 209, 211
Ueda, Makoto, 194
Ueno Hidenobu, 72
"Umi yukaba" (When we go to sea), 80
United States and the Americans, 3, 4, 8, 9, 11, 12, 13, 14, 69, 74, 82, 85, 130,137, 152, 171, 172, 176, 188, 191, 193, 194, 197, 199, 210, 211, 212, 217, 221, 226, 228–29n.12, 229n.18, 230n.23, 237n.138, 255n.416, 265n.589, 266–67n.601, 267nn.606, 608, 609, 268nn.610, 611, 612
United States-Japan Security Treaty ("Anpo"), 8, 9, 142, 222, 268n.610
United States military occupation (Okinawa), 8, 221–24, 226–27
Updike, John, 205–6

"Victory over Japan (V-J) Day," 230n.23
Vietnam War (1961–73), 8, 104, 210–11, 229nn.12, 18

Wagner, Richard, 220
Ward, Samuel A., 233n.52
Watanabe Kazuko, 225
Weihaiwei, 5, 90, 209
Weisman, Steven R., 225–26
Wetta, Frank J., 12
Whitman, Walt, 176
Whitten, Harry, 3–4
Wiesel, Elie, 207
Willson, Forceythe, "Boy Brittan," 13–14, 74–75
women's rights and status, 112–14, 127, 133, 134, 139, 141, 142, 247n.287, 251–52n.356
Women's Volunteer Labor Corps (Joshi Rōdō Teishintai), 251n.356

Wordsworth, William, 82
World War I, 1–3, 6, 102, 134–35, 144, 152, 169–71, 176, 182, 183, 186, 189, 203, 211, 213, 214, 231n.34, 254n.398, 259n.479, 261n.514, 262nn.518, 525, 265n.589
World War II, 3, 8, 81, 105, 108, 112, 113, 127, 141, 148, 149, 164, 215, 216–20, 224, 225, 226, 227, 258n.463, 267n.603. *See also* China War and Pacific War

Yamagata Aritomo, 94, 95, 96
Yamagiwa Keiji, 105
Yamamoto Fujie, 72, 75, 129, 134, 138–39, 140, 143, 250n.342
Yamanokuchi Baku, 221–22; and "Fuchin bokan Okinawa" (Unsinkable aircraft carrier Okinawa), 222; and "Ōshō" (Drafted), 10–11, 232n.46
Yano Hōjin, 49, 142, 246n.272
Yasukuni Jinja (shrine), 31, 176, 235n.88, 258n.463
Yeats, William Butler, 207
Yomiuri shinbun, 122, 130
Yorozu chōhō, 116
Yosano Akiko, 16–17, 18, 48, 68, 77, 81, 100, 107–43, 148, 189, 194, 246n.280, 247n.295, 248n.304, 250n.342, 251n.356, 252n.357, 253n.370; and "Hiraki-bumi" (Open letter), 121–22; and "Heiwa shisō no mirai" (The future of a philosophy of peace), 247n.287; and "Inochi o kezuru" (Shortening their lives), 135; and "Kimi shinitamō koto nakare" (Brother, do not give your life), 17, 48, 71, 100, 107–9, 112, 114, 118–23, 124, 131, 134, 138, 139, 140, 141–43, 148, 149, 177; and "Kōgan no shi" (Rosy-cheeked death), 127, 130–32, 135, 140; and *Man-Mō yūki* (Travels in Manchuria and Mongolia), 128, 250n.339; and *Midaregami* (Tangled hair), 114; and "Mirai no fujin nare" (Become women of the future), 247n.287; and "Nihon kokumin asa no uta" (Citizens of Japan, a morning song), 127, 133–34, 251n.356; and "Nisshin kokumin no shinwa" (Friendship between the citizens of Japan and China), 135; and "Shuppei to fujin no kōsatsu" (Women's viewpoint on the Siberian Intervention), 247n.287; and "Tōshi-shō no mondai" (The Tungssu problem), 135; and "Yama o ugoku hi" (The day the mountains moved), 114
Yosano Augyusuto (Iku), 137–38, 253n.370
Yosano Tekkan (Hiroshi), 12, 16, 46–76, 77, 78, 81, 83, 109, 110, 114, 122, 127, 128, 134, 138, 150, 200; and "Aa, Hirose chūsa" (Ah, Commander Hirose), 69–71, 76; and "Bakudan san'yūshi" (Human bombs: the three brave warriors), 12–13, 16, 69–76, 134, 138, 252n.357; and *Bōkoku no on* (Tones ruinous to the nation), 48, 66; and "Gaisenmon" (Arch of triumph), 58–59, 61, 62, 87; and "Kessha-ka" (Poem limned in blood), 62–64, 65, 67, 68, 71; and "Myōjō" (Morning star), 61, 65, 67; and "Nihon o saru uta (Song of farewell to Japan), 66, 67; and "Ryojun-guchi fūsa-tai" (The blockading squadron at Port Arthur), 68–69, 71; and "Sajō no kotoba" (Words on the sand), 51, 54, 55, 56; and *Tekkan-shi,* 61–65; and *Tōzai nanboku* (East, west, south, north), 49, 52, 53–55, 57–59
Yoshida Kin'ichi, "1967-nen Nihon o natsu" (Japan's summer of 1967), 210
Yoshimi Yoshiaki, 266n.599
Yoshimoto Takaaki, 194
Young, Louise, 251n.352
Yūri Kaoru, 128, 139–41; and *Akiko no shōgai* (The life of Akiko), 139–41

ABOUT THE AUTHOR

Steve Rabson completed a Ph.D. in Japanese literature at Harvard University in 1979. Since that year he has taught at Brown University in the Departments of East Asian Studies, Comparative Literature, and Linguistics. He has published research on the fiction of Ōe Kenzaburō and Nagai Kafū, and the poetry of Yosano Akiko, Shimazaki Tōson, and Yamanokuchi Baku. His first book, *Okinawa: Two Postwar Novellas* (Institute of East Asian Studies, University of California, Berkeley, 1989), is now in its second printing. He is currently coediting an anthology of Japanese literature, in translation, by writers from Okinawa. Between 1966 and 1968 he served in the United States Army, with overseas assignments that included eight months in Okinawa.